The Beautiful Soul

ALSO BY ROBERT E. NORTON

Herder's Aesthetics and the European Enlightenment

THE

Beautiful Soul

Aesthetic Morality in the Eighteenth Century

ROBERT E. NORTON

CORNELL UNIVERSITY PRESS

ITHACA AND LONDON

The publisher gratefully acknowledges a subvention
from Vassar College which aided in
the publication of this book.

First published 1995 by Cornell University Press.

Printed in the United States of America

⊗ The paper in this book meets the minimum requirements
of the American National Standard for Information Sciences—
Permanence of Paper for Printed Library Materials, ANSI Z39.48-1984.

Library of Congress Cataloging-in-Publication Data

Norton, Robert Edward, 1960–
    The beautiful soul : aesthetic morality in the eighteenth century
/ Robert E. Norton.
    p.   cm.
    Includes bibliographical references and index.
    ISBN 0-8014-3050-X
    1. Ethics, Modern—18th century.   2. Aesthetics, Modern—18th
century.   3. Soul.   I. Title.
BJ311.N67   1995
170'.9'033—dc20   94-37298

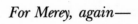

For Merey, again—

What do we long for when we see beauty?
To be beautiful. We think much happiness
must be connected with it.
— But that is an error.

—NIETZSCHE

Contents

Preface

ix

Introduction

1

CHAPTER ONE

The Advent of Modern Ethics in Britain and the Emergence
of the Idea of Moral Beauty

9

CHAPTER TWO

Beauty of Soul: Pietism and the Ideal of Moral Perfection

55

CHAPTER THREE

The Eighteenth Century and the Hellenic Ideal of *Kalokagathia*

100

CHAPTER FOUR

Wieland and Rousseau: The Figuration of the Beautiful Soul

137

CHAPTER FIVE

The Cult of Physiognomy: Physical Beauty as the Cipher
of Moral Excellence

176

CHAPTER SIX

Kant and Schiller: The Apotheosis of the Beautiful Soul

210

CHAPTER SEVEN

Goethe and Hegel: The Sublation of the Beautiful Soul

246

Epilogue

283

Bibliography

291

Index

308

Preface

Once praised as the epitome of human existence, acclaimed by poets, philosophers, and artists alike as the ultimate achievement of individual endeavor, the "beautiful soul" has by now been all but forgotten. To most ears today the phrase probably strikes faintly discordant tones, evoking paradoxical associations—if any at all. But many during the eighteenth century considered the beautiful soul to be the very symbol of enlightened humanity and devoted a substantial amount of energy to discovering how to attain this widely acknowledged good. Given the temper of the Enlightenment, however, it will surprise no one to learn that not all eighteenth-century observers were equally enthusiastic about the idea, and that some were overtly hostile to it. As the era of illumination began to dim, the accumulated weight of critical pressure that had been placed on the concept of the beautiful soul eventually caused the relatively fragile intellectual structures supporting it to collapse. And after the turn of the century, the literary record of this remarkable cultural icon—composed as it was from a set of beliefs that came to be viewed, like the time that produced them, as compromised by a naive and ill-founded optimism—gradually collected the dust of neglect and has remained virtually undisturbed ever since.

Yet the premise on which the idea of the beautiful soul was based—that a profound affinity exists between beauty and goodness, that there is a point at which aesthetic and ethical values commingle to form a new, indivisible unity—was certainly not unique to the eighteenth century. On the contrary: it has been a theme of European culture for as long as our collective memory can recall. Beginning with the earliest metaphysical speculations of ancient Greek philosophers and extending through medieval Christian

ix

thought and beyond to the revival of classical learning that introduced our own modernity, this notion, or rather this hopeful dream, that virtue could somehow be identified with beauty maintained a central place in the imagination of countless and otherwise incompatible thinkers. Even today, in an age characterized by radical skepticism toward most traditional categories of thought—and not least toward those informing the subjects of morality and aesthetics—there is renewed though perhaps unexpected interest in the possibility of combining the elements of the good and the beautiful as a way of solving our own moral predicaments.

In this book I discuss in detail only one episode of that larger history. But it was arguably the most explicitly articulated and ambitious attempt to realize the ideal of moral beauty in the two and a half thousand years of its recorded existence. In the early 1700s, inaugurating a development that closely paralleled the chronological progression of the European Enlightenment as a whole, several thinkers in England, France, and Germany began to employ terms referring to moral and aesthetic excellence to address contemporary problems of ethical philosophy. This deliberate mixing of what had commonly been viewed as properly distinct modes of discourse seemed so persuasive, or at least so attractive, that after the 1750s some version of moral beauty appeared in almost every eighteenth-century discussion of morality, whether it was in works of high philosophical seriousness or in literary texts meant for the popular market. Indeed, it was here, in the novels and plays written for the consumption and, it was hoped, the edification of the general reader, that the amalgamation of abstract moral and aesthetic qualities became personified by what only then came to be known as the "beautiful soul." It is to tracing the fortunes of this forgotten figure and discovering the reasons for its initial success and subsequent decline that this book is principally devoted.

I thank the Alexander von Humboldt Foundation for granting me a generous research fellowship to complete the manuscript of this book. Vassar College also allowed me to take a leave of absence from my teaching duties in 1992–93 so that I could concentrate my energies on writing; for that opportunity I am extremely grateful. In addition, I thank the indefatigable staff of the Interlibrary Loan Office of the Vassar College Library, the Herzog August Bibliothek in Wolfenbüttel, the Universitätsbibliothek of the Freie Universität Berlin, the McAlpin Special Collection of the Burke Library of Union Theological Seminary in the City of New York, the Internationale Forschungsstätte Europäische Aufklärung und Pietismus at Halle, and the Martin-Luther-Universität, Halle-Wittenberg. Without the assistance of these institutions this work could never have come into being.

Most especially, however, I thank the numerous colleagues and friends who, in one form or another, have enabled me to envision and write this book. Its first conception arose from a conversation I had a number of years ago with David Ellison, who posed the simple but fruitful question about the place of the beautiful soul in eighteenth-century German letters. I realized even then that my response was cursory at best, and this book represents my attempt to provide a fuller answer to his original inquiry. During my sabbatical year, Jürgen Trabant performed the minor miracle of finding a suitable place for me and my wife, Meredith, to live and work in Berlin, and in general his unfailing good humor made our stay much more enjoyable than it might otherwise have been. For their help in addressing particular issues, or for their more general encouragement, I am also indebted to Hans Aarsleff, John Ahern, William S. Anderson, Robert Brown, Elisabeth Cardonne-Arlyck, Jennifer Church, Joachim Gessinger, Christine Mitchell Havelock, Laura Haynes, Donna Heiland, Adrienne Hytier, Jesse Kalin, Molly Levine, Mark Lilla, Michael McCarthy, Charles Mercier, Mitchell H. Miller, Helmut Obst, Daniel O'Neil, Steven F. Ostrow, David M. Posner, Wolfert von Rahden, Ulrich Ricken, Arno Sames, and Johannes Wallmann. I am also happy to have the opportunity to thank Cornell University Press for its exemplary professionalism and meticulousness. Every aspect of my association with the Press has been nothing but pleasant, and I feel especially fortunate to have had as editor Bernhard Kendler. But my greatest debt, in this as in everything else, is to the person to whom I have dedicated this book.

ROBERT E. NORTON

Poughkeepsie, New York

The Beautiful Soul

Introduction

I n the last several years interest in the questions of moral philosophy has notably increased. Often ignored in favor of epistemology and logic, and even considered by some analytical thinkers as an inappropriate subject of philosophical study, ethics appears to be regaining its former status as the only truly practical discipline. But although the rediscovery of the importance of ethical inquiry is undoubtedly a positive development, the motivations for its sudden popularity have probably sprung from a more ambiguous source. Discriminating dialectitian that he was, Jean-Jacques Rousseau realized long ago that an excessive relish for models of moral probity was itself a symptom of its lack or loss. "It is in the most depraved centuries," he once pointedly wrote, "that one cherishes the lessons of the most perfect morality."[1] Although not everyone would want to claim that this century is more fundamentally depraved than any other, or that we show a particularly pronounced desire for moral instruction, most would be willing to agree that for us morality in any conventional sense has forfeited much of its traditional prestige and social function. In 1981 Alasdair MacIntyre put it perhaps most forcefully in his book *After Virtue* by stating that "we have—very largely, if not entirely—lost our comprehension, both theoretical and practical, of morality."[2] MacIntyre's diagnoses of the disorders of modern society, not to speak of the various remedies he proposes, have predictably remained controversial. Yet the powerful response he provoked is itself a sign that a shared sense of urgent concern, and possibly even of desperate confusion, has indeed arisen about the vital matter of determining how to live.

1. Jean-Jacques Rousseau, *Julie, ou la Nouvelle Héloïse*, in *Oeuvres complètes*, ed. Bernard Gagnebin and Marcel Raymond (Paris: Gallimard, Bibliothèque de la Pléiade, 1959–69), 2:26.
2. Alasdair MacIntyre, *After Virtue: A Study in Moral Theory*, 2d ed. (Notre Dame: University of Notre Dame Press, 1984), 2.

To a great degree, the collapse of moral consensus that MacIntyre describes can be seen as an extension of the intellectual climate that has prevailed in the United States and Europe since the 1960s. Principally opposed to systems of thought that rely on generalizing conceptual categories, homogeneity, and self-contained hierarchical structures for their coherence, the most influential thinkers of this period have stressed, on the contrary, radical plurality, discontinuity, and decentralization in their critiques of Western traditions of thought. That there could even be a single morality valid for all members of a social organization or an ethical code to which an individual could always adhere is incompatible with the basic tenets of poststructuralist or deconstructive thinking. Even the category of a unified, integral self that could serve as the seat of moral knowledge and action had already begun to lose its credibility in the wake of Freud's discovery of an unconscious realm of desires and drives beyond our rational control. Almost simultaneously with the appearance of MacIntyre's book, Richard Rorty remarked on the effect that this disintegration of a common moral context has had specifically on the study of literature. Instead of reading nineteenth-century novels, for example, as straightforward advocations of certain moral postulates, modern literary critics, Rorty claimed, typically "mine them for ambiguity, intertextuality, and the like, because they do not really recognize *morality* as a possible form of life. For neither the religious nor the secular and liberal morality seems possible, and no third alternative has emerged."[3] Although conveyed in less apocalyptic terms, Rorty's sanguine estimate of the moral constitution of our time thus corresponds in its essentials to MacIntyre's bleak indictment of it. So inured are postmodern critics to the moral instability of the present that they are not only unable to take past moral codes seriously on their own terms, but they also see their own experience of moral fragmentation mirrored wherever they look, with no likely substitute in sight.

But then Rorty did detect, in an article he published a few years later, a "third alternative" to the two traditional types of morality that he felt had governed behavior until this century. Expressly identifying Freud as the primary catalyst in the disintegration of familiar metaphysical conceptions of the self that characterizes modern thought, Rorty wrote affirmatively that he wanted "to focus on the way in which Freud, by helping us see ourselves as centerless, as random assemblages of contingent and idiosyncratic needs rather than as more or less adequate exemplifications of a common human essence, opened up new possibilities for the aesthetic life." Turning the destruction of the humanistic conception of the self to positive advantage, Rorty credits Freud with having liberated us from the need to discover our

3. Richard Rorty, "Freud, Morality, and Hermeneutics," *New Literary History* 12 (1980): 179–80.

preexistent "true" moral being, the basic elements of which would be reflected by the whole of humanity. For in Rorty's opinion, Freud has "helped us think of moral reflection and sophistication as a matter of self-creation rather than self-knowledge."[4] In Rorty's reading, the "loss" of a prefabricated notion of what it means to be a moral agent has granted us the freedom to invent our *own* meaning, indeed the very form of our own life. By having liberated us from the tyranny of conscious rationality, Freud has enabled us to perceive our unconscious energies as the raw material for the creation, potentially, of living works of art. Yet about precisely how this quasi-aesthetic activity of self-formation is supposed to have some inherent ethical significance, Rorty remained conspicuously silent.

Still, Rorty is not alone in the search for a way to meet the challenges of postmodern morality within the domain of a broadly defined aesthetic activity. In 1983 Michel Foucault, who himself played a major role in dismantling traditional moral frameworks by announcing the death of the autonomous, sovereign subject, expressed sentiments very similar to those of Rorty. Shortly before his death, Foucault gave an interview in which he spoke about his recent work on the ethical theories of the ancient Greeks. Foucault said that one of their main concerns was "to constitute a kind of ethics which was an aesthetics of existence. . . . I wonder if our problem nowadays is not, in a way, similar to this one, since most of us no longer believe that ethics is founded in religion, nor do we want a legal system to intervene in our moral, personal, private life." After again asserting his view that "Greek ethics is centered on a problem of personal choice, of aesthetics of existence," Foucault then made explicit what Rorty had only intimated. "What strikes me," Foucault told his interviewer, "is the fact that in our society, art has become something which is related only to objects and not to individuals, or to life. . . . But couldn't everyone's life become a work of art? Why should the lamp or the house be an art object, but not our life?"[5] The rubble left behind by the annihilation of the old, self-sufficient subject therefore became for Foucault a quarry for the artful construction of a new, postmodern identity. Like Rorty, he thus thought that an ethics for our time could be established by applying aesthetic measures to the very fabric of our lives.

It would not be difficult to cite other contemporary thinkers who believe, as Ludwig Wittgenstein also once somewhat elliptically proclaimed, that "ethics and aesthetics are one."[6] So far, however, no one seems to have

---

4. Richard Rorty, "Freud and Moral Reflection," in *Pragmatism's Freud: The Moral Disposition of Psychoanalysis*, ed. Joseph H. Smith and William Kerrigan (Baltimore: Johns Hopkins University Press, 1986), 12.
5. Michel Foucault, "On the Genealogy of Ethics: An Overview of Work in Progress," in *The Foucault Reader*, ed. Paul Rabinow (New York: Random House, 1984), 343 and 348–50.
6. Ludwig Wittgenstein, *Tractatus Logico-Philosophicus* (London: Routledge & Kegan Paul, 1963), 146, 147, proposition 6.421; cited from Richard Shusterman, "'Ethics and Aesthe-

wondered about the nature of the claim itself, or to have bothered to inquire into its origins.[7] For it is by no means the case that we automatically accept this alleged unity. Just the reverse is true: ever since the romantics insisted on the absolute autonomy of art and above all attempted to disengage art from any moralistic or even vaguely didactic intentions, we have tended to see aesthetics and ethics as opposing rather than as complementing each other. Because the new advocates of the idea have always simply asserted, but never actually demonstrated, that these two complex fields of knowledge and experience are somehow identical, or at least similar enough to be aligned, we have to infer certain unspoken assumptions. In the absence of argument, we are thus forced to reconstruct these assumptions for ourselves and if possible unearth their antecedents, for only then can we determine how—or whether—they can be applied to the present. To approach the issue in this way is of course to treat it historically, and philosophers throughout most of this century have not been particularly interested in history. But the history of the idea that ethics and aesthetics can be intelligibly conceived as being "one" is absolutely crucial to understanding why, in our own days, it has regained a respectable following and is being advanced by prominent and equally respected thinkers—and why, if it is carefully considered on its own terms, the idea must fail to offer what it promises.

It is no accident that the most recent, and most spectacular, failure to fuse the good and the beautiful took place against a comparable background of crisis. The traditional framework of religious faith, supplemented and reinforced by the secular authority of the monarchical state, had begun to betray the first indications of a diminishing power of persuasion. These two institutions had long provided a reliable network of restraints and rewards for the guidance of the subjects under their sway, and the void that many feared their dissolution would produce was consequently perceived as a grave

---

tics Are One': Postmodernism's Ethics of Taste," in *After the Future: Postmodern Times and Places*, ed. Gary Shapiro (Albany: SUNY Press, 1990), 115. I found this article in general very useful in assessing postmodern ethics. Shusterman also identifies with this morality and offers what he calls his own personal "confession" in the final paragraph of his essay: "I too subscribe to a vision of the good life that could be characterized as aesthetic: one that attempts to integrate a reasonable variety of interests and enterprises into a pleasingly shaped, dynamically developing, and organically united narrative that I would like to call my life" (134).

7. One partial exception is the remarkable book by Josef Chytry, *The Aesthetic State: A Quest in Modern German Thought* (Berkeley and Los Angeles: University of California Press, 1989). As the title of the book implies, however, Chytry is primarily concerned with the political, rather than the strictly moral, implications of making aesthetic categories universal. Although Chytry is certainly aware of its significance, ethics as such rarely appears in his account. More relevant, but rather narrowly focused, is the study by Doris Bachmann-Medick, *Die ästhetische Ordnung des Handelns: Moralphilosophie und Ästhetik in der Popularphilosophie des 18. Jahrhunderts* (Stuttgart: Metzler, 1989).

threat to social stability. There was then, as there appears to be now, a pervasive sense that the moral certainties of the past were thus endangered, if not already fatally weakened, by the decreasing influence of external control on individual lives. Several thinkers therefore attempted to identify some purely internal or subjective measures for regulating behavior that would afford the greatest possible personal freedom while at the same time preventing actions that would impinge on the freedom or well-being of others. Like the proposals advanced today by Rorty, Foucault, and others, the moral model then thought to offer the best means of fulfilling these contradictory requirements also entailed some fusion of aesthetic and ethical values. In light of such parallels, we might reasonably expect that the outcome of this earlier experiment in moral philosophy, undertaken in response to a dramatically shifting cultural context that appears to have shared so many similarities to our own, might cast some prognostic light on our present and future prospects.

This previous period in question, as the reader will have guessed, was the European Enlightenment. That the roots of our own modernity, including both its positive and negative filiations, extend into the eighteenth century is no longer a novel suggestion. But the habitual acknowledgment of our indebtedness has not always found its adequate expression in the archaeological labor of uncovering the deeper historical strata on which modern consciousness rests. This disinclination to engage with history applies particularly, and disastrously, to discussions of ethics. MacIntyre himself, who stands as one of the few exceptions to this general rule, has repeatedly criticized the "persistently unhistorical treatment of moral philosophy by contemporary philosophers in both the writing about and the teaching of the subject."[8] To explore, in turn, the reasons for this almost defiantly unhistorical attitude toward ethics, which naturally has its own specific historical causes, would require a separate study. Let it suffice to mention, as being symptomatic of this greater tendency, that in his otherwise brilliant, panoptic survey, *The Philosophy of the Enlightenment*, Ernst Cassirer devoted individual chapters to the most important developments in eighteenth-century episte-

8. MacIntyre, *After Virtue*, 11; see also 59. Jerome B. Schneewind, ed., *Moral Philosophy from Montaigne to Kant: An Anthology* (Cambridge: Cambridge University Press, 1990), 1: x, has similarly written "that there is surprisingly little secondary literature on many of the moral philosophers of the seventeenth and eighteenth centuries. This is particularly noticeable if one is looking for help in gaining a historical perspective on them. Among the innumerable studies of the ethics of Hobbes or Hume or Kant, few indeed make serious attempts to locate them in the controversies in which they took themselves to be engaging, and there are not even many critical studies of lesser figures—sometimes none at all. I came to think, therefore, that an anthology of primary material might help stimulate interest in a neglected but quite important part of the history of philosophy." This defect was also noted by David Fate Norton, *David Hume: Common-Sense Moralist, Sceptical Metaphysician* (Princeton: Princeton University Press, 1982), 10–13.

mology, theology, historiography, natural science, and aesthetics—but hardly a word to ethics.

Yet ethics was never very far from the mind of any Enlightenment thinker, and most felt that morality was, in the words of David Hume, "a subject that interests us above all others."[9] When Hume made that assertion in the late 1730s an intellectual movement was already well under way that would eventually culminate in the crystallization of a figure that personified the real fulfillment of that all-consuming subject. The beautiful soul served as the ideational node at which the ethical imperatives of the eighteenth century converged; and concentrated within this single, memorable formula, it thereby assumed a further potentiation, almost literally gaining a life of its own. And if the beautiful soul thus stood at the pinnacle of what Hume had confessed was the predominant interest of his time, then the lacuna in our historical knowledge about it is serious indeed.[10] In reconstructing the lost history of the beautiful soul I have therefore found it necessary to retrace certain segments of eighteenth-century moral philosophy in order to locate the concept of the beautiful soul within that still largely misappreciated historical and theoretical constellation. Although I concentrate on German thought during the second half of the 1700s—it is there, after all, that the beautiful soul emerged in its most distinctive and compelling form—I also discuss along the way the numerous French and English contributions to the formation of this ideal. The invention of the beautiful soul was a collective enterprise carried out by the entire European Enlightenment, and my own retelling of its history seeks to reflect that cosmopolitan diversity.

One of the most significant—and most characteristic—stages in the evolution of the beautiful soul was that it did not remain bound to the sphere of philosophical abstraction, but emerged at midcentury in most of the other major literary media as well, especially in the burgeoning narrative form, the modern novel. In an age that did not insist on the split between signifier and signified and considered the mimetic depiction of reality as the primary and, moreover, attainable goal of art, the fictional treatment of the beautiful soul lent the idea a credibility that it could never have otherwise possessed. It seemed so real, in fact, that later eighteenth-century writers no longer

9. David Hume, *A Treatise of Human Nature*, ed. L. A. Selby-Bigge, 2d ed., ed. P. H. Nidditch (Oxford: Oxford University Press, 1978), 455.
10. Only one monograph about the beautiful soul has ever appeared in any language, and it is now almost seventy years old: Hans Schmeer, *Der Begriff der "schönen Seele" besonders bei Wieland und in der deutschen Literatur des 18. Jahrhunderts* (Berlin: Emil Ebering, 1926). To my knowledge there have been only two doctoral dissertations devoted to the topic; see Heinrich Pohlmeier, "Untersuchungen zum Begriff der schönen Seele im achtzehnten Jahrhundert und in der Goethezeit" (Ph.D. diss., University of Münster, 1954), and Jeffrey Scott Librett, "Rhapsodic Dispositions: Engenderments of the Ground in the Discourse of the 'Beautiful Soul' (Shaftesbury, Kant, Hegel, Heidegger)" (Ph.D. diss., Cornell University, 1989).

thought of "beauty of soul" as nothing more than a noble, utopian ideal, which as such every person should strive to attain, but which no one could ever fully achieve. Many assumed, instead, that people not only *could* but actually *did* exist who exemplified the attributes it entailed. The most striking example of this mental shift from theoretical possibility to putative certainty was the eighteenth-century revival of physiognomy, the ancient practice of reading external traits as legible signs of inner character. For in its equation between physical beauty and moral goodness, physiognomy assumed the reality of beautiful souls.

It will become obvious that the conceptual elements joined together under the term "beautiful soul" did not issue from a single source, that the beautiful soul amounted to a composite image formed by various components borrowed from otherwise discrete realms of discourse. It is possible, however, to discern three main influences on the Enlightenment notion of the beautiful soul and to weigh independently the role of each in producing the finished portrait. But although I treat each of the individual ingredients more or less as unique, isolated forces in the first three chapters, it should nevertheless be kept in mind that it was precisely in their combined effect that the beautiful soul, as the embodiment of their convergence, gained its contemporary salience. In the opening chapter I deal almost solely with what are properly speaking the philosophical underpinnings of the notion and emphasize, in particular, British thought of the late-seventeenth and early eighteenth centuries, which is when the modern idea of moral beauty achieved its first explicit formulation. Although part of the original purpose of moral beauty was to help disentangle ethics from theology, in the second chapter I stress the continued connection between religion and morals, especially for German-speaking thinkers. In the third chapter I then focus on the final major strand of thought that substantially shaped the eighteenth-century conception of the beautiful soul: the Hellenic ideal of *kalokagathia* and its latter-day German appropriation. Following these analytic excursuses into the separate philosophical, theological, and even linguistic components of the idea of the beautiful soul, the remaining four chapters entail a more synthetic consideration of its subsequent chronological progress. Covering a period spanning little more than five decades, they demonstrate how the beautiful soul made its literary debut during the middle years of the century and won almost instantaneous and overwhelming public acceptance, and how the idea thereafter eventually gained entrance into the most exclusive intellectual circles of the day. But by the beginning of the 1800s, the limitations of the beautiful soul had already made themselves manifest to anyone who cared to notice them. Once they were openly and unmistakably pointed out by the critics of the idea, the beautiful soul retired from its long and extraordinary career and gradually retreated into its present obscurity.

This is not to say, naturally, that the impulse to apply aesthetic criteria to the entirety of human experience, or the utopian wish to erect an "aesthetic state," ended with the Enlightenment itself. In many respects, as Josef Chytry has splendidly shown, this desire continued—often enough with dire results—to dominate intellectual, cultural, and political ambitions in Germany until the present century. But my aim here is to pursue both a more modest and a more specific end. I have resurrected this supreme representative of eighteenth-century moral self-understanding in order to contribute a missing but I believe essential chapter to any comprehensive historical assessment of the European Enlightenment in its broadest definition. Yet as I have mentioned, I think that some more immediate gain might perhaps result from this enterprise as well. By contemplating the rise and fall of the beautiful soul, which was originally conceived in response to a widespread perception of moral instability and social drift, we might be better able to measure the efficacy of any similarly inspired "aesthetics of existence" at a time when far fewer certainties exist.

1

The Advent of Modern Ethics in Britain and the Emergence of the Idea of Moral Beauty

> Virtue is nothing but inward beauty;
> beauty nothing but outward virtue.
> —Sir Francis Bacon

The practitioners of Enlightenment, to say nothing of their adversaries, always remained acutely aware of the pragmatic implications of their enterprise. The final success or failure of their efforts, they well knew, would be gauged less by their speculative achievements than by the practical results they produced in shaping the conduct and welfare of every individual life they touched. They thought, or rather they passionately believed, that knowledge—the mature fruit of rational inquiry—ought never to be sought for its own sake, but that its value should be judged by its ability to change and, one may hope, to improve the various subjects to which it was applied. Despite the many real and profound differences among them, it remained true for every thinker from Locke to Kant that philosophy in particular was considered to be intrinsically unable to add anything new to the store of human knowledge. At best, it could put what we already possessed in order and—perhaps—provide a secure foundation for future endeavor. And since this reduced regimen appeared to be all that the once-proud province of philosophy could maintain, it seemed all the more imperative that it be made to perform this, its modest but proper role, in a way that had some immediate and tangible benefit.

We see a typical expression of these somewhat diminished expectations in what might initially appear to have been an improbable quarter. Well into the second half of the eighteenth century, when the first leaders of the Enlightenment had already reached the zenith of their energy and influence, and the tirelessly repeated expectation that the civilized world would one day radiate in the light of reason and truth was starting to sound more programmatic than plausible, Frederick II began to worry. The Prussian "Philosopher King," the enlightened sovereign who had rejuvenated the Academy of Sciences and Letters in Berlin, which had risen up in an astonishingly brief time to rival similar institutions in London, Paris, and St. Petersburg; the royal resident of Sanssouci, the cultivated friend and admirer of Voltaire and, indeed, of all things French—Frederick the Great had begun to show unmistakable signs of doubting the value of those very efforts which he had so long supported with his active patronage and interest. As he wrote in a letter of 1768 to Jean Le Rond d'Alembert, one of the *philosophes* he most esteemed,

> All modern endeavors in the natural sciences relating to electricity, gravitation, and chemistry have not improved the people and have not changed their moral constitution; these things are therefore a luxury. Even the natural scientists themselves have not become better people through their science! What, then, do all of those discoveries the Moderns are making mean for society if philosophy neglects the capital of morality and manners to which the Ancients devoted their every energy?[1]

Somber as it sounds, this was not so much an admission of defeat, or an intrusion of resignation into a mind that was optimistic by principle, as it was a sober recognition of the limitations inherent in those sciences which address only our physical, and thus mortal, state. With more than a slight nod in the direction of that "other" Frenchman, Rousseau, Frederick felt that without some real, perceptible effect on the lives of the people who both produced and profited from the advancement of knowledge this activity itself amounted to little more than a higher form of self-gratification. One of the most prudent investments the Prussian monarch himself had made toward increasing the "capital of morality" in his own native state was to transfer British thought to Germany (filtered though it was through the lens of French philosophy) by inviting its best continental advocates to his eastern outpost. For it had been in Britain that the modern science devoted to improving the "moral constitution" of humanity had first gained a sizable following as an independent field of philosophical endeavor.

The learned wits of the eighteenth century were fond of Cicero's remark that Socrates had been the first to bring philosophy down from the heavens and place it on the level of human concerns, but agreed that Socrates's seventeenth-century colleague Thomas Hobbes had lowered it entirely too

---

1. Cited from Adolf Harnack, *Geschichte der königlich-preussischen Akademie der Wissenschaften zu Berlin* (Berlin: Reichsdruckerei, 1900), 1:371.

far. Although the publication in 1651 of Hobbes's disturbing masterpiece, *Leviathan*, does mark the inauguration of modern ethics, it was anything but a benevolent beginning. His ideas about morality, religion, and civil society were almost immediately perceived to be so dangerous, or so repugnant, that they encountered the severest sort of censure imaginable. At the height of the resistance that quickly gathered against his work, the authorities branded Hobbes an atheist, ceremoniously banned his books and, finally, had them publicly burned.[2] Because of a generally more tolerant political and religious climate that followed in the wake of the Glorious Revolution in 1688, however—and no doubt because of the seemingly infinite human capacity to absorb and reconcile even the most antithetical ideas—Hobbes's works no longer inspired such violent opposition after the turn of the century. But throughout the next one hundred years and beyond, his name nonetheless remained notorious, and merely to mention it in any other than the most dismissive manner might well have risked suspicion—or something far worse.

This vehement and unanimously negative reaction to Hobbes may seem, on first inspection, somewhat surprising. Hobbes's attempt to disengage the study of both human and natural affairs from the doctrinal authority of the Church, coupled with his insistence that human reason alone could lay bare the inner workings of the world, should have won, one would think, nothing but unqualified support from enlightened and unprejudiced minds. In addition, and for eighteenth-century thinkers equally important, Hobbes was captivated by the question of scientific and philosophical method. Not that this interest was unique to Hobbes: Francis Bacon's *Novum Organum* of 1620 and René Descartes's *Discourse on Method* of 1637 (which differ in direction but not in temperament) are only two of the best-known examples of the almost obsessive contemporary concern with the significance of procedure. But it was the specific approach Hobbes took to the methodological problem of philosophical inquiry that ought to have recommended him to his eighteenth-century readers. In particular, Hobbes conceived of himself as strictly applying the method of mathematics to the investigation of nonmathematical problems, especially to physiological, psychological, and social studies.[3] By observing the procedures of geometrical analysis and synthesis—or what are also known as the resolutive and compositive methods—he felt that it would be possible to discover a few simple, stable

---

2. See Samuel I. Mintz, *The Hunting of Leviathan: Seventeenth-Century Reactions to the Materialism and Moral Philosophy of Thomas Hobbes* (Cambridge: Cambridge University Press, 1962), vii. For further information on the reception of Hobbes, see also Jonathan Bowle, *Hobbes and His Critics: A Study in Seventeenth-Century Constitutionalism* (London: Jonathan Cape, 1951).
3. There are very informative descriptions of Hobbes's ideas about method in Richard Peters, *Hobbes* (Harmondsworth, U.K.: Penguin, 1956), esp. 43–74, and in F. S. McNeilly, *The Anatomy of "Leviathan"* (London: Macmillan, 1968), 59–91.

laws of human nature that would have the same validity and certainty as the axioms of geometry. It is therefore not just a figure of speech, but a statement of firmly held principle, that Hobbes announces in the fifth chapter of *Leviathan*, "Of Reason and Science": "When a man *reasoneth*, he does nothing else but conceive a sum total, from *addition* of parcels; or conceive a remainder, from *subtraction* of one sum from another. . . . For REASON, in this sense, is nothing but *reckoning*."[4] To understand human behavior and society thus meant for Hobbes systematically to "subtract" all of the elements from the totality of human experience as it appeared to us in its bewildering natural complexity until one reached some irreducible core, some central, solitary constituent that Hobbes felt would necessarily be the originary moment, the basic law of its entire organization. Then, on the firm foundation of this first principle, one could proceed to reconstruct—or, in Hobbes's metaphor, to "add"—the various elements together again in order to demonstrate how the whole structure, once we have recognized its inherent organization, was uniformly ruled by this single law.

Hobbes believed he had found that most primary component of human behavior in the laws and mechanics of motion: ranging from the most minuscule atoms colliding against one another, receiving and imparting energetic movement, to the clash of entire armies caught up in the advance and retreat of combat, the elemental principle driving the world, Hobbes thought, is motion. In individual human beings this law is expressed as appetite and aversion, which denotes the motion toward or away from the objects in our purview. Whether we like to acknowledge it or not (and Hobbes felt that mainly we did not), it follows from this premise that human happiness can only be measured by the relative degree to which our desires are met and the sources of our aversions abated. With unsmiling solemnity he suggested that "we are to consider, that the felicity of this life, consisteth not in the repose of a mind satisfied. For there is no such *finis ultimus*, utmost aim, nor *summum bonum*, greatest good, as is spoken of in the books of the old moral philosophers. . . . Felicity is a continual progress of the desire, from one object to another, the attaining of the former, being still but the way to the latter" (*Leviathan*, 63). Motion, that is, or the unimpeded access to the things we wish to possess, constitutes the principle on which our happiness depends. And since Hobbes considered the "general inclination of all mankind" to be "a perpetual and restless desire of power after power that ceaseth only in death" (64), it was only reasonable that he imagined the world quite literally as a constantly moving battleground of the selfish and the egotistical ruthlessly waging war on one another in violent, unceasing competition for increasing personal power and hegemony.

4. Thomas Hobbes, *Leviathan, or the Matter, Forme and Power of a Commonwealth Ecclesiasticall and Civil*, ed. Michael Oakeshott (Oxford: Basil Blackwell, 1946), 25–26. Henceforth cited parenthetically in the text as "*Leviathan*" by page number.

The martial metaphors are entirely Hobbes's own. He was convinced that in the "natural state" of humanity—that is, before we had formed any social organization—human beings were "in that condition which is called war; and such a war, as is of every man, against every man" (82).[5] Clearly, Hobbes was deeply pessimistic about the deepest wellsprings of human motivation. He believed that if he pursued his scientifically validated analysis far enough he could show that naked self-interest ultimately fueled our every action and thought. And here, in his famous, chilling words, he drew his bleakest picture of the hypothetical "natural" condition of humanity before we had sought protection from our own self-destructive proclivities by entering into the social contract:

> In such condition, there is no place for industry; because the fruit thereof is uncertain: and consequently no culture of the earth; no navigation, nor use of the commodities that may be imported by sea; no commodious building; no instruments of moving, and removing, such things as require much force; no knowledge of the face of the earth; no account of time; no arts; no letters; no society; and which is worst of all, continual fear, and danger of violent death; and the life of man, solitary, poor, nasty, brutish, and short. (*Leviathan*, 82)

In Hobbes's geometrically patterned, mechanistically regulated, and brutally competitive universe there is obviously no room for sentimental pieties. All is cause and effect, matter in motion, means to ends, with no regard for the niceties of polite convention. "Moral life" in the natural state, according to any customary conception of ethical norms, simply would not exist.[6] "Good" and "evil," Hobbes argued, are entirely a product and function of social organization and hence totally meaningless outside that artificial context. Moreover, in the "war" that comprised the human condition before it was checked by the restraints imposed by the laws of the sovereign state, traditional Christian virtues such as charity, pity, and brotherly love were thus not only absent, but suicidal. "To this war of every man, against every man," Hobbes coolly explained, "this also is consequent; that nothing can be unjust. The notions of right and wrong, justice and injustice have there no place. Where there is no common power, there is no law: where no law, no injustice. . . . Justice, and injustice are none of the faculties neither of thebody nor mind. . . . They are qualities that relate to men in society, not in solitude" (*Leviathan*, 83). In Hobbes's secular Leviathan, then, morality is nothing more than a late-born child of practical social convenience. It is

5. Chapter 13 of *Leviathan* is titled "Of the Natural Condition of Mankind as concerning their Felicity, and Misery."
6. One of the best accounts of Hobbes's ethical theory is by Jean Hampton, *Hobbes and the Social Contract Tradition* (Cambridge: Cambridge University Press, 1986), esp. 27–57.

merely an artificial instrument of mutual control that is generated and maintained by a complex equilibrium, in which the external forces represented by the will of the state are balanced against the immediate satisfaction of individual desires. Fulfillment of these desires is thus deferred, checked not by obedient submission to a higher moral instance, but instead by an astute—and carefully "reckoning"—consciousness of the probably painful consequences attending the transgression of the sovereign's commands. Morally "good" conduct is therefore the product of the sensible wish to avoid punishment and is reinforced by the promise of long-term gain. Thus transmuted and tempered though it appears in this clinical description, the engine that drives this social machine is still raw and insatiable self-interest.

What gave his contemporary readers pause was not just what Hobbes positively asserted, though that is certainly grim enough; rather, what he omitted from his account seemed to be more expressive of his true purposes. Although he expanded with a fairly frightening complacence on what he considered to be the realities of "this life," he conspicuously avoided reference to the one to come. Indeed, his comments on received religion (and especially Catholicism) were generally laced with a generous amount of animus against what he considered to be an irredeemably corrupt and self-serving clergy who exploited the foolish superstitions of the uneducated masses. One could very well argue that by portraying the natural state of humanity as utterly and irredeemably depraved, Hobbes presents a vision that is not essentially unlike the Christian conception of the human condition immediately after the Fall, before we had learned to understand and obey the laws of God.[7] But precisely because Hobbes never explicitly establishes this connection, and because of his wish to limit his inquiry to tangible, verifiable realities, he actively sought, so it seemed, to prevent such a connection from occurring in the minds of his readers. It was instead Hobbes's express intention, and one that most of his critics felt he had fulfilled much too successfully, to present the outlines of a moral theory in his *Leviathan* that is secular in both origin and aim.

The reaction to Hobbes was immediate and massive. His reduction of human action to, at best, long-range rational self-interest flew in the face of those who preached that human beings were by nature inclined toward the sort of charitable behavior they felt was merely codified, not constructed, by Christian doctrine. But it was impossible, once Hobbes had struck his blow, to ignore his arguments or pretend that one could simply return to the state of innocence prior to the publication of the *Leviathan*. Hobbes had to be

7. See J. A. Passmore, *Ralph Cudworth: An Interpretation* (Cambridge: Cambridge University Press, 1951), 83.

met and refuted on his own ground, which meant employing, if possible, the same tools of rational analysis at the same level of methodological rigor to defend what he had tried to dismantle. Although many believed, as Bacon once famously said, that a little philosophy may promote atheism, Hobbes's opponents rested their hopes in the second half of the maxim, that real depth in philosophy would just as surely lead us back to religion. Instead, what occurred was a gradual replacement of theology with ethics, which in its philosophical guise produced so many new problems that the reason it arose in the first place—namely, to support Christian faith with reasoned argument—became lost in the attempt to justify the discipline itself.[8]

Among Hobbes's most committed and able adversaries was that loose group of thinkers now generally known as the Cambridge Platonists. They were actually more independent of one another than this label implies, and their crusade against this common enemy served more, perhaps, than anything else to unite them. All born within ten years of one another during the second decade of the seventeenth century, Henry More, John Smith, and particularly Benjamin Whichcote and Ralph Cudworth—the last-named being the most astute of the four—developed a highly rationalistic response to the problems raised by Hobbes's plain and forceful contentions.[9] Dugald Stewart, one of the best informed and, after Hume, one of the most stylistically polished among the eighteenth-century Scottish philosophers, once described Cudworth as "one of the first who successfully combated this new philosophy," adding that his thought "displays a rich store of enlightened and choice erudition, penetrated throughout with a peculiar vein of sobered and subdued Platonism."[10] Cudworth's main work on ethics, his *Treatise concerning Eternal and Immutable Morality*, remained, like almost all of his writings, an unfinished though massive fragment, and it was not published until 1731, long after his death in 1688. Its title succinctly states the broadest aim of the book: to prove that there did exist, as Cudworth asserted after

8. Cf., on this development, the informative book by Gerald R. Cragg, *Reason and Authority in the Eighteenth Century* (Cambridge: Cambridge University Press, 1964).

9. See Ernst Cassirer, *The Platonic Renaissance in England*, trans. James P. Pettegrove (New York: Gordian, 1970).

10. In Dugald Stewart, *Dissertation: Exhibiting the Progress of Metaphysical, Ethical, and Political Philosophy, since the Revival of Letters in Europe*, in *Collected Works*, ed. Sir William Hamilton (Edinburgh: Thomas Constable, 1854–60), 1:85–86. In the same passage, Stewart characterizes the general response to Hobbes in this way: "As Hobbes, in the frenzy of his political zeal, had been led to sacrifice wantonly all the principles of religion and morality to the establishment of his conclusions, his works not only gave offence to the friends of liberty, but excited a general alarm among all sound moralists. His doctrine, in particular, that there is no *natural* distinction between Right and Wrong, and that these are dependent on the arbitrary will of the civil magistrate, was so obviously subversive of all the commonly received ideas concerning the moral constitution of human nature, that it became indispensably necessary, either to expose the sophistry of the attempt, or to admit, with Hobbes, that man is a beast of prey, incapable of being governed by any motives but fear, and the desire of self-preservation."

the words of Plato, "something naturally and immutably good and just."[11] Human virtue was not just a function of the social contract, Cudworth and all of the Cambridge Platonists maintained *contra* Hobbes, but a separate, independent quality found in every man and woman, although often obscured by the blurring effect of circumstance or habit. Yet instead of constructing an ethical theory per se, Cudworth devoted most of the *Treatise* to an elaboration of the epistemology designed to bolster this primary claim. Underlying all of his arguments was the central notion that contrary to Hobbes's theory, human reason was not the product of the material forces setting matter in motion, and the mind was not simply the passive receptacle of randomly occurring external stimuli. If it were indeed the case that the mind possessed no active properties of its own, Cudworth asserted, then it would have been impossible for us ever to rise above the primitive level of pure sense perception. Instead, Cudworth wanted to show

> that there are some ideas of the mind which were not stamped or imprinted upon it from the sensible objects without, and therefore must needs arise from the innate vigour and activity of the mind itself . . . such as are the ideas of wisdom, folly, prudence, imprudence, knowledge, ignorance, verity, falsity, virtue, vice, honesty, dishonesty, justice, injustice, volition, cogitation, nay of sense itself, which is a species of cogitation, and which is not perceptible by any sense. (3:586)

It would be difficult indeed to think of some aspect of mind that this exhaustive list does not include, and Cudworth's insistence that we possess not just innate intellectual powers, but innate "knowledge" and "wisdom" as well, fared rather badly at the hands of Locke. But it is important nonetheless to appreciate the systematic quality of Cudworth's intentions. For the tenor of his thought affected, though more indirectly than through any positive influence, a significant part of the course moral philosophy later took in the eighteenth century.[12] The attempt by the Cambridge Platonists to resist Hobbes's materialist relativism and what they saw as the consequent disintegration of the traditional (that is, the theological) bases supporting moral thought did not occur, as is sometimes supposed, as the result of a flight from reality into ethereal, irrational realms. Rather, it issued from the widely shared conviction (which, in their writings, was reinforced by frequent reference to their favorite Greek philosophers, and principally to Plato and Plotinos) that

11. Ralph Cudworth, *The True Intellectual System of the Universe: wherein all the Reason and Philosophy of Atheism is confuted, and its Impossibility demonstrated, with a Treatise concerning Eternal and Immutable Morality* (London: Thomas Tegg, 1845), 3:530.
12. That Cudworth significantly stimulated the main non-Utilitarian ethical movements of the eighteenth century is the (unusual, but I think correct) argument of Passmore, *Ralph Cudworth*, 105.

the fundamental characteristics of the human mind were always and everywhere the same. In arguing for an unchanging morality, Cudworth was clearly not making the patently absurd claim that we are born, say, with a liberal education. But he did insist that we *are* given—innately and, what was the same thing in his mind, from God—the essential capacities to acquire it. Also in explicit analogy to the principles of mathematics, Cudworth reasoned that we may come only late—or conceivably never—to learn the laws of algebra, but that our knowledge or ignorance of them in no way affects their intrinsic validity and permanence. And it is on this basis (and, he thought, on this one alone) that anything like a universal system of ethics is at all possible. Nevertheless, once the epistemological conditions enabling an "eternal and immutable" morality had been established, Cudworth and his confederates did contend that it was equally necessary to imagine God as the guarantor of their conception. For, Cudworth explained, "It is not possible that there should be any such thing as morality, unless there be a God, that is, an infinite eternal mind that is the first original and source of all things, whose nature is the first rule and exemplar of morality" (3:645).

Cudworth's attempt, as well as that of the Cambridge Platonists as a whole, to shore up the ground of morality by equating reason with revelation was the logical and probably inevitable expression of an age that increasingly required sound arguments, rather than simple assurances or threats, to uphold its religious beliefs. Yet at the same time, a peculiar dialectical shift was already under way that served, if not actually to subvert these very efforts, then at least to carry them in directions their authors could never have wished for or even foreseen. For once ethics was subjected to rational inquiry, it quickly shed the last vestiges of its theological encumbrance and soon assimilated itself to these new "scientific" criteria of judgment. As Mark Pattison once noted concerning the developments taking place in the religious thought of the day, "reason was at first offered as the basis of faith, but gradually became its substitute."[13] Or, as that eighteenth-century observer Edward Gibbon also once remarked—with a satisfaction he made no attempt to conceal—in the endeavor "to reconcile the jarring interests of reason and piety," the relentless force of the former was destined finally to prevail.[14]

It was a fundamental characteristic of moral philosophy before the modern period that the justification for moral precepts had always been drawn from some external set of principles. Within the Christian context, it used to be relatively simple to answer the two most basic questions of ethics, namely,

13. Mark Pattison, "Tendencies of Religious Thought in England, 1688–1750," in *Essays* (Oxford: Oxford University Press, 1889), 2:48.
14. Edward Gibbon, *The History of the Decline and Fall of the Roman Empire*, ed. J. B. Bury, (London: Methuen, 1909–14; reprint, New York: AMS Press, 1974), 1:33.

w do I know what is good? and Why should I choose to do what is "right"
when doing the opposite might provide me with more immediate and greater gain? God told us clearly enough what our duties were, and his promises
regarding their transgression or observance were equally direct, if not always
very precise. But although the Church had ready answers to both of those
questions, the impartial arbiter of rational judgment required an explanation that carried some *internal* grounds for conviction. How *do* we, then—or,
to phrase it more cautiously, how would we—make moral distinctions or
ethical judgments in the absence of divine authority? Do we somehow simply
and innately "know" or "sense" that something is right or wrong? Or are we
really born with no more moral equipment than those miserable beings
described by Hobbes's "state of nature," who in order to prevent their mutual destruction, require the rule of commands imposed by some sacred or
secular sovereign? And, concomitantly, what *are* the true motives for ethical
behavior? Is it no more than fear of punishment and hope for reward? Or is
there a fuller, more satisfying psychological explanation, one more flattering
to our favored notions of ourselves as the unique possessors of reason, but
also well-founded enough to convince modern, skeptical minds who now
demand to be persuaded not by the force of ancient or ecclesiastical authority, but by rational argument and sound proof? It is partially in response to
such questions that John Locke wrote the *Essay concerning Human Understanding* (1690). Among its many other qualities, the *Essay* marks a decisive
moment in the history of the transition from the reliance on religious belief
to the necessity of rational conviction in moral philosophy, for it attempted
to satisfy both requirements at once.

It would be impossible to overestimate the importance of Locke's *Essay* to
the later thinkers of the Enlightenment. His philosophy, together with the
spirit (if not always the letter) of Newtonian science, left an indelible mark
on the works of almost every thinker who lived and wrote during the century
following its publication. Voltaire, in a phrase that described not so much
Locke himself as the unprecedented enthusiasm his ideas generated, once
exclaimed that "perhaps there never was a more sage, a more methodical
mind, never a more precise logician, than Locke."[15] Readers of Locke's
rambling, somewhat repetitive *Essay* admire the scope of its concerns and
the originality of its presentation, even if they rarely make such extravagant
claims about the author's considerable, but by no means infallible, logical
abilities. Yet for all of its breathless overstatement, Voltaire's aperçu reveals
an almost universal bias regarding the primary focus of Locke's philosophical contribution that with few exceptions has remained dominant to this

15. Voltaire, *Lettres philosophiques*, in *Oeuvres complètes*, ed. Louis Moland (Paris: Garnier
Frères, 1877–85), 22:121.

day. Locke's *Essay* continues, that is, to occupy a place of special distinction in the history of philosophy, but for reasons that on closer inspection contradict his broadest intentions. Usually viewed as the founder of modern empirical epistemology, Locke himself saw this philosophical project as being subordinate to other needs. As the introductory "Epistle to the Reader" explains, Locke originally sat down to write his *Essay* for a few friends who, "meeting at my Chamber, and discoursing on a Subject very remote from this, found themselves quickly at a stand, by the Difficulties that rose on every side."[16] As someone who had been present at the meeting—Locke's friend James Tyrrell—later reported it, the difficulties to which Locke referred had not been about solving the problems of perception, reflection, or sensation, or about any of the other concerns related to the specific workings of the mind that in fact came to dominate the pages of the *Essay*. Instead, his primary motivation was to secure a foundation on which "the Principles of morality, and reveal'd Religion" could rest.[17]

It is true that Locke began his *Essay* with purely epistemological concerns and that he wanted to demonstrate, as he famously wrote, "the Original, Certainty, and Extent of humane Knowledge" (I, i, § 2). But we forget (or fail to realize fully) that Locke intended such an investigation merely as the intermediate means of securing a reliable basis for the practical offices of life. For only after we have ascertained the true nature of the materials composing our "entire store" of knowledge could we then confidently advance to what Locke himself considered to be the much more important matter regarding the ends to which this knowledge could and ought to be applied. And the most important of these ends had to do, naturally enough, with the conduct of our lives, which was motivated by the universally felt desire for what Locke and his followers typically called the attainment of human happiness—both here and hereafter. As Locke phrased it, "Happiness and misery are the two great springs of human actions, and though through different ways we find men so busy in the world, they all aim at happiness, and desire to avoid misery."[18] And the means by which we could attain this "happiness" were, for Locke, equally certain: "God, . . . by an inseparable connexion, joined *Virtue* and publick Happiness together" (I, iii, § 6). By concentrating so exclusively on the purely epistemological aspects of the *Essay* (and of eighteenth-century thought in general), we have thus

16. John Locke, *An Essay concerning Human Understanding*, ed. Peter H. Nidditch (Oxford: Oxford University Press, 1975), 7. The *Essay* itself is cited parenthetically in the text by book, chapter, and paragraph numbers.
17. See John Colman, *John Locke's Moral Philosophy* (Edinburgh: Edinburgh University Press, 1983), 1. This is also the account given in Nidditch's foreword to his edition of the *Essay*.
18. Cited from the fragment "Of Ethics in general," which is printed in Peter King, *The Life of John Locke, with Extracts from His Correspondence, Journals, and Common-Place Books* (London: Henry Colburn & Richard Bentley, 1830), 2:122.

lost sight of the instrumental, and therefore auxiliary, character that these antecedent researches held for Locke and his contempories.[19] The pursuit of knowledge in and of itself was, to eighteenth-century thinkers, worse than simply worthless: pedantry was seen as a positive evil that was thought to lead to foolishness, vanity, and arrogance, and (as the fortunes of Faust vividly demonstrated) potentially to eternal damnation.[20] And it was how to avoid just such a fate that Locke and his friends most wished to discover for themselves and to promulgate among their fellow mortals. If the end of human life is indeed happiness, which is made possible only through the practice of virtue, it is obviously of no small significance that we secure the knowledge that would reliably lead us toward that ultimate goal.

Although Locke addressed particular moral issues throughout the whole of his *Essay*, it was not until the final paragraphs that he explicitly set ethics in a systematic relation to the other branches of inquiry. Here he made his well-known division of philosophy into the three areas of investigation accessible to human reason, setting forth that he was concerned with

> all that can fall within the compass of Humane Understanding, being either, *First*, The Nature of Things, as they are in themselves, their Relations, and their manner of Operation: Or *Secondly*, That which Man himself ought to do, as a rational and voluntary Agent, for the Attainment of any End, especially Happiness: Or, *Thirdly*, The ways and means, whereby the Knowledge of both the one and the other of these, are attained and communicated. (IV, xxi, § 1)

Natural philosophy, ethics, and logic, in other words, (Locke also called the third category "semiotics") described the possible fields and thus the abso-

19. A notable exception to the tendency to discount the religious and ethical impetus in Locke is the essay by Richard Ashcraft, "Faith and Knowledge in Locke's Philosophy," in *John Locke: Problems and Perspectives, A Collection of New Essays*, ed. John E. Yolton, (Cambridge: Cambridge University Press, 1969), 194–223. See also, in the same collection, the superb essay by Hans Aarsleff, "The State of Nature and the Nature of Man in Locke," 99–136. One can also still profitably consult James Gibson's book *Locke's Theory of Knowledge and Its Historical Relations* (Cambridge: Cambridge University Press, 1917).

20. See the witty, though representative, description of pedantry in no. 105 of Joseph Addison, *The Spectator*, ed. Donald F. Bond (Oxford: Oxford University Press, 1965), 1:438: "The Truth of it is, Learning, like Travelling, and all other Methods of Improvement, as it finishes good Sense, so it makes a silly Man ten thousand times more insufferable, by supplying variety of Matter to his Impertinence, and giving him an Opportunity of abounding in Absurdities. Shallow Pedants cry up one another much more than Men of solid and useful Learning. To read the Titles they give an Editor, or Collator of a Manuscript, you would take him for the Glory of the Common Wealth of Letters, and the Wonder of his Age; when perhaps upon Examination you find that he has only Rectify'd a *Greek* Particle, or laid out a whole Sentence in proper Comma's. They are obliged indeed to be thus lavish of their Praises, that they may keep one another in Countenance; and it is no wonder if a great deal of Knowledge, which is not capable of making a Man Wise, has a natural Tendency to make him Vain and Arrogant."

lute limits of human knowledge. But there is clearly a certain degree of judgment implicit in this passage. Natural philosophy can afford only what Locke termed "bare speculative Truth," but ethics enables us to put this knowledge to real, practical use. It was, he wrote, the "Skill of Right applying our own Powers and Actions, for the Attainment of Things good and useful. The most considerable under this Head, is *Ethicks*, which is the seeking out of those Rules, and Measures of humane Actions, which lead to Happiness, and the Means to practise them. The end of this is not bare Speculation, and the Knowledge of Truth; but Right, and a Conduct suitable to it" (IV, xxi, § 3). In another section of the *Essay*, Locke rendered the imperative toward moral inquiry as the basis for ethical action more explicit still: "'Tis rational to conclude, that our proper Imployment lies in those Enquiries, and in that sort of Knowledge, which is suited to our natural Capacities, and carries in it our greatest interest, *i.e.* the Condition of our eternal Estate. Hence I think I may conclude, that *Morality* is *the proper Science, and Business of Mankind in general*" (IV, xii, § 11).[21] Never before in modern times had the importance of moral knowledge in and of itself been so clearly and forcefully expressed. It had been part of the positive, though unintended, legacy of Hobbes that in their efforts to prove him wrong his critics had pushed ethics into the center of intellectual debate. Locke had merely taken the next logical, though in its consequences momentous, step by proclaiming that ethics amounted to nothing less than the single most essential concern of humanity.

Now, ethics is a notoriously slippery subject, one that always threatens to elude the grasp of even the most tenacious inquirers. And to stress its significance, although perhaps praiseworthy in itself, is not to address the difficult issues it raises. Fearing the collapse of moral stability in the aftermath of *Leviathan*, Cudworth had responded to Hobbes's reduction of human behavior to the mechanistic laws of material cause and effect merely by reasserting the existence of abstract, inborn ideas of good and evil. Whether Locke had intended it or not, by dispensing with such innate ideas, he appeared to make the already unsteady ground of moral judgment more uncertain still. An avid reader of travel reports describing distant explorations, Locke was fully conscious of the variations in ethical values among different peoples and times, and he admitted it appeared that "that passes for *Vice* in one Country, which is counted a *Vertue*, or at least not *Vice*, in another" (II, xxviii, § 11). But he also felt that the difficulties obscuring moral issues could be resolved by treating them in the same way he treated

---

21. It is characteristic that the entry for *Morale* in the *Encyclopédie, ou Dictionnaire raisonné des sciences, des arts et des métiers, par une société de gens de lettres*, ed. Denis Diderot and Jean Le Rond d'Alembert (Paris, 1751–67), 10:699, contains the very similar assertion that "la *Morale* est la propre science des hommes," and in general represents a summary of Locke's ethical views as he expressed them in the *Essay*.

all other realms of human experience. Like Hobbes in this, at least, Locke therefore looked to the method of mathematics as the guarantor of his results.[22] "*Morality*," Locke confidently announced, "*is capable of Demonstration*, as well as Mathematicks" (III, xi, § 16).[23] There is a savory irony here: in order to protect morality from the dangers of arbitrariness, but also to give ethics the stature and certainty of science, Locke thus sought to bring the study of morals into conformity—while trying simultaneously, although not always successfully, to avoid any impression of ideological collusion—with the methodological procedure advanced by the man who was considered to have embodied the greatest threat to morality itself.

Toward the end of the second book of the *Essay*, in accord with the premise that social and psychological phenomena would yield to mathematical rigor, Locke analyzed the various ways in which the mind combined the simple ideas derived from the two sources of all of our knowledge, namely, sensation and reflection. Here he showed how complex notions subsequently arose out of the various relations formed among these compound clusters of simple ideas. Among this group of complex ideas, then, were what Locke termed "moral relations," and he believed there were three primary rules or laws that served as the guides for judging "the Rectitude and Pravity of their Actions" (II, xxviii, § 6). The first, and preeminent, source of authority was the "*Divine* Law, whereby I mean, that Law which God has set to the actions of Men, whether promulgated to them by the light of Nature, or the voice of Revelation" (II, xxviii, § 8). Locke's second rule consisted in the "*Civil* Law, the Rule set by the Commonwealth," and the third concerned the so-called *Law of Opinion or Reputation*, or what Locke later referred to as the Law of Fashion (II, xxviii, §§ 9, 10, 13). In light of these three "laws," Locke thought it was possible to demonstrate how it was that we could know what was good and what was evil, and why we should desire what was abstractly good even on those occasions when it conflicted with what we believed will procure our immediate happiness. Locke's final position on the matter was categorical, if perhaps disappointingly conformable to traditional theological morality:

That God has given a Rule whereby Men should govern themselves, I think there is no body so brutish as to deny. . . . He has Goodness and Wisdom to

22. Locke occasionally encountered difficulties because of this apparent similarity to Hobbes. Richard Ashcraft cites an unpublished letter (which is contained in the manuscript collection in the Bodleian Library at Oxford University) that Newton wrote to Locke on 16 September 1693, in which he apologized to Locke "for representing that you struck at the root of morality in a principle you laid down in your book of ideas . . . and that I took you for a Hobbist." See Ashcraft, "Faith and Knowledge," 199 n. 2.

23. Locke repeated this assertion (but makes no attempt to carry out this demonstration in detail) in IV, iii, § 18, and IV, xii, § 8. On this subject, see John E. Yolton, *Locke and the Compass of Human Understanding: A Selective Commentary on the "Essay"* (Cambridge: Cambridge University Press, 1970), esp. 163–67.

direct our Actions to that which is best: and he has Power to enforce it by Rewards and Punishments, of infinite weight and duration, in another Life: for no body can take us out of his hands. This is the only true touchstone of *moral Rectitude*, and by comparing them to this Law, it is, that Men judge of the most considerable *Moral Good* or *Evil* of their Actions; that is, whether as *Duties, or Sins*, they are like to procure them happiness, or misery, from the hands of the ALMIGHTY. (II, xxviii, § 8)

Many commentators have wanted to see a contradiction in Locke's thinking on this regard, believing that his appeal to transcendent authority here violated both his "empiricist" principles, as well as his own, constantly repeated, injunction that *"Reason* must be our last Judge and Guide in every Thing" (IV, xix, § 14). It is true that for Locke rational inquiry was perfectly adequate to the discovery of the rules of moral conduct. But it remained an unquestioned premise in his mind that what human beings were capable of understanding was at every point synonymous with God's design. In Locke's view, there could therefore never be a fundamental conflict between the powers of human reason and the authority of divine revelation.[24] Locke believed that it was only because of our inability to understand, or because we have not examined carefully enough what we believed we knew, that any dissonance could ever be thought to exist between the Gospel and the world. As he wrote in the unfinished chapter "Of Ethics in General" originally intended to close the *Essay*:

To establish morality, therefore, upon its proper basis, and such foundations as may carry an obligation with them, we must first prove a law, which always supposes a law-maker: one that has a superiority and right to ordain, and also a power to reward and punish according to the tenor of the law established by him. This sovereign law-maker who has set rules and bounds to the actions of men is God.[25]

Abstract, rationally graspable moral "laws" certainly did exist in Locke's estimation; but there also had to be some being who legislated those laws. The rational contribution to making moral judgments thus mainly consisted, according to Locke, in the fairly unglamorous task of apprehending the fitness or unfitness in the relations among ideas. But Locke affirmed that in every case, all such relations that we are rationally able to discover or discern—provided that their truth has indeed been established—will correspond to the stipulations of the foremost and "sovereign law-maker," God.

But what of those other two "laws" Locke mentioned? The first, which

24. See the discussion in Yolton, *Locke and the Compass of Human Understanding*, 169, and Colman, *Locke's Moral Philosophy*, 237–38.
25. Locke, "Of Ethics," in King, *Life of John Locke*, 133.

Locke otherwise called the "Law of politick Societies," posed no particular problems because it was imposed entirely from without and applied to social or civil rather than strictly moral behavior. The case was not so clear, however, with the final rule of fashion. At one point Locke makes the revealing claim, which he does not bother to prove, that when it is invoked in a "true" manner, it is "co-incident with the *divine Law*" (II, xxvii, § 10). But Locke also recognized, as we saw earlier, that what is considered "good" or virtuous in one epoch and place, may have a completely different meaning in another, and that "the several Nations and Societies of Men" patently applied this rule in ways that conflicted with one another. It appears, however, that Locke was only slightly troubled by the potential threat of moral relativism implied by this recognition. Although he acknowledges that "the different Temper, Education, Fashion, Maxims, or Interest of different sorts of Men" causes the standard of virtue and vice to fluctuate, he believed that "as to the Main, they for the most part kept the same every where" (II, xxviii, § 11). As a way of circumventing this dilemma, Locke resorts to an argument that comes very close to the central doctrine that supplied the name to the "commonsense" school of philosophy: "Even in the Corruption of Manners, the true Boundaries of the Law of Nature, which ought to be the Rule of Vertue and Vice, were pretty well preserved. So that even the Exhortations of inspired Teachers have not feared to appeal to common Repute" (ibid.). Almost in spite of himself, then, Locke introduced an element of uncertainty at the very place where he most wanted to secure the stability of unshakable law. By substituting "is" with "ought," he attempted to salvage some sort of "law of nature" by asserting it outright, since he could not demonstrate its necessity.

No doubt sensing these and other unresolved ambiguities, Locke's friend and faithful correspondent, the Irish physician William Molyneux, repeatedly implored Locke to elaborate on the frustratingly brief remarks scattered throughout the *Essay* about the mathematical demonstrability of morality.[26] But Locke never fulfilled his friend's request, and he justified his refusal with what must have been the no less frustrating reply that "the Gospel contains so perfect a body of ethics, that reason may be excused from that enquiry, since she may find man's duty clearer and easier in revelation than

26. In Molyneux's first letter to Locke he asks that "you would think of obliging the world with A Treatise of Morals, drawn up according to the hints you frequently give in your Essay, of being demonstrable, according to the mathematical method." Cited from Locke, *Works* (London, 1823), 9:291. See also the letter of 22 December 1692 (9:299), in which Molyneux writes, "I again put you in mind of the second member of your division of the sciences, the *ars practica*, or ethics. . . . The touches you give, in many places of your book, on this subject, are wonderfully curious, and do largely testify your great abilities that way; and I am sure the pravity of men's morals does mightily require the most powerful means to reform them."

in herself."[27] Again, this statement by Locke has appeared to some as inconsistent with his allegiance to reason. In Locke's *Reasonableness of Christianity* (1695), however, the work that many have regarded as marking the beginning of the Deist movement, he did again directly address the issue concerning the foundations of morality by recalling that "a clear knowledge of their duty was wanting to mankind."[28] Much more comprehensively than he had done in the earlier *Essay*, Locke sought to show here that "whatsoever should thus be universally useful, as a standard to which men should conform their manners, must have its authority, either from reason or revelation" (142). He had recognized that his insistence that moral authority issues solely from an external source could not convince those who sought reasons for their belief. By thus placing the word of God and the powers of the human mind on such equal footing, he apparently hoped to find a path on which they could advance side by side.

Although Locke was certain that in theory an absolute uniformity existed between these two sources of moral legitimacy, he realized that in practice not everyone was equally susceptible to their respective persuasive powers. The many—the "unwashed masses"—had neither the time, the inclination, nor the ability required for deriving moral precepts from logical demonstration, but the few—the educated—would not be satisfied by anything less than strict methodological rigor. Locke thus drew a distinction in his treatment of moral fitness that was ultimately based on class or social divisions. Although he was interested in identifying the theoretical possibility of a comprehensive code of ethical behavior that was guided by eternally valid and immutable laws, he was realistic enough to recognize that only a privileged few had acquired the means (both financial and intellectual) to perceive and act according to such laws. As Locke wrote in his characteristically direct language, "You may as soon hope to have all the day-labourers and tradesmen, the spinsters and dairy-maids, perfect mathematicians, as to have them perfect in ethics this way" (146). Locke remained convinced that ordinary people would need some stimulus to good conduct of a more sensible kind.

Yet even if the majority *were* capable of following the subtleties of rational proofs, Locke still doubted that such abstract insight alone would be sufficient to promote virtue and prevent vice. There had to be some other incentive, he thought, some other attraction that sensibly led everyone, and not simply the untutored multitudes, toward a life of relative virtue. Locke saved the largest measure of his scorn for those "philosophers" who ignored the need actively to encourage the cultivation of morals and who tried to

27. Locke to Molyneux, 30 March 1696, in Locke, *Works*, 9:377.
28. John Locke, *The Reasonableness of Christianity as delivered in the Scriptures*, in *Works*, 7:138.

promote nothing more than "the excellency of virtue; and the highest they generally went, was the exalting of human nature, whose perfection lay in virtue" (149). Not one to exalt "human nature" as such, Locke went on in his dry and derisive way to mock "the philosophers" who thus tried to dispense with the Christian promise altogether:

> The philosophers, indeed, showed the beauty of virtue; they set her off so, as drew men's eyes and approbation to her; but leaving her unendowed, very few were willing to espouse her. . . . It has another relish and efficacy to persuade men, that if they live well here, they shall be happy hereafter. Open their eyes upon the endless, unspeakable joys of another life, and their hearts will find something solid and powerful to move them. The view of heaven and hell will cast a slight upon the short pleasures and pains of this present state, and give attractions and encouragements to virtue, which reason and interest, and the care of ourselves, cannot but allow and prefer. Upon this foundation, and upon this only, morality stands firm, and may defy all competition. This makes it more than a name; a substantial good, worth all our aims and endeavors; and thus the Gospel of Jesus Christ has delivered it to us. (150–51)

There may well be a "beauty of virtue," Locke admitted, but if left otherwise unadorned, it would lack proper persuasion. In the end, then, Locke fell back on the familiar and convenient Christian doctrine of future rewards and punishments to explain where we found the necessary incitements to ethical action. Locke in general thought too little of human nature (for what else had his *Essay* been but an exercise in proving how *little* we are actually able to know?) and his thinking was too firmly established within the Christian tradition for him to have believed that without the intercession of divine grace, shored up by the severity of divine justice, the human condition could ever be anything better than depraved. Both in his *Essay* and in his somewhat halfhearted attempt to reveal the "reasonableness" of Christianity, he begged as many questions as he broached, and he was never able to resolve the tension between the only two sources of moral law he acknowledged. It is ironic that although Locke had thus scorned the idea of the "beauty of virtue" as a possible solution to the dilemma of modern ethical philosophy, it was precisely this concept of moral existence that came to be seen as the best solution to the difficulties he had located but had been unable himself to surmount. Not entirely by coincidence, perhaps, one thinker who personified the sort of philosopher Locke had condemned had also once been a close acquaintance of his: Anthony Ashley Cooper, third earl of Shaftesbury.

Shaftesbury (whose grandfather, the first earl, had been a patron and friend of Locke) had received a good part of his education under the philosopher's guidance and influence, and Locke's lifelong preoccupation with the issues of ethics could not have failed to have had an effect on his gifted pupil. This indebtedness in fact became manifest when Shaftesbury published his collection of essays *Characteristicks of Men, Manners, Opinions, Times* in 1711. The book made him instantly famous, and his own influence on the eighteenth century rivaled, and in some quarters even surpassed, that of his great teacher. In Britain, Francis Hutcheson, Bishop Butler, David Hume, and many others in the Scottish school of philosophy all read and admired his works, and their own thinking betrays a profound debt to his example. The leading minds of the French Enlightenment also held his essays in extremely high regard, and one can find numerous direct references, as well as many more subtle allusions, to Shaftesbury in the writings most notably of Montesquieu, Voltaire, Diderot, and Rousseau. And in Germany, Shaftesbury's reputation reached unprecedented heights, leaving a deep imprint in the works by the major figures of the "classical" period in German letters. Lessing, Winckelmann, Mendelssohn, Wieland, Kant, Goethe, Herder, and Schiller—the list could go on—all remained his lifelong admirers.[29]

Given his acknowledged importance, it is dismaying to discover that Shaftesbury has not received as much attention as he obviously deserves, a neglect that is only partly due to the general avoidance of ethics in scholarly discussions of the period. One of the principal reasons for this relative disregard stems from the habit of seeing Shaftesbury's writings almost solely within the context of the developments that took place within eighteenth-century aesthetic theory.[30] There is certainly no denying that Shaftesbury's ideas about beauty played a significant role in the formation of a distinct sphere of philosophical inquiry devoted to the investigation of aesthetic phenomena. But it is critical to an accurate assessment not just of his thought alone but also of his influence on the thinkers who later came under his sway that one remember how central ethical concerns were to his entire philosophical enterprise and how much the debates I have sketched out so far formed the foil against which his thought took shape. As an earlier historian has correctly, although again rather one-sidedly, stated it, "Shaf-

---

29. See Stanley Grean, *Shaftesbury's Philosophy of Religion and Ethics: A Study in Enthusiasm* (Athens: Ohio University Press, 1967), x–xiii.

30. In the classic and highly influential account by Ernst Cassirer, *The Philosophy of the Enlightenment*, trans. Fritz C. A. Koelln and James P. Pettegrove (Princeton: Princeton University Press, 1951), there is hardly a word said about Shaftesbury's preoccupation with moral philosophy. One would have to assume from Cassirer's presentation, on the contrary, that Shaftesbury was interested exclusively in aesthetic concerns. As if in anticipation of objections to this one-sided emphasis, Cassirer also advances the bizarre contention that Shaftesbury "feels no kinship with contemporary philosophy . . . There is scarcely an echo here of the problems affecting his era, or of the intellectual and practical decisions with which this era is confronted" (313). See the corrective comments by John Andrew Bernstein, *Shaftesbury, Rousseau, and Kant: An Introduction to the Conflict between Aesthetic and Moral Values in Modern Thought* (London: Associated University Presses, 1980), 21–22.

tesbury is emphatically a Moral Philosopher."[31] That is true enough; but to be even more precise, Shaftesbury deliberately linked ethical and aesthetical matters, always treating the good and the beautiful as belonging together in a symbiotic and indivisible unity.

Another reason for the general misunderstanding of Shaftesbury originates in his stance toward philosophical method itself, which we have already seen to have been an issue of paramount significance to almost every other contemporary philosopher. One of the most often quoted, and in the absence of further qualification most often misrepresented, passages from the *Characteristicks* is Shaftesbury's statement that the "most ingenious way of becoming foolish, is *by a System*."[32] Many critics have taken this remark to mean that Shaftesbury rejected not only systematic thought of the venerable scholastic variety, but also that under the impress of the supposedly more mystical elements in the works of the Cambridge Platonists, he wished to dispense with rational argument altogether in favor of a more intuitive, subjectivist approach to philosophical matters.[33] Yet nothing could be further from the case: although Shaftesbury did cultivate a digressive, even rhapsodic prose style that dramatically departed from the dry syllogistic procedures of school philosophy, he would never have considered jettisoning reason itself, which he recognized as humanity's distinctive, and most precious, possession.[34] As Shaftesbury rhetorically asks in "The Moralists," "is not Thought and Reason *principal* in Man?" (*Characteristicks*, 2:307). The emphasis on the rational basis of all human action and thought resides at the heart of Shaftesbury's entire philosophy. What Shaftesbury *did* object to was the belief that systematic knowledge in and of itself, divorced and abstracted from practical life, already constituted wisdom. He argued, rather, that if knowledge were not always brought to bear on what mattered to us

31. Thomas Fowler, *Shaftesbury and Hutcheson* (New York: G. P. Putnam's Sons, 1883), 63.
32. Anthony Ashley Cooper, third earl of Shaftesbury, "Soliloquy: or Advice to an Author," in *Characteristicks of Men, Manners, Opinions, Times*, 2d ed. (London, 1714), 1:290. Henceforth cited parenthetically in the text as "*Characteristicks*" by volume and page number.
33. Typical of many German treatments of Shaftesbury is the assessment given in one of the very few studies devoted to the notion of the "beautiful soul" (*schöne Seele*), namely, the unpublished doctoral thesis by Heinrich Pohlmeier, "Untersuchungen zum Begriff der schönen Seele," who writes that "Shaftesbury attacks rationalism and empiricism, as forms of both thought and life, from the inside, and he opposes the rational-instrumental worldview with an aesthetic one that is founded in nature and that enthusiastically summons the irrational powers of humankind" (12). But this view is not confined to German scholars alone; see, for example, David Summers, *The Judgment of Sense: Renaissance Naturalism and the Rise of Aesthetics* (Cambridge: Cambridge University Press, 1987), 106.
34. See the evenhanded treatment of this issue by Grean, *Shaftesbury's Philosophy*, 8–9. Grean's study is commendable for its synthetic presentation of the various arguments scattered throughout Shaftesbury's works, but it pays too little attention to the context from which his thought arose. The same can be said of the book by Wolfgang H. Schrader, *Ethik und Anthropologie in der englischen Aufklärung: Der Wandel der moral-sense-Theorie von Shaftesbury bis Hume* (Hamburg: Felix Meiner, 1984).

most, if we did not with every step ask what value our study had for the conduct of our affairs, we would indeed be nothing more than foolish. And it was in this commitment to the application and practical employment of knowledge, as opposed to the fruitless collection of dead and useless data, that his philosophy most profoundly confirmed, and simultaneously surpassed, the ultimate intentions of his former mentor, Locke.[35]

These cautionary words notwithstanding, there is certainly some justice in claiming that Shaftesbury opposed several tendencies he detected in Locke's thinking. But the person he most particularly disagreed with was Hobbes. In Shaftesbury's first publication—characteristically, a preface to the selected sermons of Benjamin Whichcote, the founding father of the Cambridge Platonist school—he spoke directly about Hobbes's effect on ethics, which he deemed "has done but very ill service to the moral world."[36] And it was toward the correction of this "ill service" that a major portion of Shaftesbury's energies was directed. But he also thought that Locke's apparently dispassionate investigations into the mechanisms of human knowledge had not just hindered but actively harmed the cause of morality. In an often quoted letter containing his declaration of belief in the existence of certain universal and eternal principles of human virtue, Shaftesbury accused Locke of having destroyed the basis of morality by denying those very qualities to the human mind:

> It was Mr. Locke that struck the home blow: for Mr. Hobbes's character and base slavish principles in government took off the poison of his philosophy. 'Twas Mr. Locke that struck at all fundamentals, threw all order and virtue out of the world, and made the very ideas of these (which are the same as those of God) *unnatural*, and without foundation in our minds. *Innate* is a word he poorly plays upon; the right word, though less used, is *connatural*. For what has birth or progress of the foetus out of the womb to do in this case? The question is not about the time the *ideas* entered, or the moment that one body came out of the other, but whether the constitution of man be such that, being adult and grown up, at such or such a time, sooner or later (no matter when), the idea and sense of order, administration, and a God, will not infallibly, inevitably, necessarily spring up in him.[37]

35. See R. L. Brett, *The Third Earl of Shaftesbury: A Study in Eighteenth-Century Literary Theory* (London: Hutchinson, 1951), 79, who insists that Shaftesbury "radically" disagrees with Locke, and that there were "profound differences between his own and Locke's philosophy."

36. Benjamin Whichcote, *Works* (Aberdeen: J. Chalmers, 1751; reprint, New York: Garland Publishing, 1977), 3:iv.

37. Letter to Michael Ainsworth, 3 June 1709. Cited from *The Life, Unpublished Letters, and Philosophical Regimen of Anthony, Earl of Shaftesbury*, ed. Benjamin Rand (London: Swan Sonnenschein, 1900), 403. Whereas Shaftesbury dispenses with Hobbes here in rather summa-

What is most immediately striking about this passage is that far from endorsing any abandonment of logic and rational standards, Shaftesbury attempted on the contrary to ward off the potential encroachment of relativism into moral philosophy. For as he and everyone else feared, such arbitrariness would have signaled the most dangerous threat to ethical theory as a whole. We thus find him insisting on an even greater degree of uniformity in human manners and on an even more prominent role for reason in the regulation of our lives, than Locke, skeptical realist that he was, had been ready to allow. Still, it is apparent that Shaftesbury had grievously misread Locke, especially when he seemed to accuse Locke of having reduced moral behavior to mere habit or custom, or even to something resembling the nonrational activity of instinct in animals. But it is a misreading that, like most misunderstandings, is also productively revealing of the person making the mistake. "According to Mr. Locke," Shaftesbury continued in the same letter, "virtue has no other measure, law, or rule, than fashion and custom; morality, justice, equity, depend only on law and will . . . Experience and our catechism teach us all! I suppose 'tis something of like kind which teaches birds their nests, and how to fly the minute they have full feathers."[38] Whatever its other faults—and selective quotation is only one of them—this description is not the complaint of a person who wishes to abandon the paradigms of reason.

The distinction Shaftesbury made in his letter, even though he had rather uncharitably distorted Locke's own thought itself, is nevertheless vital to understanding the import of Shaftesbury's moral philosophy as a whole. Although he asserted that there necessarily existed some "innate"—or as Shaftesbury put it, "connatural"—capacity in the human mind that makes it constitutionally possible for us to distinguish between right and wrong, what he was most particularly *not* claiming (and what Locke had also, though less concisely, disputed) is that we come into the world already supplied with some specific, determinate notion of good and bad. He was not arguing, in other words, that we possess some innate notion of the *content* of virtue. Rather, he wished to stress that the capacity to make such a moral judgment at all is an inherently and supremely human quality and

---

ry fashion, he does deal with him more directly in his works. Although he does not mention his opponent by name, in the essay "*Sensus Communis*: An Essay on the Freedom of Wit and Humour" (in *Characteristicks*, 1:115), Shaftesbury argues for a more complex view of human nature than Hobbes seems to have been willing (or able) to give; he notes that it is "a common Saying, that *Interest governs the World*. But, I believe, whoever looks narrowly into the Affairs of it, will find, that *Passion, Humour, Caprice, Zeal, Faction*, and a thousand other Springs, which are counter to *Self-Interest*, have as considerable a part in the Movements of this Machine. . . . 'Tis of too complex a kind, to fall under one simple View, or be explain'd thus briefly in a word or two. The Studiers of this *Mechanism* must have a very partial Eye, to overlook all other Motions besides those of the lowest and narrowest compass."
38. Letter to Michael Ainsworth, 3 June 1709. In Shaftesbury, *The Life*, 404.

has its basis in the faculty of reason that we do in fact possess from birth. The question is not whether we have the means to make such judgments or not—for as far as Shaftesbury was concerned, that was self-evident. What is crucial is how this faculty was formed. "One who aspires to the Character of a Man of Breeding and Politeness," Shaftesbury thus wrote in one of his essays, "is careful to form his Judgment of Arts and Sciences upon right Models of *Perfection*" (*Characteristicks*, 1:338). In conformity with the contemporary concern about the utility and purpose of knowledge, Shaftesbury expressed impatience with what he thought were pedantic and pointless inquiries into the ways in which we acquired ideas, and he pressed for greater consideration of the actual ends to which they might be applied. So although he believed that human beings are indeed born equipped with all of their essential defining attributes, he argued (as had, of course, Locke and many others before him) that these faculties are not yet fully formed at birth and that we have to develop and train them in order to fulfill their merely latent potential. Here, then, we have a closer sense of what Shaftesbury meant by the word "connatural": "Who wou'd not endeavour to *force* Nature as well in this respect, as in what relates to a *Taste*, or *Judgment* in other Arts and Sciences? . . . If a natural *good* Taste be not already form'd in us; why shou'd not we endeavour to form it, and become *natural?*" (1:339). Shaftesbury could therefore call "taste" (which he aligned here with the activity of "judgment") "natural" because both taste and judgment were the product of rational effort and of the conscious, formative effect of the will, all of which were themselves dependent on what he deemed to be the "natural," or inborn, defining characteristics of humanity.

We see here for the first time the complete acceptance, and even the attempt toward a resolution, of that inherent but as yet unacknowledged tension within moral inquiry between the dictates of reason and those of revelation which we detected in Cudworth's philosophy and which Locke tried to evade by merely positing, but not proving, their identity. Once the source of moral knowledge had been identified as residing wholly within the human sphere, rather than in an external code of ethical behavior, ethics became irrevocably disengaged from its century-old dependency on religion. Although Shaftesbury never renounced his Christian faith and even asserted that "the Perfection and Height of Virtue must be owing to *the Belief of a God,*" he still recognized the logical necessity of separating religion and morality in philosophical discussions of either one. Shaftesbury always insisted on the importance of inquiring into "what *Honesty* or Virtue is, consider'd by itself" (2:76–77). From this point onward, then, throughout the eighteenth century and well into the modern period, the focus of ethical inquiry would remain trained on the inner, decidedly human psychological conditions that enable us to recognize the morally good and that lead us to realize this recognition in and through our actions.

Shaftesbury's views concerning the connection between reason and virtue obviously imply certain assumptions about humanity that were shared by the Cambridge Platonists and indeed were common to practically all of the advocates of the Enlightenment. They all took it for granted that despite what they considered the relatively superficial differences caused by the various climates and cultures in which human beings subsist, the basic components of human nature are everywhere fundamentally the same. It was, for example, on this unspoken premise that he founded his assertion that no matter the country or era, "*Virtue* has the same fix'd Standard. The same *Numbers, Harmony,* and *Proportion* will have place in Morals; and are discoverable in the *Characters* and *Affections* of Mankind; in which are laid the just Foundations of an Art and Science, superior to every other of human Practice and Comprehension" (1:353). This universality, which Shaftesbury saw as the guarantor of the very possibility of morality, is thus based not on particular beliefs or customs, but in the abstract constitution—the "numbers" —of unchanging human reason itself.

I have emphasized the thoroughly rational strain in Shaftesbury's writings primarily in order to modify the traditional conception of what many readers have thought to have been his most original contribution to the history of philosophy: his notion of the "moral sense."[39] Most often the "moral sense" is described as some noncognitive or nonrational mode of perception, supposedly functioning much in the way in which the ear immediately responds to sound or the eye registers light.[40] Although generally attributed to Shaftesbury, the term really gained its greatest currency through Francis Hutcheson's much more patient and thorough exposition of its meaning. In fact, Shaftesbury himself rarely used the term, although he did often speak of an intellectual "sense," but most often in ways such as the following:

> In a Creature capable of forming general Notions of Things, not only the outward Beings which offer themselves to the Sense, are the Objects of the Affection; but the very *Actions* themselves, and the *Affections* of Pity, Kindness,

39. See, however, the second chapter in Ernest Lee Tuveson, *The Imagination as a Means of Grace: Locke and the Aesthetics of Romanticism* (Berkeley and Los Angeles: University of California Press, 1960), "The Origin of the 'Moral Sense'," esp. 46–55, in which Tuveson speculates that Thomas Burnet was actually the true author of the notion.

40. See, for one example among many others, the account given by Monroe C. Beardsley, *Aesthetics from Classical Greece to the Present: A Short History* (New York: Macmillan, 1966; reprint, Tuscaloosa: University of Alabama Press, 1975), 179, who writes: "The theory . . . which Shaftesbury gave the name 'moral sense,' was his contribution to eighteenth-century ethical theory, and at the same time to aesthetics. . . . Its essential feature is that it grasps its object immediately, without reasoning."

Gratitude, and their Contrarys, being brought into the Mind by Reflection, become Objects. So that, by means of this reflected Sense, there arises another kind of Affection towards those very Affections themselves, which have been already felt, and are now become the Subject of a new Liking or Dislike. (*Characteristicks*, 2:28)

Obviously the emotions (sentiments, sensations, and so on) played a significant role in Shaftesbury's account of human and specifically moral experience, but he never saw them in isolation from our ability to make rational sense of such experience. It is only by means of what he called a "reflected sense" that we become aware of the sort of immediate sensory perceptions that Shaftesbury mentioned and, depending on whether they are pleasant or not, entice us to seek either their prolongation or avoidance. Developed in its most complex way, this intermingling of pleasure (which for Shaftesbury meant only the sorts of charitable affections he listed above) and rational reflection become the mechanism by which virtuous action is produced. Only when Shaftesbury's notion of the so-called moral sense is understood in this way can his emphasis on the regulation of reason in our affairs be grasped (which he stressed much more emphatically and more often than the vague term "sense"). Shaftesbury, so frequently elliptical and elusive on other matters, was always very explicit in this regard. "Worth and Virtue," he expressly wrote, "depend on a knowledge of *Right* and *Wrong*, and on a use of Reason, sufficient to secure a right application of the Affections" (2:35).[41] He could hardly have stated his intentions more clearly.

One can detect an explicit influence of Neoplatonic doctrine in Shaftesbury's conviction, which he often repeated, that the "*Pleasures of the Mind*" are "superior to those of *the Body*" (*Characteristicks*, 2:100). And this belief led him to a first definition of how we can attain permanent—which for him meant virtuously maintained—felicity: "It follows, that the natural Affections duly establish'd in a rational Creature, being the only means which can procure him a constant Series or Succession of the mental Enjoyments, they are the only means which can procure him a certain and solid *Happiness*" (2:101). Thus the sensation of pleasure—albeit "duly established" and rationally regulated—occupies the central place of Shaftersbury's moral theory. Constantly abstracted and refined, our most exquisite pleasure ultimately arises from the contemplation of actions that issue from a mind that is itself the product of such ceaseless "exercise" and deliberate self-fashioning. And

41. In light of such assertions, it becomes difficult to call him a "sentimentalist," which is understood as "one who held, as Shaftesbury was taken to believe, that morality is ultimately a matter of feeling rather than of knowledge." Cited from Jerome B. Schneewind, ed., *Moral Philosophy from Montaigne to Kant: An Anthology* (Cambridge: Cambridge University Press, 1990), 2:504.

the mental instrument by which we discern what "affections" are enjoyable —that is, "good"—is the mental faculty Shaftesbury called taste.

In all that Shaftesbury wrote there is a concern for what he referred to as the connection and "balance" of every part that belonged to any greater whole.[42] "Nothing surely is more strongly imprinted on our Minds," he wrote in this regard, "or more closely interwoven with our Souls, than the Idea or Sense of *Order* and *Proportion*" (2:284). The notions of "order," "proportion," and "harmony," which are among the most often recurring words in all of Shaftesbury's works, are very closely aligned, in fact in most instances identical, with his idea of beauty. We perceive these qualities through the faculty that Shaftesbury, like his compatriot Joseph Addison, had defined as "taste." In a famous letter for the *Spectator*, dated 19 June 1712, Addison noted that taste, which is "the utmost Perfection of an accomplished Man," can be called "*that Faculty of the Soul, which discerns the Beauties of an Author with Pleasure, and the Imperfections with Dislike.*"[43]

Shaftesbury recognized that "taste" is not an ability that comes naturally, but one that can be acquired only through patient and careful discipline. If it is so trained and shaped, however, it can well become "natural" in his peculiar sense of the term. "How long e'er a true *Taste* is gain'd!" he once mused; "How many things shocking, how many offensive at first, which afterwards are known and acknowledg'd the highest *Beautys!* For 'tis not instantly we acquire the *Sense* by which these Beautys are discoverable. *Labour* and *Pains* are requir'd, and *Time* to cultivate a natural Genius, ever so apt and forward" (*Characteristicks*, 2:401). For those who are accustomed to romantic notions of unfettered originality and unreflective spontaneity as constituting genius, the suggestion that a "natural Genius" could be "cultivated" must appear strange indeed.[44] But it formed the cornerstone of Shaftesbury's moral theory: for once we accept that judgment can thus be taught to respond to "Beautys" (or, for that matter, to their opposite) outside of ourselves, then it seems a small step to learn to apply this same faculty to the judgment of what occurs within us. "Taste" thus turned inward becomes the mechanism by which we watch over and control our own interior: "The Moral Artist, who . . . is thus knowing in the inward Form and Structure of his Fellow-Creature, will hardly, I presume, be found unknowing in *Himself*, or at a loss in those Numbers which make the Harmony of a Mind. For *Knavery* is mere *Dissonance* and *Disproportion*" (*Characteristicks*, 1:207–8)[45]

42. See, for example, Shaftesbury, "An Inquiry concerning Virtue, *or* Merit," in *Characteristicks*, 2:174.
43. Addison, *The Spectator*, 3:527–28.
44. See Grean, *Shaftesbury's Philosophy*, 256, as an example of the attempt to trace the romantic notion of the artistic genius to Shaftesbury.
45. This notion of "inner harmony," or as Shaftesbury sometimes called it "interior numbers," was perhaps an ironic allusion to the mathematical demonstrability of morals, which he, like his

Moral viciousness therefore results, Shaftesbury concluded, from the failure to recognize and rectify psychological or social disharmony. Put more pointedly still, at a certain level Shaftesbury thought that evil was no more, or rather no less, than the detestable consequence of bad taste.

Once Shaftesbury felt that he had established the intellectual basis of moral judgment, he saw the way clear to advance to a definition of the qualities to which this faculty responded. He had already explained that happiness relies on a variety of intellectual pleasure, and that pleasure is produced by the perception of symmetry, order, proportion—in short, of beauty. By again constructing an analogy between internal and external qualities, he thought that the same criteria that applied to corporeal beauty could also be placed on the inner, immaterial realm:

> Scarce is there any-one, who pretends not to know and to decide What is *well-bred* and *handsom.* There are few so affectedly clownish, as absolutely to disown *Good-breeding,* and renounce the Notion of a Beauty in *outward Manners* and *Deportment.* With such as these, whereever they shou'd be found, I must confess, I cou'd scarce be tempted to bestow the least Pains or Labour, towards convincing 'em of a *Beauty* in *inward Sentiments* and *Principles.* (*Characteristicks,* 3:179)

This hypothesis of an abstract, nonphysical beauty (which, in a clever rhetorical ruse, Shaftesbury claimed was so easy to prove convincingly that it would be an insult to both himself and his readers to do so) prepares the supporting ground for the most innovative idea of his entire moral theory. In a crucial distinction, Shaftesbury similarly asked: "Is Beauty founded then in *Body* only; and not in *Action, Life,* or *Operation?*" (2:403). The use of the singular in the last three nouns is important, for it refers not to particular "actions" or deeds, but to *activity* itself, and it is in this conception of beauty as being expressed in, or rather expressive of, a certain rational activity that we find the central doctrine of his ethics.

In one of the exchanges between Theocles and Philocles in "The Moralists" —a work that, more than any other, Shaftesbury self-consciously wrote in the style of a Platonic dialogue—Theocles asks about what we admire as being "beautiful" in works of art, or in medals and coins. Philocles agrees that it is not the material from which these things are made that elicits our praise and affection; rather, it is the evidence of the skill, or "*Art,*" that went

---

predecessors, also thought possible. See also where he wrote: "We have cast up all those Particulars, from whence (as by way of Addition and Subtraction) the main *Sum* or general Account of Happiness, is either augmented or diminish'd. And if there be no Article exceptionable in this Scheme of *Moral Arithmetick*; the Subject treated may be said to have an evidence as great as that which is found in Numbers, or Mathematicks" (*Characteristicks,* 2:173).

into their creation. Beauty, then, is not a tangible property of things, but the perceptible imprint of a rational mind on matter. Beauty is the evidence of an active formation of some substance into a shape that is determined by a consciously molding mind. Or as Theocles phrases it in preeminently Platonic fashion, "the Beautifying, not the Beautify'd, is the really *Beautiful*" (2:404). Things that bespeak the application of taste, in Shaftesbury's definition of the term, and not the things themselves, are thus those objects which may be thought to wear the attributes of beauty. "*The Beautiful, the Fair, the Comely*, were never in the *Matter*, but in the *Art* and *Design*; never in *Body* it-self, but in the *Form* or *Forming Power*. Does not the beautiful *Form* confess this, and speak the Beauty of *the Design*, whene'er it strikes you? What is it but *the Design* which strikes? What is it you admire but Mind, or the Effect of *Mind?* 'Tis *Mind* alone which forms" (2:408).

Consequently, the most praiseworthy manifestation of beauty—indeed, according to Shaftesbury, the only instance of "true" beauty—occurs only in a mind that has trained its formative powers *on itself*, that has made *itself* the object of its power to impose order and harmony on external matter. This is what Shaftesbury described as that

> Order of Beauty, which forms not only such as we call mere Forms, but even *the Forms which form*. For we our-selves are notable Architects in Matter, and can shew lifeless Bodys brought into Form, and fashion'd by our own hands: but that which fashions even Minds themselves, contains in it-self all the Beautys fashion'd by those Minds; and is consequently the Principle, Source, and Fountain of all *Beauty*. (2:407–8)

There is, admittedly, some ambiguity here about who or what this last power is that "fashions even minds themselves." It is conceivable that Shaftesbury meant to suggest God as that prime creator. But it seems most likely that he wanted to say that the ability we all have as rational legislators of our own will to shape matter according to our own desires can be applied reflectively to itself. And it is in this activity that not solely the central law of beauty can be found, but its most satisfying and meaningful manifestation as well.

It is only now, by keeping in mind the preceding arguments about the place of reason and education in forming judgment or taste, and by recalling his idiosyncratic definition of the "natural," that we can understand Shaftesbury's comments at the end of "The Moralists." It is here that he summarizes his notion of moral beauty, which, in a marginal annotation, he calls here for the first—and only—time "Beauty of Soul":

> Is there then . . . a natural Beauty of *Figures*? and is there not as natural a one of Actions? No sooner the Eye opens upon *Figures*, the Ear to *Sounds*, than

straight *the Beautiful* results, and *Grace* and *Harmony* are known and acknowledg'd. No sooner are Actions view'd, no sooner the *human Affections* and
Passions descern'd (and they are most of them as soon descern'd as felt) then
straight *an inward* Eye distinguishes, and sees *the Fair* and *Shapely*, *the Amiable*
and *Admirable*, apart from the *Deform'd*, *the Foul*, *the Odious*, or *the Despicable*.
How is it possible therefore not to own, "That these *Distinctions* have their
Foundation *in Nature*, the Discernment it-self is *natural*, and from Nature
alone?" (2:414–15)

Those people who are virtuously good, who are morally beautiful—or, in
other words, those who evidence the mental labor of having applied their
will to the formation of their characters—will immediately or naturally show
themselves as such, according to Shaftesbury, to those who have likewise
undergone similar exertions. If, as increasingly appeared to be the case,
religion could no longer provide the absolute rule for morality, then it was
necessary to produce some other real incentive for people to prefer to
desire and do what is good over what is evil. For as history has proven with
depressing thoroughness, it is evident that vice holds allurements that virtue
"unendowed," as Locke had phrased it, can hardly hope to match. In Shaftesbury's understanding of moral goodness, however, virtue is "naturally"
adorned by the qualities of beauty that arouse our affections, and that it is
on the uninterrupted experience of these rationally validated sensations
that our real happiness rests. As he wrote on another occasion (and underscoring once again his commitment to models of reasoned persuasion):
"There is not, I presume, the least degree of Certainty wanting, in what has
been said concerning the Preferableness of the *mental Pleasures to the sensual*. . . . Nor is there less Evidence in what has been said, of *the united Structure
and Fabrick of the Mind*, and of those Passions which constitute *the Temper*, or
Soul; and on which its Happiness or Misery so immediately depend"
(2:173–74). And it is in this "united structure and fabric"—or, in a word,
the "beauty"—of the soul, that the happiness which is synonymous with
virtue consists.

Given the inherent difficulties in achieving this state, it is evident that
Shaftesbury espoused what one can only call an elitist, and specifically aristocratic, conception of moral duty. By contrast, Locke had recognized the
necessity of developing a moral theory that would embrace not just an elect
minority comprising the educated and noble classes. Locke had proposed,
albeit accompanied by a generous amount of condescension, the outlines of
a rationally informed theological morality that relied on the regulative power of rewards and punishments, which could, he thought, address the needs
of both the "common people" and the intellectuals alike. Shaftesbury, however, who was himself an unapologetic member of the noble class (and

whom Locke, we remember, had served in the distinctly subordinate role as private tutor), simply excluded from serious consideration those unhappy multitudes who had not enjoyed the benefits of a liberal education and had thus not already achieved a certain sufficient degree of moral autonomy. As Shaftesbury explained it, "the mere Vulgar of Mankind . . . stand in need of such a rectifying Object as *the Gallows* before their Eyes" (1:127), with the clear implication that "gentlemen" would never require such a crude inducement.[46]

Yet if one tries to acknowledge, rather than condemn or explain away, the frankly aristocratic foundations of his philosophy, the logical or internal attractions of Shaftesbury's suggestions become immediately obvious. His numerous enthusiastic readers eagerly adopted the proposal that moral goodness possesses all of the attributes of beauty, and that all people (all people of refined sensibilities, that is) are infallibly attracted to beauty *cum* virtue and vice versa. For many, indeed, Shaftesbury thus seemed to offer a sound solution to the main quandaries of early eighteenth-century ethical philosophy. External agency was no longer required because we were given, in his view, complete autonomy and control over our moral lives, and our success or failure to attain virtue was therefore measured in purely human, in fact eminently personal, terms. Similarly, Shaftesbury's conviction that beauty exerts a natural and irresistible attraction on all who perceive it (provided, once again, that they have enjoyed the sort of education that would enable them to be sensible of it in the first place) appeared to clear up the problem concerning the grounds of motivation in ethical action. If we have properly trained our "taste" and have thus adequately exercised the appropriate faculties of our mind, we will always and unerringly desire what is good because it is at the same time beautiful, that is, in conformity, or harmonious, with our "natural" constitution. It is an ingenious, and almost irresistible, theory. Most, it fact, did not even try to resist: throughout the following one hundred years, British moral philosophy—and hence, because of its enormous influence on the Continent, that of Germany and France as well—remained preoccupied, indeed almost obsessed, with the notion and meaning of "moral beauty."

The thinker who made the most ambitious attempt to systematize and thereby secure Shaftesbury's arguments about the relation obtaining between beauty and virtue was Francis Hutcheson, a transplanted Irishman teaching at Glasgow University. In 1725 he published his first work, which carried a lavishly baroque title that deserves to be, but rarely is, reproduced in full: *An Inquiry into the Original of our Ideas of Beauty and Virtue; in two*

46. Terry Eagleton, *The Ideology of the Aesthetic* (Oxford: Basil Blackwell, 1990), 35–36, makes some interesting comments on the dialectical interplay of Whiggish political theory and the unabashedly aristocratic Neoplatonism in Shaftesbury's thought.

treatises, in which the Principles of the late Earl of Shaftesbury are explained and defended, against the Author of the Fable of the Bees; and the Ideas of Moral Good and Evil are established, according to the Sentiments of the Ancient Moralists with an Attempt to introduce a Mathematical Calculation in subjects of Morality.[47] Besides asserting Hutcheson's opposition to the most recent representative of a kind of Hobbesian theory of egoistic morality—namely Bernard de Mandeville, whose *Fable of the Bees* Hutcheson had explicitly mentioned— the title announces his belief that the two "ideas" of beauty and virtue are in some essential way connected with each other. Yet almost every interpreter of Hutcheson's work has read the *Inquiry* with an exclusive interest in either its ethical theory or its contribution to aesthetics, often strenuously discounting, or at least trying to minimize, the significance of one or the other of its two parts.[48] Virtually no one has seen—or wanted to see—these two aspects of Hutcheson's work as existing in a necessary and mutually supporting relationship.[49] But there must have been something more than a superficial reason in Hutcheson's mind for treating both aesthetics and ethics so prominently in the same work. It was in fact his primary aim (although certainly not his only one) to explain and promote just that concept of moral beauty which Shaftesbury had reintroduced into modern ethical thought. Hutcheson obviously felt that it was the only way to give a logically satisfactory account of the psychological basis underlying human morality, one that dispensed with the need to introduce the external authority of a deity, but did not require one to posit, in the fashion of Cudworth and his confederates, specific "innate" ideas in the mind.

There has been, however, a further obstacle to a fuller appreciation of Hutcheson's philosophy, one that is similar to the circumstances described in connection with the thought of Shaftesbury himself. Until recently, Hutcheson was uniformly thought to have promoted a strictly "noncogniti-

47. The second edition of the following year (and all subsequent reissues of the book) bore the much shorter title, *Inquiry into the Original of our Ideas of BEAUTY and VIRTUE; In Two Treatises. I. Concerning BEAUTY, ORDER, HARMONY, DESIGN. II. Concerning MORAL GOOD and EVIL.*

48. This tendency to split the *Inquiry* and its explicitly stated intention into two discrete halves has occasioned startlingly divergent views of Hutcheson's book. Beardsley, *Aesthetics*, 185, for example, calls the *Inquiry* simply the "first modern essay in philosophical aesthetics," and Beardsley's analysis concentrates exclusively on this aspect of the work. On the other hand, in D. F. Norton's *David Hume: Common-Sense Moralist, Sceptical Metaphysician* (Princeton: Princeton University Press, 1982), 63, we read that "Hutcheson's interest in the sense of beauty is decidedly subsidiary," and Norton also pitches his (otherwise informative) examination accordingly.

49. The discussion in the book by William Robert Scott, *Francis Hutcheson: His Life, Teaching and Position in the History of Philosophy* (Cambridge: Cambridge University Press, 1900), 182–97, also fails to describe the connection between beauty and virtue as central to Hutcheson's theory.

vist" theory of morals and aesthetics.[50] Although readers during Hutcheson's own day obviously did not use this word to describe his proposals, they likewise suspected that he had tried to dilute the intellectual consistency of morality by injecting a disturbing number of subjective variables into his account of how we make moral judgments. He was imagined to have believed, in other words, that by virtue of a special "moral sense" we somehow "feel," or immediately and unreflectively perceive, moral emotions rather than rationally or cognitively apprehend moral qualities. In the most simplistic reading, Hutcheson was thus made to seem to advocate the sort of subjectivism (and hence potential relativism) in both ethical thought and practice that he in fact most ardently sought to combat. As the reference in the title of his book to the application of a "mathematical" method to morality should alert us, however, Hutcheson was anything but a straightforward "emotivist" with no interest in rational rules and definitions (even if the avowal of an adherence to mathematical models was hardly novel at the time).[51] Rather than seeking to diminish the part played by reason in moral judgments, Hutcheson displayed on the contrary an abiding faith in the existence of objective, identifiable criteria for morality—or, in his own words, the "Reality of Virtue."[52]

Although his theory is carefully set forth and proleptically guarded at great length against possible attack in his book, the argument Hutcheson presents is actually relatively simple. Following the dictates demanded by the contemporary "mathematical" method of psychological explanation, Hutcheson begins his demonstration by analyzing all human behavior into its two main components, which he (without making any claim here, either, to originality) identifies as "pleasure" and "pain." He also divides the experience of these two fundamental sensations into what he calls "sensible" and "rational" categories, stating, as had his Platonizing mentor, that the latter

50. One of the most influential expositions of Hutcheson's philosophy, especially as it affected Hume, is by Norman Kemp Smith, *The Philosophy of David Hume: A Critical Study of Its Origins and Central Doctrines* (London: Macmillan, 1941), 29 and passim, who contends that Hutcheson viewed "moral and aesthetic judgments as nonrational, resting exclusively on feeling." This view is also defended in an article by William Frankena, "Hutcheson's Moral Sense Theory," *Journal of the History of Ideas* 16 (1955): 356–75. In a series of articles and in his book, David Fate Norton has contested this interpretation, arguing that Hutcheson always insisted on the role of reason in making these judgments, and that the so-called moral sense must be understood as resting on this basis. See "Hutcheson's Moral Sense Theory Reconsidered," *Dialogue* 13 (1974): 3–23; "Hutcheson on Perception and Moral Perception," *Archiv für Geschichte der Philosophie* 59 (1977): 181–97; and "Hutcheson's Moral Realism," in *David Hume*, 55–93. Norton's arguments, in turn, have been criticized by Kenneth P. Winkler in his article "Hutcheson's Alleged Realism," *Journal of the History of Philosophy* 23 (1985): 179–94, to which Norton responded in the same issue of that journal on pages 397–418.

51. On this aspect of Hutcheson's thought, see Norton, *David Hume*, 55–93.

52. Francis Hutcheson, *An Inquiry into the Original of Our Ideas of Beauty and Virtue*, 2d ed. (London, 1726; reprint, New York: Garland, 1971), xi.

sort of pleasures are superior to the fleeting impressions of sense. "Thus we find ourselves pleas'd with a *Regular Form*," Hutcheson concludes, "and we are conscious that this Pleasure necessarily arises from the Contemplation of the Idea, which is then present to our Minds" (xiii). Since Hutcheson additionally subscribed to the notion that the basic structure of the human mind never varied, he held that certain sorts of ideas, just as certain sorts of objects, would always and necessarily elicit either pleasant or unpleasant reactions from us. But it is important to emphasize the thoroughly rational conception Hutcheson espoused, and that at every point he was speaking of our perception of ideas and of the attendant intellectual processes, not of purely emotional response. With this caveat in mind, one can understand the following well-known, but often misunderstood, passage:

> These *Determinations* to be pleas'd with any Forms, or Ideas which occur to our Observation, the *Author* chuses to call SENSES; distinguishing them from the Powers which commonly go by that Name, by calling our Power of perceiving the *Beauty* of *Regularity, Order, Harmony*, an INTERNAL SENSE; and *that Determination* to be pleas'd with the Contemplation of those *Affections, Actions,* or *Characters* of *rational Agents*, which we call *virtuous*, he marks by the name of a MORAL SENSE. (xiii–xiv)

Once he had accepted this initial proposition, Hutcheson thought it was possible to explain how we are motivated to desire the good—that is, to find it pleasing and to respond accordingly—and to avoid evil. Here Hutcheson only seems to retreat to a position reminiscent of that taken by Locke by making, as it were, recourse to divine intervention; but their solutions are in no way alike. Whereas Locke had said that we directly received specific, identifiable moral laws from God, even though we may be able to discover them by reason alone, Hutcheson claimed that God merely gives us a certain mental constitution that only potentially enables us to perceive the beauty— or the "order" and "harmony"—of virtue: "The *AUTHOR* of *Nature* has much better furnish'd us for a virtuous Conduct, than our *Moralists* seem to imagine, by almost as quick and powerful Instructions, as we have for the preservation of our Bodys. He has made *Virtue* a *lovely Form*, to excite our pursuit of it; and has given us *strong Affections* to be the Springs of each virtuous Action" (xv). Far from being simply some auxiliary component of his work, or nothing more than a misplaced embellishment to an otherwise sober treatise on ethics, the first half of the *Inquiry* had the vital task of showing that we do possess a natural "sense" of beauty, thus laying the conceptual ground for the second section of the book. For the second part illustrates how this sense guides us in perceiving and attaining "moral beauty," and it therefore represents an essential and indispensible part of the larger design. Indeed, as Hutcheson defined it, our natural, immediate response to the "beauty" of virtue *guarantees* that we will seek goodness for its own sake, and not for some ulterior motive stemming from some sort of Hobbesian sense of self-interest: "This *moral Sense*, either of our *own* Actions, or of those of *others*, has this in common with our other Senses, that however our Desire of *Virtue* may be counterballanc'd by *Interest*, our Sentiment or Perception of its *Beauty* cannot" (126). It is beauty, in other words, and nothing else, that ensures an unimpeachable virtue. Hutcheson therefore saw beauty and moral goodness not just as constituting an inseparable unity, as being fused together in a vital, necessary affinity. He believed that this was the one and only way to stabilize and sustain a moral theory in the absence of transcendent commands.

Hutcheson was obviously well aware that with the advancement of the notion of an "internal" or "moral sense," he had decided to adopt an unusual nomenclature to elaborate his theory, and it was above all this terminology which prompted both puzzlement and criticism among his many readers. Hutcheson himself admitted that "this *moral Sense* of *Beauty* in *Action* and *Affections*, may appear strange at first View" (xv). But it is apparent that Hutcheson had wished mainly to solve a purely logical problem, and not to divide the mind into a theoretically endless number of discrete and independent "senses." Most of all he did not want to give the impression that he discounted, much less denied, the active regulation of reason in moral judgment and action. He simply wanted to demonstrate that all ethical theories with an exclusively human focus necessarily *imply* something like a "moral sense" as a logical requirement even if they do not explicitly incorporate it in fact.

Otherwise, Hutcheson's opinions about the actual nature of beauty— basically that it consists, as he repeatedly wrote in classically good fashion, in "Uniformity in Variety"[53]—and his ideas about the mechanism of the "moral sense," which responds to the pleasing perception of such an ordered regularity, are not particularly new or illuminating. All of his elaborations served to support his governing thesis. Hutcheson argued at length, for instance, about how education, customs, and habitat could and did influence the functioning of this sense. But the very fact that every person and every culture responded in some internally consistent way to both beauty and ugliness and hence, he thought, to good and evil as well, no matter what the particular manifestation of these qualities may be, was itself proof of the

---

53. See, for example, *Inquiry*, 82–83, where Hutcheson defines the *"internal Sense"* as *"a passive Power of receiving Ideas of Beauty from all Objects in which there is Uniformity amidst Variety."*

universal existence of such a sense, even though it was not evidence of its uniform constitution. As Hutcheson explained:

> Had we no *natural Sense* of *Beauty* and *Harmony*, we could never be prejudic'd in favour of Objects or Sounds as *Beautiful* or *Harmonious*. *Education* may make an unattentive GOTH imagine that his *Countrymen* have attain'd the Perfection of *Architecture*, and an Aversion to their Enemys the ROMANS, may have join'd some disagreeable Ideas to their very Buildings, and excited them to their Demolition; but he had never form'd these Prejudices, had he been void of a *Sense* of *Beauty*. (92)

Although it is filled with many interesting discussions of individual examples of moral excellence and depravity, the rest of the *Inquiry* primarily represents the extended attempt to justify these general remarks and thus need not occupy us further.

Despite its conceptual limitations, Hutcheson's theory proved to be extraordinarily influential, and like many of his other works, the *Inquiry* was soon translated into all of the major European languages. Diderot, for instance, devoted a large section of his *Encyclopédie* article on beauty ("Beau") to a discussion of Hutcheson's theory. In 1756 Lessing published a translation of another book by Hutcheson, the *System of Moral Philosophy*, with the inaccurate but telling title *Sittenlehre der Vernunft* (Moral doctrine of reason). Lessing's friend, Moses Mendelssohn, also carefully studied and commented on Hutcheson's works, and in Kant's announcement for his courses during the winter semester of 1765–66, he noted that he would be using Hutcheson's proposals, as well as those of Shaftesbury and Hume, as his point of departure in his lectures on ethics.[54]

Naturally, not all of the reactions to Hutcheson's work were this positive, and most of the negative responses tended to focus, as he had himself predicted, on his unorthodox use of the term "sense." But his equation of virtue with beauty also encountered decided opposition among his critics, particularly those who sought to defend a system of morals that still drew its principles and justification from traditional Christian theology. Whether or

54. See Immanuel Kant, "Nachricht von der Einrichtung seiner Vorlesungen in dem Winterhalbenjahre von 1765–1766," in *Werkausgabe*, ed. Wilhelm Weischedel (Frankfurt am Main: Suhrkamp, 1968), 2:914–15. Kant wrote: "The essays of Shaftesbury, Hutcheson, and Hume—which, while incomplete and faulty, have nevertheless advanced the furthest in the inquiry into the first principles of all morality—will receive the precision and completion they lack. And by always considering both historically and philosophically that in moral theory [*Tugendlehre*] which *actually happens* before showing what *should happen*, I will make the method clear according to which one has to study human beings. . . . This method of ethical investigation is a beautiful discovery of our times, and it was (if one considers it in its entire scope) completely unknown to the ancients."

not Shaftesbury or Hutcheson had found it possible to reconcile their moral theory with a fairly orthodox Christian belief was immaterial to their detractors. They saw in the concept of moral beauty nothing less than a mortal threat to their faith. In 1726 John Balguy, an English divine, published "A Letter to a Deist, Concerning the Beauty and Excellency of Moral Virtue, and The Support and Improvement which it receives from the CHRISTIAN REVELATION." Although the "Deist" to whom he addressed the letter was Shaftesbury, Balguy mentioned Hutcheson's recently published *Inquiry* as well, and two years later published another work, *The Foundation of Moral Goodness*, which took more direct aim at Hutcheson himself. As the title of the "Letter" fairly unambiguously revealed, Balguy upheld the view that only the belief in eternal rewards and punishments can serve as an adequate, which is to say truly persuasive, stimulus to virtuous conduct. He specifically disputed that the perception of some beauty, however defined, could perform this important task, and he based his assessment on his simple observation of "how small a Proportion of Mankind are capable of discerning, in any considerable Degree, the inward Beauty and Excellence of Virtue."[55] Rejecting the aristocratic attitude of Shaftesbury, as well as its more placative abstract codification in Hutcheson's work, Balguy sought to exercise his pastoral function by embracing the morally degenerate and socially dispossessed within the fold of ethical concern. He doubted that these and other unfortunates would be much moved by airy speculations about harmony and just proportion. "Alas!" Balguy sighed over such troubled souls, "their Reason is exceedingly darkened and depraved; and their Moral Sense must be grown very languid, if it be not quite lost. Represent to a vicious Man the Beauty of Virtue, you speak to him in a Language that he does not understand" (15).

Of course, it could be argued that Balguy himself did not understand the logical import of Hutcheson's notion of the moral sense, and had Hutcheson decided to do so, he could have dispatched Balguy's objections with relative ease. A more serious threat to Hutcheson's theory (or, more precisely, to that of its progenitor, Shaftesbury) came in the form of a fellow Irishman, Dean George Berkeley, future bishop of Cloyne. In 1732 Berkeley published *Alciphron, or, the Minute Philosopher*, which he had written in Newport, Rhode Island, during his three-year sojourn in the Colonies. Subtitled *An Apology for the Christian Religion, against those who are called Free-Thinkers*, the book thus made no pretense to impartiality, but openly announced its opposition to Deism, with which, as we have already observed in the case of

55. John Balguy, "A Letter to a Deist," in *A Collection of Tracts Moral and Theological* (London: J. Pemberton, 1734), 13.

Balguy, Shaftesbury was then closely identified. By then well practiced in the art of polemics, Berkeley used *Alciphron* to deliver an at times subtle, at times plainly scornful, attack on the principles upheld by the so-called minute philosophers, most particularly Mandeville and Shaftesbury.[56] This somewhat surprising juxtaposition was evidently designed to underscore Berkeley's belief in the similarity of the final effect—rather than the real substance—of their views. For it was an influence that, as Berkeley categorically claimed in the "Advertisement" to his book, would do no less than to "unhinge the principles of morality, and destroy the means of making men reasonably virtuous."[57]

Although there is no question, as we will see, that Berkeley distorted Shaftesbury's philosophy, the same could also be said about the common contention that in the words of Sir Leslie Stephen, Berkeley's *Alciphron* itself "is the least admirable performance of that admirable writer."[58] Because Stephen's judgment has been widely and uncritically accepted, this work, as well as Berkeley's participation in the English eighteenth-century ethical debates generally, has been almost totally ignored.[59] But what Berkeley positively *did* do, and what no one had done before him with such skill and conviction, was to make the concept of "moral beauty" a *problem* by subjecting it to a sustained and rigorous examination. After the appearance of *Alciphron*—and despite Berkeley's intentions—the notion that virtue and beauty were at bottom somehow identical became a fixed part of eighteenth-century ethical discourse in Britain and, later, abroad. Although various factions would later advance their favorite arguments to defend or to deny this reputed identity, the very debate itself assured that the notion of an inner, "moral beauty" remained firmly established at the center of the intellectual, and thus larger cultural, transformations taking place during the European Enlightenment.

It is revealing, yet also paradigmatic, that in the Third Dialogue (which is

56. The first word in the phrase "minuti philosophi," which comes originally from Cicero's *Tusculan Disputations*, means "small in degree of importance, slight, petty, minor; (of persons) small-minded, ignoble." Cited from P.G.W. Glare, ed., *Oxford Latin Dictionary* (Oxford: Oxford University Press, 1982).

57. George Berkeley, *Alciphron, or, the Minute Philosopher*, in *Works*, ed. A. A. Luce and T. E. Jessop (London: Thomas Nelson, 1948–57), 3:23. Henceforth cited parenthetically in the text as "*Alciphron*" by page number.

58. Leslie Stephen, *History of English Thought in the Eighteenth Century*, 3d ed. (London: John Murray, 1902), 2:43.

59. There is to my knowledge only one full-length study of Berkeley's ethics, and that is by Paul J. Olscamp, *The Moral Philosophy of George Berkeley* (The Hague: Martinus Nijhoff, 1970), who himself remarks (whether the pun was intended or not) on "the minute amount of writing on the subject" (4). Similarly, in the extensive collection of essays recently brought out by Walter E. Creery, ed., *George Berkeley: Critical Assessments*, 3 vols. (London: Routledge, 1991), there is not a single article discussing Berkeley's moral theory.

entirely devoted to a discussion of Shaftesbury, *alias* Alciphron) Berkeley concentrated his critique on the connection between beauty and virtue that Shaftesbury and his followers had advocated.[60] Among the many other items of potential discord in Shaftesbury's thought, Berkeley had thus astutely perceived the one element on which his nontheologically motivated moral theory hinged. But instead of simply asserting the opposite view, as for example Balguy had done, Berkeley sought to attack the fundamentals of the theory itself, and he demanded—in the voice of Euphranor, Alciphron's principle antagonist—to know above all else "what sense it is in which you understand the beauty of virtue. Define it, explain it, make me to understand your meaning, so that we may argue about the same thing" (*Alciphron*, 119).

Clearly, Berkeley held all of the cards: he enjoyed the distinct—and distinctly unfair—advantage of being able to supply his opponent with his arguments and he thus enjoyed the delicious opportunity of compelling his antagonist to portray his own opinions in a less than favorable light. And Berkeley made masterful use of the dialogue form to expose the ambiguities underlying the concept of moral beauty and the ways in which we were able to judge it. He communicated the majority of his criticisms indirectly, by lending Alciphron words that, although they do not wholly misrepresent Shaftesbury's theory, are so selective in their emphasis and detail that they effectively distort Shaftesbury's original intentions. A typical instance of Berkeley's procedure can be seen in the following passage, in which he let Alciphron recite a synopsis of his (that is, the *faux* Shaftesbury's) views:

> A man needs no arguments to make him discern and approve what is beautiful; it strikes at first sight, and attracts without a reason. And as this beauty is found in the shape and form of corporeal things; so also is there analogous to it a beauty of another kind—an order, a symmetry, and comeliness, in the moral world. And as the eye perceiveth the one, so the mind doth, by a certain interior sense, perceive the other; which sense, talent, or faculty is ever quickest and purest in the noblest minds. . . . To relish this kind of beauty there must be a delicate and fine taste; but, where there is this natural taste, nothing further is wanting, either as a principle to convince, or as a motive to induce men to the love of virtue. (117)

60. Although commentators on *Alciphron* (what few of them there are) have tended to identify the character of Alciphron solely with Shaftesbury, I am inclined to think that Berkeley may have also had Hutcheson in mind. This is suggested by Berkeley's repeated reference to the phrase "moral sense," which Shaftesbury used but once and which plays, as we know, a far more prominent role in Hutcheson's work. And it is possible, perhaps, that the more recent publication of Hutcheson's book also represented to Berkeley the increasing, and increasingly dangerous, acceptance of what he considered to be an insidious philosophy.

There is much that is by now familiar in this account, but also a great deal that is misleading. First is the implication that what Alciphron calls this "certain interior sense" operates entirely without assistance from our rational faculties, that it functions in us, as Berkeley had him depict it, "without reason." But as we have discovered, Shaftesbury did not hold this simplistic view; he insisted instead that the word "sense" was merely a metaphor explaining what was indeed the product of rational effort and deliberate, careful training. Of course, if we were not human beings and did not in some sense "naturally" possess the equipment to develop this faculty of moral "sense" or trained discernment, which Shaftesbury (as well as several others) had likened to "taste," then all attempts to cultivate it would clearly be in vain. But Shaftesbury did not identify the latent presence of this "taste" with its fully formed realization, as Berkeley implied he did; it was only a potential that, as such, could go untapped.

Lower down the polemical register, Berkeley attempted to portray Alciphron-Shaftesbury as an aloof representative of the noble class. He sought to discredit Shaftesbury by typing him as someone who indulged in frivolous pursuits that were attractive precisely because they were commonly unattainable to the multitudes, and thus as someone who looked down on simple people and their need for religion with a supercilious gaze. To that end, Berkeley had Alciphron utter such mindless comments as: "The refined moralists of our sect are ravished and transported with the abstract beauty of virtue. They disdain all forensic motives to it; and love virtue only for virtue's sake. Oh rapture! oh enthusiasm! oh the quintessence of beauty!" (120–21). There was, to be sure, good reason to accuse Shaftesbury of having favored an exclusionary model of moral philosophy, and, as we know, Berkeley was not the first to have faulted him for it. But had Shaftesbury really written such trite banalities, not only would he have deserved the scorn Berkeley heaped on him, he would also have never achieved the considerable reputation and influence that he did.

As things stood, however, Berkeley was free to fashion Alciphron into a straw man, and his spokesman Euphranor had no difficulty in disposing of the flimsy arguments put forward by his insubstantial opponent. Since this seemed to be the point on which all else depended, Berkeley had Euphranor first inquire into the nature of that external beauty which Alciphron had said we perceive "with the eye" and which provided the analogy to the internal or "moral" beauty we apprehended "with the mind." Imitating the shrewd modesty and probing ignorance of Socrates, Euphranor exclaims: "O Alciphron, it is my weakness that I am apt to be lost and bewildered by abstractions and generalities, but a particular thing is better suited to my faculties. . . . Be pleased then to inform me, what is it we call beauty in the objects of sense?" (123). After weakly suggesting that beauty consisted in a certain symmetry or proportion pleasing to the eye, Alciphron finds himself helplessly at the mercy of Euphranor's relentless logic. He analyzes each of the terms in Alciphron's "definition" and then rightly concludes that "proportions . . . are not, strictly speaking, perceived by the sense of sight, but only by reason through the means of sight" (124). No distinction exists, that is, in the means of perception themselves; and in each case it is reason itself, not some real or imagined "sense," that performs the business of judging. No one, including Shaftesbury, could possibly have disagreed with this proposition, but Alciphron is confounded by it.

But about the main issue at stake there existed a surprising degree of accord between Berkeley and Shaftesbury. Despite Berkeley's efforts to expose and deride the logical flaws within the ethical theory that claimed moral beauty as both the motivation and manifestation of virtue, he did not dispute that this variety of "beauty" existed, or even that resorting to it was an inappropriate way of speaking about moral states or actions. At one point, Berkeley-Euphranor thus freely admits that he thought that "there is a beauty of the mind, a charm in virtue, a symmetry and proportion in the moral world. This moral beauty was known to the ancients by the name of *honestum* or *to kalon*" (118). Berkeley did not necessarily disagree that one could regard virtue as being somehow "beautiful"; he resisted Shaftesbury's efforts to found his ethical theory on this perception and our reaction to it alone.[61] Pitting a conscientious professionalism against Shaftesbury's gentlemanly amateurism, Berkeley sought to demonstrate the deficiencies of Shaftesbury's philosophy, as we have seen, by examining each of its necessary components: first, the question of a "sense" that supposedly immediately perceives and approves of beauty and, second, the nature of beauty itself. But through Berkeley's criticism, the concept of moral beauty—whatever it might ultimately prove to be—had irrevocably entered the main current of philosophical ethics.

In one further respect, Berkeley advanced the discussion surrounding moral beauty decisively by introducing yet another element to the already complex equation. We have seen how Euphranor, in his attempts to understand Alciphron's meaning, had identified the notion of moral beauty with the Greek word *to kalon*. Although it has become a commonplace to mention Shaftesbury's indebtedness to Plato and Plotinus, Shaftesbury himself, in conformity with contemporary practice, rarely mentioned any of his predecessors or antagonists by name, nor did he ever explicitly refer to this concept by the Greek word.[62] It thus fell to Berkeley to be the first in the

61. See also Olscamp, *Moral Philosophy*, 168.
62. Josef Chytry, *The Aesthetic State: A Quest in Modern German Thought* (Berkeley and Los Angeles: University of California Press, 1989), 72, for example, mentions "Shaftesbury's

eighteenth century to recognize and to enunciate one of the main historical dimensions of the debate about beauty of the soul.[63] It turns out that Berkeley was especially well equipped for this task: he was not just a formidable speculative thinker, but also a scholar of considerable acumen and depth, and his first position came to him in 1712, at the age of twenty-eight, when he was appointed Junior Greek Lecturer at Trinity College in Dublin.[64] It was on the basis of this youthful philological training that in a subsequent section of the Third Dialogue of *Alciphron*, Berkeley has Crito (who is on the side of Euphranor and positive religion) remind his interlocutors of the classical origins underlying the concept of moral beauty. Crito explains that "Aristotle distinguisheth between two characters of a good man; the one he calleth *agathos*, or simply *good*; the other *kalos kagathos*, from whence the compound term *kalokagathia*, which cannot, perhaps, be rendered by any one word in our language" (133). As we will see in the third chapter of this book, not only is the Greek compound noun *kalokagathia* difficult to render into English—forcing us to adopt some clumsy coinage such as "beauty-and-goodness"—the Greeks themselves seemed to have had notable trouble deciding what the word actually meant. But Crito goes on to say, despite these terminological difficulties in interpreting Aristotle's ethical system, "His sense is plainly this: . . . *kalos kagathos* is that man in whom are to be found all things worthy and decent and laudable, purely as such and for their own sake, and who practiseth virtue from no other motive than the sole love of her own innate beauty" (134).

But what Berkeley was willing to accept from Aristotle was quite different from the demands he made of the Stagirite's modern expositors. Despite his willingness to entertain speculation about the springs for moral behavior, he still remained unconvinced by the notion that the perception of beauty alone could move us to perform virtuous acts. In the end, as much as he conceded that virtue may be vaguely pleasing to behold and hence could in this way be considered somehow "beautiful," Berkeley finally resorted to the well-worn, yet still serviceable, argument that "reward and fear of punishment are highly expedient to cast the balance of pleasant and profitable on

concept of *kalokagathia*," creating the impression that Shaftesbury himself used this term, which he never did.

63. It is interesting that one of Berkeley's friends was Thomas Blackwell, whose *Enquiry into the Life and Writings of Homer* (London, 1735) was the first work on the Greek bard that tried to explain his epics according to historical information that was then available about Homer's Greece.

64. See John Wild, *George Berkeley: A Study of His Life and Philosophy* (New York: Russell & Russell, 1962), 67. In the same place, Wild comments: "Nothing . . . is more essential for an understanding of Berkeley's 'development' than his growth in his understanding of the meaning and importance of Platonism, though it has been hitherto strangely neglected by commentators."

the side of virtue" (119). But as is often the case in the annals of polemical dispute, Berkeley's efforts produced a result that ran counter to his hopes. The very vigor with which he criticized the concept of moral beauty and its ability to deliver the ground for an autonomous morality, as well as the relatively unimaginative cast of his counterproposal, served to make the notion all the more attractive, or at least worth serious consideration, in the eyes of succeeding writers.

Throughout the next two decades, until well into the 1750s, there thus continued to appear a large number of works on both moral and aesthetic matters in which the notion of moral beauty was taken for granted, even if its final significance and value remained contested. In 1744, for instance, James Harris published his *Three Treatises, The First Concerning Art, The Second Concerning Music, Painting and Poetry, The Third Concerning Happiness*, which he dedicated to his uncle—the late earl of Shaftesbury. In the last of the three "treatises," Harris wrote at length, but not with much originality, about "Moral Artists" and "this *moral, mental*, and *original Beauty*."[65] Similarly, in 1751 Henry Home—better known as Lord Kames—anonymously issued his *Essays on the Principles of Morality and Natural Religion*, the fourth chapter of which is titled "Of the Different Orders of Moral Beauty."[66] On the whole one can class Home among the adherents of the notion that we possess some kind of a "moral sense," which he defined in express reference to its response to beauty as follows: "This peculiar feeling, or modification of beauty and deformity in human actions, is known by the name of *moral beauty*, and *moral deformity*. In it consists the *morality* and *immorality* of human actions; and the power or faculty, by which we perceive this difference among actions, passes under the name of the *moral sense*" (50).[67] And in 1752, writing under the pseudonym of Sir Harry Beaumont, Joseph Spence published *Crito; or, A Dialogue on Beauty*, a short work that finds a relatively minor place in the long line of eighteenth-century Shaftesburian dialogues. Although it cannot be said that Spence in any way contributed to the philosophical advancement of the concept, his *Crito* is nevertheless an indication of the virtual ubiquity of the notion that, "as Virtue is the supreme Beauty, so is Vice the most odious of all Deformities."[68] Finally, Richard Price pub-

---

65. James Harris, *Three Treatises, The First Concerning Art, The Second Concerning Music, Painting and Poetry, The Third Concerning Happiness*, 4th ed. (London: C. Nourse, 1783), 188 and 212; see also 214–221, and 234–38.
66. Henry Home (Lord Kames), *Essays on the Principles of Morality and Natural Religion* (Edinburgh: R. Fleming, 1751), 69–76.
67. Norton, *David Hume*, 176, remarks dismissively, but accurately, that "Kames's views in morals are almost entirely derivative."
68. Joseph Spence, *Crito; or, A Dialogue on Beauty* (London, 1752; reprint, New York: Garland, 1970), 59. Given the title of the essay, it is perhaps not surprising that Spence fre-

lished his influential *Review of the Principal Questions of Morals* in 1758, which recapitulated and critiqued many of the foregoing developments. Even though Price was one of the most talented and subtle opponents of the "moral sense" school itself, he also accepted that there was a "Beauty and Deformity of Actions," even as he strenuously objected in particular to Hutcheson's arguments relating to their precise function and place in moral judgments.[69]

But it was at the beginning of that fruitful decade, in 1751, that there appeared what was probably the most important work in philosophical ethics of the mid-eighteenth century: David Hume's *Enquiry concerning the Principles of Morals*.[70] Unfortunately, this work did not fare much better in contemporary esteem than Hume's first (and, as many still believe, more important) book of philosophy, the *Treatise of Human Nature*, which appeared in three volumes in 1739–40. The publication of the earlier *Treatise* excited so little interest at the time that, as Hume famously lamented, it seemed that the work "fell *dead-born from the Press*."[71] But despite the equally disheartening reception accorded to his *Enquiry* (it too, he reported, "came unnoticed and unobserved into the World"), Hume made the extraordinary claim at the end of his life that the *Enquiry* was, "of all my writings, historical, philosophical, or literary, incomparably the best" (4). Whatever the merits of Hume's self-assessment might be, it should at least caution us about dismissing the significance of this book, as compared to the *Treatise*, too quickly.[72]

---

quently referred to Plato, as in the following passage: "And yet all the Profusion of Beauty I have been speaking of, and even that of the whole Universe taken together, is but of a weaker nature in Comparison of the Beauty of Virtue. It was extremely well said by *Plato*, That if Virtue was to appear in a visible Shape, all Men would be enamoured of her: And it seems as if the *Greeks* and *Romans* in general had had this Idea of her Beauty, because the Goddess of Virtue, and the Goddess of Wisdom (which was often taken for one and the same Thing among them, as well as in our Sacred Writings), were always represented with the greatest and most commanding Beauty. The same appears yet stronger from their using the Words Good and Beautiful indifferently for each other; as if all Beauty was contained in Goodness" (57–58).

69. Richard Price, *A Review of the Principal Questions of Morals*, ed. D. Daiches Raphael (Oxford: Oxford University Press, 1948), 57–68. Interestingly, Price uses a quotation from Plato's *Phaedo* as an epigraph proclaiming the "identity of the highest beauty and good."

70. Yet, as J. L. Mackie, *Hume's Moral Theory* (London: Routledge & Kegan Paul, 1980), vii, writes, "Hume's moral theory has been relatively neglected, compared with other parts of his philosophy."

71. Cited from Hume's autobiography, David Hume, *My Own Life*, in *Letters*, ed. J.Y.T. Greig (Oxford: Oxford University Press, 1932), 1:2.

72. For a fairly typical expression of the reasons for preferring the *Treatise* over the *Enquiry*, see Mackie, *Hume's Moral Theory*, 157: "Hume thought that the failure of the *Treatise* to attract much attention was due to its defects of style, and the *Enquiry* was certainly a much more polished work. But in improving the presentation of his moral theory Hume smoothed off too many corners, and softened or suppressed some of his most significant

When he wrote the *Enquiry*, Hume was able to look back over the half-century of ethical debate that we have just reviewed, and with his customary clarity and discrimination he neatly isolated the main terms that had characterized the exchange of opinion thus far. "There has been a controversy started of late," he began in his reassuringly measured manner, "concerning the general foundation of Morals; whether they be derived from Reason, or from Sentiment; whether we attain the knowledge of them by a chain of argument and induction, or by an immediate feeling and finer internal sense."[73] With these swift, sure strokes, Hume accurately summarized the conceptual basis of the conflict, and with his *Enquiry* he proposed to clear away some of the confusion that threatened to arrest all future investigation. Far from encouraging mere skeptical resignation—which is still often imagined to have been his primary, though negative, legacy—Hume sought to advance a positive thesis that would aid not only in fostering a more adequate philosophical understanding of morals, but would perhaps also fulfill the practical dictates of the Enlightener's role by helping to promote a greater level of virtuous conduct in society at large. In view of his consciousness of the high social purpose upholding moral theory, it is all the more expressive of the newly won respectability enjoyed by the concept of moral beauty that it found its way into Hume's most general declaration concerning the final goal of all ethical inquiry: "The end of all moral speculations is to teach us our duty," he uncontroversially concluded, "and, by proper representations of the deformity of vice and beauty of virtue, beget correspondent habits, and engage us to avoid the one, and embrace the other" (172).

Rather than continue the tradition that had posited "reason" and "sentiment" as the opposite, and mutually exclusive, grounds for moral knowledge, Hume suggested that we see them as necessary and complementary correlates. Like the Stoics and Shaftesbury before him, Hume felt that rational calculations alone are incapable of providing the necessary motivation for virtuous actions. Even the barest knowledge of history, as well as a sufficiently honest examination of ourselves, will serve to disabuse us of the notion that human beings are always willing—or often even able—to exercise rational control over their sensuous desires and appetites. Yet Hume also realized, since we *are* human beings—that is to say, uniquely rational agents—and thus not wholly subject to the vagaries of passion and sensation, that there has to be a balance between these two major influences on the determination of our conduct. He therefore agreed that the final guide

---

arguments." For a slightly different view, see Norton, *David Hume*, 121–26; but on the whole Norton also heavily favors the *Treatise* in his discussion of Hume's moral philosophy.

73. David Hume, *Enquiries concerning Human Understanding and concerning the Principles of Morals*, ed. L. A. Selby-Bigge, 3d. ed., rev. P. H. Nidditch (Oxford: Oxford University Press, 1975), 171.

in pronouncing an action good or evil "depends on some internal sense or feeling, which nature has made universal in the whole species" (173). But, Hume immediately added, in most instances this "internal sense" is, by itself, not an adequate guide and required the greater governance of reason. It is thus necessary, he wrote, "to employ much reasoning, in order to feel the proper sentiment; and a false relish may frequently be corrected by argument and reflection. There are just grounds to conclude, that moral beauty partakes much of this latter species, and demands the assistance of our intellectual faculties, in order to give it a suitable influence on the human mind" (173).[74] The final product, then, of human sentiment that has been tempered or cultivated by an active, reasoning mind is nothing other than— moral beauty.

With Hume's *Enquiry* we thus reach a kind of momentary pause in the story I have been retelling. It has become apparent that Hume did not add any substantially new insights to the discussion that Shaftesbury had begun about the possibility of an autonomous morality and about the prominent place moral beauty held in that theory. But he did clarify several implications it contained by attempting to resolve some of its inner tensions. The fundamental problem concerned not whether rational *or* emotional faculties provided the means of determining morality. Rather, it was a matter of resolving what exactly reason *and* sentiment contribute and how they operate in concert with each other. As Hume put it, the "elegant Lord Shaftesbury, who first gave occasion to remark this distinction, . . . is not, himself, entirely free from the same confusion."[75] Indeed, as Shaftesbury's theory has emerged here, Hume did not appreciably advance beyond its fundamental position, even though he stated it and its consequences much more incisively and consistently. In fact, even as he gently rebuked Shaftesbury for his lack of precision, Hume himself seems to have recognized that by more rigorously locating the distinct but elemental roles played by *both* reason and sentiment in making moral knowledge, he had only elaborated an argument that had already been present, however dimly, in the works of his aristocratic predecessor.

With Hume, then, we attain a temporary caesura in a development that had begun a hundred years earlier with the challenge of Hobbes's materialist philosophy. In some ways, Hume and Hobbes were not as dissimilar as they would first appear. Like everyone else who thought about the matter, Hume felt obliged to announce, as the subtitle of his *Treatise* proclaimed, that he, too, wanted to "attempt to introduce the experimental method of

74. One of the most recent accounts of Hume's moral philosophy, Jan Rohls, *Geschichte der Ethik* (Tübingen: J.C.B. Mohr, Paul Siebeck, 1991), 261, describes Hume's ethics as "antirationalistic and intuitive."
75. Hume, *Enquiries*, 171.

reasoning into moral subjects." And both philosophers dispensed with the necessity of appealing to divine authority as the guarantee for morally good conduct, looking instead to the psychological mechanisms responsible for regulating human behavior in morals and everywhere else. But though their means were similar in several important respects, their conclusions were utterly different. One of the consequences of this difference was that Hume, very much unlike Hobbes, enjoyed a generally favorable reputation both at home and abroad. He was particularly well received in Germany, where religion and the Enlightenment coexisted, as we will presently see, in a much less fractious union than had been the case in the British isles.

2

Beauty of Soul:
Pietism and the Ideal
of Moral Perfection

What obstacle then remains to hinder the soul from
recalling the primal beauty which it abandoned,
when it can make an end of its vices?
—St. Augustine

The conception of moral beauty that emerged within early
eighteenth-century British philosophy had arisen, naturally enough,
in response to a specific intellectual and social context. As a consequence, its indebtedness to this particular frame of reference at first slowed,
but did not ultimately prevent, the exportation of the notion and its many
implications to the Continent. When these ideas did begin to make their
eastern migration in the late 1720s and 1730s, the first to welcome them to
their shores were the French, with the anglophilic Voltaire foremost among
them. Indeed, many French thinkers embraced everything written in the
language of Newton and Locke with a passion that approached the sort
of enthusiastic zeal they took care to deplore in others. Although Deism
(which, as we have seen, more than a few thought lurked behind the facade
of moral beauty) had by then already lost much of its momentum in England, many French thinkers still eagerly appropriated this British brand of
a rationalized natural theology in the hope that it would provide potent new
weapons to combat an entrenched and well-fortified state religion.[1] The
ideologically sclerotic Cardinal Fleury confirmed their partial success when
he described the period of the Regency (1714–23) as the time when "that
pile of offensive books came across the sea and inundated France, or rather
poisoned all of those among us who make grand claims about the power of

1. See Norman L. Torrey, *Voltaire and the English Deists* (New Haven: Yale University Press,
1930), and Dorothy B. Schlegel, *Shaftesbury and the French Deists* (Chapel Hill: University of
North Carolina Press, 1956).

the mind."[2] The situation was different in Germany, however, where the effect of British philosophy in general, including the specific problem of the ostensible beauty of virtue, did not begin to make itself felt in any significant way until the middle of the century. Yet there was another, indigenous tradition of "inward beauty" within German thought that, paradoxically, had its origin in precisely that sphere of belief to which the British philosophers had formulated their theory of "moral beauty" as an alternative.

PIETISM AND INNER REBIRTH

Often thought to have been thoroughly, if not singularly, secular, the eighteenth century exhibited far more signs of a vital belief than the usual slogans would seem to admit. It is true that certain central aims of the Enlightenment program, especially in its more radical (and particularly French) manifestations, represented an unrelenting attack against the religious "superstitions" that the Church—as Hobbes and many others were convinced—opportunistically fed and manipulated. But it is equally certain that actual atheism remained confined to a relative minority. In truth the traces of religion in the early eighteenth century were pervasive and profound: the music of Bach, the novels of Richardson, even the scientific researches of both Leibniz and Newton are unthinkable outside the context of Christian belief. To perceive its effects one does not need to summon the sort of dogged ingenuity that Carl Becker displayed in his attempt to expose the Christian paradigms that he felt surreptitiously upheld the "true faith" of eighteenth-century skeptics, namely, the euphemistic "religion of humanity."[3] An eclectic and somewhat diffuse notion of "humanity" did become a kind of cultic catchword for many of the leading thinkers of the later Enlightenment, and in some cases the advocacy of that idea approached the kind of religious fervor that Becker suspected the *philosophes* of hypocritically harboring. But during the first fifty years of the century and even beyond, the "true faith" not only of the superstitious multitudes, but of a majority of the intellectuals as well, remained the much more properly named religion of Christianity. It became, it is true, less important to the most outspoken and original thinkers of the day to adhere to the letter of institutional observance than to cultivate the spirit of personal devotion. Most often, in fact, they deemed the Church to be an increasingly intrusive impediment to an individual, and individually acquired, relation to God. But for all of their principled insistence on autonomy and freedom in

2. Gotthard Victor Lechler, *Geschichte des englischen Deismus* (Stuttgart, 1842; reprint, intro. Günter Gawlick, Hildesheim: Georg Olms, 1965), 446.
3. Carl L. Becker, *The Heavenly City of the Eighteenth-Century Philosophers* (New Haven: Yale University Press, 1932), 37.

making decisions about even the most weighty religious matters, eighteenth-century writers lived in a world whose widest boundaries were still largely circumscribed by common Christian categories. At midcentury, David Hume —to be sure, with a liberal dose of self-conscious irony—expressed the predicament this way: "To be a philosophical skeptic is, in a man of letters, the first and most essential step towards being a sound, believing Christian."[4] It had never before been more difficult for people to be sound, believing Christians, but they were not an endangered species—yet.

This is not to imply, of course, that a placid uniformity of doctrine and practice prevailed in the religious life of the eighteenth century. Although the European states were no longer waging devastating wars over confessional lines as had been the case in the century before, the Enlightenment continued to witness fiercely acrimonious controversies about the most basic tenets of belief. As we have already seen, the attempts by some British philosophers to disengage morality from religion and to offer a justification of ethical action based on an understanding of human nature alone did not mean that they denied the reality of the Christian God, or even less that they rejected the general validity of religious thought. But those closer to, and certainly those within, the clergy sensed a real threat in such overfine distinctions. They responded to the challenge by trying to prove that an awareness of assured reward and equally certain punishment was a far more potent and persuasive impetus to good conduct than, for example, some abstract appreciation of beauty. Naturally, one can see these conflicts themselves as an early indication of what we, from our latter-day perspective, know to have been an inevitable, albeit gradual, erosion of faith. As Mark Pattison once keenly observed, "When an age is found occupied in proving its creed, this is but a token that the age has ceased to have a proper belief in it."[5] That may very well be true. But it bears repeating that throughout the eighteenth century, despite bitter and, for the participants, sometimes dangerous disputes, the Christian religious tradition, though constantly modified to meet changing expectations and needs, continued to exert a— indeed, arguably still *the*—dominant influence on European society. It left no aspect of contemporary political, artistic, or intellectual life unaffected, and nowhere, perhaps, was its living presence more in evidence than in German-speaking lands.

4. David Hume, *Dialogues concerning Natural Religion*, in *Essays and Treatises on Several Subjects* (London: J. Jones, 1822), 2:575. These words are spoken by Philo, but most scholars agree that this character represents Hume. On the vexed problem of Hume's by no means clear views on religion, see the essay by Keith E. Yandell, "Hume on Religious Belief," in *Hume: A Re-evaluation*, ed. Donald W. Livingston and James T. King (New York: Fordham University Press, 1976), 109–25.
5. Mark Pattison, "Tendencies of Religious Thought," in *Essays* (Oxford: Oxford University Press, 1889), 2:53.

Given the charged climate of mutual suspicion that so frequently characterized the relationship between the representatives of the Enlightenment and those who adhered to the Christian religious tradition, it can come as no surprise that the expression of belief itself did not always take entirely traditional forms.[6] One of the most powerful forces shaping German culture in particular during the seventeenth and eighteenth centuries was the decidedly unconventional movement known as Pietism. Pietism derived a great deal of its primary attraction from the sincere efforts of its first advocates to reinvigorate what in their view had become a rather complacent, and some thought even corrupt, Lutheran orthodoxy. In its purest embodiment, Pietism was an attempt, one might say, to reform the Reformation. Yet although most historians of the period will readily concede that Pietism played a crucial role in the greater development of eighteenth-century German culture, there is a relative lack of reliable studies about this extremely rich episode in intellectual and ecclesiastical history.[7] As a result, references to Pietism frequently probe no deeper than the thin surface of received opinion, and more often than not a mere phantom of Pietism is made to serve some other, ideologically motivated, end. Much of what *has* been written about Pietism has also overemphasized its relationship to medieval mysticism and thus its presumably irrational, or at least anti-intellectual, bias. And depending on the general orientation of the respective commentator, these aspects are then portrayed in either a positive or a negative light.[8]

6. On the situation in Germany generally, see Karl Barth, *Protestant Theology in the Nineteenth Century: Its Background and History* (Valley Forge: Judson Press, 1973), the entire first half of which is devoted to the eighteenth century.

7. The most famous—as well as infamous—study is the highly tendentious and critical work by Albrecht Ritschl, *Geschichte des Pietismus*, 3 vols. (Bonn: Adolph Marcus, 1880–86). Although Ritschl condemned, at great and painstaking length, the Pietist tradition as being principally indebted to medieval mysticism and hence as being fundamentally at odds with Lutheran doctrine, his work stands as a unique monument to erudition and thoroughness that has not been matched subsequently by either his apologists or his critics. All too often, scholars of the period make the obligatory reference to some vaguely "Pietistic" influence (whether in a positive or negative sense) without ever consulting original texts, basing their knowledge instead on second- or even third-hand information. One of the worst—and, it appears, in literary circles most often cited—examples of this sort of practice is the essay by Hans R. G. Günther, "Psychologie des deutschen Pietismus," *Deutsche Vierteljahrsschrift* 4 (1926): 144–76. However, mainly owing to the offices of Martin Schmidt, F. Ernest Stoeffler, and Johannes Wallmann, a resurgence of serious scholarly interest in Pietism began in the 1950s that has already yielded important results in changing our perception of its essence and goals.

8. The study by Rudolf Unger, *Hamann und die Aufklärung: Studien zur Vorgeschichte des romantischen Geistes im 18. Jahrhundert*, vol. 1 (Halle: Niemeyer, 1925), has had an enormous influence on the perception of eighteenth-century "irrationalism" in general, and of Hamann and the *Sturm und Drang* movement in particular. His comments on Pietism (on 34–38 and 76–82) concentrate on its connection with the "inward intensity of German emotional life" (34) and are typical of his nationalistic attempt to identify an "anti-

But if we wish to understand Pietism itself, as well as its substantial role in determining moral thought in eighteenth-century Germany, we will have to look at the writings of the Pietists anew. Although there were what one would call "mystical" elements in the thought of its earliest representatives, Pietism did not principally represent a passive retreat from social responsibility into a purely contemplative regard of the divine. Just the opposite was the case: all Pietists were deeply concerned about what they saw as the degeneration of morality and religious faith in their fellow human beings. Many viewed it as their holy obligation to remedy these and other perceived ills of modern society by performing direct and essential services for those who were less fortunate than themselves. Most significant, they felt that without reestablishing their own inner relationship to their God—without first, so to speak, "reforming" themselves—they would be unable, even unqualified, to aid those in greater need. But this latter imperative, actively fulfilling one's Christian duty toward the disadvantaged and weak, always remained their largest goal. The later Pietists in particular thus built—often at tremendous personal cost—housing, orphanages, and schools, as did August Hermann Francke in Halle, the city that soon became the center of the Pietist movement; they trained theologians and future pastors at the university they helped found there in 1694; and, as in the case of the tireless Count Nikolaus Ludwig von Zinzendorf and his Moravian settlement at Herrnhut, they established entire communities based on their conception of service and good works.[9] Seventeenth-century divines liked to insist that "theologia habitus practicus est" [theology is a practical discipline] and no one better embodied the truth of this motto than their Pietistic brethren.

Philipp Jakob Spener, who lived from 1635 to 1705, is generally considered to have been the founder—some have said the patriarch—of German Pietism.[10] Distrusting both the inner integrity and outward effectiveness of existing ecclesiastical institutions, Spener began to organize small groups of

---

Enlightenment" (which almost always meant anti-French) development in late-eighteenth-century German thought. For a negative assessment of the same development (but based, I believe, on a mistaken interpretation of Pietism in the first place), see the book by Koppel S. Pinson, *Pietism as a Factor in the Rise of German Nationalism* (New York: Columbia University Press, 1934). To my knowledge, the first study to confront these issues directly and refute the shallow assertions about the supposedly extreme "subjectivism," "asceticism," "mysticism," and so on, said to have characterized or have been promoted by Pietism, is the excellent book by F. Ernest Stoeffler, *The Rise of Evangelical Pietism*, Studies in the History of Religions, vol. 9 (Leiden: E. J. Brill, 1965), esp. 9–23.

9. See the richly detailed and evenhanded account by F. Ernest Stoeffler, *German Pietism during the Eighteenth Century*, Studies in the History of Religions, vol. 24 (Leiden: E. J. Brill, 1973). See also Carl Hinrichs, "Der Hallische Pietismus als politisch-soziale Reformbewegung des 18. Jahrhunderts," in *Zur neueren Pietismusforschung*, ed. Martin Greschat (Darmstadt: Wissenschaftliche Buchgesellschaft, 1977), 243–58.

10. On this epithet, see Martin Schmidt, "Speners 'Pia Desideria': Versuch einer theologischen Interpretation," in Greschat, *Zur neueren Pietismusforschung*, 113.

like-minded people in the 1670s to read and discuss the Bible as well as selected devotional texts. Out of this activity grew the so-called *collegia pietatis*, which eventually developed into more or less formal vehicles for the broader dissemination of Pietistic practices and attitudes.[11] Every movement has its manifesto, and it was Spener's rather brief but trenchantly written *Pia Desideria* (Pious desires) of 1675 that inaugurated what only later came to be known as Pietism.[12] And even though Spener was an extraordinarily prolific writer, it is for this single work that he is still remembered today. But Spener—as he modestly, though perhaps a little too frequently, admitted himself—was not so much an original thinker as he was an effective synthesizer and promulgator of opinions that his predecessors had voiced during the first part of the seventeenth century. First among these acknowledged forerunners was the Lutheran theologian Johann Arndt, who was born in 1555 and died in 1621. Spener could never find enough superlative terms of description for Arndt; at one point he even lauded him as "the precious, gifted, and sainted John Arndt."[13] Given the esteem in which he held Arndt, it is understandable that Spener originally wrote his *Pia Desideria* as the preface to a reissue of a collection of sermons that Arndt had first published in 1616, *Postilla; Oder, Auslegung der Sonntages und aller Festen Evangelien* (Postille, or exegesis of Sunday and all feast-day gospels).[14] But the work that secured Arndt's own fame and influence was his *Vier Bücher vom Wahren Christenthum* (Four books on true Christianity), which appeared between 1605 and 1610. Before we return to a consideration of Spener himself, we should therefore begin with an examination of this work, which Spener professed was his favorite book after the Bible, and which for a long time remained one of the most popular books of devotion in the history of the Protestant church.[15]

If Spener was the person who consolidated Pietism into an identifiable

11. On the history and function of the *collegia pietatis*, see Stoeffler, *Rise of Evangelical Pietism*, 237.

12. Originally (and for some still today) the word "Pietist" carried a pejorative connotation and was used disparagingly by the Pietists' opponents. The people to whom the label was applied sought to diffuse its power by using it themselves to refer to one another, whereupon the word entered into the general vocabulary and gradually became the accepted, and more or less neutral, name of the sect.

13. Cited from Philip Jacob Spener, *Pia Desideria*, trans. and ed. Theodore G. Tappert (Philadelphia: Fortress Press, 1964), 117.

14. Indicative of the uncertain state of some of the scholarship devoted to the subject, Gerhard Kaiser, *Pietismus und Patriotismus im literarischen Deutschland: Ein Beitrag zum Problem der Säkularisation* (Wiesbaden: Franz Steiner, 1961), 9, erroneously asserts that Spener intended his work to be a foreword to Arndt's more famous work, *Vom Wahren Christenthum*.

15. Johannes Wallmann, *Philipp Jakob Spener und die Anfänge des Pietismus*, Beiträge zur historischen Theologie 42 (Tübingen: J.C.B. Mohr, Paul Siebeck, 1970), 14, mentions that from the time of its first appearance, in 1610, to the publication of Spener's *Pia Desideria* sixty-five years later, there were no fewer than forty-nine editions or reprints of Arndt's *Vom Wahren Christenthum*.

and viable program, then it was Arndt who delivered many of the theological means for him to do so.[16] Inside the parish church in the North German town of Celle where Arndt is buried, there is an inscription on his tombstone that describes him as "a true lover of Jesus" and as "a lover of inner Christianity."[17] This epitaph could serve as a leitmotif to his treatise *Vom Wahren Christenthum*, in which he first expressed what would later become the familiar articles of the Pietistic credo. Here, as in all of his teachings, Arndt sought above all to regain the lost momentum of the Protestant revival by stripping away the encumbrances of ritual and dogma that he thought threatened to obscure one's individual, and inwardly experienced, relationship to God. But beyond simply reestablishing this deeply personal communion, Arndt wished to refocus the energies of religious observance into an instrument not just of private devotion but, moreover, of radical personal transformation. If the essential relationship was that between the individual soul and God, then it followed that the true meaning of any "reformation" would consist in its ability to reshape or refashion a soul into a new form that best served this end. In the first book in *Vom Wahren Christenthum*, Arndt therefore categorically called for "an entirely inward, new human being" to replace the fallen, old, and worldly one.[18] According to Arndt, we should strive not just to make ourselves *better* but, moreover, to create in ourselves a completely *different* inner organization. It was here, in the introspective, almost obsessive care given to the continued effort to improve and cultivate one's inner being (but always for external—and, it should go without saying, eternal—purposes), that Arndt's theology, and that of Pietism as a whole, acquired its greatest importance for contemporary religious and ethical life. And it was also this inward focus that eventually allowed its characteristic habit of mind to be carried over to other, less sectarian, realms.

The initial stage in the all-important process of conversion thus amounted to a kind of existential crisis, an absolute abandonment of one's familiar, and by definition debased, state of being. Arndt stipulated that such a complete conversion is not possible until one has undergone genuine repentance and felt true—that is to say, truly painful—remorse for past sins, transgressions, and unholy desires. "Repentance occurs," he thus wrote, "not only when one takes leave of coarse external sins and refrains from them; but when one goes into oneself and changes and betters the innermost bottom of one's heart" (*Vom Wahren Christenthum*, 16). This aim was to

16. Stoeffler, *Rise of Evangelical Pietism*, 202, actually asserts that the "father of Lutheran Pietism is not Spener but John Arndt."
17. Cited from the *Allgemeine Deutsche Biographie* (Leipzig: Duncker & Humblot, 1875–1912), 1:549.
18. Johann Arndt, *Vier Bücher vom Wahren Christenthum* (Magdeburg: C. L. Faber, 1727), 23. Henceforth cited parenthetically in the text as "*Vom Wahren Christenthum*" by page number.

remain at the center of the Pietist doctrine. Almost two centuries later, in one of the last works published before he died, Immanuel Kant (who like so many of his German-speaking contemporaries had also grown up in a devoutly Pietistic household) offered the following vivid description of this struggle for repentance, or *Bußkampf*, that was supposed to initiate conversion:

> According to the Pietist hypothesis, the operation that separates good from evil (of which human nature is compounded) is a supernatural one—a rending and contrition of the heart in *repentance*, a grief (*maeror animi*) bordering on despair that can, however, reach the necessary intensity only by the influence of a heavenly spirit. Man must himself beg for this grief, while grieving over the fact that his grief is not great enough (to drive the pain completely from his heart). Now, as the late Hamann says: "This descent into the hell of self-knowledge paves the way to deification." In other words, when the fire of repentance has reached its height, the amalgam of good and evil *breaks up* and the purer metal of the *reborn* [*Wiedergebornen*] gleams through the dross, which surrounds but does not contaminate it, ready for service pleasing to God in good conduct. This radical change, therefore, begins with a *miracle* and ends with what we would ordinarily consider natural, since *reason* prescribes it: namely, morally good conduct.[19]

Although Kant himself—or at least the Kant of the second critique—was unwilling to place the "morally good conduct" that should result from this conversion on any other ground except that of reason, he gladly accepted that the final goal, and presumably the content as well, of virtue was the same. In any case, Kant made explicit here that in practical terms the Pietistic conversion possessed an inherently ethical meaning, apart from any other personal rewards there might have been.

Naturally, for Arndt himself the desirability of the end of conversion was never in doubt; reaching it was the problem. The transformation, or what Kant called the "radical change," that had to take place in the breast of the true believer was, according to Arndt, literally (or as literally as such things can ever be seen) a "rebirth" (*Wiedergeburt*) of our inner person.[20] In the concrete and colorful language that he had inherited from Luther, Arndt explained that

> there are two births experienced by a Christian, the old fleshly, sinful, damned, and accursed birth that descends from Adam and by which the seed

19. Immanuel Kant, *The Conflict of the Faculties. Der Streit der Fakultäten*, trans. Mary J. Gregor (New York: Abaris Books, 1979), 99–101; translation slightly modified.
20. On the meaning of the *Wiedergeburt*, and on the centrality of this concept for Pietism generally, see Martin Schmidt, *Pietismus*, 3d ed. (Stuttgart: W. Kohlhammer, 1983), esp. 14–22.

of the serpent, the image of Satan, and the earthly, bestial human race propagates itself: And the spiritual, holy, blessed, consecrated New Birth that comes from Christ and by which the seed of God, the image of God, and the heavenly human being, formed in the image of God, is spiritually propagated. (*Vom Wahren Christenthum*, 10)

The associations that Arndt exploited here are more pronounced in the original: God provided the "image" (*Bild*) and thus literally the goal and the content of our spiritual formation (*Bildung*).[21] This connection between *Bildung* and religious transformation will become more important as we continue; for the moment it is enough to note the literary source of these images or *Bilder*. For again like Luther, Arndt placed constant emphasis on a return to the Bible—God's testament to humanity—as the most direct and assured way of advancing toward the eventual regeneration he described. Maintaining the metaphorical equation of physical procreation and spiritual genesis, Arndt thus proclaimed that "the word of God is the seed of the new birth" (*Vom Wahren Christenthum*, 11).[22] For Arndt and his many followers, reading the Bible, both alone and in the presence of others, thus did not mean receiving instruction from a distant and disengaged preceptor; it represented the act of communing directly with the divine, living presence himself through his Scripture. Not incidentally, attending immediately to the word of God conveniently dispensed with the need for the intercession of priests and of other official clergy. But by receiving the divine linguistic "seed," the Scripture also, and more important, immediately engendered the "new inner being," it set into motion the spiritual *Bildung* that was the ultimate aim of Arndt's theology.

In seeking to modify the received perception of Spener as a wholly innovative thinker, one should also avoid the opposite extreme of exaggerating Arndt's own originality. Despite, or perhaps because of, his desire to rekindle the torch that Luther held aloft for his followers, Arndt had no desire to remove himself from a lineage he regarded as constituting the only "pure" or "true" Christianity. Thus in addition to the works of Luther, those of other well-known German Protestant writers such as Valentin Weigel, Philipp Nicolai, and Johann Tauler, all of whom had also written extensively about the necessity of spiritual "rebirth," are given a prominent place and copiously cited throughout *Vom wahren Christenthum*.[23] Arndt also adopted and modified the notion of an "imitatio Christi" in the conduct of one's life

21. On this etymological link in the history of the word, see Rudolf Vierhaus's "Bildung," in *Geschichtliche Grundbegriffe: Historisches Lexikon zur politisch-sozialen Sprache in Deutschland*, ed. Otto Brunner, Werner Conze, and Reinhart Koselleck (Stuttgart: Ernst Klett, 1972), 1:509.
22. In creating this analogy, Arndt referred to 1 Peter 1:23, which reads: "You have been born anew, not of perishable seed but of imperishable, through the living and abiding word of God."
23. See also Stoeffler, *Rise of Evangelical Pietism*, 204.

made famous by the work of that name by Thomas à Kempis. But in conformity with the ubiquitous analogy between physical and spiritual genesis, Arndt understood this internalization of the model of Christ very much in the sense of achieving the *unio mystica* described by other medieval theologians. Arndt wrote that the new inner being was, as it were, conceived through the union of Christ with our soul, and from this spiritual embrace resulted the embryo of our new, reformed constitution. It was in passages like these that Arndt's rhetoric conspicuously drew on the kind of highly charged erotic vocabulary that tends to elicit knowing smiles from twentieth-century readers, who no doubt too quickly detect in it a naive transference of poorly sublimated desires. Arndt exclaimed:

> The soul is a pure bride of Christ, which loves nothing else in the world other than Christ: For His sake you must despise and forsake in your heart everything that is in the world so that you will become worthy of being loved by Christ, your bridegroom. The love that does not love Christ alone and is not fond of Him in all things is an adulteress and not a pure virgin: The love of Christians shall be a virgin. (*Vom Wahren Christenthum*, 59)

The imagery Arndt employed here and throughout *Vom Wahren Christenthum* to illustrate the stages required for spiritual rebirth took its primary inspiration from the Song of Songs and the tradition of its exegesis.[24] From the beginning of its existence, the Song of Songs had exerted a profound effect on European conceptions of conjugal love, and had awakened so much interest, or caused so much uneasiness, that virtually an entire genre of interpretative literature had grown up around it by the time Arndt formulated his own version of "true Christianity." The Song of Songs was, for example, the focus of a ten-volume commentary written by Origen between 240 and 245 (of which only a part has survived); it inspired a series of famous sermons by St. Bernard, the twelfth-century French abbot of the Cistercian monastery of Clairvaux; and, most recently for Arndt, it preoccupied the sixteenth-century Spanish Saints Teresa of Avila and John of the Cross.[25] One of very few places in the Bible that frankly addresses the subject of sexuality, the Song of Songs represents a curious and plainly unnerving anomaly in the canon, a strangely foreign presence that interpreters of the Bible have tried, almost from the beginning, to explain in terms that either avoided or minimized its obvious liter-

24. Still the most comprehensive book on the subject and its history is Marvin H. Pope's, *Song of Songs: A New Translation with Introduction and Commentary* (Garden City, N.Y.: Doubleday, 1977).
25. See Ann W. Astell, *The Song of Songs in the Middle Ages* (Ithaca: Cornell University Press, 1990), 8–10.

al meaning.[26] The preferred method of reading this book was simply to invert the poles of signification: whatever seemed to speak of physical matters was represented in an allegorical light as pointing to the spiritual sphere. But the question of the bride's beauty in particular, which plays such a prominent role in the poem, received some of the most imaginative exegetical attention to be found within the whole of biblical commentary.

Early Christianity had, to say the least, a somewhat strained relation to the concept, and even more so to the actual phenomenon, of beauty. Most of the Church Fathers harbored deep suspicions about its all too apparent connection with the vain and transient pleasures of the world. They thus regularly associated beauty—the "shining gloss that fadeth suddenly"—with the decay and death that unavoidably attended all things of this earth. But in the wake of St. Augustine's Platonic theology, they also distinguished between different orders of beauty, asserting on the one hand that there was a merely physical beauty that inevitably withered and perished. Yet on the other hand, they thought that there also existed a certain spiritual beauty based on the goodness and the love of God, which, like the soul saved by divine grace, enjoyed the permanence of eternal life. St. Bernard of Clairvaux, for instance, adopted this view in his sermons on the Song of Songs, and wrote at length about the necessity of making one's soul "beautiful" to resemble the example of God so that he would willingly receive his spiritual bride. "The prophet says, 'The Lord is king, he is clothed in beauty.' How can he but desire a like garment for his Bride, who is also his likeness? And the closer the likeness, the dearer she will be to him." Somewhat disappointingly, when St. Bernard considered what the qualities might be that produced such inner beauty, he proposed, not very helpfully, that one might think of it in terms of "honor":

> Let us elucidate what we mean by honor, and wherein it may be found; so
> that the soul's beauty may shine forth even more. It is integrity of mind,
> which is concerned to keep the innocent reputation with a good conscience,
> and not only, as the Apostle says, to provide things good in the sight of God,
> but in the sight of men also. Happy the mind which has clothed itself in the
> beauty of holiness and the brightness of innocence, by which it manifests its
> glorious likeness, not to the world but to the Word, of whom we read that he

26. Johann Gottfried Herder, for example, who was also one of the most prominent German theologians of the eighteenth century, explained that it was merely due to cultural differences that we read the book as having any sexual significance at all: "And, behold, people have wanted to drive away precisely that passage in the Song of Songs which so delicately celebrates it [i.e., modesty] and to turn words of innocence into despicable double entendres, which according to all sources, both old and new, the Orient did not know or endure; rather, the Orient spit them back as filth and shame into the faces of us civilized, double-entendre-loving Europeans." See Johann Gottfried Herder, *Lieder der Liebe*, in *Sämmtliche Werke*, ed. Bernhard Suphan (Berlin: Weidmann, 1877–1913), 8:509–10.

is the brightness of eternal life, the splendor and image of the being of God.[27]

This manner of interpreting—one is tempted to say "explaining away"—the Song of Songs subsequently became common practice, especially among the members of the Cistercian order, and its influence on Arndt's theology, even in the slighter details of linguistic usage, is obvious. Thus there arose during the Middle Ages a substantial body of literature nominally devoted to unraveling the meaning in the Song of Songs in which the beauty of the soul that was united with Christ was expounded on, which in turn had a profound effect more broadly on how individual spiritual life in general was envisaged.[28] The most important writer to continue this tradition in Germany was an early Pietist and follower of Arndt by the name of Joachim Lütkemann.

Although now almost completely forgotten, Lütkemann, who lived from 1608 to 1655, was one of the most influential Lutheran theologians of his day, and during his lifetime his influence rivaled, indeed even briefly surpassed, that of Arndt himself.[29] So great in fact was Lütkemann's prestige and popularity that it was his main work of 1643, the *Vorschmack Göttlicher Güte* (Foretaste of divine goodness), rather than one of Arndt's, that was intensively read and discussed in the first Pietist conventicles—the *collegia pietatis*—that Spener founded in Frankfurt some thirty years after Lütkemann's book appeared.[30] It is thus all the more significant that the sixteenth chapter of Lütkemann's book, its conceptual culmination, deals explicitly with what he called the beauty of believing souls.[31]

27. Bernard of Clairvaux, *On the Song of Songs*, vol. 4, trans. Irene Edmonds, intro. Jean Leclerq (Kalamazoo, Mich.: Cistercian Publications, 1980), 206–8.
28. Roland E. Murphy, *The Song of Songs: A Commentary on the Book of Canticles or The Song of Songs*, ed. S. Dean McBride Jr. (Minneapolis: Augsburg Fortress Press, 1990), 25, writes: "Bernard's *Sermones in Canticum* are . . . at once the crowning achievement of the approach to the Song initiated by Origen and the superlative contribution of monastic theology to Christian spirituality." See, however, the fastidiously disdainful comments on Bernard and on his relationship to Pietism in Ritschl, *Geschichte des Pietismus*, 1:46–61. See also Walter Müller, *Das Problem der Seelenschönheit im Mittelalter: Eine Begriffsgeschichtliche Untersuchung* (Bern: Paul Haupt, 1923), and Max Freiherr von Waldberg, *Studien und Quellen zur Geschichte des Romans, vol. 1, Zur Entwicklungsgeschichte der "schönen Seele" bei den spanischen Mystikern* (Berlin: Emil Felber, 1910).
29. See Stoeffler, *Rise of Evangelical Pietism*, 219. One probable reason that Lütkemann has been ignored by literary historians is that he is not mentioned in the list of sources in the influential book by August Langen, *Der Wortschatz des deutschen Pietismus*, 2d ed. (Tübingen: Niemeyer, 1968), 477–80.
30. See Wallmann, *Philipp Jakob Spener*, 278–79.
31. Even Ritschl, *Geschichte des Pietismus*, 2:86–87, although generally critical of Lütkemann, grants that the book reaches a rhetorical and conceptual high point in this chapter. It is also worth noting that in the only other monograph on the beautiful soul, the book by Schmeer, *Der Begriff der "schönen Seele,"* 63, we read that "evidence for the frequent use of the expression 'beautiful soul' in Pietism has never yet been provided. It is only a vague assumption

The influence of Arndt's views and of the common tradition on which they both drew is plainly visible throughout Lütkemann's work. Like Arndt, he saw the *Wiedergeburt* as the essential moment in a person's spiritual life, and he argued that everything in a pious soul should be directed toward achieving this central experience. But Lütkemann seemed to be much more interested than Arndt in the actual means by which the soul experiences its union with Christ and in the inner manifestation of its successful completion. Of one thing, in any event, Lütkemann was utterly certain: if the "conversion" did not occur, the disfiguring mark of original sin exhibited an aspect that was precisely the opposite of beauty. Following the tradition of exegesis St. Augustine had begun, Lütkemann thought that, although God had originally created us in his own image and hence given us a "beautiful soul" in his likeness, we no longer possessed that first form. As Lütkemann explained it, "Although one cannot deny the human soul to have been created in exceedingly great beauty, one must also confess, that—alas!—a great change has occurred, and that the soul has become exceedingly ugly. For since it has turned from God to the devil, the image of God has ceased to shine in it, and it is filled with the image of the loathsome devil."[32] The only way to regain this lost beauty is to submit to that elemental experience leading to inner edification: "The soul is brought to such beauty not only through cleansing and clothing it, but also through a new birth" (*Göttliche Güte*, 1:547). Thus the rebirth that had played such a major role in Arndt's theology became in Lütkemann's hands the means toward achieving the specific result of beauty of soul.

So far, however, Lütkemann had not written anything that was not already contained, either directly stated or in implicit terms, in Arndt's earlier work. Where Lütkemann made his own contribution was in his efforts to respond to the obvious, but previously avoided question: "In what does this beauty of soul consist?" (1:545). Lütkemann offered a five-part answer; the first and most important of the attributes Lütkemann assigned to the beauty of soul was justice. Here, then, and for the first time in the Pietist literature, Lütkemann explicitly thematized the connection between internal moral beauty and external moral duty:

> When we have seized Christ with his justice, then we also receive at the same
> time the disposition of Christ, who gives us a new heart and mind, and makes
> our soul fertile for all that is good, so that the soul is not only just in Christ,
> but that it begins to become sanctified in and of itself. The justice of Christ is

made on the basis of the general emotional temper of Pietistic views and in particular of Zinzendorf." The following discussion provides that evidence and supports that assumption.
32. Joachim Lütkemann, *Der Vorschmack Göttlicher Güte Durch Gottes Gnade*, ed. Philipp Julius Rehtmeyer (Braunschweig: Rudolph Schröder, 1720–25), 1:543. Henceforth cited parenthetically in the text as "*Göttliche Güte*" by volume and page number.

the sole natural beauty of the new inner person: the gifts of the Holy Spirit, sanctified desire, patience, and humility are the ornament of the new person. Thus does the new inner person stand before God, like a beautiful virgin in exquisite attire. (1:546)

This emphasis on the virtues that accompany, or are presumably identical with, the assumption of inner beauty had been almost completely missing in Arndt's account and was destined to become one of the elements that survived his baroque emphasis on self-annihilation in the name of spiritual renewal. The Pietists of the eighteenth century, who could afford to be less apocalyptic than their seventeenth-century predecessors (Arndt, Lütkemann, and Spener, it should be remembered, had all lived through at least part of the ruinous Thirty Years' War), found the idea of enhancing or enriching their beauty of soul a more congenial means of self-definition than utter inner devastation and gradual regrowth.

Because the founding fathers of Pietism also saw themselves as combating a Protestant orthodoxy that had, in time, become comfortable with the corrupting apparatuses of position and power, the early voices of Pietism demanded a highly rigorous ethical standard, and they remained highly sensitive to all forms of pretense and insincerity. Lütkemann thus made the further point that although a person may seem to be virtuous to others, what truly matters will be invisible to all but God: "Beauty of the soul is an internal beauty . . . one should not think, therefore, that the holiness [*Heiligkeit*] of the soul consists in external pomp and ceremony. External holiness without inner purity of the heart is nothing but hypocrisy [*Scheinheiligkeit*]" (1:551). But Lütkemann thought that true beauty of soul, which only the grace of Jesus Christ can bestow, overshadows not only the original innocence of Adam, but also exceeds that of the angels. Beauty of soul, that is, is nothing less than the last step toward personal divinity.

The actual content informing Lütkemann's notion of virtue, and that of most later Pietist writers as well, rested firmly on New Testament, and specifically on Pauline, ethical principles.[33] Central, therefore, to their thinking was a belief in the perfectibility of human virtue, which Lütkemann again described in reference to our ability to model ourselves after the example of Christ. Citing 2 Corinthians I 3:18, he wrote that "we recognize that the beauty of soul may, so to speak, grow and increase" (*Göttliche Güte*, 1:555).[34] By trying to internalize the qualities of Christ, by clothing our soul with his garments, we gradually become ever more appropriately adorned for the sight of God. Nor is this virtue simply a matter of private ethics; it also

33. See Stoeffler, *Rise of Evangelical Pietism*, 20–21.
34. On this aspect of Pietist thought, see ibid., 18.

provides the basis for a larger civic moral code. As this transformation takes place, the beauty of soul begins to shine forth for others to see as well. At the close of the chapter on the beauty of believing souls, Lütkemann enumerated all of the moral qualities that such a "reborn" soul would possess, and he used the image of a "golden chain" to demonstrate how these virtues are linked together in a continuous, and necessary, whole:

> As soon as one's soul is purified by the blood of Christ, then it is crowned with a diadem, and the diadem is the victory over the devil and over the world. The soul is ornamented with hope toward God, with peace and joy in the Holy Spirit—these can be the jewels and the armbands. It carries a golden chain of various virtues, all connected as links, and one link is joined to the other: to chastity, moderation; to moderation, truth; to truth, honesty; to honesty, justice; to justice, love; to love, kindness; to kindness, charity; to charity, meekness; to meekness, patience; to patience, humility. That is a chain for the new inner person, and its brilliance can also be seen externally. (*Göttliche Güte*, 1:561–62)

Although this beautiful brilliance was based quite specifically on moral qualities, Lütkemann and the later Pietists did not speak, as the British philosophers would, of a specifically "moral beauty," but rather always of a "beauty of soul." The main reason seems obvious: the Christian focus in general on the soul almost predetermined this way of formulating the issue. Yet as we will see, the consequences of this difference in phraseology, at first seemingly negligible, proved to be an important stage in the subsequent development in the eighteenth century of the figure of the "beautiful soul."

If we now turn to Spener himself, it is possible to see the *Pia Desideria*—the charter text of Pietism—not so much as an absolute beginning, but as a consolidation and refinement of the ideas set forth by Arndt, Lütkemann, and many others. The power and influence of Spener's own work therefore owed less to any new insights it might contain than to its generally superior organization, to its avoidance of the monotonous repetition that was painfully typical of comparable works that preceded it, and to a smooth rhetorical polish that emanated the calm self-assurance of truth. If, besides this stylistic superiority, Spener's book represented any appreciable advance over the ideas of his predecessors, then it would have to be in the more moderate and sober tone he struck with respect to the nature of the inner life. Broadly speaking, Spener seems to have directed his pastoral energies more toward the solution of particular societal, and not simply theological, problems than toward the composition of tracts for purely personal devotion. In this, he exemplified that commitment to practical affairs and social reform which would especially characterize the later adherents of Pietism. Far from enclosing himself in mystical reveries enshrouded in blissful ignorance of worldly concerns, Spener was very much aware of contemporary intellectual and philosophical developments. Not only was he fully conscious of them, he took active part in them as well: in 1653, at the University of Strasbourg, Spener defended his master's thesis, in which he critically examined the thought of none other than the seventeenth-century bête noire of ethical philosophy, Thomas Hobbes.[35]

Although Spener endorsed the general notion of conversion, or inner "rebirth," and its numerous attendant implications, he did not dwell on the luxuriant furnishings of the "interior castle," as St. Teresa had memorably termed it. Most noticeably, Spener relegated the doctrine of the spiritual union with Christ, the *unio mystica* that had enthralled the imaginations of his predecessors, to the margins of his work. Consequently, he does not mention beauty of the soul anywhere in the *Pia Desideria*. Although he wrote, following Arndt and his school, that the "whole Christian religion consists of the inner man or the new man," he was much more vitally interested in the effect that this "new" constitution would have on the practice of real virtue. To ensure that this end was actually achieved, Spener went on in the same passage to propose that

> works be so set in motion that we may by no means be content merely to have the people refrain from outward vices and practice outward virtues and thus be concerned only with the outward man, which the ethics of the heathen can also accomplish, but that we lay the right foundation in the heart, show that what does not proceed from this foundation is mere hypocrisy, and hence accustom the people first to work on what is inward (awaken love of God and neighbor through suitable means) and only then to act accordingly.[36]

Like Lütkemann, Spener thus certainly wanted the reforms, which he piously desired, to take place first of all in the hearts of his followers. But Spener seems to have thought that the idea of beauty, which Lütkemann himself was never able to describe except by making analogies to the realm of physical appearance, would detract from the serious business of contrition and real moral change. Virtually every page of the *Pia Desideria* demonstrates Spener's concern for the pragmatic application of the principles he

35. Spener's thesis was titled *Dissertatio de Conformatione creaturae rationalis ad creatorem*; he wrote it, however, not in response to Hobbes's *Leviathan*, but in response to the *Elementa philosophica de Cive*, which had appeared four years earlier, in 1647. On Spener's thesis, see Wallmann, *Philipp Jakob Spener*, 71–77.
36. Spener, *Pia Desideria*, 116–17.

had abstractly delineated. He never tired of repeating that "because theology is a practical discipline and does not consist only of knowledge, study alone is not enough, nor is the mere accumulation and imparting of information" (112). Although such statements are often taken to indicate Spener's—and hence Pietism's—anti-intellectualism, they were meant in the positive sense of advocating real action in the place of indulgence in ineffectual contemplation. And in no other sphere was action more necessary, Spener and his adherents believed, than in securing public and private morals—which philosophers and theologians alike had long called the only "practical philosophy."

Spener's pragmatism is expressed in other, perhaps more important ways, too—ways that underscore the probable causes not just for the success of his book alone, but also for the Pietist movement itself. Ultimately this popularity allowed his ideas to enter the more secular mainstream of eighteenth-century German society at large. "We are not living in a Platonic state," Spener at one juncture rather unnecessarily pointed out, "and so it is not possible to have everything perfect and according to rule." Despite this, our congenital fallibility, he went on to write that although "we shall never in this life achieve such a degree of perfection that nothing could or should be added, we are nevertheless under obligation to achieve some degree of perfection" (80). The act of spiritual reformation, shorn of the perhaps compromising, or at least somewhat delimiting, erotic vocabulary, thus became abstracted and instrumentalized in Spener's account into an easily assimilable mechanism by which the soul could be tailored, as had he put it, "according to rule."

The idea of perfection, modified though it was in Spener's advocacy of a merely relative improvement, resides at the center of Pietist, indeed of Christian, ethics.[37] From its very beginnings—as in the Sermon on the Mount, in which Jesus exhorted his listeners that they must be perfect, "as your heavenly Father is perfect" (Matthew 5:48)—striving to attain perfection had been a defining moment of Christian morality. This imperative appears repeatedly in Pietist moral and paedogogical works. The person who succeeded Spener as the most important representative of the Pietist faith, August Hermann Francke, wrote in fact an entire treatise titled *Von der Christen Vollkommenheit* (On the perfection of Christians). And it was this ideal of moral perfection that provided the most important bridge spanning contemporary religious and philosophical conceptions of our duty as ethical beings.

37. Cf. John Passmore, *The Perfectibility of Man* (New York: Charles Scribner's Sons, 1970), and the somewhat less useful book by R. Newton Flew, *The Idea of Perfection in Christian Theology: An Historical Study of the Christian Ideal for the Present Life* (Oxford: Oxford University Press, 1934).

THE BIRTH OF PHILOSOPHICAL AESTHETICS

As great as its influence was on the minds and actions of countless eighteenth-century Germans, it need hardly be said that Pietism was not the only, or even the most important, thread in the dense fabric of social and intellectual life. During the first half of the century, the rationalistic school of thought that came to be known as the "Leibniz-Wolffian philosophy" formed the common framework within which the educated members of German society addressed philosophical concerns.[38] Although Wolff later became a favorite target of ridicule as a model of prolix and sterile pedantry, his effect on the disciplines of logic, metaphysics, and ethics during his own generation was nothing short of astonishing. It would be no exaggeration to say that until well after the 1760s, anyone who engaged in abstract reasoning in Germany did so by and large according to the rules prescribed by Wolff. But whereas Wolff's own religious beliefs basically conformed to the tenets of Christianity, he did not enjoy the same authority when it came to questions of faith as he did in matters of metaphysics. Even though the leading advocates of Pietism and Wolffian thought at the turn of the century, namely, Francke and Wolff himself, both claimed Halle as their base of operations, the two camps coexisted in an often uneasy and fractious relationship. When, on 8 November 1723, following what initially seemed a relatively minor misunderstanding, Friedrich Wilhelm I of Prussia ordered Wolff to leave Halle within forty-eight hours or face hanging, the Pietists were not only quite happy to witness his fall and subsequent flight, they had even played an active role in bringing both about.[39] But the union of philosophical sophistication with soundness of theological doctrine seemed to have achieved a state of perfectly balanced accord in the figure of Wolff's great mentor, Gottfried Wilhelm Leibniz, who once programmatically wrote of himself: "I begin as a philosopher, but I end as a theologian."[40]

Although God and religious issues more generally command a greater

38. Max Wundt, *Die deutsche Schulphilosophie im Zeitalter der Aufklärung* (Tübingen: J.C.B. Mohr, Paul Siebeck, 1945), 150, explains that the phrase "Leibniz-Wolffian philosophy" had a negative connotation in Wolff's mind, and that he sought—to no avail, as it turned out—to prevent its use.

39. See the account in Lewis White Beck, *Early German Philosophy: Kant and his Predecessors* (Cambridge: Harvard University Press, 1969), 259. The main instigator of Wolff's banishment was a theologian at the university by the name of Joachim Lange; see Bruno Bianco, "Freiheit gegen Fatalismus: Zu Joachim Langes Kritik an Wolff," in *Zentren der Aufklärung, vol. 1, Halle: Aufklärung und Pietismus*, ed. Norbert Hinske (Heidelberg: Lambert Schneider, 1989), 111–55. On Wolff's relationship more generally to Pietism, see Carl Hinrichs, *Preußentum und Pietismus: Der Pietismus in Brandenburg-Preußen als religiös-soziale Reformbewegung* (Göttingen: Vandenhoeck & Ruprecht, 1971), 388–441.

40. Gottfried Wilhelm Leibniz, "Trois dialogues mystiques inédits de Leibniz," ed. Jean Baruzi, *Revue de Métaphysique et de Morale* 13 (1905): 13.

degree of interest in Leibniz's thought than in that of most other modern philosophers, it is difficult, if not impossible, to determine the precise nature of his religious beliefs. Some have actually claimed that Leibniz, accomplished courtier that he was, considered his creed to be nothing more than a professional accoutrement and that he wore his religion like a wig, changing it as the circumstances and his own convenience demanded. There may be some justice to this assessment, but in this extreme form it requires considerable qualification. The idea of God as such is an integral, though admittedly highly abstract, part of all of Leibniz's writings; indeed, his entire intellectual edifice would collapse if that central support were somehow removed. And given his repeatedly proven political dexterity, one can readily imagine that, had he really wanted to do so, Leibniz could have found some suitable way of downplaying or sidestepping the issue altogether. It is certainly true that Leibniz moved with apparent ease among representatives of both the Catholic and Protestant orthodoxy, and he even exchanged a series of letters with several Pietist leaders, most notably with Spener himself.[41] In religion, as in the many other realms of thought and experience that occupied his interest, Leibniz entertained a generous and diverse set of beliefs that, when individually examined, may indeed appear to conflict with one another. But to assume the essential sincerity, if not the depth, of his faith in the Christian God, however eclectic his conception might have been, is nonetheless a prerequisite for a full appreciation of his thought as a whole.

The uncertainty obscuring Leibniz's position on the basis of both religion and morality has at least one very simple source, and it plagues our understanding of all other aspects of his thinking as well: the unusually private and fragmented nature of his philosophy. The long and somewhat tedious *Théodicée* (Theodicy) of 1709 was the only book Leibniz published during his lifetime, and with the further exception of a handful of essays, he set forth the entirety of his thought in personal letters and in short, frequently occasional pieces he never published but intended for the equally private edification of particular patrons or scholarly acquaintances. As a result, he never set down a detailed presentation of his thinking, even though isolated comments about individual issues are scattered throughout all of his works, commingled with his reflections on a thousand and one other subjects. Leibniz, in theoretical terms one of the most systematic of philosophers, neglected to leave the world with a full exposition of his system. One is therefore forced to resort to the otherwise unsatisfactory practice of culling quotations from a variety of sources, some of them written at large intervals

41. The relation between Leibniz and Pietism was first explored in an article by Ernst Troeltsch, "Leibniz und die Anfänge des Pietismus," in *Aufsätze zur Geistesgeschichte und Religionssoziologie* (Tübingen: J.C.B. Mohr, Paul Siebeck, 1925), 488–531.

from one another, in order to piece together a reasonably coherent account of any one element of his philosophy.[42]

Perhaps partly because of these considerable obstacles to grasping the real scope of his oeuvre, but also because of the pervasive indifference to eighteenth-century moral philosophy in studies of the period, Leibniz's theory of ethics in particular has received very little critical attention.[43] Yet the evidence of Leibniz's preoccupation with questions of moral philosophy is everywhere: his most famous works, the *Discourse on Metaphysics*, which he wrote (but did not publish) in 1686, as well as the *Principles of Nature and Grace, Based on Reason* and the *Principles of Philosophy, or, the Monadology*, both of which he wrote (yet also never published) in 1714, two years before his death—all conclude with a précis of his ethical theory.[44] As one would expect, the idea of God, forever at, or in any case near, the heart of Leibniz's writings, formed a focal point of his ethical thought as well. But Leibniz's God—unlike, for instance, Locke's—is no stern judge, who enforces morality by parceling out salvation and eternal damnation. Nor is Leibniz's God a surrogate lover, who seduces us into virtue with the attractions of bliss. Leibniz's God is a civilized, rational deity who exerts indirect control through the positive example of his own benevolent perfection, representing the ideal to which everyone ought to aspire. As he once wrote in a letter to Duke Rudolf August of Brunswick, Leibniz's ethical theory was "grounded, not on hope or fear, but solely and alone on the beauty and perfection of God."[45]

The idea of perfection constituted one of the most important principles upholding the whole of Leibniz's thinking, and it assumed an equally central status in his ethical philosophy as well. The functional significance he accorded to the notion of perfection becomes immediately apparent in all of his major works, especially in the *Principles of Nature and Grace* and the *Monadology*, which commentators have understood as the most succinct summaries of his entire philosophical system. As Leibniz never tired of writing in these and other works, an omnipotent and omniscient God is at once the

42. The situation is further complicated by the lack of a modern edition of Leibniz's complete works. The *Akademie* edition, although begun in 1923, shows no sign of nearing completion.

43. This is also the complaint voiced by the author of one of the very few works on the subject; see John Hostler, *Leibniz's Moral Philosophy* (London: Duckworth, 1975), 9. In his edition of Leibniz's works in translation, Loemker also alludes to the lack of studies devoted to Leibniz's ethical thought; see Gottfried Wilhelm Leibniz, *Philosophical Papers and Letters*, trans. and ed., Leroy E. Loemker, 2d ed. (Dordrecht, Holland: D. Reidel, 1969), 68.

44. See Hostler, *Leibniz's Moral Philosophy*, 9.

45. Onno Klopp, *Correspondance de Leibniz avec l'électrice Sophie de Brunswick-Lunebourg* (Hanover: Klindworth, 1874), 2:65; cited in Leroy E. Loemker, "The Ethical Import of the Leibnizian System," in *The Philosophy of Leibniz and the Modern World*, ed. Ivor Leclerc (Nashville: Vanderbilt University Press, 1973), 209.

ground and goal of all existence, and whatever degree of perfection we find in this world receives that quality by being derived from its divine Author. But it was in a short sketch, which Leibniz wrote sometime between 1694 and 1698 and is alternately titled "On Wisdom" or "On Happiness," that we find his most concise discussion of how these issues relate to the problem of how we should and can conduct our lives.

This typically condensed and suggestive essay betrays Leibniz's weakness for moving with perfunctory speed to the matters that interested him most at the expense of systematic thoroughness (a fault, incidentally, for which Wolff would more than compensate). Leibniz began by defining wisdom as the science of happiness—hence the confusion about the title of the work—and asserting that the attainment and preservation of happiness was the end of all human existence. In the deductive, syllogistic method he preferred, Leibniz went on to stipulate that a soul's happiness consists in being in a state of permanent joy, which in turn is caused by pleasant thoughts. Pleasure, finally, has its basis in any perceived excellence or perfection (which Leibniz had enigmatically defined as any "heightening" of being), whether we experience this perfection through sensation or apprehend it by the mind alone. In a passage that uncannily prefigures much of the debate that would begin about a decade later in England, Leibniz grants that we seem to respond to these phenomena in an immediate or intuitive fashion, but adds that further investigation would show that our reaction has a rationally identifiable source. "We do not always observe wherein the perfection of pleasing things consists," he admitted, "or what kind of perfection within ourselves they serve, yet our feelings [Gemüt] perceive it, even though our understanding does not. . . . But those who seek the causes of things will usually find a ground for this and understand that there is something at the bottom of the matter which, though unnoticed, really appeals to us."[46] Like other late admirers of Plato, Leibniz carefully distinguishes between the fleeting pleasures of the senses—which if not enjoyed in moderation, soon lead to satiety and in the end to revulsion—and the permanent pleasures we derive from intellectual and spiritual pursuits. In accord with this rigorously rational conception of the most lasting, and thus preferable, sort of pleasure and happiness available to us, Leibniz was convinced that "nothing serves our happiness better than the illumination of our understanding" and that "there springs from such knowledge an enduring progress in wisdom and virtue, and therefore also in perfection and joy, the advantage of which remains with the soul even after this life" (426). A committed rationalist even here, in the consideration of the greatest bliss known to humanity,

46. Gottfried Wilhelm Leibniz, "On Happiness," in Loemker, *Philosophical Papers and Letters,* 425.

Leibniz felt that the best way to describe this state of perfected fulfillment was to say that it consisted in a kind of "harmony."

To illustrate his notion of harmony and the effect that he felt the perception of order invariably had on us, Leibniz drew not, as we might expect, on mathematics or geometry, or on any other scientific discipline, but on an art form, specifically on the "beautiful example" of music.

> Everything that emits a sound contains a vibration or a transverse motion such as we see in strings; thus everything that emits sounds gives off invisible impulses. When these are not confused, but proceed together in order but with a certain variation, they are pleasing. . . . Drum beats, the beat and cadence of the dance, and other motions of this kind in measure and rule derive their pleasurableness from their order, for all order is an aid to the emotions. And a regular though invisible order is found also in the artfully created beats and motions of vibrating strings, pipes, bells, and indeed, even of the air itself, which these bring into uniform motion. Through our hearing, this creates a sympathetic echo in us, to which our animal spirits respond. This is why music is so well adapted to move our minds, even though this main purpose is not sufficiently noticed or sought after. (425–26)[47]

Not the perceptible phenomena themselves—that is, in this example, the actual audible sounds—but rather the *relation* in which these phenomena stand to one another, which in turn evinces the human imposition of form onto matter, is what constitutes the pleasure we experience while listening to music. As a description of that regular order to which Leibniz later on in the essay lends the familiar term "harmony," music—often called the most abstract of the arts—was thus truly a beautiful, and beautifully appropriate, model.

Although it is unclear to whom precisely Leibniz addressed "On Happiness," it was undoubtedly some august personage attached to one of the courts at which Leibniz served during his life. For judiciously sprinkled throughout the essay are repeated—and in their purpose rather transparent —references to people of high birth, as when he comments that "no one can rise more easily to a higher stage of happiness than can persons of rank." This shameless fawning on his noble patrons emerges in the course of the essay in more subtle ways as well, and one can even detect a practical or political significance in those places where Leibniz appears to have been operating with purely metaphysical concepts alone. Resuming, for example, his efforts to delineate in rational terms what we normally only indistinctly

47. Plato—whom Leibniz greatly admired—also considered music as being ideally suited to "move our minds" and, in fact, lead us toward virtue and inner beauty; see Plato, *Republic*, 3.401c–402a.

feel, Leibniz further unraveled the components of his proof, claiming that "perfection shows itself in great freedom and power of action, since all being consists in a kind of power; and the greater the power, the higher and freer the being." Quite apart from its philosophical import, no prince or monarch had ever received a more palatable justification for amassing ever greater amounts of wealth and political influence.

Still, Leibniz was not really composing a self-serving pamphlet celebrating greed and domination, nor did he espouse anything resembling a Hobbesian theory of polity and human behavior. The categories he used to describe his ethical ideal have, fortunately, the redeeming quality of being sufficiently nuanced and abstract to be read on a variety of levels at once. Following the passage just cited, Leibniz further explained that the greater any power (that is, the larger any single being or corporate entity), the wider its physical compass and the more numerous its individual constituents—all of which this "power" enfolds within its unifying embrace, thus representing a synthesized totality in singular form. "Now unity in plurality is nothing but harmony [Übereinstimmung]," Leibniz continued, "and since any particular being agrees with one rather than another being, there flows from this harmony the order from which beauty arises, and beauty awakens love." Very much in the same terms with which Shaftesbury and Hutcheson would soon argue for an autonomous morality, Leibniz thus equated harmony, or a unity in variety, with beauty, and he also suggested that an irresistible attraction emanated from its perceived presence in both physical objects and other human beings. Finally, Leibniz concluded the main line of his argument with an impetuous rhetorical flourish, issuing forth a torrent of conceptual appositions in rapid succession, claiming that "we see that happiness, pleasure, love, perfection, being, power, freedom, harmony, order, and beauty are all tied to each other, a truth which is rightly perceived by few."[48] Although it is probably not possible to establish a precise hierarchy among each one of these terms, all of which Leibniz saw as being profoundly related, it is perhaps more than a coincidence that the last word in the list, the culminating note in a crescendo of correlative concepts, is beauty.

Although the aesthetic element in Leibniz's philosophy has not completely escaped notice, its position within his ethical theory has, like that theory itself, suffered from undue neglect.[49] But, as the essay "On Happiness" amply shows, Leibniz clearly conceived of the ideal of moral perfection

48. Leibniz, "On Happiness," 426.
49. See, for example, Wilhelm Dilthey, "Leibniz und sein Zeitalter," in *Gesammelte Schriften* (Stuttgart: B. G. Teubner; Göttingen: Vandenhoeck & Ruprecht, 1959), 3:65. See also Alfred Baeumler, *Das Irrationalitätsproblem in der Ästhetik und Logik des 18. Jahrhunderts bis zur Kritik der Urteilskraft* (Halle: Max Niemeyer, 1923), 38. The only person to have remarked on the aesthetic aspect of Leibniz's moral philosophy in particular is Loemker, "Ethical Import," 220, who briefly discusses the "aesthetic character of Leibniz's ethics."

as possessing an eminently aesthetic quality, and his entire theory rested on this assumption. Leibniz thought that we are to pursue happiness by seeking to achieve a balance of our passions and desires, an equilibrium of our wishes and inclinations, or by attempting to establish what he called, following the Greeks and particularly the Stoic philosophers of antiquity, an inner "harmony." As in Leibniz's example of music, we are to arrange the various components of our inner life in a harmonious and balanced composition, and it is the degree of skill and intelligence with which we dispose the powers of our soul, rather than the intrinsic nature of those powers themselves, that elicit the admiration and love—that is, cause pleasure—in those who witness our actions.

Since Leibniz wrote but did not publish "On Happiness" several years before Shaftesbury's *Characteristicks* appeared, the affinities between the views expressed independently by these two philosophers are nothing short of remarkable. And when Shaftesbury did publish his work in 1711, Leibniz was among the first to comment on the similarities, saying that, while reading the three volumes, he "was surprised to find a great number of thoughts which agree with my own principles."[50] Besides their shared notions of the importance and the effect of beauty in morals, it has also become apparent that they both adopted an unabashedly aristocratic, not to say elitist, posture toward humanity. In another short piece titled "Discours sur les beaux sentiments," Leibniz similarly wrote that "the soul is beautiful [*l'âme est belle*] when it is good and great at the same time."[51] Much more directly than before, Leibniz here asserted that we have two different types of internal powers, or powers of the soul: those which are natural and those which we acquire through conscious, purposeful effort. "Nature forms us," he wrote, "but art perfects [*achève*] us" (366–67).[52] Leibniz used the word "art" not in our modern meaning, as in reference to works of art, but in the sense of human skill, dexterity, or talent. It is true, he wrote, that such mastery and application will not be able to augment the powers that nature has produced. "Art," rather, bundles our innate natural capacities to form a distinctively human, which is to say rational, design. "Art reunites and employs the powers that nature had scattered and misdirected," Leibniz explained. "Our spirits are by nature scattered, and from the time we are born we are diverted by a thousand trifles that divide our attention. Only art can reunite and give direction to our thoughts" (367).[53] As the instrument or expression of human reason, art is thus the activity responsible for creating the

50. Loemker, *Philosophical Papers and Letters*, 629.
51. Cited from Jean Baruzi, *Leibniz. Avec de nombreux textes inédits* (Paris: Bloud, 1909), 365.
52. With regard to this and other passages in this essay by Leibniz, I have profited from the discussion and the translations in Loemker, "Ethical Import," 220–21.
53. See also ibid., 221.

perfection necessary to happiness and morality, and its manifestation, as Leibniz wrote, is a soul that is correspondingly "beautiful." In these and other comments, then, Leibniz clearly displayed a philosophical stance that would justify considering him, as James Engell puts it, "the Shaftesbury of the Continent."[54]

But despite their resemblances, one should not forget or ignore the no less substantial differences separating these two philosophers.[55] Unlike Shaftesbury, Leibniz did not wish for his theory to serve as a substitute for an ethical code grounded in Christian theology. In the essay "On Happiness," he specifically stated that the end of this moral self-fashioning and of the pleasure we take in its deliberate operation was that it led us to a constantly renewed awareness of the divine origin and prime exemplar of all perfection. The true goal of virtue, Leibniz always insisted, was that it carried us forever toward a recognition of "the chief source, the course, and the purpose of everything, and the incomprehensible excellence of that Supreme Nature which comprises all things within it."[56] Unlike Shaftesbury's attempt to perform at least a logical separation of ethics and theology, the idea of a divine Being never strayed far from the middle of Leibniz's thought, and in his moral theory, too, God forever provided the reason and focus for inquiry.

Although Christian Wolff, Leibniz's temperamentally more moderate protégé, largely tried to extricate his philosophy from such doctrinal strictures, he never allowed himself to indulge in the sort of intoxicating speculative flights that Leibniz himself habitually undertook. Trained in mathematics (his first teaching post was in Halle as a professor of the subject), Wolff's sensibilities tended in other directions. He mainly concerned himself with elaborating and systematizing—usually at great and numbingly meticulous length—what his predecessor had sketched out in his characteristically broad and hasty strokes. One may therefore detect an interesting parallel between Wolff's relationship to Leibniz and the one we noted between Spener and his mentor, Arndt. Both were relatively unoriginal thinkers, writers whose talents tended toward synthesis and distillation, which allowed them to reach a larger and more varied audience. Their fame and influence thus far exceeded, at least during their own lifetimes, the comparable effect of their respective teachers. Both Wolff and Spener also took a much more

54. James Engell, *The Creative Imagination: Enlightenment to Romanticism* (Cambridge: Harvard University Press, 1981), 25.

55. Without further substantiating his opinion, Cassirer sought to locate this difference at precisely the point that I have identified as constituting their similarity, and he made the odd and plainly incorrect assertion that "for Leibniz, the concept of beauty was a peripheral problem, for Shaftesbury it was a central one." See Ernst Cassirer, *Freiheit und Form: Studien zur deutschen Geistesgeschichte* (Darmstadt: Wissenschaftliche Buchgesellschaft, 1975), 85.

56. Leibniz, "On Happiness," 427.

directly pragmatic approach to the issues of religion and ethics than the men they admired. And whereas Leibniz had written virtually all of his works in French and Latin, the languages of the educated elite, Wolff published many of his books in the vernacular German as part of his broader didactic aims. A direct consequence of this shared practical sobriety was that Wolff, like Spener, also more or less completely dispensed with the concept of beauty when dealing with questions of ethics. In its place, the concept of perfection became for both the absolute standard according to which one ought to measure moral goodness. Before Wolff in fact published in 1720 his chief work of moral philosophy, the ponderously titled *Vernünfftige Gedancken von der Menschen Thun und Lassen, zu Beförderung ihrer Glückseligkeit* (Rational thoughts on human actions for the promotion of their happiness), he exchanged a number of letters with Leibniz on this very topic. As Wolff candidly and somewhat urgently wrote in May 1715 in one such missive, "I need the notion of perfection for dealing with morals."[57]

Nevertheless, although it seems that Wolff never used the phrase "moral beauty" itself in any of his writings, he did help promote a separation of theology and ethics that had already begun to occur under the banner of that concept in both England and France. And Wolff's general adoption of Leibniz's ideas to formulate his own conception of moral perfection, and of the attraction and pleasurable effect such perfection aroused in those who observed it (either in themselves or in others), bears more than a merely superficial resemblance to the conceptual tradition underlying the notion of moral beauty itself.[58] Although he never approached, and in fact disapproved of, the rhapsodic style cultivated by Leibniz and Shaftesbury, the ideas Wolff developed nonetheless stand in marked contrast to the usual perception of him as nothing more than a dry rationalist who completely discounted the role of sensation in philosophical investigation. As he explained in the same letter to Leibniz,

When I see that some actions tend toward our perfection and that of others, whereas other [actions] tend toward our imperfection and that of others, the sensation of perfection excites a certain pleasure [*voluptas*] and the sensation of imperfection a certain displeasure [*nausea*]. And the emotions [*af-*

---

57. Gottfried Wilhelm Leibniz, *Philosophical Essays*, ed. and trans. Roger Ariew and Daniel Garber (Indianapolis: Hackett, 1989), 231.
58. I have found only one use of the word "beauty" in connection with goodness in Wolff's writings, and that occurs in the (unpaginated) preface to his work on ethics; see Christian Wolff, *Vernünfftige Gedancken von der Menschen Thun und Lassen, zu Beförderung ihrer Glückseligkeit*, 4th ed. (Frankfurt and Leipzig, 1733; reprint, ed. Hans Werner Arndt, Hildesheim: Georg Olms, 1976), § 10 of the foreword to the third edition: "No one has made freedom of the will more useful than I have just done and no one has proven more distinctly how virtue receives therefrom its beauty and reward, and vice its disgrace and punishment."

fectus], by virtue of which the mind is, in the end, inclined or disinclined, are modifications of this pleasure and displeasure; I explain the origin of natural obligation in this way. As soon as the perfection toward which the action tends, and which it indicates, is represented in the intellect, pleasure arises, which causes us to cling more closely to the action that we should contemplate. And so, once circumstances overflowing with good for us or for others have been noticed, the pleasure is, at last, inclined toward appetition. And from this inborn disposition toward obligation, I deduce all practical morals, properly enough.[59]

This passage, as relatively brief as it is, accurately summarizes the whole of Wolff's moral philosophy. The central maxim of his ethics consisted of one fairly simple injunction: do that which increases both your own perfection as well as that of your neighbor and refrain from the opposite.[60] And since Wolff thought, as did Leibniz (and Descartes) before him, that the perception of perfection caused us to experience pleasure, then it followed that those things which caused pleasure—or, more generally, produce happiness—were good and hence valuable in and of themselves. The stimulus to morally good conduct thus seemed unproblematic to Wolff. There was, he felt, a natural law implied in our attraction to perfection, and if we exercise our rational faculties as God meant for us to do, there will be no obstacle to attaining durable felicity in this life. Similarly, he held that there is a natural joy, or pleasure, that we experience while observing moral perfection. Thus, although Wolff did not actually invoke the category of "moral beauty" by name, he was nevertheless clearly operating with its implications, and he described moral action and motivation in implicitly aesthetic terms. Pleasure—either voluptuous sensate stimulation or the more abstract enjoyment of an intellectual kind—therefore stood at the root of his ethical system, just as, incidentally, it would reside at the heart of philosophical aesthetics, which a talented student of Wolff by the name of Alexander Gottlieb Baumgarten was to invent in the 1740s.

Wolff of course realized that there are some people who do not act entirely according to the dictates of reason, that there are those who require, as he put it in the preface to his *Vernünfftige Gedancken*, a "slavish fear of the power and violence of a superior to prevent them from doing what they would like to do." But he argued that to control all people in this way is to treat them no better than animals (*Vieh*) and that by such Hobbesian means one achieves, at best, no more than a merely external habituation to

59. Leibniz, *Philosophical Essays*, 231–32.
60. For a useful summary of the main points of Wolff's moral philosophy, see Josef Schmucker, *Die Ursprünge der Ethik Kants in seinen vorkritischen Schriften und Reflektionen* (Meisenheim am Glan: Anton Hain, 1961), 35–42.

the performance of good actions, but not the establishment of true and lasting inner virtue. It is much more in keeping with the dignity of human beings, he wrote, who are distinguished from beasts precisely by their possession of reason and volitional freedom, that they should strive to acquire an intellectual understanding of the nature of good and evil, and to learn, if necessary, to act according to the one and to avoid the other. "Reasonable and rational human beings," Wolff confidently proclaimed, "need no other form of obligation than the natural one." It was this sort of categorical faith in the power of unaided, if not wholly untutored, human reason to guide human actions that secured Wolff's credentials as the first German "Aufklärer"—and prompted gleeful and savage parodies of his thought by Voltaire and many others.

But Wolff did not seem to be aware that he was operating with conflicting categories in his moral philosophy, incompatible elements that, considered together, threatened the very integrity of his system. Unlike his colleagues in Britain who had placed the concept of beauty at the center of their ethical theories, Wolff wanted to preserve a metaphysical and moral hierarchy with God at the summit, and he thus relied solely on the intellectualistic concept of perfection to provide the structural support to his conception. Morality, for Wolff, is mainly a matter of the right application of the understanding.[61] Not that he thought it possible for mere human beings to attain the absolute perfection exemplified by God alone. Like Spener in this as well, Wolff admitted that "since the greatest perfection is unique to God and can be communicated to none of his creatures, then it is also not possible that human beings, even if they daily apply all of their powers to it, can ever reach that state. They can thus never attain more than that they advance from one particular perfection to another and avoid imperfection more and more. And that is the highest good that they may attain."[62] Yet Wolff still retained the nonrational element of pleasure as an important, in fact arguably the secretly decisive, part of his ethical thought. But whereas this apparent tension between the respective powers of reason and sense in the governance of our actions was explicitly thematized in British moral philosophy, Wolff never addressed it as such. There was some consolation, however, in Wolff's silence. For like a speck of sand that stimulates an oyster to produce a pearl as protection against the intruding body, the conceptual irritant to the Wolffian system represented by the conflicted notion of pleasure prodded a new form into existence that transcended in both beauty and interest the host that had originally fostered it.

---

61. See the discussion on this issue by Thomas P. Saine, *Von der Kopernikanischen bis zur Französischen Revolution: Die Auseinandersetzung der deutschen Frühaufklärung mit der neuen Zeit* (Berlin: Erich Schmidt, 1987), 149–52.
62. Wolff, *Vernünfftige Gedancken*, § 44 of the foreword to the third edition.

The problem, though still unarticulated as such, largely stemmed from the basic premises and methods of Leibniz-Wolffian philosophy itself. As has become apparent, the thinkers who embodied this tradition approached every object of inquiry by trying to make it fit within their preconceived metaphysical and, above all, religious hierarchy, one in which God is the pinnacle of Being and that from which everything else is derived. In purely logical terms, this scheme obviously placed severe limitations on subjective or individual freedom of thought; in epistemological terms, this scheme confined very narrowly the possibilities for the discovery of new knowledge. Taking his lead from Leibniz, and from Descartes too, Wolff felt that he could classify the whole of human cognition, and in this specific case all aspects of human morality, according to a small set of criteria that describe the varying degrees of clarity and distinctness with which one can analyze any given idea or perception into its constituent components. As Wolff emphasizes in his preface, "I have made the effort above all to demonstrate a distinct concept of the virtues and vices." At the lowest level of this epistemological framework are the undifferentiated impressions of sense, the brute facticity of sensory experience that exists as such before the intellect processes it into the discrete and identifiable classes of knowledge. It is evident that pleasure—or in Wolffian terminology, the immediate, indistinct sensation we receive when confronted by perceptible perfection, or by the harmony produced by a unity in plurality—belongs to this lower order of being, and Wolff apparently never found an adequate way to accommodate his theory to this inescapable, but nonsystematizable, fact of existence.[63] This inability, or perhaps unwillingness, to grapple with the epistemological problem presented by the phenomenon of sensate pleasure as such seemed all the more compromising to the closed structure of his thought in that his ethical theory rested on its efficacy. It would be jumping ahead of ourselves to note that Kant, more than half a century later, sought to solve this particular question by insisting that morality could have no purpose, motive, or law outside itself. A first provisional solution, however, came from within the ranks of the Wolffian school itself.

Alexander Gottlieb Baumgarten, generally considered Wolff's most accomplished follower, was by no means unusual in his fundamental allegiance to the prevailing metaphysical orthodoxy. Equally common among German philosophers of his day was Baumgarten's devotion to the Christian faith, and, in addition to his logical acumen, he was also noted for the Christian tranquillity and kindness of his demeanor. But unlike Wolff, who had every reason to harbor misgivings about Pietism, Baumgarten felt no

---

63. See the perceptive comments on this issue by Schmucker, *Die Ursprünge der Ethik Kants,* 41–43.

threat from the Pietist fold. For he had grown up in a strictly Pietistic environment along with his older brother, Siegmund Jakob Baumgarten, who managed to be simultaneously a Wolffian and a Pietist theologian of no small repute. (Voltaire in fact once bestowed upon Siegmund Baumgarten the admittedly rather ambiguous distinction, considering its source, of having personified the "crown of German scholarship.")[64] Indeed, their father died when they were still quite young, and they were both sent to be raised and educated in none other than Francke's orphanage in Halle.[65] Although one can only speculate on this point, perhaps it was in part because of this intense and early exposure to the Pietistic atmosphere, in which the notion of inner beauty played such an important role, that the younger Baumgarten became the first person to attempt to integrate the study of aesthetic phenomena into the existing structure of Wolffian dogmatic metaphysics. It is inviting to imagine that, albeit on a plane of great theoretical abstraction, Wolffian thought and Pietism, and in particular the doctrines of moral perfection and the Christian notion of beauty of the soul, thus found a productive synthesis in the form of Baumgarten's mature philosophy of aesthetics.

In 1750, after having written several learned and moderately influential books on the disciplines usually taught by university professors of philosophy (Kant, for example, used Baumgarten's earlier *Metaphysica* and *Ethica* for many years as the bases for his own lectures on these subjects), Baumgarten published the first volume of his *Aesthetica* and, by that gesture, inaugurated a minor philosophical revolution. Although, as we have seen, Leibniz had very much been occupied by both the idea and the phenomenon of beauty, he had never really enlarged on his brilliant, but cursory asides; and Wolff, characteristically, had ignored the issue altogether. Baumgarten thus became the first to use the traditional taxonomy of Wolffian logic to investigate exactly what Wolff had neglected to incorporate convincingly into his system: sensation. Baumgarten accordingly called this new branch of inquiry "aesthetics" after the Greek word for physical perception, especially the sense of taste. At its inception, therefore, aesthetics had little to do with its later incarnations in which the study of art formed the primary focus of interest; it spoke, rather, and less dramatically, to a deficiency in Wolffian epistemology. In some respects, then, the advance Baumgarten made with his *Aesthetica* went no further than an incremental amplification of the inherent, though previously unexplored, possibilities within his

64. For Voltaire's comment, and on Siegmund Baumgarten generally, see the *Allgemeine Deutsche Biographie*, 2:161.
65. On the education of Alexander Baumgarten, see Bernhard Poppe, *Alexander Gottlieb Baumgarten: Seine Bedeutung und Stellung in der Leibniz-Wolffischen Philosophie und seine Beziehungen zu Kant* (Borna-Leipzig: Robert Noske, 1907), 9–14; and Beck, *Early German Philosophy*, 283–84.

adopted frame of reference. Whereas Wolffian philosophy dealt almost exclusively with the realm of "clear" and "distinct" ideas that we apprehended with our "superior" faculties of mind, Baumgarten proposed considering those realms of experience—the "confused" perceptions of sensation, passion, feeling, and so on—which we receive through our "inferior" faculties of sense. And if truth is the end of logic, then it naturally follows that beauty is the end of aesthetics, and it was in expanding on this basic insight that Baumgarten made his own significant contribution.

Curiously, there is a fundamental ambiguity running through Baumgarten's *Aesthetica* about the final aim of the book itself. This uncertainty appears in the opening paragraph of the work, in which Baumgarten declared that aesthetics was both the "theory of sensation"—or as he expressed it in the recondite vocabulary of Wolffian psychology, the theory of "lower cognition" (*gnoseologia inferior*)—and that it was additionally, as he wrote, "the art of thinking beautifully [*ars pulchre cogitandi*]."[66] These two claims, however, seem mutually contradictory: the first implies the objective or "scientific" study of sensation that is expected of an academic philosopher. But the second suggests that the *Aesthetica* will teach us how to make beautiful—that is, how to perfect—the subjective faculties that fall under the rubric of sensation, and that is something else again. How, his readers wondered, did the author of the *Aesthetica* conceive of its real purpose? Was it a new philosophy or a new pedagogy, a way of knowing or a way of doing? Johann Gottfried Herder, for one, felt that these two very distinct intentions had to be sharply separated and that aesthetics could claim validity only if taken in the former sense of a strict and objective science.[67]

Because of the primacy granted to epistemological over ethical concerns in most modern accounts of the period (a hierarchy of values eighteenth-century thinkers themselves did not endorse), what no one seems to have appreciated is that Baumgarten intended to accomplish *both* goals at once. He wanted, in the first place, to provide a theoretical justification for turning sensation into an object of serious inquiry and thus to put it on a sure, philosophical footing. At the same time, he wished to demonstrate how one could raise those faculties engaged by the objects of sense to a degree of relative refinement and perfection—to show us how to become, as it were, *virtuosi* of feeling, just as logic supposedly could help us become masters of

---

66. Alexander Gottlieb Baumgarten, *Theoretische Ästhetik: Die grundlegenden Abschnitte aus der "Aesthetica" (1750/58)*, trans. and ed. Hans Rudolf Schweizer (Hamburg: Felix Meiner, 1983), § 1.

67. See Johann Gottfried Herder, "Plan zu einer Aesthetik," in *Werke*, ed. Ulrich Gaier et al. (Frankfurt am Main: Deutscher Klassiker Verlag, 1985), 1:659–76, in which Herder castigates Baumgarten primarily for failing to make this distinction. See also my comments on this problem in *Herder's Aesthetics and the European Enlightenment* (Ithaca: Cornell University Press, 1991), 176–87.

thinking. The cultivation and ordering into a harmonious disposition of the faculties that respond to sensate stimuli thus stood as the ultimate aim of Baumgarten's work. "The goal of aesthetics," he unequivocally announced, "is the perfection of sensate cognition as such, by which is meant beauty."[68] With regard to his broadest purpose, Baumgarten thus planned for his aesthetics to provide a kind of instruction manual for achieving an adequate measure of intellectual or inner beauty. In so doing, Baumgarten elevated the concept of inner beauty—as well as the discipline meant to aid in achieving it—to a level of philosophical legitimacy that, in German-speaking lands at least, it had never previously enjoyed.

Without entering into the further complexities of his book—which, as interesting as its many arguments are, also resembles the work of his teacher in its rather verbose and punctilious attention to detail—we can still appreciate the historical place of Baumgarten's achievement. Considered as the launching of a new branch of philosophy that would soon spawn whole libraries devoted to the subject, the *Aesthetica* in many ways does not appear to be a very auspicious beginning. Often, in fact, Baumgarten now receives no more credit for the development of aesthetic philosophy than that of having first given it its name. But his effect on contemporary thought was, although not exactly electric, far from insignificant. Most important was his decisive move away from the ancient habit of concentrating entirely on the work of art itself and of thereby deriving the rules that artists had to obey. Instead, his insistence on making the perceiving subject the locus of theoretical attention set the course that almost every subsequent aesthetic philosopher would take. As a consequence, Baumgarten's work also conforms to that general tendency we have discovered in which the prescription and aim of inner beauty, indeed of all moral standards, were no longer dependent on some external authority such as God or the state, but rather found their confirmation solely from within. And since the perceiving subject that Baumgarten described was someone who, ideally, "thought beautifully," Baumgarten's ideas could not have failed to find their way into, and thus also substantially contribute to, the growing literature on the ideal of the beautiful soul itself.

Conspicuously, however, Baumgarten did not link in any explicit fashion morality or ethics with the character of the person he called a "successful" (or, literally, a "happy") asthetician (*felix aestheticus*). He confined himself instead to brief and fairly unhelpful observations on the subject, such as

---

68. Baumgarten, *Theoretische Ästhetik*, § 14. Significantly, Herder singled out this passage in his critique of Baumgarten and wrote his own version of the Latin original: "Aesthetices finis non est perfection sed *scientia* cognitionis sensitivae" [The goal of aesthetics is not the perfection, but the *study* of sensate cognition]; see Herder, "Plan zu einer Aesthetik," in *Werke*, 1:670.

when he wrote in the section that described how to train aestheticians (*disciplina aesthetica*) that "the most important parts of beautiful education are those sciences that deal with God, with the universe, with humanity—above all as concerns our moral station—with history (without excluding myth), with antiquities, and the essence of linguistic and artistic means of expression."[69] The real connection between Wolffian philosophy and the ethical theories that depended on the notion of moral beauty was established in the decade after Baumgarten's book appeared. Yet instead of an easy amalgamation, this convergence of philosophical traditions produced a collision of incompatible assumptions and methods. The result was that not just Kant, but the whole of German philosophy awoke from its dogmatic slumber, or rather—to stay with the Pietistic phraseology that is probably even more apt—the encounter engendered an offspring that although bearing the unmistakable traits of its progenitors, gradually grew into a completely new and individual being.

The preoccupation with method that we noted in the British philosophers of the late seventeenth and early eighteenth centuries did not begin to acquire the same sort of urgency or interest in Germany until the 1740s, when the newly installed Frederick II initiated his reform of the foundering academy in Berlin. Although Leibniz had created the institution in 1700, it had remained slavishly beholden to the precepts of his own thinking and Wolff's subsequent systematization of it, and had thus not been able to rise to real European prominence. By bringing in such famous scholars and scientists as Jean Le Rond d'Alembert, Pierre-Louis Moreau de Maupertuis and, of course, the tireless Voltaire, all of whom had appointed themselves the promoters and defenders of Newtonian science, the young king of Prussia introduced to the Germans the spirit and method of English philosophy—albeit with a decidedly French accent. Although these new ideas were certainly not completely unknown in Germany during the first half of the century, they had been unable to prevail over the Wolffian doctrine. But the institutional visibility that French and English philosophy received through Frederick's energetic reorganization of the academy soon precipitated a profound change in the direction of German thought as a whole.[70]

One of the innovations that Frederick brought to the academy was the establishment of a division—or as it was called, a "class"—dedicated to what was termed "philosophie spéculative." In addition to the usual separate classes devoted to experimental philosophy, mathematics, and "belles-

69. Baumgarten, *Theoretische Ästhetik*, § 64.
70. For an indication of the sea change that began to occur during the 1740s, see the list of works translated into German after the middle of the century in Wundt, *Die deutsche Schulphilosophie*, 270–71.

lettres," which the Berlin academy had in common with the institutions in London and Paris that had served as its models, the Berlin academy was unique in possessing this "speculative" class whose subject was logic, metaphysics, and—most notably—ethics.[71] We have already seen that Frederick showed himself to be particularly concerned about the moral constitution of his subjects and about the greater moral purpose of scientific research, and it is thus not surprising that this commitment would be reflected in the organization of the program of the learned society in which he took active interest. As it happened, one of the momentous reorientations of modern German philosophy that his academy helped to inaugurate likewise began not with questions of ontology or epistemology (although these disciplines always played at least an auxiliary role) but rather with a consideration of ethics.

At regular intervals, the Berlin academy organized essay contests, frequently in response to topics that had arisen in its regular plenary discussions, and it officially invited all who wished to participate to submit essays addressing the subject that had engaged its collective interest. Because of the distinctive openness that the members of the academy cultivated regarding the more "speculative" issues, these prize questions often articulated problems that had otherwise attracted little institutional, which is to say officially sanctioned, notice. Thus these contests soon became national and even international events, attracting essays from some of the finest European minds of the day (199). On 28 May 1761, the academy posed the question for its prize contest for 1763, announcing that the members of the academy wished to know "whether metaphysical truths in general, and in particular the first principles of natural theology and morality, are capable of the same distinct proofs as geometric truths; and, if they are not capable of such proofs, what the actual nature of their certainty is, what degree of certainty one can achieve; and whether this degree is sufficient for complete conviction?"[72] That seemingly simple question touched on most of the basic problems of eighteenth-century moral philosophy. Hobbes, Locke, Wolff, and Hume, as different as they otherwise were, shared the hope that one could apply the methodological rigor of mathematics to moral philosophy, and thus guarantee its status as a strict and scientifically secure discipline.

---

71. See the informative article by Hans Aarsleff, "The Berlin Academy under Frederick the Great," *History of the Human Sciences* 2 (1989): 197–98. Aarsleff mentions that in the article on academies written for the first volume of the *Encyclopédie* in 1751, d'Alembert made special mention of the Berlin academy as having "this unique quality that it embraces even metaphysics, logic, and ethics, which no other academy includes among its topics."

72. Cited from Hans-Jürgen Engfer, *Philosophie als Analysis: Studien zur Entwicklung philosophischer Analysiskonzeptionen unter dem Einfluß mathematischer Methodenmodelle im 17. und frühen 18. Jahrhundert* (Stuttgart: Friedrich Frommann Verlag; Bad Cannstatt: Günter Holzboog, 1982), 26.

Although all of these thinkers had explicitly held out the possibility of reducing morality to a small set of basic laws or principles comparable to those of mathematics in their simplicity, regularity, and universal validity, none had so far managed to provide a compelling and full treatment of ethics that answered to those stated criteria. The prize question posed by the academy was meant to settle, finally, that long outstanding account.

Among the numerous participants in the contest were the gifted mathematician Johann Heinrich Lambert, the literary critic Thomas Abbt, and Immanuel Kant. Prevailing over these impressive competitors, Moses Mendelssohn won the prize with his essay "Ueber die Evidenz in metaphysischen Wissenschaften" (On evidence in the metaphysical sciences), which was published under the auspices of the academy in 1764.[73] Although the historical importance of all of the essays by these thinkers for the later development of philosophical method in Germany has been frequently acknowledged, few have mentioned their pivotal status for the subsequent character of German ethical thought.[74] In particular, these texts stand as the most important bridge linking the German philosophical school with the British tradition of ethics, and especially with its conception of moral beauty.

Although Mendelssohn felt most comfortable with the theoretical apparatus he had inherited from Leibniz and Wolff, he had also devoted himself to a careful and sympathetic study of the principal works of the major English philosophers, above all those of Locke, Shaftesbury, and Hutcheson. In the early 1760s, for example, Mendelssohn had been busy trying to translate Shaftesbury's works, but soon abandoned the project. "My translation has been stuck for a few weeks now," he complained in a letter to Thomas Abbt on 22 February 1762. "The Lord is an obstinate Englishman who frequently refuses to accept a German coat."[75] Through his reading of the British philosophers, Mendelssohn had grown accustomed to equating the Wolffian conception of "the most perfect virtue" with what he also called in a previous work "this infinite beauty of the soul."[76] Before completing the prize essay,

73. See Alexander Altmann, *Moses Mendelssohn: A Biographical Study* (Philadelphia: Jewish Publication Society of America, 1973), 112–18, for a description of the events surrounding Mendelssohn's participation in the contest.

74. Among the more useful discussions of this transition is the fine book by Engfer, *Philosophie als Analysis*, esp. 26–67. See as well the study by Paul Arthur Schilpp, *Kant's Pre-Critical Ethics*, 2d ed. (Evanston: Northwestern University Press, 1960), 22–40, and that by Keith Ward, *The Development of Kant's View of Ethics* (New York: Humanities Press, 1972), 26–31.

75. Moses Mendelssohn, *Gesammelte Schriften: Jubiläumsausgabe*, ed. Fritz Bamberger et al. (Stuttgart: Friedrich Frommann Verlag; Bad Cannstatt: Günter Holzboog, 1972–), 11:296.

76. See Moses Mendelssohn, "Die Idealschönheit in den schönen Wissenschaften," in *Schriften zur Philosophie, Aesthetik und Apologetik*, ed. Moritz Brasch (Leipzig, 1880; reprint, Hildesheim: Georg Olms, 1968), 2:283. Henceforth referred to in the text by volume and page number. This essay was first published as no. 66 of the *Briefe, die neueste Literatur betreffend*, which appeared on 8 November 1759.

Mendelssohn had therefore spent a good deal of his intellectual energy thinking about the relationship between the beautiful and the good; he even used that phrase as the title of another of his earlier essays ("Die Verwandtschaft des Schönen und Guten"), which he wrote sometime between 1757 and 1760. But ever the epistemologist, Mendelssohn did not concern himself so much with the relations obtaining between the good and the beautiful themselves as with the similarities in how we perceive them. He was interested, that is, in the parallels he detected between the psychological or epistemological processes that occur in the mind when we perceive moral and aesthetic phenomena. Recalling perhaps Shaftesbury's use of the concept of taste—which, though it seems to react immediately to the objects it encounters, really stands under the regulation of our rational faculty—Mendelssohn similarly asserted that in addition to the realm of art, "there is also a taste in morals, for morals, too, have their beauty and ugliness" (2:287). But Mendelssohn certainly knew of the criticism that had been brought to bear on this line of reasoning, especially the criticism against its later development in Hutcheson's philosophy. For Mendelssohn liberally, if somewhat patronizingly, quoted Hutcheson this essay, noting at one point that his "theory rests on solid ground, but it needs some explanation" (2:288).

In providing the rudiments of such an explanation, Mendelssohn showed himself to be unwilling to forsake the primacy of rational judgment in distinguishing truth from falsehood, good from evil, and beauty from ugliness, even though he granted that in practical terms we are primarily guided by what he called "*bon-sens*, sensation, and taste." If we were to analyze every seemingly immediate, unreflective judgment we made about the goodness or beauty of an action into the individual cognitive constituents that underlie that judgment, Mendelssohn reasoned, then we would see that it presupposed a complex chain of separate logical operations and thus entirely conformed to the same rational paradigms that governed all of our thought. Only through a process of habituation, in which we learn to perform these intermediary steps quickly and without being consciously aware of them, do we have the impression that we determine, for example, what is good and what is beautiful without making recourse to reflective consideration.[77] Mendelssohn thus viewed the functioning of the "moral sense" in much the same way that Baumgarten described aesthetic judgment. He saw it, namely, as a mental operation that works according to the same rules as logical reasoning and that can be resolved into logical categories, but that actually takes place on the plane of "sensate" experience, in the realm of feelings,

77. Mendelssohn makes the same argument, although in greater detail, in his "Rhapsodie oder Zusätze zu den Briefen über die Empfindungen," in *Schriften zur Philosophie*, 2:133–35.

emotions, passions, and so forth. In this way, Mendelssohn created the theoretical possibility of embracing the new ideas coming from abroad while retaining the familiar framework of German dogmatic metaphysics.

This eclectic mixture of resources is also apparent in the fourth section of Mendelssohn's prize essay, "Über die Evidenz," in which he addressed, as he wrote, the "first principles of ethics." Like the German thinkers who had most immediately influenced his thought, and in direct response to the terms in which the academy had formulated its question, Mendelssohn stated his conviction that one can prove these principles "with geometric precision and validity." Similarly, he believed that "there are also general basic rules [analogous to the axioms and laws of geometry] according to which [human beings] should decide what they should do or should not do, and these general basic rules are the *laws of nature*" (1:91). Entirely in keeping with his rationalistic conception of the mechanisms regulating our moral behavior, Mendelssohn then announced (in words that clearly left an impression on Kant) that the first "general practical maxim, the first law of nature" was as follows: "*Make your internal and external state, as well as that of your neighbor, in the proper proportion, as perfect as you can*" (1:92). Here, as in Wolff's ethical philosophy, the striving after the attainment of perfection in oneself and its encouragement in others constitutes the ultimate goal of all ethical action. And once more taking his lead from Wolff, Mendelssohn also allowed that pleasure, which he likewise defined as the sensible experience of perfection in its physical manifestation, provided both the stimulus and motivation for moral conduct. But Mendelssohn added a decisive additional element to the list his predecessor had drawn up:

> A being that is endowed with freedom can choose between various objects, or representations of objects, that please it. The basis of this pleasure [*Wohlgefallen*] is the perfection, beauty, and order that it perceives, or believes to perceive, in the desired object. . . . The observation of perfection, beauty, and order grants us pleasure [*Lust*], but that of imperfection, ugliness, and disorder imparts displeasure. Thus, order, beauty, and perfection can provide the motives [*Beweggründe*] by which a free being is determined in its choice. These motives do not impose any physical coercion on the free being, for it chooses according to pleasure and internal effect. But they do, nevertheless, imply a moral necessity, according to which it becomes impossible for a free mind to find pleasure in imperfections, ugliness and disorder. (1:93)

Although Mendelssohn did not claim that beauty was the sole impetus responsible for setting moral deeds in motion, he did think it important enough to set it next to perfection and order as the three main goods that we as beings furnished with both reason and freedom of will, would—indeed, as paradoxical as it sounds, *must*—rationally choose when we perceived them.[78] Mendelssohn described this process specifically as an instantiation of a "natural law." Thus according to his conception of ethical action, every free human agent stands under the moral (which, in this case, also meant natural) obligation to bring forth as much perfection, beauty, and order as possible in one's own internal and external condition as well as in that of others. With Mendelssohn, in other words, the accession to moral beauty had become a kind of categorical imperative.

After Mendelssohn had established the general maxim according to which all ethical action must be, and certainly could be, rationally measured, he felt it was safe to venture into the more difficult depths surrounding sensation's role in moral judgment. On the whole, the argument he advanced in "Über die Evidenz" regarding the role of sense in ethical reasoning derives from the theory—itself substantially dependent on English empiricist psychology—that he had put forward in his earlier writings. Mendelssohn concluded that

> conscience is the acquired skill [*Fertigkeit*] of correctly distinguishing good from evil, and the sense of truth is the skill of correctly distinguishing the true from the false, by means of indistinct reasoning. They are, in their domain, what taste is in the realm of the beautiful and the ugly. A practiced taste immediately finds what slower criticism can only gradually illuminate. With the same speed conscience decides, and the sense of truth judges, what reason cannot analyze into distinct conclusions [*Schlüsse*] without laborious reflection. (1:100)

Although this passage may sound like a concession to nonrational or emotivist theories, in reality Mendelssohn never called reason into question; he merely tried to explain how we actually go about making practical decisions in everyday life. Here, as anyone would be able to confirm, we do not compare our reactions to events with abstract laws and rules; rather, we seem to respond immediately, without reflecting on our experience. But as one of the many precursors to Freud, Mendelsohn argued that this apparent immediacy is deceptive, for it really conforms to patterns prescribed by unconscious laws. "This inner feeling [*innere Gefühl*], this sensation of good and evil, of true and false, acts according to unchanging rules, according to correct principles, but according to principles that have been incorporated into our temperament through continuous practice and that have been, as it

78. See the informative comments on Mendelssohn's argument in Beck, *Early German Philosophy*, 330–31, and in Alexander Altmann, *Moses Mendelssohns Frühschriften zur Metaphysik* (Tübingen: J.C.B. Mohr, Paul Siebeck, 1969), 358–59.

were, transformed into flesh and blood" (1:100). This is an elegant solution to the problem of moral judgment that Hume, a few years earlier, had also outlined in comparable terms, and the decision made by the members of the academy to award the prize to Mendelssohn indicates that they, too, were favorably impressed.

Mendelssohn thus carried the day in the academy's contest with a contribution that although it took creative cognizance of the impulses issuing from British moral thinkers, still stayed well within the confines marked out by traditional German metaphysics.[79] It was, however, the essay written by Mendelssohn's closest competitor, Kant, that indicated the direction that German philosophy as a whole would later take. Although there are certainly some similarities between the basic conceptions underlying the two works, the main and most critical difference between them resides in their methodological orientation. Whereas Mendelssohn adhered to the belief in the theoretical possibility of making the method in all philosophical disciplines, including ethics, coincide with that of mathematics, Kant—here far more consequential in his reading of recent British and French thinkers than Mendelssohn had been—decisively broke with this established precedent. In his submission to the contest, "Untersuchung über die Deutlichkeit der Grundsätze der natürlichen Theologie und Moral" (An inquiry into the distinctness of the principles of natural theology and morals), he categorically announced that "nothing has been more harmful to philosophy than mathematics; or better, there is nothing more harmful than the idea of imitating mathematics as a method of thinking where it cannot possibly be used."[80] Instead, Kant suggested that one replace this deductive method with the inductive one advocated by Newton. For as Kant confidently, even defiantly, put it, "the genuine method of metaphysics is, in fundamentals, identical with that which was introduced into natural science by Newton and

79. That Mendelssohn maintained this compromise position is nicely shown in his 1774 essay "Anweisung zur spekul. Philosophie, für einen jungen Menschen von 15 bis 20 Jahren" (Introduction to specul.[ative] philosophy for a young person between 15 and 20 years of age), in *Gesammelte Schriften*, 3.1.305–7, in which he says, on the one hand: "Above all things the young person must have studied the basic principles of geometry; . . . only the stricter synthetic method of the ancient Greek [Euclid] is of great use to the budding philosopher. . . . A further introduction to logic can be found in *Wolff's Art of Thinking Rationally*." Yet, on the other hand, Mendelssohn wrote at the end of the essay: "Practical philosophy, however, is of far greater importance by being immediately associated with the happiness of humanity, and it gives a good head as much to reflect upon as the heart, to examine oneself with all due severity, and to educate [*bilden*] oneself toward virtue and true wisdom. . . . The ancients, it seems to me, are in this respect the best teachers; yet the English have also done a great deal here that is indispensible to the lover of wisdom."
80. Immanuel Kant, "An Inquiry into the Distinctness of the Principles of Natural Theology and Morals," in *Critique of Practical Reason and Other Writings in Moral Philosophy*, trans. and ed. Lewis White Beck (Chicago: University of Chicago Press, 1949), 269. Henceforth cited parenthetically in the text as "*WMP*" by page number.

which had such useful consequences there" (*WMP*, 271). With that statement, the history of moral philosophy separating Hobbes's *Leviathan* from this essay by Kant came to an abrupt and dramatic close. Basically suggesting the substitution of the process of synthesis, which had by then come to be seen as synonymous with dogmatic and erroneous thinking, with the practice of analysis, which not least by virtue of having been advocated by Newton enjoyed enormous prestige as the only "true" procedure of inquiry, Kant's methodological proposal amounted in its effect to a fundamental reorientation, even a revolution, in how German philosophy was conducted.[81]

Thus the larger methodological significance of Kant's essay for the subsequent development of German philosophy far outweighs the comparatively few comments it contains about moral philosophy, which are reserved for the last pages of the work and by their very brevity betray a lack of real engagement with the subject. Abbreviated as they are, however, his remarks about the psychological mechanisms governing moral judgment, and the degree of certainty with which we can hope to attain knowledge of good and evil, warrant attention. For Kant's argument is notable not only for its apparently complete acceptance of the British moral theories—Kant mentioned that Hutcheson and otherwise unspecified "others" had made some "excellent observations" on the issue of "moral feeling" (*WMP*, 285)[82]—but also in view of his somewhat pessimistic assessment of the susceptibility of this "moral feeling" to rational analysis. Kant agreed in principle with Mendelssohn that it was the responsibility of the philosopher to illuminate the unconscious processes of perception, the performance of which habit or "practice" have obscured. But he did not share Mendelssohn's confidence that all of the individual elements composing the "feeling for the good" could be resolved into their primary constituents and principles. Kant wrote, ironically still using the technical terminology of the Wolffian school whose methodological premises he had just repudiated, "it is a task of the understanding to resolve the compounded and confused concept of the good and to make it distinct by showing how it arises from simpler sensations of the good. But if the sensation of the good is simple, the judgment, 'This is good,' is completely indemonstrable and a direct effect of the consciousness of the feeling of pleasure associated with the conception of the object" (*WMP*, 284). Again, at the very end of the essay, Kant conceded that as far as he was concerned, "it is still to be settled whether it is simply the cognitive faculty or whether it is feeling . . . which decides the basic princi-

81. I discuss in detail this change in the conception of philosophical method during the first half of the eighteenth century in *Herder's Aesthetics and the European Enlightenment*, esp. 11–38.
82. See Dieter Henrich, "Hutcheson und Kant," *Kant-Studien* 49 (1957): 49–69.

ples of practical philosophy" (285). Probably because of this impasse, which Kant seemed to have encountered in defining the principles of moral philosophy, he did not return publicly to these problems for another twenty years, that is, not until 1785, when his *Grundlegung zur Metaphysik der Sitten* (Foundations of the metaphysics of morals) appeared. But he did not entirely forsake this field of inquiry in the meantime, and evidence of his continued preoccupation with ethical concerns can even be found in his next published work, which appeared in the same year of 1764: *Beobachtungen über das Gefühl des Schönen und Erhabenen* (Observations on the feeling of the Beautiful and Sublime).

In light of the preceding discussion, however, the title of the work should alert us that even though Kant was writing not about how we perceived the good, but instead about how we appreciated what is beautiful, he was still referring to the same related set of difficulties by using "feeling" as a central point of departure. Although he anticipates here in part the stance he would assume in his critical work, Kant's mature moral philosophy is hardly recognizable in his effusive contention that

> true virtue can be grafted only upon principles such that the more general they are, the more sublime and noble it becomes. These principles are not speculative rules, but the consciousness of a feeling that lives in every human breast and extends itself much further than over the particular grounds of compassion and complaisance. I believe that I sum it all up when I say that it is the *feeling of the beauty and the dignity of human nature*. The first is a ground of universal affection, the second of universal esteem; and if this feeling had the greatest perfection in some one human heart, this man would of course love and prize even himself, but only so far as he is one of all those over whom his broadened and noble feeling is spread. Only when one subordinates his own inclination to one that has been expanded in this way can our charitable impulses be used proportionately and bring about the noble bearing that is the beauty of virtue.[83]

To appreciate the force and relative novelty of Kant's statement, and to remind ourselves that it was by no means self-evident that he should have spoken so positively of "the beauty of virtue," one has only to consult the work that had first made the juxtaposition of beauty and sublimity popular: Edmund Burke's *Philosophical Enquiry into the Origin of Our Ideas of the Sublime and Beautiful*, which had appeared in 1757, a few years before Kant wrote his essay on the subject. In general, Burke displayed little interest in the arts

83. Immanuel Kant, *Observations on the Feeling of the Beautiful and Sublime*, trans. John T. Goldthwait (Berkeley and Los Angeles: University of California Press, 1965), 60; translation slightly modified.

themselves; he concentrated instead on the qualities of both nature and humanity that gave rise to the kinds of "ideas" mentioned in his title. Given this focus, it seems almost inevitable that Burke eventually had to confront the issue, as the heading to the eleventh section of the *Enquiry* reads, concerning "How far the idea of BEAUTY may be applied to VIRTUE." Typically, Burke expressed his opinion in clear and unmistakable terms:

> The general application of this quality to virtue, has a strong tendency to confound our ideas of things; and it has given rise to an infinite deal of whimsical theory; as the affixing the name of beauty to proportion, congruity and perfection, as well as to qualities of things yet more remote from our natural ideas of it, and from one another, has tended to confound our ideas of beauty. . . . This loose and inaccurate manner of speaking, has therefore misled us both in the theory of taste and of morals; and induced us to remove the science of our duties from their proper basis, (our reason, our relations, and our necessities,) to rest it upon foundations altogether visionary and unsubstantial.[84]

During the "critical" phase of his own thinking, Kant would also come to endorse this view, at least as it concerned the necessity of strictly separating the theory of taste from that of morals and of founding our duties entirely on reason. But in his pre-critical *Observations* he clearly seems to have considered the notion of moral beauty an important component in establishing an autonomous ethical philosophy. It gave a motive of moral action that as Kant at this stage in his philosophical development still believed, reason alone could not supply.

There are several plausible reasons for Kant's decision in the 1760s to accept the implications attached to the conception of what he had called "the beauty of virtue." We have already noted that Kant was raised and educated in a Pietistic atmosphere that for those other eighteenth-century Germans who had also been exposed to it gave rise to an almost natural association of moral purity and goodness with a kind of beauty of soul.[85] It is possible, though not strictly demonstrable, that these early experiences formed Kant in a way that made it easier or more natural for him to conceive of virtue in these terms. And although Kant subsequently adopted a much more critical stance toward the British school of thought in which this moral

84. Edmund Burke, *A Philosophical Enquiry into the Origin of Our Ideas of the Sublime and Beautiful*, ed. James T. Boulton (Notre Dame: University of Notre Dame Press, 1968), 112.
85. The influence of Kant's Pietistic background on the tenor of his thought is mentioned by almost all commentators. The most informative account is offered in the still useful biography by J.H.W. Stuckenberg, *The Life of Immanuel Kant* (London: Macmillan, 1882), esp. 9–25. See also Schilpp, *Kant's Pre-Critical Ethics*, 49–51; Ward, *Kant's View of Ethics*, 3–4; and Roger J. Sullivan, *Immanuel Kant's Moral Theory* (Cambridge: Cambridge University Press, 1989), 6–7.

principle had been promoted, he put equal distance between himself and the Wolffian tradition that advocated the idea of perfection as the basic principle of morality. Two decades later, in the *Foundations of the Metaphysics of Morals*, he had this to say about the "ontological concept of perfection": "It is empty, indefinite, and consequently useless . . . ; it inevitably tends to move in a circle and cannot avoid tacitly presupposing the morality which it ought to explain" (*WMP*, 99). At the same time, however, Kant granted that "the moral feeling is nearer to morality and its dignity, inasmuch as it pays virtue the honor of ascribing the pleasure [*Wohlgefallen*] and esteem for her directly to morality, and does not, as it were, say to her face that it is not her beauty but only our advantage which attaches us to her" (99).[86] The distinction Kant made here is subtle: the activity of moral feeling, which responds to the perception of morality, is preferable to the purely rational process of confirming the presence or absence of perfection because moral feeling does not calculate any gain that might flow from that perfection, but reacts merely and immediately to the "beauty of virtue" itself. The process that had been taking place over the past century in German ethical philosophy, in which the concept of perfection had gradually begun to cede its categorical place to the ideal of moral beauty as the end toward which one ought to strive, had thus, with Kant, been finally decided in favor of the latter.[87] During the following decades, the notion of the beauty of virtue, recommended by such impressive credentials, rapidly gained admission into all of the literary and cultural capitals within the entire European republic of letters.

We end up, then, by returning to our point of departure, in which the importance of religion, not merely for the idea of the beauty of soul, but more generally for the tenor of German eighteenth-century ethical thought at large, had made itself more than manifest. And Kant certainly represented no exception to this general rule. In spite of his rigorous distinctions between the various branches of knowledge and action, and his later insistence that the moral law had to be entirely autonomous and derive its

---

86. Translation slightly modified. Kant obviously wavered in his opinion of this school of thought, as evidenced by a brief comment he made in his Inaugural Dissertation of 1770, in which he airily commented that "Epicurus, who reduced the criteria of morals to the feeling of pleasure or displeasure, is therefore quite rightly condemned, along with certain moderns who, like Shaftesbury and his school, follow him in a much less thorough manner." Cited from Lewis White Beck, *Kant's Latin Writings: Translations, Commentaries, and Notes*, in collaboration with Mary J. Gregor, Ralf Meerbote, John A. Reuscher (New York: Peter Lang, 1986), 158. But Ward rightly points out, in *Kant's View of Ethics*, 22–23, that "beauty and dignity are central to Kant's approach to ethics," and that "Kant did not change his early view that morality was intimately associated with the feeling of the beauty and dignity of human nature."
87. On Kant's repudiation of the Wolffian concept of perfection, see Dieter Henrich, "Über Kants früheste Ethik: Versuch einer Rekonstruktion," *Kant-Studien* 54 (1963): esp. 421–29.

justification solely from freely applied human reason, his profoundly religious attitude made it probably inescapable that his ethics would reflect his earliest memories and values as well. In the preface to the second edition of the *Critique of Pure Reason* of 1781, for instance, Kant revealed that he had intended to accomplish with his critical labors something that Locke had also wished to perform with his own *Essay*. Kant wrote that there were many potential rewards to be gained from establishing metaphysics on a solid scientific ground. "But, above all," he explained, "there is the inestimable benefit, that all objections to morality and religion will be forever silenced."[88] That is, Kant explicitly understood his critical labors to be part of a large-scale defense of these basic human concerns. And in one of his last works, *Religion within the Limits of Reason Alone* of 1793, he claimed that although morality contained its laws wholly within itself, "morality . . . leads ineluctably to religion."[89] Yet it is worth reminding ourselves that Kant's conviction that morality and religion were inextricably related was not, as some have assumed, atypical for the Enlightenment at large, but rather an expression of its deepest tendencies and hopes.[90]

It thus appears that Kant unified within the generous architecture of his philosophy the diverse, and in some ways even incongruous, eighteenth-century systems of thought and belief that had advanced beauty of soul as a central part of their ethical program. The customary image of Kant as an abstracted and remote thinker far removed from the quotidian events and concerns of his day bears little resemblance to reality. Although he generally tried to avoid becoming embroiled in the fiercely contested, but frequently trivial, polemical skirmishes that were common throughout the century, he nonetheless actively participated in the intellectual developments of his time. As we have seen, at every stage of his own intellectual evolution, his thought was very much shaped by the main currents of contemporary thinking. German rationalist philosophy, or rather its embodiment in Wolffian paradigms; English and French psychology enlivened by an empirical attachment to the tangible nature of things; and an introspective habit of mind inherited from his observant Pietist upbringing: all of these forces contributed, both directly and in more circuitous ways, to the construction of the imposing edifice represented by his later critical philosophy. And although Kant never raised the concept of moral beauty itself to the level of

88. Immanuel Kant, *Critique of Pure Reason*, trans. Norman Kemp Smith (New York: St. Martin's Press, 1965), 30.
89. Immanuel Kant, *Religion within the Limits of Reason Alone*, trans. Theodore M. Greene and Hoyt H. Hudson (Chicago: Open Court, 1934), 5. The religious basis of Kant's ethics is especially emphasized by Ward, *Kant's View of Ethics*, who sums up his argument by saying that Kant's moral philosophy was "religious in origin and articulation" (174).
90. See Sullivan, *Immanuel Kant's Moral Theory*, 10: "Contrary to the prevailing Enlightenment temper, Kant also defended our need and right to religious faith."

sustained critical attention, it did inhabit the recesses of the massive structure of his thought. It makes an appearance here and there, at infrequent intervals; but sometimes—as at the conclusion of the first part of the third critique, the *Critique of Judgment*—it assumed a place of preeminent importance. Indeed, there is good reason to believe that Kant, like so many others of his time, continued to the end to view the achievement of a symbiosis of morality and beauty as the greatest and most important goal of human striving.

Yet there was one other major cultural transformation then under way that contributed to the complex development of the ideal of moral beauty, but one that seems to have affected Kant, if at all, only very marginally. As we will discover, the Enlightenment's rediscovery of ancient Greece, which permeated almost every other aspect of eighteenth-century life—from literature, to architecture, to sculpture, and painting—did not leave its philosophy untouched either.

3

The Eighteenth Century and the Hellenic Ideal of *Kalokagathia*

> The Beautiful is not different from the Good; the Beautiful
> *Is* the Good that shows itself to us pleasingly veiled.
> —Goethe

Religion and philosophy alone, whether in conflict or in their (rarer) moments of accord, were not of course the only sources for the raw materials either of contemporary consciousness in its entirety or of the particular ideal that concerns us here. As the century in Europe progressed, a knowledge of classical antiquity—although it had always been the obligatory acquirement of the savant and had recently become a fashionable embellishment of leisured gentlemen—began to take on an even greater role in shaping both public and private life. Although the educated citizens of the Enlightenment were generally convinced of the cumulative superiority of their own civilization, the extraordinary accomplishments of ancient Greece and Rome still loomed large in their minds. The impression left by antiquity was in fact so deep that eighteenth-century thinkers sometimes seemed to submit their every action and thought to the crucible of classical sensibility, producing a complex amalgam of diffidence and familiarity that to modern tastes, is as compelling as it is odd. Rousseau, who personified to a representative degree this singular means of self-definition, described in his *Confessions* how in his youth he was so "continuously preoccupied with Rome and Athens, living as one might say with their great men," that he often thought of himself "as a Greek or Roman."[1] Yet even when eighteenth-century writers rebelled against the perceived tyranny of the past, they still paid indirect tribute to the ancients, for it was more often than not a rebellion against Horace or Homer than against some more recent authority. And although their admiration of antiquity was nearly always genuine despite its being virtually requisite for social and intellectual respectability, eighteenth-century enthusiasts were not pre-

1. Jean-Jacques Rousseau, *The Confessions*, trans. J. M. Cohen (London: Penguin, 1953), 20.

vented by pious notions about the inviolate sanctity of the past from tailoring the historical record to suit their immediate needs. They thus regarded classical culture, in other words, as a rich quarry, and they happily mined what they wanted, shaped it to fit their current requirements, and slagged off, or simply ignored, what they were unable to use. And it was this deliberate and highly selective adoption of ancient art and thought that in strictly dialectical terms, helped in turn to mold the eighteenth century itself as a whole.

What is initially most striking, however, about this intimate and carefully cultivated relationship is how much the first half of the century was beholden to ancient Rome, and how the second half and beyond was to ancient Greece. Although thinkers in the early part of the century tended to speak indiscriminately of a uniform "antiquity," they more often meant, even if unconsciously, its Latin rather than its Greek constituents. One major reason for this imbalance had to do with the obvious but important fact that Rome—from the military conquests of the Roman legionnaires to the millennial reign of the Holy Roman Empire—had possessed an immediate, tangible influence on all of the governments and even the languages of Europe that Greece had never matched. Until the eighteenth century, all but a few books were written in Latin, and anyone who wanted to pursue a profession in theology, jurisprudence, medicine, or philosophy had no choice but to learn this language that though technically "dead," still showed signs of a tenacious vitality. "People often admired Greek literature from a distance, like an Alp," one historian has written of this period, "but they were at home in Latin."[2] The works of Virgil and Horace, Ovid and Caesar, Lucretius and Cicero thus formed the main staple of the Augustan Age, and their language resonated with accents familiar to those who were conversant in the common culture of Europe. But suddenly at midcentury the writings of Homer, Herodotus, Xenophon, and most particularly those of Plato began to lose much of their forbidding, alpine aspect and together with the other major Greek writers they provided the principal inspiration for the ascent of Hellenism.

Naturally, this does not mean that Greek authors were not read until 1750, or that after that year Latin writers were promptly dropped. Alexander Pope's translation of Homer's *Iliad*, which appeared in six volumes between 1715 and 1720, as well as Christoph Martin Wieland's translation of Cicero's collected letters, which appeared between 1808 and 1812, are only two among innumerable examples demonstrating that such rigid boundaries did not exist or, at least, that they were by no means universally

2. Gilbert Highet, *The Classical Tradition: Greek and Roman Influences on Western Literature* (Oxford: Oxford University Press, 1949), 348.

respected. But as a general tendency and not as an absolute rule, it remains true that in the course of the mid-1700s, for England and especially for the German-speaking countries, Greece began to supplant Rome as the place where humanity was thought to have reached its highest conceivable stage of development. Well into the next century, when this displacement had already been largely completed, Shelley—one of the leading English graecophiles—asserted that "the human form and the human mind attained to a perfection in Greece which has impressed its image on those faultless productions, whose very fragments are the despair of modern art."[3] And it was this glorified vision of Greece and its art that had become the goal that Shelley and those of his generation strove to attain and, if possible, surpass.

This dramatic shift in the perception of Greece is perhaps most vividly demonstrated by the change of opinion regarding Plato that took place during the hundred-odd years in question here. With few, though certainly significant exceptions, the thinkers of the early eighteenth century displayed a remarkable and unrelenting hostility toward the philosophy of Plato. For many representatives of the Enlightenment, Plato's works were the epitome of the very type of imprecise, even mystical thinking that they most ardently opposed, whether they detected it in the venerable writings of the ancients or in the superstitious beliefs of their own benighted contemporaries. By his insistence that the source of truth was to be found in some transcendental realm far removed from physical reality, Plato represented the very antithesis to the scientific, empirically grounded principles upheld by those whose heroes were Newton and Locke. Lord Bolingbroke, who would come to exert such a powerful sway over the mind of Voltaire and who himself professed allegiance to Bacon and Newton, succinctly summed up the attitude of his time when he asserted that "Plato treated every subject, whether corporeal or intellectual, like a bombast poet and a mad theologian."[4]

The accusation that Plato's writings were obscure and pompous had become by Bolingbroke's day something of a commonplace. Samuel Parker, who was bishop of Oxford during the late seventeenth century, had already sounded this theme in a polemical work of 1666 that was aimed at his colleagues at Cambridge and disingenuously claimed to be a *Free and Impartial Censure of the Platonick Philosophie.* "*Plato* and his Followers," Parker wrote, "have communicated their Notions by Emblems, Fables, Symbols, Parables,

3. Percy Bysshe Shelley, "Preface to Hellas," in *The Complete Works*, ed. Roger Ingpen and Walter E. Peck (New York: Charles Scribner's Sons, 1926–30), 3:8.
4. Henry St. John Bolingbroke, *On the Practical Attempts that have been made to reform the Abuses of Human Reason*, in *Works* (London, 1809), 6:116. In a footnote to this sally, Bolingbroke cites as his source a passage from Bacon's *De Interpretatio Naturae*: "Tumidus poeta, theologus mente captus."

heaps of Metaphors, Allegories, and all sorts of Mysticall Representations (as is vulgarly known). All of which upon the account of their Obscurity and Ambiguity are apparently the unfittest signes in the world to expresse . . . Philosophical Notions and discoveries of the Natures of things."[5] To an age that was sensitive to the "abuse of words," as Locke had put it in his *Essay*, it was only natural that Plato's supposedly lax use of language was seen to reflect badly on the systematic quality of his thought, and other detractors were quick to point out this defect as well. In his *Dissertation on the Phaedon* of 1733, Charles Crawford (who, incidentally, took particularly outraged offense at Plato's homosexuality) also found the ancient Greek thinker wanting in the rigors of modern method. He declared in the hyperbole of self-righteous indignation that Plato was "the most wild and inconsistent author that ever wrote, who instead of a rational system of philosophy, raised by the observation of the phaenomena of Nature, constructed a fantastic hypothetical one of imagination, and corrupted the true springs of knowledge."[6] Plato deserved our sternest censure, in other words, because he had not bothered to read Newton.

Far more weighty, however, than the familiar assertions that Plato had indulged in poetic and thus imprecise language—although this reproach was certainly serious enough to the mind of the true *philosophe*—was Bolingbroke's charge that Plato had mixed theology with his metaphysics. There was, to be sure, nothing new in this claim by itself: as recently as the Renaissance in Italy, Marsilio Ficino and the other members of the Platonic Academy in Florence had viewed Plato (albeit positively) not just as a religious, but specifically as a proto-Christian, philosopher.[7] But in the Age of Reason, thinkers preferred their knowledge assembled into and reduced to discrete and definable classes; the confusion of categories they perceived in Plato's writings aroused their most severe misgivings. And among those thinkers especially who prided themselves on their own liberation from doctrinal authority, it certainly did not help to foster confidence in Plato that one of these categories had unmistakably religious roots.

No one stated these reservations more clearly, or with more plain distaste, than Voltaire. In his characteristically partisan and polemical *Philosophical Dictionary* of 1765, for instance, Voltaire concentrated his invective on the

---

5. Samuel Parker, *A Free and Impartial Censure of the Platonick Philosophie, Being a Letter Written to his much Honoured Friend Mr. Nath. Bisbie*, 2d ed. (Oxford: Oxford University Press, 1667), 71.
6. Cited from Timothy Webb, *English Romantic Hellenism, 1700–1824*, Literature in Context (Manchester: Manchester University Press, 1982), 61.
7. See D. P. Walker, *The Ancient Theology: Studies in Christian Platonism from the Fifteenth to the Eighteenth Century* (Ithaca: Cornell University Press, 1972), 10. Cf. also Paul Oskar Kristeller, *The Philosophy of Marsilio Ficino*, trans. Virginia Conant (New York: Columbia University Press, 1943).

fateful connection that had been forged between Platonism and Christianity. He began his entry on Plato by claiming that "the fathers of the church during the first four centuries were all Greeks and Platonists"; but, he wrote, as a salutary corrective "you find not one Roman who wrote for Christianity, or who had the slightest tincture of philosophy."[8] For Voltaire—whose favorite self-description was that of a "noble Roman" and whose love of Cicero in particular led him to effuse that the Roman orator had composed "the two most beautiful works that were ever written by mere human wisdom"[9]—for this self-proclaimed pagan the simple observation that no Roman favored Christian doctrine was already condemnation enough (18:181). But even if one disregarded the Christians' weakness for Plato, Voltaire thought that the Greek philosopher's works alone provided enough evidence to convince anyone of their lack of merit. Voltaire mused that the *Timaeus*, Plato's highly metaphysical and theological cosmography, was "almost the only one that Dacier has not translated, and I think the reason is because he did not understand it, and that he was afraid of exposing to clear-sighted readers the face of this Greek divinity, who is adored only because he is veiled" (20:224). Concluding an ironically incredulous account of the contents of *Timaeus*, Voltaire sighed with mock exasperation that "no philosopher in a madhouse [*petites-maisons*] has ever reasoned so powerfully" (20:227).

Voltaire always had a personal agenda, but in this case a majority of his compatriots shared his antipathy. Greek thought in general and the philosophy of Plato in particular seemed markedly uncongenial to almost all of the writers who represent the French Enlightenment.[10] It is true that in France, as in both England and Germany, admiration for Socrates remained largely unaffected by the predominant prejudice against Plato. Many *philosophes*, among them Diderot and d'Alembert, plainly enjoyed identifying with the Athenian gadfly, whom they frequently described as having been persecuted, like themselves, by mean-spirited and corrupt authorities for having dared to expose ignorance and speak the truth.[11] But others, such as d'Holbach, would not even give Socrates the benefit of the doubt and con-

8. See Voltaire, *Dictionnaire philosophique*, in *Oeuvres complètes*, ed. Louis Moland (Paris: Garnier Frères, 1877–85), 20:224.
9. Voltaire was specifically referring to the *Tusculan Disputations* and *The Nature of the Gods*.
10. On the resistance of French thinkers to Greek philosophy, and particularly to that of Plato, see Paul Shorey, *Platonism Ancient and Modern* (Berkeley and Los Angeles: University of California Press, 1938), especially 153–168; and on the almost completely Roman orientation of France throughout the last half of the century, see Harold T. Parker, *The Cult of Antiquity and the French Revolutionaries: A Study in the Development of the Revolutionary Spirit* (Chicago: University of Chicago Press, 1937), esp. 17–20.
11. On Diderot's identification with Socrates, see Jean Seznec, *Essais sur Diderot et l'antiquité* (Oxford: Oxford University Press, 1957), esp. the first chapter, "Le Socrate imaginaire," 1–22. See also Arthur M. Wilson, *Diderot* (New York: Oxford University Press, 1972), 446 and 476.

demned him along with the principal transmitters of his ideas. In words that remind us what purists the French *philosophes* could be when it came to questions concerning philosophical method, d'Holbach wrote that Socrates's "principles, as they have been presented to us by his disciples Xenophon and Plato, although adorned with the charm of poetic eloquence, offer to the mind nothing but confused concepts and poorly determined ideas, presented with the *élan* of a brilliant imagination, but hardly able to provide us with real instruction."[12] Likewise, Montesquieu, who characteristically approached the matter by considering its historical implications, also disliked not only Plato but all of ancient Greek thought. In the article on the Greeks in his *Pensées diverses*, he found that "the same error permeated the Greeks' entire philosophy," resulting in what he testily termed "bad physics, bad morality, bad metaphysics." The "error" the Greeks had consistently committed, Montesquieu wrote, arose from their habit of hypostatizing certain concepts into timeless and unchanging quantities without realizing the historical and even subjective variability of their terms. "Plato and Socrates deceived themselves with their beauty, their goodness, and their wisdom. . . . The terms the beautiful, the good, the noble, the perfect, are attributes of objects that are relative to the beings who think them. It is important to get this principle firmly in one's head."[13] The condescension Montesquieu clearly meant to convey with this last, curt line seems calculated as a final pronouncement on what by then had become a wearisome debate about the respective merits of the ancients and moderns. As far as Montesquieu was concerned, the moderns easily possessed the advantage in the sciences and all other purely intellectual endeavors. But he conceded that the ancients had displayed remarkable skill in poetry and the arts and that within this sphere, their accomplishments still deserved our notice and praise. Nevertheless, Montesquieu surely intended it as no compliment when he wrote on another occasion that Plato was one of the four greatest poets who ever lived (2:464).[14]

And yet despite the opposition of these and many other powerful antagonists, few other philosophers affected the thought of the later eighteenth century as much as Plato did. It is well known that Plato was Rousseau's favorite philosopher, and the presence of Plato's thought can indeed be felt throughout all of his writings.[15] But in this high regard for the Greek sage,

12. Paul Henri Thiry, baron d'Holbach, *La morale universelle ou les devoirs de l'homme fondés sur sa nature* (Amsterdam, 1776; reprint, Stuttgart: Friedrich Frommann Verlag; Bad Cannstatt: Günter Holzboog, 1970), 1:ii.

13. Charles de Secondat, baron de Montesquieu, *Oeuvres complètes* (Paris: Hachette, 1862), 2:457.

14. The other three, interestingly enough, were Montaigne, Malebranche, and Shaftesbury.

15. See, on the influence of Plato on Rousseau, Charles William Hendel, *Jean-Jacques Rousseau: Moralist* (Oxford: Oxford University Press, 1934).

Rousseau was hardly, as Peter Gay would have it, "a lonely voice in the Enlightenment."[16] As the eighteenth century entered its second half, Plato's works began, on the contrary, to command once more the sort of attention and admiration among the intellectual elite that they had not experienced since the Renaissance. And perhaps predictably, it was precisely those aspects of Plato's philosophy for which he had been criticized by the thinkers of earlier decades—now interpreted more sympathetically and applied to different ends—which also allowed his thought to undergo a genuine renascence of interest and appreciation. Instead of faulting him for using vague metaphors and inadequately defined terms, writers suddenly began to laud the subtlety and profundity of his style. Instead of reproaching him for mingling religious speculations with scientific thinking, these new supporters praised Plato for his recognition that human needs and hopes extended beyond the material realm. And most important, the weight Plato lent to moral behavior and to the elevated purpose of the individual life—which accorded to the human soul a dignity and worth fully equal to (and, some argued, even greater than) its status in Christian theology—this moral emphasis attracted with a virtually irresistible force those thinkers of the late eighteenth century who were searching for an ethical standard that did not necessarily reject, but could logically dispense with, theocentric morality.

The positive appropriation of Platonic thought had, of course, never disappeared altogether from the European intellectual tradition. The Cambridge Platonists, who had provoked the Reverend Parker's not very impartial censure, had been only the most recent examples of its vital and unbroken continuity. And the enormous success achieved by the works of Shaftesbury, the Cambridge reverends' most celebrated and accessible follower (and whom Johann Gottfried Herder once memorably called "the amiable Plato of Europe"),[17] created a context that permitted a rebirth of general interest in Plato. It was, for instance, no doubt partly due to Shaftesbury's tremendous influence on the Scottish school of philosophy that during the first half of the century Plato's thought did not meet with the sort of antagonism in Edinburgh that it still encountered in most other European capitals. We thus find all of the principal representatives of eighteenth-century Scottish thought, primarily Hutcheson, Adam Ferguson, Adam Smith, and Thomas Reid, referring frequently and approvingly to Plato. In his *Essay on Original Genius* of 1767, for example, a fellow Scotsman by the name of William Duff wrote that "of all the Philosophers of antiquity, Plato possessed the most copious and exuberant imagination,

16. Peter Gay, *The Enlightenment: An Interpretation* (New York: Alfred A. Knopf, 1966–69), 1:83. Gay goes on to admit, however, that despite the *philosophes*' ill treatment of Plato "the Enlightenment was permeated with Platonic ideas."

17. Johann Gottfried Herder, *Auch eine Philosophie der Geschichte zur Bildung der Menschheit*, in *Sämmtliche Werke*, ed. Bernhard Suphan (Berlin: Weidmann, 1877–1913), 5:490.

which, joined to a certain contemplative turn of mind, qualified him for the successful pursuit of philosophical studies." As became typical for the mid-century rehabilitation of Plato, Duff praised the Greek philosopher for possessing exactly those qualities which before had earned him nothing but repudiation and scorn. In fact, Duff even asserted that Plato's philosophy had an immediate benefit for the conduct of life by being "calculated to elevate and to expand the soul; to settle, to sooth, to refine the passions; and to warm the heart with the love of virtue."[18] And as we will discover, it was in this capacity, namely, in its reputed ability to "elevate" and "refine" the soul in the interest of promoting virtue, that Plato's thought had its greatest influence during the following decades.

But farther to the south, in England, where Plato was still received with more skeptical ambivalence and where the attraction of the practical sobriety represented by Roman models prevailed for much of the century, it took longer for the new enthusiasm for Plato and for the rest of Greek philosophy to take hold. "Plato is unfashionable," someone could still write in the March 1762 edition of the London *Monthly Review*. "The number of Platonic readers is now very inconsiderable."[19] One of the main reasons why there were so few "Platonic readers" in England was that unlike in Scotland and Ireland instruction in Greek at the schools and universities during the eighteenth century ranged from indifferent to nonexistent. Given this obvious lack of interest and motivation, it is not very surprising that no one bothered to render Plato's works into English until 1804, when Thomas Taylor, a somewhat eccentric autodidact who gave himself the epithet "the Platonist," finished the translation that Floyer Sydenham had begun a few decades earlier but never completed.[20] But it was just at this time, during the rise of English romanticism, that Plato finally fully entered the intellectual current, sweeping along William Wordsworth, Samuel Taylor Coleridge, William Blake, and Shelley himself.[21] Resistant at first to the attractions of Greece, England remained all the more captivated by its spell for the next one hundred years.

18. William Duff, *An Essay on Original Genius and Its Various Modes of Exertion in Philosophy and the Fine Arts, Particularly in Poetry* (London, 1767; ed. John L. Mahoney, Gainesville, Fla.: Scholars' Facsimiles & Reprints, 1964), 104–5.
19. Cited from M. L. Clarke, *Greek Studies in England, 1700–1830* (Cambridge: Cambridge University Press, 1945), 112.
20. Ibid., 117. For a short but informative characterization of Taylor, see the introduction to Thomas Taylor, *Selected Writings*, ed. Kathleen Raine and George Mills Harper (Princeton: Princeton University Press, 1969).
21. On the development of Plato studies in England during the nineteenth century, see Frank M. Turner, *The Greek Heritage in Victorian Britain* (New Haven: Yale University Press, 1981), esp. the last chapter, "The Victorian Platonic Revival," 369–446. There are also useful insights in the article by the same author, "Why the Greeks and not the Romans in Victorian Britain?" in *Rediscovering Hellenism: The Hellenic Inheritance and the English Imagination*, ed. G. W. Clarke (Cambridge: Cambridge University Press, 1989), 61–81. For a representative romantic opinion of Plato, see Percy Bysshe Shelley, "On the Symposium, or Preface to the Banquet of Plato. A Fragment," in *Complete Works*, 7:161.

Yet for Germany the revival of Hellenism, and especially the accompanying reappraisal of Platonic and Neoplatonic philosophy, seemed to acquire an even greater significance than it had for any other part of Europe.[22] Indeed, it coincides and in many ways is synonymous with that most brilliant period of modern German culture which we identify as Weimar Classicism.[23] Considering the tremendous importance that these later thinkers and artists invested in the ideal of Greece, the signs in Germany, too, were initially anything but auspicious. The most widely read book of poetics to issue from Germany during the eighteenth century—the much maligned but furtively consulted *Versuch einer Critischen Dichtkunst*, which the Leipzig professor Johann Christoph Gottsched first published in 1730—contained almost no Greek examples; the majority of the sources were in either Latin or French. In 1733 Greek literature was still totally absent from the curriculum at Gottsched's university, and a newly matriculated student by the name of Johann Jakob Reiske, who was later to become one of the most distinguished orientalists of his day, decided to study Arabic because he could find no one to help him learn the language of Homer.[24]

But within the next fifty years this situation underwent a complete reversal, with late-eighteenth-century German-speaking poets and philosophers making Greece the primary focus of their collective cultural aspirations. Throughout the rest of the century and for much of the next, Greece served, in effect, as both a catalyst and a substitute in the German search for self-definition. And in striving to form themselves according to their image of Greece—which necessarily consisted of genuine historical knowledge, fanciful projection, and sheer, empty conjecture—these German writers and artists produced a body of work that is extraordinary in its diversity and power, but also, as we will see, in the overwhelming sense of alienation it both explicitly and indirectly conveys. The Pietistic habit of mind, which emphasized the incorporation of an external model in the process of self-renewal, helped them to focus on the plaster copies of ancient statues and

22. There is an astonishing and desperate lack of studies on the rise of Platonism in Germany in the eighteenth century; one of the very few is the brief but informative essay by Max Wundt, "Die Wiederentdeckung Platons im 18. Jahrhundert," *Blätter für deutsche Philosophie* 15 (1941): 149–58.

23. One of the most informative and balanced accounts of the German infatuation with Greece is by Henry Hatfield's *Aesthetic Paganism in German Literature: From Winckelmann to the Death of Goethe* (Cambridge: Harvard University Press, 1964). Equally objective, though brief, is the article by Manfred Fuhrmann, "Die *Querelle des Anciens et des Modernes*, der Nationalismus und die deutsche Klassik," in *Classical Influences on Western Thought, A.D. 1650–1870: Proceedings of an International Conference Held at King's College, Cambridge, March 1977*, ed. R. R. Bolgar (Cambridge: Cambridge University Press, 1979), 107–29.

24. See Humphrey Trevelyan, *Goethe and the Greeks* (Cambridge: Cambridge University Press, 1941), 3. For information on Reiske, see Conrad Bursian, *Geschichte der classischen Philologie in Deutschland von den Anfängen bis zur Gegenwart* (Munich: R. Oldenbourg, 1883), 1:407–16.

the few texts that survived (which were all that most Germans ever experienced of Greece) as the revered icons of yet another, secular conversion. Late-eighteenth-century Germans also wished to undergo a radical "rebirth," but they wanted to be reborn as Greeks.

Although it is impossible to attribute this change to any single person or cause, surely the most passionate and persuasive spokesman for the new perception of Greece was Johann Joachim Winckelmann. It would be difficult to exaggerate Winckelmann's influence on the German understanding of Greece, and it is a force that filtered though it is, still makes itself felt even today. It is almost equally difficult to imagine the enormity of the personal and institutional obstacles he was obliged to overcome in order to achieve that influence. Like the Englishman Thomas Taylor, Winckelmann was of necessity virtually self-taught in Greek, and since he lacked reliable or even available texts, he frequently had to work with anthologies or excerpts he had copied out himself.[25] But despite these impediments, he soon acquired enough Greek to read all of the works of Homer, Sophocles, Herodotus, and, most particularly, the dialogues of Plato.[26] Although scholars continue to debate about the actual degree to which Winckelmann was influenced by Plato, there is no denying that Plato's thought and even his rhapsodic prose style pervade all of Winckelmann's published works.[27]

But Winckelmann was not so much the cause as he was the most visible symptom of a larger cultural transformation. Had he been completely alone in his new appreciation of Plato and Greek culture, or had he not had a receptive audience, his works obviously would never have achieved the overwhelming success they did. The greater reasons for the turn away from Rome and toward Greece during the middle of the eighteenth century—for which, as we have just seen, the perception of Plato played a pivotal role—are as various as they are necessary for an adequate understanding of the period. At about the middle of the eighteenth century, historical studies were attracting renewed interest in the wake of the works of Montesquieu, Voltaire, and Hume. These writers represented what has been called a new school of "philosophic history" that was characterized by the desire to trace

25. See the informative account in Barbara Maria Stafford, "Beauty of the Invisible: Winckelmann and the Aesthetics of Imperceptibility," *Zeitschrift für Kunstgeschichte* 43 (1980): 65–78.
26. See Rudolf Pfeiffer, *History of Classical Scholarship from 1300 to 1850* (Oxford: Oxford University Press, 1976), 167. On Winckelmann's favorite Greek authors, see Carl Justi, *Winckelmann und seine Zeitgenossen*, 2d rev. ed. (Leipzig: F.C.W. Vogel, 1898), 1:139–51.
27. Ernst Cassirer, *Freiheit und Form: Studien zur deutschen Geistesgeschichte* (Darmstadt: Wissenschaftliche Buchgesellschaft, 1975), 127–39, argues for a decisive Platonic influence on Winckelmann. In an article by Christine Mitchell Havelock, "Plato and Winckelmann: Ideological Bias in the History of Greek Art," *Source* 5 (1986): 5, we read the similar claim that "Winckelmann's new and most original contribution to the history of Greek art was the imposition of Platonic theory upon its development."

the development of humanity as a whole.[28] Instead of tirelessly collating endless data about wars and the reigns of forgotten monarchs, the new philosophical historians wished to lay bare the real but hidden causes of human behavior and development. In its first manifestations, enthusiasm for Greece also stemmed primarily, and fairly innocuously, from this same historical desire to uncover what were thought to be the "original" and, hence, "true" sources of Roman and thus European civilization. "The Greeks were the teachers of the Romans," Diderot once observed, "the Greeks and Romans have been ours."[29] To pass beyond Rome to Greece thus meant, for the earliest advocates of Hellenism, a return to the origins of culture itself.

Historians and philosophers of the eighteenth century were peculiarly fascinated by origins, for reasons that were what one might be tempted to call romantic as well as philosophical. The connotations of freshness, vitality, simplicity, and uncorrupted purity they associated with the concept of origins proved irresistible to an age that was notoriously impatient with what it felt were its own decrepit and oppressive institutions. But another, and more important, element of the appeal that origins exercised over the minds of eighteenth-century writers can be found in an eminently rational source. To seek the origins of any idea or thing implied a rigorous adherence to the analytic, which is to say the only reliably "scientific," method of inquiry. The analytical procedure, in the contemporary understanding of the term, sought to explain every phenomenon by isolating all of its constituent elements until one reached some irreducible, or "original," core, thereby producing a secure basis on which one could then build further knowledge. For the historian of the mid-eighteenth century, who perceived such a fundamental significance in origins, to investigate Greece thus meant no less than to perform the first essential step in what they felt must be an accurate or "analytical" history of the Western world. The same impulse that had revolutionized the study of morality and held out for the first time the possibility of defining human virtue in the absence of divine injunctions—namely, the attempt to apply "scientific" principles of observation and evaluation to the study of psychological and social phenomena—thus led to a similar revolution in the understanding of the past. Yet besides being identical in their methodological impetus, the revitalization in both ethics and history turn out to be even more closely related. For the return to Greece, in addition to

28. On the tenor of the new style of philosophic history that arose at the middle of the century, see the essay by Arnaldo Momigliano, "Gibbon's Contribution to Historical Method," in *Studies in Historiography* (New York: Harper & Row, 1966), esp. 42–43.
29. Denis Diderot, *Plan d'une université pour le gouvernement de Russie*, in *Oeuvres complètes*, eds. Jules Assézat and Maurice Tourneux (Paris: Garnier Frères, 1875–77), 3:477. Cited from Gay, *Enlightenment*, 1:94.

satisfying mere curiosity about the supposed beginnings of civilization, was also driven by the desire to discover in the past a moral model that could be used to address the issue of how to live in the present.

The German "rediscovery" of Greek culture and art during the 1750s arose in part from this impulse to search for the origins of social institutions with the hope that these beginnings might shed some light on their current condition. In his epoch-making essay, "Gedancken über die Nachahmung der Griechischen Wercke in der Mahlerey und Bildhauer-Kunst" (Thoughts on the imitation of Greek works in painting and sculpture) of 1755, Winckelmann accordingly emphasized above all else the Greeks' originality—or perhaps more accurately, their historical primacy—when he wrote the now-famous introductory words: "Good taste, which is spreading into ever more corners of the world, first began to form under the Greek heavens." Throughout the first paragraphs of his essay, Winckelmann's main object was thus to persuade his readers that the Greeks should command our interest and respect not only because they had discovered and perfected the representation of beauty, but also—or more important, precisely because—they were the first to have done so. The Greeks' generative power was in fact so great, Winckelmann asserted, that even the "inventions of foreign peoples made their way to Greece, so to speak, only as first seeds and assumed a different nature and shape." In a studied and spiteful allusion to the Roman poet Virgil, Winckelmann finally proclaimed that the "purest sources of art are opened: happy is he who finds and enjoys them. To seek these sources means to travel to Athens."[30]

Yet as the century came to a close, a new tone began to make itself heard in German descriptions of Greece. Whereas the predominantly antiquarian, historical interest in the Greek contribution to the development of modern society prevailed during the first phase of the German involvement with Greek culture, this relative degree of intellectual detachment soon gave way to a more subjective response to the fact of its irretrievable loss. In a way, this sense of melancholy which arose from contemplating the faded and distant glory of Greece can be seen as a logical consequence of those very historical researches. As German scholars and poets accumulated ever more knowledge about the past grandeur of Greece, and as the image of its history became fuller and more richly detailed, the inescapable realization of its disappearance seemed to make it recede even farther into the unattainable distance of historical time. Schiller's elegiac poem "Die Götter Griechen-

30. See Johann Joachim Winckelmann, "Gedancken über die Nachahmung der Griechischen Wercke in der Mahlerey und Bildhauer-Kunst," in *Kleine Schriften. Vorreden. Entwürfe*, ed. Walther Rehm (Berlin: Walter de Gruyter, 1968), 29. Winckelmann was possibly alluding to the famous line in Virgil: "Felix qui potuit rerum cognoscere causas" (*Georgics*, 2.1.490).

lands" (The gods of Greece) of 1788 was one of the first, and certainly one of the most affecting, expressions of this new sentiment in Germany.

> Schöne Welt, wo bist du? Kehre wieder,
> Holdes Blütenalter der Natur!
> Ach, nur in dem Feenland der Lieder
> Lebt noch deine fabelhafte Spur.
> Ausgestorben trauert das Gefilde,
> Keine Gottheit zeigt sich meinem Blick,
> Ach, von jenem lebenwarmen Bilde
> Blieb der Schatten nur zurück.[31]

[Beautiful world, where are you? Return, cherished blossom-age of nature! Alas, your legendary trace lives on only in the fairy land of songs. The field mourns, its life extinguished, no divinity shows itself to my gaze; alas, only the shadow remains of that life-warm image.]

Yet, although Schiller clearly mourned the passing of the Greek world, he gathered some consolation from the thought that it had found some refuge from total oblivion in the extant works of art that commemorate its former splendor. In a poem written five years later by Hölderlin, however, one notices a remarkable shift and intensification of feeling. In his work—simply titled "Griechenland"—Hölderlin also lamented the death of the Greek gods. But unlike Schiller, who always remained mindful of his commitment to the present, Hölderlin abandoned himself much more fully to the enchantment of identifying with an idealized version of the vanished land. In his poem he spoke, for instance, of "my Plato" (in the similarly intimate terms that Goethe's Werther had used to refer to "my Homer") as someone who had created "paradises." And it was precisely the overbearing intensity of Hölderlin's identification with the projected ideal world of Greece and of his yearning to be redeemed by its perfection that caused him to grasp at the only means he possessed to commune with this dead and distant past. Since it was obvious that the inhabitants of Schiller's "beautiful world" were never going to return, Hölderlin presented his poetic persona as being seized by the desire to join them in their eternal slumber:

> Attika, die Heldin, ist gefallen;
> Wo die alten Göttersöhne ruhn,
> Im Ruin der schönen Marmorhallen
> Steht der Kranich einsam trauernd nun;

31. Friedrich Schiller, "Die Götter Griechenlands," in *Sämtliche Werke*, ed. Gerhard Fricke and Herbert G. Göpfert (Munich: Carl Hanser, 1958–59), 1:172.

Lächelnd kehrt der holde Frühling nieder,
Doch er findet seine Brüder nie
In Ilissus heilgem Thale wieder—
Unter Schutt und Dornen schlummern sie.

Mich verlangt ins ferne Land hinüber
Nach Alcäus und Anakreon,
Und schlief' im engen Hause lieber,
Bei den Heiligen in Marathon;
Ach! es sei die lezte meiner Thränen,
Die dem lieben Griechenlande rann,
Laßt, o Parzen, laßt die Scheere tönen,
Denn mein Herz gehört den Todten an![32]

[Attica, the Heroine, has fallen; where the old sons of the Gods lie in peace, in the ruins of the beautiful marble halls, the crane now stands alone and mourns; smiling, the cherished Spring returns below, but he never finds his brothers in the holy vale of Ilissus—they slumber under rubble and thorns.

I long for the distant land, for Alcaeus and Anacreon, and I would rather sleep in the narrow house [i.e. the grave], with the holy ones in Marathon; alas! let this be the last of my tears I've shed for dear Greece; let, oh Fates, let the shears clash, for my heart belongs to the Dead!]

Although Hölderlin represents German "graecomania" at its most morbid extreme, his works nevertheless—or rather, for that very reason—provide moving testimony of the degree to which the idea of Greece had taken hold of the German imagination by the turn of the century.

As it came to occupy this psychologically important position, Greek culture, or the image of timeless perfection it increasingly came to represent, was progressively portrayed as transcending the historical fate that otherwise irrevocably determined every other people. In a peculiar reversal, the very historical impetus that first ignited interest in Greece literally disengaged itself at the height of German preoccupation with Hellenic culture. Sensing, perhaps, that scrupulous fidelity to the available historical facts would finally remove the Greeks forever to the realm of an unattainable and unrepeatable past, they simply exempted Greece from the laws of history. Just at the moment, that is, when some sort of accurate, informed understanding of the Greeks was actually becoming possible again for the first time since

32. Friedrich Hölderlin, "Griechenland. An St.," in *Sämtliche Werke,* ed. Friedrich Beissner and Adolf Beck (Stuttgart: J. G. Cottasche Buchhandlung, 1946–85), 1:180.

antiquity, the Germans refused to lift the mythical veil. Instead, they created the Greeks after their own image while pretending, or perhaps truly believing, that they were doing just the opposite.

One can observe this peculiar mechanism at work in an essay by Wilhelm von Humboldt, one of the most fervent, yet also well-informed, graecophiles of the period. In his "Geschichte des Verfalls und Unterganges der griechischen Freistaaten" (History of the decline and fall of the Greek free states), which he wrote in 1807 but never published, Humboldt announced categorically that one did not study Greek history in the same way that one studied the past of other peoples, for "the Greeks step entirely out of the circle of history." Indeed, Humboldt went on to write with perfect confidence, "only in them do we find the ideal of that which we ourselves would like to be and to bring forth. If every other part of history enriches us with human intelligence and human experience, then we derive from the contemplation of the Greeks something that is more than earthly—indeed, something almost divine."[33] Humboldt's deliberate, even defiant, ahistoricism was typical of German thinking at the turn of the century. We see it in representative form in one of Goethe's conversations with Eckermann in 1827, in which the poet similarly stated this belief not only in the historical singularity of the Greeks, but in the uniquely eternal nature of their cultural accomplishments as well: "However much we value foreign literatures," he averred,

> we must not cling to one in particular and try to take that one as our model. We must not think the Chinese, or the Serbian, or Calderon, or the Nibelungen can be that. If we are in need of a model, we must always go back to the ancient Greeks, in whose works the object of representation is always beautiful humanity [der schöne Mensch]. Everything else we must look at from a purely historical standpoint, and take in what is good in it as far as may be."[34]

The Greek myth had by then become so powerful that Goethe appears not to have even noticed the contradiction in his words. He actually seems to have thought, or was driven by a half-conscious need to believe, that unlike other peoples, the Greeks and their achievements escaped the bonds of historical time and, almost in the manner of Platonic Forms, that they alone existed in a sphere removed from finitude and decay.

Most historians have assumed that Winckelmann's often repeated exhortation—that "the only way for us to become great, indeed, if it is possible, to become inimitable, is to imitate the ancients"—was meant to

33. Wilhelm von Humboldt, "Geschichte des Verfalls und Unterganges der griechischen Freistaaten," in Gesammelte Schriften, ed. Albert Leitzmann (Berlin: B. Behr, 1903–18), 3:188.
34. From a conversation on 31 January 1827; cited from Trevelyan, Goethe and the Greeks, 270.

apply to the imitation of art works alone.[35] Even if Winckelmann had in fact been thinking exclusively of art, the German writers who came after him in fact understood his words in a much broader, although very specific, sense. What Winckelmann intended, or at any rate was taken to mean, was that his fellow Germans should imitate the Greeks not just in creating works of art, but in everything else they did. At first, to be sure, a much more realistic and detached sentiment prevailed in the German appreciation of Greece, an attitude one finds, for example, in Herder's *Ueber die neuere Deutsche Litteratur* of 1767. "Of course we can learn much from the Greeks," he cautiously advised as he witnessed the first wave of Winckelmannian enthusiasm wash over Germany, "of course we can take them as models; but let us make imitations that are appropriate to our time: otherwise everything will become a caricature!"[36] But in later decades, German writers and artists came to believe that it was possible not just to create imitations of "Greek" works of art, but to become in every way like the Greeks themselves—or at least like the unhistorical and idealized image they had selectively constructed of the Attic character. But this practice did not of course run counter to Winckelmann's intentions. In their efforts to recreate themselves according to their notion of Greek humanity, late-eighteenth-century German intellectuals actually heeded the deepest meaning of his call by beginning to regard and treat themselves, in effect, as living works of art. As if to improve on Pope's well-known phrase, Goethe had claimed that the proper aim of the Greeks had been not merely to study "Man," but to create and portray "beautiful humanity." To take the Greeks as a model thus meant not just to imitate their works of art but to internalize what were thought to be their essential attributes. The German attempt to revivify Greece entailed at its core the endeavor to become, as they ardently believed the Greeks to have been, "beautiful human beings."

Residing at the center of this extraordinary development in late-eighteenth-century German culture there was a particular concept—or rather a constellation of concepts that went by a single name—defining the highest human aspirations. And it was an idea that rested on explicitly aesthetic foundations. But the Greek revival took root in soil that had been prepared by the other philosophical, religious, and political forces that we have already witnessed here. Having been given official sanction through the auspices of the newly reorganized academy in Berlin, British moral philosophy and especially its insistence on the "beauty of virtue" had begun to find an interested and sympathetic German audience by the 1760s at the latest. There was also a more native receptivity, since most intellectuals in German-

35. Winckelmann, "Gedancken über die Nachahmung," in *Kleine Schriften*, 29.
36. Johann Gottfried Herder, *Ueber die neuere Deutsche Litteratur. Fragmente*, in *Sämmtliche Werke*, 1:306.

speaking lands had been raised in Pietist households. Many of them had early grown accustomed to thinking of morality not only in terms of a complete inner transformation but moreover as a process in which one makes the soul more beautiful in the eyes of God. By the middle decade of the eighteenth century in Germany, an idea of beauty that went beyond the sphere of art alone had thus assumed a place in the very center of the collective imagination. No longer merely the means of making one's external environment more pleasant or merely bearable, beauty was becoming the measure by which the ultimate aim of humanity itself was judged. The new contribution to this larger equation, the specifically Greek element in this eclectic mixture, was the peculiar Hellenic concept of *kalokagathia*.

The urge to uncover the historical substratum of modern culture, which had provided one of the original motives for the eighteenth-century interest in Greece, had also been operative at the first moment in which this word occurred in the Enlightenment context. Berkeley, we remember, notes in his *Alciphron* that the earl of Shaftesbury's ideas owed more than he admitted to this concept. The Irish dean was thus the first to establish the historical connection between contemporary ethics and ancient philosophy which would become explicit several decades later. The word and its implications appear to have first entered German thought at a conscious level in 1758 by way of a short and early work by Wieland, "Plan einer Akademie zu Bildung des Verstandes und des Herzens junger Leute" (Plan for an academy for the cultivation of the heart and mind of young people). Although the general focus of Wieland's essay on pedagogical issues was fairly typical of its time, his particular perspective on the problem was, as we will see, entirely new.

It already amounted to a significant innovation that Wieland derived the authority for his educational reform not simply from the writers of antiquity (which had usually meant, as we know, the Romans) but specifically and primarily from the Greeks. Wieland claimed that "their entire method of education and instruction was very different from our modern ways," and it becomes clear that he considered these "modern ways" in every way inferior to the practices of the ancient Greeks.[37] Instead of forcing their pupils to fill their minds with grammar and empty words, the Greeks trained their youth, Wieland explained, to exercise and develop all of their physical and mental abilities, for the Greeks believed that we come into this world, so to speak, as "embryos" that must first be formed (*ausgebildet*) into human beings. Without this necessary discipline, the Greeks felt that both body and soul would remain weak and indolent and that the whole organism would lack the coordination, agility, and strength (again, in both the physical and moral

37. Christoph Martin Wieland, "Plan einer Akademie zu Bildung des Verstandes und des Herzens junger Leute," in *Gesammelte Schriften*, ed. Deutsche Kommission der Königlich Preußischen Akademie der Wissenschaften (Berlin: Weidmann, 1909–), 4:183.

senses) to achieve happiness and success in life. Central to the Greeks' educational efforts, Wieland concluded, was the attempt to produce young men (women were not part of their plan) who embodied this latter ideal:

> The goal, therefore, of their education was to form or cultivate [*bilden*] their young citizens into that which they termed *kalokagathia*. By this word they understood all of the excellences and perfections that distinguish a free and noble human being from a slave and from a human-like animal; it encompassed all of the qualities and talents that elevate and beautify a person and make one fit to fulfill a noble role in life. To this end, which alone is worthy of human nature, they inculcated in their youth as early as possible a taste for the beautiful and the good, along with the best moral and political notions. (4:185)

Here Wieland presented the essential ingredients of his pedagogical plan with the clarity and simplicity that later became recognized as the distinctive hallmarks of his style. Influenced as much (and arguably more) by Shaftesbury and Hutcheson as by Plato and Xenophon, Wieland freely combined concepts he had borrowed from a variety of modern and ancient sources. Conspicuous throughout the essay, for example, is Wieland's insistence on the practical emphasis of Greek philosophy and his repeated contention that education and moral instruction could not be separated. Rather than indulge in "clever speculations," the Greeks, Wieland claimed, "wanted to raise virtuous citizens for the state, they saw philosophy as a discipline for the soul [*Gemüt*], which is necessary for every person, because everyone has ideas that he must learn to enlighten, inclinations to guide to the best final purpose and to their proper objects, emotions to control, faults to correct, and virtues to enhance" (4:185). Although this sounds more like a description of the eighteenth-century estimation of the function performed by philosophy, that was partly Wieland's point. He approached Greek thought—or what he took to be Greek thought—with the same practical attitude he had praised in it. For he did not suggest that the pupils of his academy study the Greeks with the sole aim of acquiring knowledge about the past for its own sake. Rather, they should apply the lessons they learned from the Greeks to their *own* lives, with the immediate purpose of improving their moral, and not simply their intellectual, constitution.

As the full title of the "Plan einer Akademie" clearly states, Wieland thought that the moral betterment he proposed would require cultivation of both the "understanding" and the "heart." He held that it was necessary to appeal to the emotional as well as the rational faculties of those one wanted to improve. The most expedient and important instrument in fulfilling this twofold demand, and one that he thought suffered from scandalous neglect in the Germany of his time, was the art of speaking and writing well. "Plato," Wieland exclaimed, "was called the Homer of philosophers because of his sublime eloquence" (4:187). Wieland considered language unique because it was the only vehicle for communicating the ideas that could be grasped by the rational mind alone; yet it could also be crafted into beautiful forms and hence appeal to the sentiment as well. And it is here that Wieland most obviously drew on the contemporary theoretical resources that had grown up around the concept of moral beauty. Making this connection explicit by mentioning Shaftesbury by name, Wieland continued his discussion of Greek education by stressing the importance of taste not just in judging works of art, but also in making the practical decisions of everyday existence. "They well knew," he said of the Greeks,

> how closely good taste—this lively and delicate ability to perceive the True, Harmonious, or Beautiful by a kind of feeling and inner sense—how closely this faculty was related to sound reason, to the regularity of the soul, and to the politeness of manners; and how it is practically impossible to possess the latter qualities, as much as they belong to humanity, without the former. They thus required of a noble and well-bred boy that he be *kalos kai agathos*, a Virtuoso, as the most brilliant and finest of all modern writers, Shaftesbury, expresses it. (4:188)

Instruction in all of the arts and sciences, then, with constant reference to their practical consequence and use, was supposed to establish an equilibrium in the breast of the pupil, a balance of mind and heart, of reason and feeling, that would be pleasant to behold and beneficial in its effect. Such a person would be, that is, both beautiful and good—or would embody, in a word, what the Greeks had called *kalokagathia*.

As interesting as Wieland's essay is on its own merits, it might well have escaped later notice had not Gotthold Ephraim Lessing, who was then rapidly becoming one of the most formidable and feared critics of his day, subjected Wieland's views to a vigorous, though somewhat misguided, attack. In a review that he wrote in January 1759 for the *Briefe, die neueste Literatur betreffend* (Letters concerning the most recent literature), Lessing critically examined the conclusions Wieland had reached about the methods and aims of ancient education. Demonstrating the sort of polemical passion in treating questions of esoteric scholarship that he would later use to such great effect in his *Laokoon* of 1766, Lessing rudely chided Wieland for his ostensible lapses in historical fidelity to the sources. Above all, he objected that Wieland had made an inadmissibly generous, as well as highly anachronistic, definition of *kalokagathia*. In the tenth letter of the *Literaturbriefe*, Lessing sarcastically claimed that he "would be very eager to learn

from him of a single piece of evidence that this *kalos kagathos* meant anything other than what we call a 'handsome good man.' "38

Yet Lessing himself was also driven by more than merely antiquarian
interests, and his criticism of Wieland rested partially on his own different
philosophical allegiances. A lifelong adherent of the Leibniz-Wolffian
school of thought, Lessing espoused a much more rationalistic view of how
virtue and wisdom ought to be attained: "The great secret of making the
human soul perfect through practice . . . consists solely in maintaining the
constant effort of reaching the truth through one's own reflection" (8:24).
But Lessing was even more vehement in rejecting Wieland's equation of the
term *kalos kagathos* with Shaftesbury's notion of the "Virtuoso." Obviously
sensing the same threat to Christianity that Shaftesbury's compatriots had
also detected in his essays, Lessing gladly acknowledged the Englishman's
philosophical talent, only to wrap his praise in a cloak of condemnation.
Accusing Wieland of having protested his own adherence to the Christian
faith too much (in a nasty aside, Lessing remarked that "people often boast
about things they don't even have so that they will at least *seem* to have
them"), Lessing found Wieland's frequent citation of the English lord itself
a damning presence: "Shaftesbury is the most dangerous enemy of religion
because he is the finest. And may he otherwise have as many good qualities
as anyone could wish, Jupiter disdained the rose in the mouth of the serpent" (8:26–27).39

Several years later, in 1767, Herder took up the threads of this disagreement, but he sought to take a more conciliatory route by approaching it in a
different, yet—for him—entirely characteristic, way: by inquiring into the
history of the disputed word itself. In a section of his *Fragmente* titled "Von
der Griechischen Litteratur in Deutschland" (On Greek literature in Germany), he referred to Lessing's quarrel with Wieland and he wondered if
both had not made the same error of failing to realize the historical contingency of the term and that its meaning, even during antiquity, had never
been permanently fixed or even stable. Herder stated categorically that not
only in Greek, but "in every language all of the words that express the actual
character of the age are subject to change, and, it seems to me, this is
precisely the case with *kalos kagathos*."40 He correctly noted that the term

---

38. Gotthold Ephraim Lessing, *Briefe, die neueste Literatur betreffend*, in *Sämtliche Schriften*, ed.
Karl Lachmann and Franz Muncker (Stuttgart: G. J. Göschen; Berlin: Walter de Gruyter,
1886–1924), 8:22.
39. Lessing's words are strongly—and in view of his erudition undoubtedly deliberately—
reminiscent of Robert Bellarmine's comment in the sixteenth century that of all the pagan
thinkers Plato was the closest to Christianity, and for that very reason he was the most
dangerous to the faith. See James Hankins, *Plato in the Italian Renaissance* (Leiden: E. J. Brill,
1990), 1:13.
40. Herder, *Ueber die neuere Deutsche Litteratur*, in *Sämmtliche Werke*, 1:303.

does not occur in the oldest Greek writings, but that it is a "word from the age of beautiful prose and of fine political manners." In fact, as Herder likewise accurately observed, it did not appear until the fifth century in Athens, and "the Athenians, who strove to attain this political culture, had it (*kalos kagathos*) constantly on their tongues; and it was to them, as a scholastic writer would say, 'summa omnis laudationis!' And it thus certainly necessarily entailed more than our notion of an attractive good man" (1:304). Lessing had thus unquestionably delimited the meaning of the term far too severely. But Herder's sense of historical propriety also prevented him from accepting Wieland's facile equation of the Athenian *kalos kagathos* with Shaftesbury's "virtuoso." "Even if there once was an age in Athens when connoisseurship in the arts, a taste for poetry and 'belles lettres,' a fine tone in society, and a critical spirit in policy and antiquities were the ruling fashion, I can never convince myself that the *kaloi kagathoi*, in Shaftesbury's broad understanding of the word, flourished at that time." The only way to discover its original meaning, Herder thought, would be to undertake a full comparative historical study of the concept and its implications.

"But," he rhetorically asked, "why make so much fuss about a word?" For Herder, who was then already laying down the conceptual foundations that would inform his *Abhandlung über den Ursprung der Sprache* (Treatise on the origin of language) of 1770, much more depended on the attempt to define this word than simply the satisfaction of philological curiosity. Like so many other Enlightenment philosophers, Herder had become convinced that language and thought were necessarily and inseparably connected, that knowledge about the linguistic workings of the mind was indispensible to understanding human culture as a whole. "One can never say too much about a word," he thus insisted, and especially about one "that had always been the expression of their character and the epitome of their laudations. The explanation of such words unlocks for us the way they thought and governed themselves, their attitudes and morals, in short the secret of their nationality, without which we always judge a people poorly, learn about them poorly, and imitate them even worse" (1:306). The admonitory tone here hints at, and thus cautions against, the fateful attraction that this "word"— which the Greeks had used to describe the most perfect and meritorious manifestation of humanity—would come to exert on the minds of his compatriots. Yet neither Herder nor any of his contemporaries ever provided the comprehensive historical analysis he had urged, even though he never forgot or forsook the Greek concept itself.[41] It seems appropriate, then, to undertake what Herder advised long ago and to inquire into the peculiar

41. Herder briefly returned to the idea of *kalokagathia* in 1795, toward the end of his career, in the fifth collection of his *Briefe zu Beförderung der Humanität*, in *Sämmtliche Werke*, 17:376–79.

meaning and social significance of the phrase *kalos kagathos*, which Werner Jaeger, in his *Paideia*, called "the highest cultural ideal of the classical period of Greece."[42] We might then be in a better position to appreciate the meaning of its revival more than two thousand years later during the "classical period" of Germany.

To modern observers it has often appeared profoundly expressive of the Hellenic character that the notion of the "beautiful-and-good" assumed the preeminent position it did in the culture of ancient Greece. For a people so obviously and willingly beguiled by beauty in all of its forms that the very idea of beauty acquired the status of a highest good, it appeared perfectly consistent to transfer, by analogy, the value they attached to beauty to everything else they admired and prized. In addition to the more conventional uses of the word, in which only the external appearances of natural phenomena are described as being "beautiful," one encounters numerous examples throughout Greek literature in which objects that perform their designated function in an exemplary way, or actions that give rise to some desirable or beneficial result, are called *kalos*. One reads, for instance, about shields that are "beautiful for defence" and javelins that are "beautiful for swift and powerful hurling."[43] But by combining the idea of *kalos* with the notion of *agathos*, or what more straightforwardly means "good," the Greeks obviously wanted to express an idea that they felt could not be communicated by either term alone. Even in purely lexical terms *kalokagathia* presents a peculiar, in fact singular, case in the Greek language. It is unique in being a substantive made up of two adjectives joined by a simple conjunction.[44] Yet as an abstract compound noun *kalokagathia* clearly constituted for the Greeks an independent conceptual unity—or, one might object, literally a linguistic "confusion" of two properly distinct spheres—and they used it to express their notion of what was most excellent, admirable, and worthy of emulation in the character of a human being. It is perhaps no less telling of their national character that the Greeks themselves seemed somewhat trou-

42. Werner Jaeger, *Paideia: The Ideals of Greek Culture*, trans. Gilbert Highet (New York: Oxford University Press, 1939–44), 2:412.
43. See Xenophon, *Memorabilia and Oeconomicus*, Loeb Classical Library (1923), 3.8.4–5. The *Memorabilia* and the *Oeconomicus* are henceforth cited parenthetically in the text. See also the discussion of the difficulties in translating the Greek *to kalon* into English and its range of application in W.K.C. Guthrie, *A History of Greek Philosophy* (Cambridge: Cambridge University Press, 1962–81), 4:177–78. In the book by Kenneth James Dover, *Greek Popular Morality in the Time of Plato and Aristotle* (Oxford: Basil Blackwell, 1974), 41–45 and 69–73, there is a full account of the various meanings attached to the word *kalos* and to its antonym *aiskhros*, or "ugly."
44. See Julius Jüthner, "Kalokagathia," in *Charisteria: Alois Rzach zum achtzigsten Geburtstag dargebracht* (Reichenberg: Gebrüder Stiepel, 1930), 99.

bled by the formal instability of the term, and they repeatedly sought, though with varying degrees of success, to define it in a satisfactory way.

As Herder had already recognized, *kalokagathia* had not always existed in the Greek vocabulary, nor was its meaning stable after it came into common use. Originally the word seems to have been applied solely to those who enjoyed high or noble birth, which the Greeks—and as history has shown more than once, not only they—assumed would express itself in superior intellectual, moral, and even physical qualities. Having been granted the leisure and the means to cultivate their bodies as well as their minds, the Greek aristocracy were able to perfect their physical appearance through gymnastic exercises, adorn their exterior with fine garments and jewelry, and polish their manners in society. Thus beautiful to behold, the wealthy became, as it were, hypothetically "good" as well, just as we still also say that a person comes from a "good" family when we mean from a rich, or at least a socially well positioned, one.[45] Initially used in this way by the commoners to designate the "upper ten thousand," at the beginning of the fifth century B.C.in Athens, the members of the noble class themselves began to use the word to distinguish themselves from those who did not have the privileges of high birth. Anyone could become "good" who possessed the necessary will and self-discipline, but the nobleman alone could inherently claim a native right to that supreme quality of being both beautiful-*and*-good.[46]

But as it became all too apparent to the later Greeks that nobility in itself was no guarantee for the presence or continued maintenance of the virtues, the question of how to acquire and preserve that distinction gradually came to occupy an ever more prominent place in thinking about *kalokagathia*. If it was not a quality that was somehow innate, then it followed that people could be trained to acquire it, or that it could come as the result of *paedaia* or education. Once education was considered essential to the attainment of *kalokagathia*, the term soon took on the quality not so much of an attribute found in the highborn, but of the unfolding, the development, and the purposeful channeling of certain capacities within the individual.[47] The

---

45. This is the, I think very plausible, thesis offered by Julius Walter, *Die Geschichte der Ästhetik im Altertum ihrer begrifflichen Entwicklung nach dargestellt* (Leipzig: O. R. Reisland, 1893), 133.
46. See Jüthner, "Kalokagathia," 118. That this way of thinking was by no means limited to the aristocratic families of antiquity is demonstrated by a self-description of Louis XIV, the most admired and emulated monarch of the Enlightenment: "To be King is to be the summit of superiority and the elevation of rank is all the more assured when it is supported by unique merit. The great interval which virtue puts between [other men] and him [the king], exposes him in the most beautiful light and with utmost glitter in the eyes of the whole world." *Oeuvres de Louis XIV* (Paris: Treuttle & Wurtz, 1806), 2:67–68; quoted in Carol Blum, *Rousseau and the Republic of Virtue: The Language of Politics in the French Revolution* (Ithaca: Cornell University Press, 1986), 23.
47. I have profited considerably from the discussion of the ethical import of *kalokagathia* by Leopold Schmidt, *Die Ethik der alten Griechen* (Berlin: Wilhelm Hertz, 1882), 1:328–34. See

dual emphasis on the exemplarity of the *kalos kagathos*, as well as on the importance of consciously emulating and thereby internalizing his traits, is neatly demonstrated in a speech to "Euragoras," which the famed Athenian orator Isocrates had written sometime around 370–365 B.C.and which was almost certainly known to every Greek writer of the time. "I know," Isocrates declaimed, "that honourable men [*kalous kagathous*] pride themselves not so much on bodily beauty as they desire to be honoured for their deeds and their wisdom; for those who do not choose to be slothful, but desire to be good men, it is easy to imitate the character of their fellow-men and their thoughts and purposes."[48] It was therefore not so much the external beauty associated with a well-proportioned body, expensive clothes, or a noble name that later came to constitute the praiseworthy attributes of the *kalos kagathos*, but rather some internal qualities that were expressed in "deeds." Instead of representing a title one simply inherited, *kalos kagathos* thus came to be seen, by the middle of the fourth century at the latest, as a designation of distinction that one had to earn by conscious and continuous exertion. But then the question quite naturally arose of how the education toward *kalokagathia* should be conducted, and more crucially, so that one might more surely reach that desired end, what its exact nature was supposed to be.

The basic uncertainty about the final significance of the term, and yet the Greeks' simultaneous unwillingness to forfeit a favorite idea, is reflected in the works of one of the most influential exponents of *kalokagathia*, the Athenian philosopher and general Xenophon, who was an almost exact contemporary of that other great student of Socrates, Plato.[49] By nature a man of action and pragmatic inclinations, Xenophon enjoyed during the eighteenth century the reputation of having been Socrates's most sober and thus more biographically reliable disciple.[50] In all of Xenophon's discussions of *kalokagathia*, the "good" thus outweighs the "beautiful" in the balance of the term's conflicting conceptual components—as one would perhaps expect from a man who was concerned with the more practical affairs of life such as planting crops or waging wars.[51] Morally good behavior can

---

also the somewhat less helpful doctoral thesis by Hermann Wankel, "Kalos kai agathos" (Ph.D. diss., University of Würzburg, 1961).

48. Isocrates, "Euragoras," in *Works*, Loeb Classical Library (1945), 3:45–47.

49. Jüthner, "Kalokagathia," 100, mentions that although no occurrence of the word can be documented before Xenophon, it must have already been in use quite a long time because Aristophanes, who lived from 445 to 385, derived a verb from the noun.

50. For a thorough discussion of the so-called Socratic Problem, see Jaeger, *Paideia*, 17–27, and Guthrie, *Greek Philosophy*, vol. 3, esp. 327–59.

51. See the section on the aristocracy in Max Wundt, *Geschichte der griechischen Ethik* (Leipzig, 1908–11; reprint, Aalen: Scientia, 1985), 1:80–81, where we read that "war and battle were the proper activities of a man in the Mycenian era, which continued to have an influence long after the nomadic period and into the more settled times. The highest good for a

under the best of circumstances produce immediate and tangible benefits, whereas beauty, though pleasant, usually brings much less material rewards. Still, Xenophon did depict Socratic *kalokagathia*, or rather its manifestation in virtuous conduct, as a goal worth pursuing for its own sake. In the *Memorabilia*—in which Xenophon recorded his "recollections" of Socrates by presenting them, as did Plato, in dialogue form—we thus read that the men who followed Socrates did so "not that they might shine in the courts or the assembly, but that they might become gentlemen [*kaloi te kagathoi*], and be able to do their duty by house and household, and relatives and friends, and city and citizens. Of these not one, in his youth or old age, did evil or incurred censure" (1.2.48). Although the emphasis on the virtue of these men is plainly evident, what Xenophon meant by "duty" is still left to the reader to discover. And this omission was not hidden from Xenophon himself. In both of his principal Socratic works, the *Memorabilia* and the *Oeconomicus*, he frequently portrayed Socrates as searching for some clarification of what the "beautiful-and-good" was in itself or, failing this, for a person who was said to embody its properties.

One thing was certain: the citizens of Athens regarded the possession of *kalokagathia*, whatever its true nature might be, as a goal one should spare no trouble in trying to attain. In the *Memorabilia*, for example, Socrates speaks at one point to a certain Euthydemus about the nature of slavishness. This deplorable state was caused, Socrates argues, not by ignorance of particular things but by ignorance, more generally, of "the beautiful and good and just," and he stressed that to avoid or remedy such ignorance "we must strain every nerve to escape being slaves" (4.2.22–23). Recognizing the constant vigilance and effort involved in realizing this ideal, Euthydemus replied that he followed "a philosophy that would provide me with the best education in all things needful to one who would be a gentleman [*kalokagathias*]" (4.2.23). Indeed, throughout Xenophon's works there are men, such as Critobolus in the *Oeconomicus*, who "long to deserve that title" (6.12). And Socrates himself, as Xenophon portrayed him, was constantly engaged in trying to lead others toward it, always "putting others to the test, and convincing them of error and exhorting them to follow virtue and gentleness [*kalokagathian*]" (4.8.11). But showing how everyone longed to be or to possess *kalokagathia*, only demonstrates its universally acknowledged social value; it does not tell us what it actually was.

The question of what constituted a *kalos kagathos* also provides the main

---

nobleman was still the laurel of the hero. . . . One legacy of that earlier heroic period was the view maintained by the nobility that, in addition to war and gymnastic exercises, no serious work was worthy of a man. The only exceptions . . . were two activities, which stood in the closest proximity to the martial life of the nobility: horse breeding and hunting." Suitably, Xenophon also wrote highly influential treatises on these latter two occupations.

focus of interest in Xenophon's *Oeconomicus,* but here, too, the answer we are offered, although more detailed, is still frustratingly vague. The *Oeconomicus* not only reveals Xenophon's preference for practical matters, it also lays bare the limits of his abilities to illuminate or even to explore the inner contradictions of the ideal he evidently espoused. In this work, Xenophon depicts a man named Critobulus as conversing with Socrates about all aspects of estate management, and in order to illustrate his notions about the most advantageous way to arrange domestic affairs, Socrates promises his friend "a complete account of an interview I once had with a man whom I took to be really one of those who are justly styled 'gentlemen' [*kalos te kagathos*]" (6.12). This man is Isomachus, a wealthy and noble farmer, and he talks with Socrates at length about how he educated his wife and about various particulars of his household economy. But when pressed to comment on why he is universally known as a *kaloskagathos,* Isomachus merely enumerates the undeniable agrarian, domestic, and martial virtues he upholds, all of which refer, however, more to physical than to strictly moral discipline. "If a man has plenty to eat, and works off the effects properly," Isomachus tells Socrates, "I take it that he both insures his health and adds to his strength. By training himself in the arts of war he is more qualified to save himself honourably, and by due diligence and avoidance of loose habits, he is more likely to increase his estate" (11.12). Thrift, moderation, and industry, all cultivated with an eye toward capital growth: the person Xenophon described through the mouthpiece of Isomachus can hardly be said to correspond to some lofty ideal of perfect humanity. On the contrary, it irresistibly evokes the image of a prosperous nineteenth-century bourgeois merchant such as one finds, say, in Thomas Mann's *Buddenbrooks* rather than the proud and noble Greeks Winckelmann adored. But despite his relative lack of metaphysical profundity, Xenophon nevertheless drew a vivid picture of one version of the *kalos kagathos* that serves at least as an indication of the consuming contemporary desire to attain that highest, though apparently elusive, distinction among one's Athenian peers.

Xenophon's testimonial credibility concerning the life and teachings of Socrates rested, at least for eighteenth-century readers, on his relatively simple diction and on his general avoidance of abstract speculation. One of the Enlightenment's most eloquent American spokesmen, Thomas Jefferson, esteemed Xenophon and mistrusted, even disliked, Plato in equal measure. As Jefferson once put the matter with his typical bluntness: "Of Socrates we have nothing genuine but in the Memorabilia of Xenophon; for Plato makes him one of his Collocutors merely to cover his own whimsies under the mantle of his name."[52] But others were more tolerant in their views.

52. From a letter to William Short, 31 October 1819, in Thomas Jefferson, *Writings,* ed.

Herder, for instance, saw Socrates' two most prominent pupils as providing necessary complements, and once remarked in a somewhat clumsy, but evocative, metaphor that Xenophon had clothed his teacher in the "garment of nature," whereas Plato had lent him "the wings of high ideas."[53] And it was in this capacity, as the thinker who persuasively insisted that the true nature of our being was located in its transcendental aspect, that Plato assumed a decisive role in shaping the ideal of the *kalos kagathos* that the eighteenth century adopted as its own.

Although Plato's penchant for linguistic and stylistic purity appears to have prevented him from actually using the compound noun *kalokagathia* itself (he did, however, frequently speak of *kaloi kagathoi*), its implications nonetheless suffuse his writings.[54] So pervasive are its traces that it does not seem extravagant to claim that the essence of the concept, if not the term itself, inhabits the center of Plato's thinking about human nature. To consider the place occupied by the concept of the "beautiful-and-good" in Plato's dialogues, one must therefore see it in the larger context of Plato's views about the most elevated nature and aims of humanity.

Plato's conception of the phrase *kalos kagathos*, much more so than that of his predecessors, contains a strongly marked ethical component. In the *Gorgias*, for instance, Polus and Socrates speak about good and evil, with Socrates emphasizing the necessity of the former for happiness. Polus disputes his teachers's eudaemonism, saying that "many men who do wrong are happy," and he names as an example Archelaus, son of Perdiccas, who was ruler of Macedonia.[55] When Polus asks Socrates whether he considers the tyrant happy or wretched, Socrates confesses he cannot judge since he doesn't know how Archelaus stands with regard to "education [*paideia*] and justice." Polus is surprised to hear that happiness rests on these two things, to which Socrates replies in explanation that "the man and woman who are noble and good [*kaloi kagathoi*] I call happy, but the evil and base I call wretched" (470e).[56] If Archelaus is indeed wicked, Socrates concludes, he

---

Merrill D. Peterson (New York: Literary Classics of the United States, 1984), 1430–31. Jefferson seems never to have felt anything but disdain for Plato. In a letter to John Adams of 5 July 1814, he reported that he had been "reading seriously Plato's republic" and complained that his study "was the heaviest task-work I ever went through." In describing his "wading thro' the whimsies, the puerilities, and unintelligible jargon" of the *Republic*, he remarked that he continually asked himself how the world could have admired "such nonsense" for so long (1341).

53. Johann Gottfried Herder, *Ueber die neuere Deutsche Litteratur*, in *Sämmtliche Werke*, 1:219.

54. The only occurrence of the word *kalokagathia* in the Platonic corpus is in the so-called *Definitions*, which is now considered apocryphal.

55. Plato, *Gorgias*, 470d. All further references to Plato are henceforth cited in the text by page and page subdivision of the standard reference (the 1578 Stephanus edition of the works of Plato).

56. See Jaeger, *Paideia*, 2:133–34, in relation to this passage and its relevance for Plato's conception of *kalokagathia*.

will necessarily be miserable, for only those who possess *kalokagathia* are and can be happy.

But Plato's particular conception of beauty in all of its manifestations also gives the first element of that phrase a weight it lacks in most other accounts. Whereas, in the works of other writers, the *kalos* is mainly subsumed under the category of the Good—whatever that might finally be—in Plato the relation is frequently reversed, making the Beautiful the dominant component. As he put it in a famous passage from the *Philebus*, "We find that the good has taken refuge in the character of the beautiful" (64e). It was this intermingling, even identification, of beauty and goodness, though prefigured in the word itself, which Plato's Socrates was the first to have made into an independent subject of reflection. Taken for granted for as much as a century or more before Socrates lived, the merging of the beautiful and the good only became a problem when Plato showed Socrates literalizing the two concepts again in his effort to try to understand their metaphorical commingling.

Before we can advance to Plato's concept of beauty-and-goodness, however, we have to examine, if only briefly, his view of the soul and of its most important, indeed, its defining activity, the process of understanding itself. The most characteristic trait of Socrates is his intellectualism. For Socrates the acquisition of knowledge meant not simply the accumulation of facts, but moreover the assimilation of oneself to the nature of that knowledge. In the *Phaedo*, for example, the dialogue depicting Socrates' final hours, Plato showed Socrates seeking to console his sorrowful friends by arguing for the immortality of the soul. He begins by saying that he is "convinced that if we are ever to have pure knowledge of anything, we must get rid of the body and contemplate things by themselves with the soul by itself" (66d). As long as we keep the soul pure and uncontaminated by the body, Socrates explained, it can escape the fate of bodily decay and attain the unsullied state of changeless permanence. Only the body is subject to death, and the greater the distance that we put between ourselves and physical concerns, the greater our chances of preserving our souls from eternal perdition. And the purity one ought to seek, the avoidance of distracting physical pleasure, corporeal defilement, is merely another name Socrates uses for wisdom; indeed, as he says, "Wisdom itself is a sort of purification" (69c). Socrates always describes the attainment of true knowledge, and hence the aspiration toward the goal of immortality, as a process that begins when the mind raises itself above the sphere that is subject to the forces of variation, inconsistency, and dissolution. All that is timeless, unchanging, and uniform constitutes the proper attributes of the soul, and by communing with what is thus immortal, the soul partakes of the same.

The result of this careful vigilance over oneself, which Socrates advocated and maintained, is therefore a kind of adequation to the objects of contemplation. By steadfastly concentrating on the immaterial realm that alone constitutes knowledge or wisdom, the soul gradually assumes, or assimilates itself to, those very qualities that characterize it. Knowledge of the good, therefore, is tantamount to virtue itself; as the example of Hippias indicates, Socrates could not imagine that anyone who knows what the "good" is will fail to heed its inherent demands, because the soul has already adequated itself to that knowledge. The same is true of one who truly knows what "beauty" is.[57] "There is one way, then," Socrates says, "in which a man can be free from all anxiety about the fate of his soul—if in life he has abandoned bodily pleasures and adornments, as foreign to his purpose and likely to do more harm than good, and has devoted himself to the pleasures of acquiring knowledge, and so by decking his soul not with a borrowed beauty but with its own—with self-control, and goodness, and courage, and liberality, and truth—has fitted himself to await his journey to the next world" (114d–e). In addition to providing a short description of Plato's notion of the way to ensure passage to the world beyond, this passage demonstrates how the soul that bedecks itself with its "own beauty," by devoting itself to the pursuit of the knowledge of virtue, becomes in this way beautiful-and-good, or *kaloskagathos*.

If in the *Phaedo* beauty seems to be the crucial and culminating moment in the soul's assumption of wisdom and, hence, of deathlessness, in the *Phaedrus* beauty acquires the even more momentous function of putting us in mind of the eternal Ideas, or Forms, themselves. Socrates often speaks in the *Phaedo* of "absolute realities, such as beauty and goodness" (76d) and "absolute beauty and goodness" (77a), and he once cryptically remarks that "it seems to me that whatever else is beautiful apart from absolute beauty is beautiful because it partakes of that absolute beauty, and for no other reason" (100c). What Plato appears to have meant here was that in addition to things that are beautiful, there is also something separate called beauty, by virtue of which these individual things can be said to have that quality. Plato thus held that there is an abstract, general Idea that stands behind every phenomenal manifestation of that Idea in reality. In the *Phaedrus*, then, Socrates explicitly singles out Beauty as the only idea or form that possesses a perceptible guise. As opposed to other abstract ideas, such as Justice, Temperance, Courage, and so on, Beauty alone has a physical correspondent in nature that thus makes it the privileged mediator pointing the way from the world of sense to that of the soul (250d).[58] Physical beauty, in Plato's universe, marks only one station on the way to that higher, unchang-

57. See Jan Rohls, *Geschichte der Ethik* (Tübingen: J.C.B. Mohr, Paul Siebeck, 1991), 47–48.
58. See the discussion of this passage in Guthrie, *History of Greek Philosophy*, 4:426–27.

ing, eternal Beauty that exists beyond the boundaries of corporeal nature. But to show what an effect even the beauty of body can have on us—and thus to prove its power to perform this marvelous leap into further reaches—Plato lapsed into the kind of rhapsodic language that earned him so many unflattering epithets in later centuries. Plato writes that if someone who has been trained in Socratic wisdom "beholds a godlike face or bodily form that truly expresses beauty, first there come upon him a shuddering and a measure of that awe which the vision inspired, and then reverence as at the sight of a god" (251e–252b). It is thus not a work of art—Plato was famously suspicious of the arts—and not a natural landscape, but the human figure, and specifically that of a handsome young boy, that is the conduit leading to a realization of true, eternal—and eternalizing—beauty.

The *Phaedrus* culminates in this account of the "yearning for him in whom beauty dwells," that is, the experience and effect of love, or *eros*. But in this dialogue Plato described love, and the perception of beauty that incites it, almost solely from the perspective of the individual who already possesses a measure of inner beauty himself; otherwise, it would not be possible for the realization of the Forms to occur. In the *Symposium*, by contrast, Socrates broadens the scope of inquiry and asks, "What good can Love be to humanity?" (204c). In attempting to answer this question, the *Symposium* tries to show how the love described in the *Phaedrus* is meant to perform its vital universal task.

As we have already seen, it would be difficult to overestimate the importance that Plato accorded to the concept of beauty, but in the *Symposium*, as always, it is an idea that depends for its coherence and interest on a complex network of related notions. The "banquet" that lends the dialogue its name is held at the house of the dramatist Agathon, and he and his guests, including Socrates, spend the evening discussing love. In his response to Agathon's suggestion that it is that which is "the most beautiful and best," Socrates first tries, typically, to define his terms. When we love, we clearly love something, and Socrates agrees that what we love is beauty and that "the good and the beautiful are the same" (201c). But here Socrates professes confusion, and it is this declaration that introduces that central section of the *Symposium* in which he recounts his conversation on the same subject with the Mantineian priestess, Diotima.

In Socrates' account of this conversation, Plato presented his fullest exposition of the purpose and power he attached to beauty. Diotima begins by pointing out that love is not precisely a longing for the beautiful itself, as Socrates had somewhat naively assumed—or so he coyly admits. Rather, love is a desire for propagating, or procreating, that which manifests itself as beauty, with a view toward ensuring its—and one's own—continued existence. Love, in other words, is the realization or the expression of the desire for immortality. To explain what she means, Diotima then makes a distinction between those who carry out their "procreancy" through the body—that is, those who found families and have children—and those "whose procreancy is of the spirit rather than of the flesh" (209a), and whose "offspring" (to extend Plato's metaphor) are thus of a more ethereal, but in Plato's view obviously a superior and more perdurable, kind.[59]

How this "procreancy of the spirit," this abstract paternity takes place constitutes the ideal essence of the relationship that always ought to obtain between mentor and protégé, teacher and student. It is important to stress the unequal status of the two participants in this equation, for one clearly plays a more or less passive, and the other a decisively active role. One is *led* to an awareness and understanding of what Plato termed the True, but only rarely, if at all, does it seem possible for someone to find that realm without the aid of such a guide. But it is critical that the education be properly performed; it is, in fact, quite literally a matter of life and death. The elder philosopher seeks to escape the effects of his physical mortality by inculcating his values, wisdom, and character—in short, by imparting his soul—in the young man or boy he has chosen as his spiritual partner. Instruction in philosophy—the "love of wisdom"—and most especially Socrates' method of performing philosophy by engaging others in dialogue, exchange, conversation, is thus the medium by which the otherwise entirely distinct realms of physical impermanence and particularity and of transcendent eternal truth are reconciled.

One of the first lessons the protégé must learn, Diotima says, is to distinguish between body and soul, between what is merely contingent and what is inalterably true, between the fleeting pleasures of sense and the permanent joys of eternity. This is most easily accomplished by attending to the complex nature of beauty itself—which, as we know, is unique in that it resides in both the physical and ideational spheres and serves as the only direct means of overcoming the chasm separating the two—and specifically by discriminating between physical and moral beauty. As Diotima puts it, the young pupil "must grasp that the beauties of the body are as nothing to the beauties of the soul, so that wherever he meets with spiritual loveliness, even in the husk of an unlovely body, he will find it beautiful enough to fall in love with and to cherish—and beautiful enough to quicken in his heart a longing for such discourse as tends toward the building of a noble nature" (210b–c).

The preceptor begins his instruction by teaching his young companion to love some individual instance of beauty "so that his passion may give life to noble discourse" (210a) and so that he will learn to value both the beautiful

59. See the account in H. I. Marrou, *A History of Education in Antiquity*, trans. George Lamb (New York: Sheed & Ward, 1956), esp. chap. 3, "Pederasty in Classical Education," in which Marrou comments on this section of the *Symposium* and writes, 31, that in ancient Greece "*paedeia* found its realization in *paiderasteia.*"

object and the love it inspires. The preceptor then shows his charge that in addition to the one object of his affection, beauty exists in other things and people as well, so that it becomes possible, by means of this comparison, for him to see that there must be some hidden cause that allows us to say that so many things that are otherwise completely different are "beautiful." The second lesson, in other words, amounts to an initiation into the logical procedure of induction. Following this process, the philosopher then leads his companion from a consideration of physical beauty to an appreciation of the more abstract beauty inhering in "laws and institutions," in the "sciences" (210c), and in all branches of knowledge, until one finally begins to approach an understanding of the idea or form of beauty itself, or what Socrates calls "absolute" or "universal beauty." "And so," he reports Diotima as having said, "when his prescribed devotion to boyish beauties has carried our candidate so far that the universal beauty dawns upon his inward sight, he is almost within reach of the final revelation. And this is the way, the only way, he must approach, or be led toward, the sanctuary of Love" (211b–c).[60] It is at this point, when the initiate has attained the highest level of abstraction, when he has stripped all remaining empirical dross from the idea of beauty and it stands revealed to him in its absolute purity and timeless perfection, that the philosopher reaches his goal. "When he has brought forth and reared this perfect virtue, he shall be called the friend of god, and if ever it is given to man to put on immortality, it shall be given to him" (212a).

This is, in nuce, Plato's vision of humanity's most important task.[61] The development of inner beauty, which is identified with "perfect virtue," in oneself and in the soul of one's beloved, is the greatest achievement possible for an individual. Thus "beauty," the first half of *kalokagathia*, not only took on an instrumental function in Plato's moral philosophy that it had never had before, but it gained a new, abstract meaning of extraordinary richness and subtlety. Yet despite the suggestiveness of his conception, the reader is left with the uneasy feeling that we still have no clear idea of precisely *how*, or even whether, beauty and goodness form a unity, and nowhere else in Plato's dialogues does Socrates address this issue.[62]

60. See Jaeger, *Paideia*, 2:194.
61. See ibid., 195: "The humanistic significance of the doctrine put forward in *The Symposium*, that Eros is man's instinctive urge to develop his own higher self, needs no exegesis here. The thought recurs in *The Republic*, in another form: Socrates says the purpose of all paideia is to help the inner man to rule over man. Humanism is based on this distinction between man the individual as given by nature, and man the higher self. It was Plato who made it possible for humanism to have this philosophical foundation, and it was *The Symposium* in which it was first laid down."
62. R. C. Lodge, *Plato's Theory of Ethics. The Moral Criterion and the Highest Good* (London: Routledge & Kegan Paul, 1928), 62, notes, with admirable understatement, that Plato's argument concerning the exact degree to which aesthetic qualities are evidence of moral worth is "not quite so clear" and, when pressed, presents "certain difficulties."

In those of his works which most obviously bear the stamp of Plato's influence, Aristotle acknowledged, even as he critically analyzed, the accepted use of *kalokagathia*. In his *Magna Moralia*, for instance, Aristotle wrote (without offering any further elaboration) that "there is a phrase . . . which is not badly used of the completely good man, namely, 'nobility and goodness' [*kalokagathia*]."[63] Similarly, in the *Eudemian Ethics*, he defined *kalokagathia* as a general term that designates the quality of a person in whom all of the virtues are present and developed to the greatest degree. "About each excellence [*arete*] by itself we have already spoken; now since we have distinguished their natures separately, we must describe clearly the excellence that arises out of the combination of them, what we have already called nobility-and-goodness [*kalokagathia*]" (1248b7–11).[64] To illustrate how this quality was different from mere *agathos*, Aristotle explained:

> There are some who think one should have excellence but only for the sake of the natural goods, and so such men are good (for the natural goods are good for them), but they have not nobility and goodness [*kalokagathia*]. For it is not true of them that they acquire the noble for itself, that they choose acts good and noble at once—more than this, that what is not noble by nature but good by nature is noble to them; for objects are noble when a man's motives for acting and choosing them are noble, because to the noble and good man the naturally good is noble. (1249a1–7)

It is telling that here, at the very moment Aristotle announces his intention to "describe clearly" the nature of *kalokagathia*, his prose becomes extremely dense.[65] What he seems to have been saying is that, whereas those people who are merely "kalos" seem to be good since they do "good deeds," they do so only in order to obtain the so-called natural goods (for example, wealth, social position, power, honor, glory, and so on). To outside observers, such people will appear to be truly meritorious, but they actually perform virtuous acts mainly for self-interested motives. The *kalos kagathos*, in contrast, is "good" solely and singly for the sake of the good itself. He loves virtue for itself and not for the rewards it potentially brings. (The last

63. Aristotle, *Magna Moralia*, in *Complete Works*, ed. Jonathan Barnes (Princeton: Princeton University Press, 1984), vol. 2, bk. 2, chap. 9, p. 1911. All further references will be to the page, column, and line, according to the standard Bekker edition. Thus the passage just quoted would be cited as follows: 1207b20–23.

64. A note to the Loeb edition reads, "*Kalokagathia*, like 'nobility,' connotes both social status and moral excellence; so *kalokagathia* may be rendered 'gentleman.'" In Aristotle, *The Athenian Constitution, The Eudemian Ethics, On Virtues and Vices*, Loeb Classical Library (1935), 469n.

65. See the comments on this passage, and on the concept of *kalokagathia* in Aristotle generally, in Anthony Kenny, *Aristotle on the Perfect Life* (Oxford: Oxford University Press, 1992), 9–15 and 19–22, and Stephen A. White, *Sovereign Virtue: Aristotle on the Relation between Happiness and Prosperity* (Stanford: Stanford University Press, 1992), 235–43.

part of the argument puts forward the tenuous claim that for such a person, even those things which are "naturally" good are, as it were, "ennobled" by association and made absolutely good through the *kalos kagathos* because of his disinterested inner disposition.) Such a man is therefore not just "good," but enjoys the additional advantage of being virtuous for its own sake, or "noble-and-good."

As this unliteral translation of *kalos kagathos* accurately emphasizes, however, it is striking how completely Aristotle tried to eliminate any remnant of beauty from his conception of *kalokagathia*. Although he had retained the word as the master trope, so to speak, of moral discourse, and identified it with the pinnacle of ethical existence, he did so by entirely excluding its formerly inherent, even constitutitive, aesthetic connotations. In other works, in fact, Aristotle went out of his way to claim, as he wrote in his *Metaphysics*, that "the good and the beautiful are different" (1078a31). Significantly, it is also in the passage immediately following this last statement that he undertook one of his most searching critiques of Plato's theory of Ideas.

Although Aristotle thus tried to alleviate the dissonance of this idea by dispensing with, or reducing the significance of, one of its two components, he nevertheless retained and defended the word itself, thus guaranteeing its continued existence throughout the Hellenistic period. The thinker who not only revived the aesthetic meaning of *kalokagathia*, but also took the concept to a new and unprecedented plane of abstraction and generality, was Plotinos. Born in Egypt in A.D. 205, Plotinos went to Rome when he was forty and gave lectures on philosophy there, which his disciple Porphyry collected and published after his death in 270. Gathered into six groups of nine treatises each (hence the name of the collection, *Enneads*), these lectures are widely considered to mark the most important document of what in the eighteenth century first became known as Neoplatonism.

The most famous of all of Plotinos's works is the sixth lecture, or book, of the first *Ennead*, which he devoted to an examination of beauty. The Platonic heritage of Plotinos's thought emerges from the very first assumption that the physical realm is only one, and decidedly the lowest, sphere of potential experience. "On rising from the domain of the senses to a superior region," Plotinos wrote, "we also discover beauty in occupations, actions, habits, sciences, and virtues."[66] Much more consequentially than Plato had done, however, Plotinos inquired into how corporeal and immaterial beauty were either similar or different, and above all how we are able to perceive their varying qualities. It was, in fact, partly this emphasis on the psychological

66. Plotinos, *Complete Works*, ed. Kenneth Sylvan Guthrie (Alpine, N.J.: Platonist Press, 1919), 1:40.

process itself that made Plotinos so attractive to his later, and especially his eighteenth-century, readers. He thought, for example, that "the soul appreciates beauty by an especially ordered faculty, whose sole function it is to appreciate all that concerns beauty, even when the other faculties take part in this judgment" (1.6.3). Although he did not call this separate faculty "taste," it was clear that he had created a theoretical space which that invention could fill almost a millennium and a half later.

Likewise, Plotinos had a great deal to say about the effect beauty has on those who perceive it. "The sentiments inspired by beauty are admiration, a gentle charm, desire, love, and a pleasurable impulse" (1.6.4). But since this reaction could equally describe our response to either physical or intellectual phenomena, Plotinos then asked: "What do you feel in presence of the noble occupations, the good morals, the habits of temperance, and in general of virtuous acts and sentiments, and of all that constitutes the beauty of souls?" (1.6.5). Here Plotinos had explicitly revived the tradition of *kalokagathia* by equating, as the word intrinsically demanded, the qualities defining virtue with those producing the effect of beauty. Conforming to the necessity of being more direct and specific than one's predecessors, which is both the burden and the privilege of all epigones, Plotinos thus won the distinction of being the first to call this state "beauty of soul."

He was also the first to try to describe its opposite. As a convenient way of making his positive meaning more concrete, Plotinos tried to set forth what constituted an "ugly soul." After listing all of the faults and vices that mar the souls of the depraved, Plotinos singled out the main cause of spiritual deformity, and hence of evil, as stemming from sensuality. Much more radically than even Socrates had done, Plotinos argued for the total disengagement of the soul from all physical interests. "The soul becomes ugly," he bluntly stated, "by mingling with the body, confusing herself with it, by inclining herself towards it. For a soul, ugliness consists in being impure, no longer unmingled, like gold tarnished by particles of earth" (1.6.5). Thus only those who cultivate this pure spirituality itself, unsullied by any earthly or sensual concern, are able to aspire to the highest stage of moral being and can themselves hope to acquire beauty of soul. The "beauty" that had originally been seen as an exclusively physical attribute, and with Plato at least had been given the compromise status of mediating between the tangible, visible world and the domain of Ideas, had thus become for Plotinos an entirely abstract category. In Plotinos's ascetic universe, virtue is possible only by abandoning the last vestige of physical being. "The purified soul, therefore, becomes a form, a reason, an incorporeal and intellectual essence" (1.6.6). As we will see, this tendency, already strongly evident in Plotinos, toward ever increasing degrees of abstraction in the conception of beauty of soul (which the eighteenth-century advocates of the ideal, I will argue, inevitably came to share) eventually led to so many internal contradictions that, in the end, they finally imperiled the idea itself.

Or perhaps they were there from the very beginning. Although everyone seems to have been uneasy about the word *kalokagathia* itself, this discomfort did not prevent the finest minds of the day from using it, even though they, too, were apparently at a loss to say what it actually meant. Plotinos's flight into the upper reaches of abstraction is, in a way, his own veiled answer to the challenge the word implicitly posed. Whereas Aristotle had instinctively sought to suppress its aesthetic aspect in his explanation of the term, Plotinos not only returned to a Platonic position by shifting considerable argumentative weight back onto the concept of beauty, he also transformed that concept itself into something so nebulous and diffuse, so thoroughly divorced from verifiable reality, that it became impossible to prove him wrong—or for that matter, to prove him right. What was needed was a leap of faith: real, immortal, unblemished beauty existed, in Plotinos's version, if you believed in it.

The proximity of these ideas to Christian theology is not coincidental, and Plotinos himself constantly envisioned an experience of a divinity as both the point of reference and the final aim of his philosophy. Indeed, it provided the motive for moral behavior. "Being supreme beauty, and the first beauty," Plotinos wrote of his God, "He beautifies those who love Him, and thereby they become worthy of love. This is the great, the supreme goal of souls; this is the goal which arouses all their efforts, if they do not wish to be disinherited of that sublime contemplation of the enjoyment of which confers blessedness, and privation of which is the greatest of earthly misfortunes" (1.6.7). Through this experience of ecstasy, this blissful communion with the divine presence, we become enchanted by the spectacle of that "supreme beauty" and strive to preserve that blessed state by making our souls resemble his perfection. The basis of virtue is thus secured by our desire to maintain this nearness to God. Plotinos's conception of morality could not have failed to recommend him to those of his enlightened readers who, themselves unwilling to relinquish their religious convictions, found in his works a profoundly metaphysical theory coupled with a theological doctrine that without too many concessions to either one, could be accommodated to a Christian context.

But Plotinos was too much of a psychologist to be satisfied with the simple declaration that beauty of soul arises solely as the result of an ecstatic vision of God. He felt that one could, in fact that one *must*, as he said, "train this interior vision" and gradually prepare oneself to behold the dazzling beauty of the divinity. And it was here that Plotinos departed most decisively from the teachings of Plato, with great consequences for the eighteenth-century conception of beauty of soul. Instead of insisting, as Plato had done, that we must stand under the guidance of an elder and more experienced mentor who would gradually lead us to an understanding of the eternal verities, Plotinos thought it possible for an individual to achieve this wisdom, and all of its attendant moral qualities, without external assistance. This is not to say that he did not recognize the importance of the relationship between an older mentor and a boyish protégé, and he wrote that "a worthy man, perceiving in a youth the character of virtue, is agreeably impressed, because he observes that the youth harmonizes with the true type of virtue which he bears within himself" (1.6.3). But according to Plotinos, this was not the exclusive, or arguably even the best, way of attaining that character oneself. Instead, he suggested that untutored, individual contemplation alone, the reflective turn toward the interior realm, would suffice in leading us to the final goal. Not by accident, Plotinos compared this process of self-cultivation to the work of a sculptor:

> Withdraw within yourself, and examine yourself. If you do not yet therein discover beauty, do as the artist, who cuts off, polishes, purifies until he has adorned his statue with all the marks of beauty. Remove from your soul, therefore, all that is superfluous, straighten out all that is crooked, purify and illuminate what is obscure, and do not cease perfecting your statue until the divine resplendence of virtue shines forth upon your sight, until you see temperance in its holy purity seated in your breast. (1.6.9)

Thus the habit that eighteenth-century thinkers acquired of regarding and treating themselves as works of art in the name of imitating the Greeks was inspired by a precedent within that ancient tradition itself. But although this conscious self-fashioning took place with the explicit intention of increasing the virtue of the soul thus affected, it still remained obscure how a "statue," however perfect a creation it may be, could be good. Plotinos himself, like all of his predecessors, did not, or more probably could not, answer this crucial question, apparently having decided to leave that issue for his own disciples to resolve. Nevertheless, his demand that to become virtuous we retreat wholly within ourselves and transform our innermost souls into objects of exquisite beauty established a pattern of ethical behavior that survived for centuries thereafter. Adulterated though it inevitably became by other, more contemporary influences, it also left its distinctive mark on Enlightenment ethics, and in particular on its dearest creation, the beautiful soul.

CHAPTER

4

Wieland and Rousseau:
The Figuration of the Beautiful Soul

Literature does not please by moralizing us; it moralizes us
because it pleases.

—H. W. Garrod

We have now reached the approximate midpoint in our investigation of moral beauty, or beauty of soul, in eighteenth-century thought. In chronological terms we have also arrived at the middle decade of the century. The 1750s mark, in fact, a kind of culmination not simply to the particular development we have been following thus far but also in some sense to the internal trajectory of the Enlightenment as a whole. These ten years bear witness to a remarkable series of attempts— epitomized by the publication of the *Encyclopédie*—to harness and synthesize the diverse strands of contemporary thought in science, ethical philosophy, theology, aesthetics, and epistemology that we have been exploring. Partly because of this intense concentration of intellectual and creative activity, it appeared to many who participated in this enormous enterprise that answers to the most pressing questions that humanity faced might soon be within its grasp. Indeed, it was arguably the Enlightenment's finest moment; confidence in the human ability to understand, shape, and control almost every aspect of human life and destiny was at its apogee. To those who lived at midcentury, it appeared that the cultivation of reason and its application to all private and collective affairs had grown closer than ever before to finally bearing fruit in the form of true liberty and lasting happiness.

But the state of fruition is a paradoxical one. For as the organic analogy equally well illustrates, the moment of ripeness also marks the onset of decay. Such a downward turn did not manifest itself immediately; the Enlightenment actually enjoyed a long and respectable senescence. Nevertheless, the confidence in the still largely unfathomed power of the mind to comprehend and transform the world that characterized the century at its zenith soon showed signs of faltering. It is ironic, yet fitting, that the first volume of the *Encyclopédie*—that vast compendium of contemporary knowledge celebrating the advancement of learning and civilization—appeared in 1751. For this was the same year in which Rousseau published his first *Discours*, which passionately attacks the very advances in the arts and sciences that the *Encyclopédie* acclaims. Rousseau asserted that these achievements had produced nothing but the most deleterious consequences for essential human virtue. This irony is made even more pronounced when we remind ourselves that, as a contributor to the *Encyclopédie*, Rousseau had also helped to promote the very phenomenon he now decried. In a similar but more subtle way the reevaluation of the concept of moral beauty also began precisely when it had been generally accepted as a cultural ideal. Even though, or possibly because, the concept of moral beauty remained fashionable among the educated classes of Europe for several decades after the 1750s, at the advent of its apparent apotheosis the conception of a morally based "beauty of soul" already bore the unmistakable traces of the strains that would lead to its eventual collapse as a viable means of self-definition.

The most significant change in the concept of moral beauty that occurred at midcentury was its descent from the heights of abstract reflection and its assumption of human form. The general philosophical category of "moral beauty" was replaced by the more personalized and more personally appealing figure of the "beautiful soul." The seemingly trivial change signaled nothing less than the difference between merely *possessing* the attributes of perfect virtue—a way of phrasing the matter that makes room for its conceivable loss—and that of more essentially *being* those qualities themselves, which clearly expresses the greater permanence of intrinsic identity. One can only *have* "moral beauty," but one can *be* a "beautiful soul." The primary catalyst for this shift of ontological emphasis had to do with the medium in which the ideas about beauty of soul were now being expressed. No longer locked within the airless chambers inhabited by disputing theologians and academic philosophers, the beautiful soul now stepped out into the vital world of literature.

It was probably inevitable that the fascination with the concept of moral beauty that had seized so many thinkers during the first part of the eighteenth century should have sooner or later found its way into popular literature. The emphasis on psychological and emotional experience, the concentration on the gradual development and refinement of character, and the plainly flattering portrait it offered of the human potential for virtuous conduct and its inherently pleasing effect—all the primary defining features of moral beauty seemed to be precisely tailored to the requirements, as well as the possibilities, of literary art. "Questions of virtue have an inherently narrative focus," Michael McKeon has perceptively written, "because they are concerned with genealogical succession and individual progress, with how human capacity is manifested in and through time."[1] But not just any fictional form would do, and it may have been more than simply fortuitous that the beautiful soul entered the mainstream of literary culture just as the modern novel appeared in Europe. Released from the plane of the philosophical treatise, the beautiful soul was better, or in any case more convincingly, realized in the space of the novel. The novel alone allowed, and even demanded, a greater specificity, more psychological immediacy, and a concreteness of detail than would have been possible in either dramatic or lyrical treatments of the concept. What did not become immediately apparent, however, was that the third and final stage in this logical progression—that is, the actual transformation of a living human being into a "beautiful soul"—would not follow as easily as the sequence suggests. In more than a few respects, the beautiful soul and the novel seem to have been made for each other—indeed, the novel remained, perhaps, its true and only home.

But even the first step leading from metaphysics to fiction proved to be more difficult to take than one might initially imagine. Whereas we now take for granted that the boundaries between philosophy and literature are more permeable than previously assumed and that each discipline can illuminate the other's obscurities, this willingness to mix the modes and objects of discourse had been generally foreign to the thinkers of the early eighteenth century. The first phase of any serious intellectual endeavor, they felt, required the strict separation of all of the elements under investigation in order to obtain the simplicity and clarity they typically associated with truth. And many felt that literature, because of the equivocation of its terms and its excessive emphasis on emotional or subjective states, did not provide a reliable vehicle for the communication of abstract ideas, let alone for the dissemination of truth. Moreover, the novel somehow seemed especially suspect, having been employed mainly to depict matters that most considered to be of doubtful value. In 1745 Georg Friedrich Meier, a professor of philosophy and former student of Baumgarten, expressed the prevailing view by writing that "many others before me have already noted that the accursed novels . . . are completely ruining taste in Germany."[2] Almost twenty years later, Diderot—who was himself guilty of having frequently

1. Michael McKeon, *The Origins of the English Novel: 1600–1740* (Baltimore: Johns Hopkins University Press, 1987), 212.
2. Georg Friedrich Meier, *Untersuchung einiger Ursachen des verdorbenen Geschmacks in Deutschland* (Halle, 1745), 25; cited from Werner Krauss, "Zur französischen Romantheorie des 18. Jahrhunderts," in *Nachahmung und Illusion*, ed. Hans Robert Jauß (Munich: Eidos, 1964), 70. See also Wolfgang Martens, *Die Botschaft der Tugend. Die Aufklärung im Spiegel der deutschen Moralischen Wochenschriften* (Stuttgart: J. B. Metzler, 1968), 505, who concludes: "Apart from very few exceptions, novels were considered inappropriate reading for people who were virtuous, for those who lived according to the dictates of reason and religion, and for those who were concerned about good taste."

violated the rigid boundaries between literature and more "serious" subjects —likewise remarked that it was still true that people viewed the genre with considerable distrust. "By the word 'novel,'" he wrote, "one has understood to this day a fabric of chimerical and frivolous events, the reading of which was dangerous to taste and morals alike."[3] It is thus symptomatic that the two writers who first transferred the discussion of moral beauty from the philosophical into the fictional realm frequently found themselves being accused, at the very least, of confusing their purposes, and probably of actively promoting the more threatening sort of dissolution Diderot described.

"I feel that I must have seemed to be a marvelous, inconceivable, enigmatic man, a fanatic in the eyes of some, a hypocrite in the eyes of others, inconsistent to serious and dull-witted minds, a lunatic to the men of the world, a poet to philosophers, a philosopher to poets, superficial to pedants, ridiculous or perhaps contemptible to mediocre minds."[4] Although these words could very well have been written by Rousseau, who throughout his life felt he was unfairly persecuted by an uncomprehending and frequently hostile public, they come, instead, from Wieland, the one German writer who most resembled Rousseau, if not in temperament, then certainly in the overall constitution of his mind and commitments. Much like Plato, whom they both supremely admired, Rousseau and Wieland have been perceived at various intervals as inconsistent, eclectic, and irrational fantasts; as either idle dreamers or dangerous threats to society; and above all as poets pretending to be philosophers, or philosophers aspiring to poetry. Yet even if one considers the situation more dispassionately, the extent to which Wieland and Rousseau shared common interests and similar backgrounds, even allowing for the sorts of similarities usually found among contemporaries, is in fact extraordinary. They both maintained a profoundly Christian sensibility throughout their lives, even though, with increasing age, they gradually modified their religious beliefs in the direction of a deistically tinged rationalism. Both were deeply marked by the examples set by the lives and works of ancient authors, and as we have noted, Platonic philosophy in particular occupied a dominant place in their thought. Both men were also deeply concerned with the problems of pedagogy, and they both wrote works on the subject of education that won them universal recognition: Wieland's *Der goldene Spiegel* was instrumental in bringing about his summons to the court of Weimar, and Rousseau's educational novel *Émile* remains one of the most famous—some might say notorious—works of its kind to this day.

3. Denis Diderot, "Éloge de Richardson," in *Oeuvres complètes*, ed. Jules Assézat and Marice Tourneux (Paris: Garnier Frères, 1875–77), 5:212–13.
4. Letter to Zimmermann, 26 April 1759, in Christoph Martin Wieland, *Briefe*, ed. Hans W. Seiffert (Berlin: Akademie, 1963–), 1:431.

🐛

But by far the most decisive link between these two writers in the course of their intellectual endeavors was their almost obsessive concern with both private virtue and public morality. Even in an age that never tired of speaking about the centrality of moral issues in the general management of human affairs, Wieland and Rousseau stand out in their singular and unceasing devotion to the problems of ethics. As Rousseau melodramatically exclaimed in the introduction to the first *Discours*: "It is Virtue that I am defending."[5] However paradoxical the motives behind his effusive declaration may have been—and with Rousseau nothing is ever as simple as it seems—this single sentence could have stood as the motto of his entire creative life. And even though Wieland's rather more forgiving conception of morality lacked Rousseau's (at least theoretically) rigorous severity, Wieland likewise made the question of virtue a constant focus of his writing. Finally, and most significant, both Rousseau and Wieland, each for his own compatriots, also evolved into the most influential poets—or perhaps one could even say the prophets—of the late-eighteenth-century cult of the beautiful soul.

Two works—two novels—will occupy the majority of our attention here, Wieland's *Geschichte des Agathon* and Rousseau's *Julie: ou, la Nouvelle Héloïse*. Rousseau's *Julie*, published in 1761, appeared before the first edition of Wieland's *Agathon*, which came out in two parts in 1766 and 1767, but Wieland had already began to explore the novelistic implications of the beautiful soul in the 1750s, several years before Rousseau's work was published. For this reason, the internal development of the ideas in these two novels is not reflected in their dates of publication. As we will discover, Wieland sought what was in many ways a positive solution to the problem of the beautiful soul by trying to reconcile its many, and often conflicting, elements into a unified, harmonious whole; he tried in effect to stabilize and promote what had already become a recognized cultural ideal. Wieland thus treated the beautiful soul in what essentially amounted to a retrospective fashion, gathering together the various traditions of thought that had previously been devoted to the philosophical and religious expositions of beauty of soul. And although his perspective on the problem evolved and changed throughout the following years in several significant respects, he never abandoned the notion entirely. Rousseau's presentation, on the other hand, is a far more complex case, but it is one that for all of its tortuous ambiguity,

5. Jean-Jacques Rousseau, "*Discours* qui a remporté le prix à l'Académie de Dijon. En L'année 1750. Sur cette Question proposée par la même Académie: Si le rétablissement des Sciences et des Arts a contribué à épurer les moeurs," in *Oeuvres complètes*, ed. Bernard Gagnebin and Marcel Raymond (Paris: Gallimard, Bibliothèque de la Pléiade, 1959–69), 3:5.

anticipates more accurately the course actually taken by the concept of the beautiful soul than does Wieland's rather hopeful projection. For although Rousseau also yearned to believe in the possibility of establishing and maintaining a society of beautiful souls, his portrayal of such a state, seemingly despite his best efforts to the contrary, exposed some of the fatal flaws in the very ideas that were meant to provide its foundation. The subsequent fortunes of the concept of moral beauty—having been made tantalizingly, almost beckoningly real in these and many other literary evocations of beautiful souls they inspired—thereafter oscillated between elevated utopian hopes and skeptically ironic reminders of the human incapacity to attain the perfection that the ideal inherently required. But it was not for another half-century and more, not until after the Enlightenment had finally exhausted its original momentum, that the beautiful soul—from the beginning a diaphanous and immaterial presence—followed the path of the Enlightenment's own waning and at last disappeared altogether.

WIELAND AND THE ALLEGORY OF THE "SCHÖNE SEELE"

Wieland has not fared well at the hands of posterity. Oddly enough, the Germans themselves bear the primary responsibility for the neglect his works had suffered until only relatively recently. This rejection of Wieland, although part of a larger and more complicated social phenomenon, seems to have stemmed for the most part from the degree to which he identified with the European Enlightenment itself. Throughout his life, Wieland read widely and sympathetically in all of the major French, English, Italian, Greek, and Roman—as well, one should add, as German—literary and philosophical traditions, and from an early age onward he cultivated an intellectual cosmopolitanism that was supported by personal inclination and reinforced by principled conviction. During his lifetime, and partially because of the scope of his interests, Wieland enjoyed even greater fame and influence than any other German-speaking writer, including both Goethe and Schiller. Goethe in fact later acknowledged Wieland's efforts to lend pliancy and grace to their native language, and he applauded the contributions Wieland had made toward fashioning German into a modern literary medium of European stature. "All Upper Germany is indebted to Wieland for its style," Goethe expansively remarked to Eckermann in the 1820s, "it has learned much from him; and the ability of expressing itself correctly is not the least."[6] Yet as the nineteenth century progressed and as the collec-

6. Johann Peter Eckermann, *Gespräche mit Goethe in den letzten Jahren seines Lebens* (Leipzig: Brockhaus, 1868), 168. See also Eric A. Blackall, *The Emergence of German as a Literary Language, 1700–1775* (Cambridge: Cambridge University Press, 1959), 415.

tive consciousness in German-speaking countries grew belligerently nationalistic, Wieland's broadly European, instead of exclusively German, orientation grew increasingly intolerable to readers who were anxious to assert their unique and autonomous German past. Wieland was accused of an ever expanding variety of sins, including fostering a shallow eclecticism; favoring French "civilization" to Germanic "culture" (a reproach that implied a censure of the artificial, even decadent, overrefinement ostensibly typical of the French); and investing far too much confidence in the "superficial" conception of reason supposedly advocated by the Enlightenment at the expense of appreciating the "deeper" emotional, which is to say nonrational, forces of humanity. For a long time, then, German literary historians habitually treated Wieland as an unfortunate aberration, as the very antithesis of authentic "Germanness," and many sought to dismiss him as having been, at best, a second-rate and eccentric scribbler.[7]

But what scholars of earlier generations considered a debilitating fault now allows us, at a greater remove, to recognize Wieland as having been one of the most representative figures of his day. Precisely because of his attunement to the complex skein of contemporary intellectual and artistic concerns, Wieland literally embodied that tendency toward a unification or reconciliation of religion, philosophy, and the sciences that was mentioned earlier as typifying the general tenor of the Enlightenment at midcentury. But in spite of the profusion of influences that contributed to the formation of his mind and art as a whole, one can isolate three major moments that fundamentally determined the shape of Wieland's intellectual universe. And it was out of this fertile matrix that his own peculiar notion of the "schöne Seele," or beautiful soul, was born.

A native of the upper-Swabian imperial town of Biberach, Christoph Martin was the son of a pastor, Thomas Adam Wieland, who had received his training in Halle in the 1720s. The ties to this city, and to its peculiar religious atmosphere, were even more intimate than this connection suggests: a woman from Biberach who was related to the Wieland family was the wife, it so happens, of the Pietist educator August Hermann Francke.[8]

7. As an indication that this view has been by no means confined to prewar scholarship, see Wolfgang Pfeiffer-Belli, *Geschichte der deutschen Dichtung* (Freiburg: Herder, 1954), 364, who writes, "With regard to poetic genius Klopstock is superior to Wieland, with regard to moral greatness Lessing also overshadows the friendly and sanguine Swabian. Wieland was also not a forward-looking genius, leading into wonderful, distant lands, yet, being the master of assimilation that he was, he did accompany [!] the development of the German spirit from Brockes and Haller up to Romanticism. His many poetic trifles, dramas, novels and translations reflect, not in depth, but in scope, the entire eighteenth century. He always remains refined, charming, tasteful, witty. Whoever concerns himself with him will not be deeply moved, but will always have the impression of being in good company. But who still reads old Wieland today?"

8. Friedrich Sengle, *Wieland* (Stuttgart: Metzler, 1949), 15. See also Uwe Blasig, *Die religiöse*

Raised in a domestic atmosphere that placed primary stress on the transformative experience of spiritual "rebirth," a process ultimately culminating in the assumption of inner beauty, Wieland always associated strongly religious and particularly Pietistic connotations with the "schöne Seele." The Christian context was likewise present, even if abstracted to a remote level of metaphysical generality, when Wieland asserted, as he often did, that moral perfection (or *Vollkommenheit*) represented the end of human striving. But as one of the first European writers during the eighteenth century to find a new appreciation for Plato and for Greek culture generally, Wieland also seemed to experience no difficulty in integrating the teachings of the ancients into his system of faith. The Hellenic ideal of *kalokagathia*, along with its many auxiliary assumptions, thus provided, as we have already seen, the second main source from which Wieland drew the inspiration for his own most ambitious cultural aspirations. And finally, the British school of moral philosophy, begun by Shaftesbury and carried on most prominently by Hutcheson and Hume, acquired an almost canonical status for Wieland at the very outset of his career. Until his death in 1813, he appears never to have wavered in his conviction that Shaftesbury had possessed one of the finest minds of modern times.[9] These three cultural currents—which themselves of course owed much to one another—merged in Wieland's mind and, in their common insistence on our moral duties, substantially defined his image of the ultimate nature and purpose of humanity.

In 1752, at the age of nineteen, Wieland left the university at Tübingen, where he had just completed his studies, and headed farther south. He traveled to Zurich at the invitation of the highly regarded Swiss literary critic, Johann Jacob Bodmer, who took the young man into his house with the intention of acting as his mentor—in the literary, but also, apparently, in the Platonic sense. Bodmer seems to have fancied himself as something of modern-day Maecenas, having already played the part of munificent patron to Klopstock not long before. But Bodmer had made unreasonable demands on the poet, expecting almost total subjugation to his own aesthetic and religious sensibilities, and his relationship with Klopstock soon ended in mutual resentment and misunderstanding. Although Wieland also left Bodmer's house within two years of his arrival, his departure was less tumultuous than Klopstock's had been, and he always expressed sincere gratitude for the generosity and genuine kindness that his former benefactor had

---

Entwicklung des frühen Christoph Martin Wieland (Frankfurt am Main: Peter Lang, 1990), esp. 44–49.

9. On the much-studied relationship between the two writers, see Charles Elson, *Wieland and Shaftesbury* (New York: Columbia University Press, 1913), 9–10. This book can be complemented by Herbert Grudzinski, *Shaftesburys Einfluss auf Chr. M. Wieland: Mit einer Einleitung über den Einfluss Shaftesburys auf die deutsche Literatur bis 1760* (Stuttgart: Metzler, 1913).

shown him.[10] For having been granted the freedom and peace to work without serious interruption or material care, he had been able to expand on the studies he had undertaken at the university. Most important, it was there, in Bodmer's richly stocked library, that Wieland taught himself Greek.

After he had taken leave of Bodmer in 1754, Wieland decided to remain in Zurich and become a private tutor. He soon entered a small circle—somewhat unimaginatively dubbed by its members the "Tuesday Society"—of mainly older women who shared both his literary and religious preoccupations and who seemed especially enamored of Platonic philosophy. The nature of their weekly meetings appears to have been not entirely unlike that of Spener's *collegia pietatis*, and their purpose must have been comparable as well. Although much admired by these sensitive souls, Wieland and his precocious pedagogical zeal did not always meet with unquestioning appreciation. When Ewald von Kleist visited Zurich in early 1753, for example, he wrote a grumpy letter to Ludwig Gleim saying he had met "a certain Wieland" who had struck him as a "simpleton [*Pinsel*] who wants to reform the world and doesn't even have a beard yet."[11] In his newly acquired role as a spiritual guide to his female friends, Wieland (who if not entirely beardless, was still barely twenty) thought he had at last found the opportunity, and the audience, to put his evolving moral ideas to practical test. And during the middle of the decade he composed several essays with just that goal in mind, even though he recognized there were some mutual benefits involved. As he wrote in a letter to his friend Johann Georg Zimmermann in 1758: "The women were at the time my main intellectual and spiritual inspiration. Without three women in particular I would never have written the 'Nature of Things,' the 'Moral Letters,' the 'Tales,' 'Sympathies,' 'Theages,' and even the 'Christian Emotions.' "[12]

Wieland thus sought to exercise an educational, almost pastoral, role within this small, select society of women, and these writings were meant to serve as the instruments of their spiritual edification and inner "reformation." In light of their purpose, it is all the more important that in almost

10. See John A. McCarthy, *Christoph Martin Wieland* (Boston: Twayne, 1979), 24–25.
11. Ewald von Kleist, *Werke*, ed. August Sauer (Berlin: Gustav Hempel, n.d.), 2:222. Cited in Sengle, *Wieland*, 54.
12. Cited from the notes to Christoph Martin Wieland, *Werke*, ed. Fritz Martini and Hans Werner Seiffert (Munich: Carl Hanser, 1964–68), 3:821. In another letter, this one from 11 January 1757, we read: "The few ladies with whom I have some acquaintance here are all over forty years old; no one was ever a great beauty, all deserve the highest esteem owing to their unaffected virtue; one of them has a great deal of wit and liveliness, she is very well read, but does not reveal it to people who are not her intimate friends except through an exemplary modesty—another has a truly angelic innocence and goodness of heart, everything that one understands by the words *beauty of soul*, coupled with a modesty that veils the worth of her heart and her many natural abilities and merits" (3:957).

every one of the works Wieland named, the question of beauty, and specifically of inner or moral beauty, occupied the center of interest. Having
remained at the margins of philosophical literature for more than half a
century, moral beauty had thus, in Wieland's work, finally moved into the
forefront of attention. One of the first essays he wrote during this period was
a short work of 1754 called "Timoklea. Ein Gespräch über scheinbare und
wahre Schönheit" (Timoklea. A dialogue on apparent and true beauty).
Adhering to the literary form made famous by Plato and recently revived by
Shaftesbury, Wieland also drew on the substance of their ideas. The dialogue consists mainly of a discussion between Timoklea and Socrates about
how to distinguish the two types of beauty mentioned in the title. Socrates
states as a matter of course "that the source of beauty is to be sought in the
soul" and not in physical attractions, and that this beauty emanates from, or
even corresponds to, moral goodness.[13] Socrates goes on to stipulate that
the person who would deserve such a description would have to place every
action, thought, and desire in the service of virtue, which alone constitutes
human happiness. At one point toward the end of the dialogue, however,
Wieland has Socrates ecstatically conjure up a vision in which he touches on
a matter that clearly lay foremost in Wieland's own mind. "But if we recognize in someone the virtue, as I have described it, in its full beauty, then we
have to admit that human nature is capable of great excellence. And how
beautiful, how like supernatural realms, would an entire world full of such
people be!" (S4:63).

As this brief passage suggests, Wieland—ever mindful of the possible
utility and practical application of his ideas—had already begun to consider
what an ethical code based on the concept of moral beauty might look like
when it was adopted by real human agents and not confined to religious or
philosophical tracts. Timoklea herself responds in the appropriate fashion,
and after listening to Socrates finish his rhapsodic paean to virtue, she
remarks that her heart was "full of desire for this lofty and intellectual
beauty, that flows out of a resolute goodness of the soul" (S4:64). Timoklea,
it is clear, will go out into the world, fortified by Socrates' wisdom and
embark on her own attempt to refashion herself, to remodel her soul, so
that she will be able to take her place in the ideal society that Socrates had so
persuasively portrayed. But although Wieland hoped the members of his
circle would follow Timoklea's example, he realized that it would not always
be so easy to move or convince his readers to undergo the labor required to
become, themselves, beautiful souls.

That Wieland continued to think about this difficulty emerges in the

13. Christoph Martin Wieland, "Timoklea. Ein Gespräch über scheinbare und wahre
Schönheit," in *Sämmtliche Werke*, Suppl. (Leipzig: Göschen, 1794–1811), suppl. vol. 4, p. 55
(henceforth S4:55).

"Platonische Betrachtungen über den Menschen" (Platonic reflections on humanity) of 1755. Wieland began the essay by locating humanity on the great chain of being: "Human beings stand, so it seems, in the middle of the endless ladder of living and animate creatures, and they connect the world of spirits with the immeasurable animal kingdom" (S4:67). It is, of course, the possession of reason that gives humanity its superiority over animals, and it is reason that teaches us "the eternal laws of order and perfection" (S4:69). Most of all, "virtue is produced by the influence of reason on the heart," and "what is more beautiful than a *virtuous* human being?" (S4:71–72). But the same degree of reason, and hence of virtue and beauty, was obviously not everywhere in evidence, and in order to make his analysis more refined, Wieland sought to divide humanity into five discreet groups. Starting with base, sense-bound creatures barely distinguishable from beasts (and which constituted, Wieland found himself forced to admit, the largest portion of humanity), Wieland gradually ascended the scale of human types, enumerating their unique qualities as he went. Subscribing to the Enlightenment antipathy toward pedantry and useless knowledge, Wieland assigned scholars, or "speculative minds," merely to the third category. Instead of using their talents and energy for the benefit of all humankind, Wieland wrote, "they count the sands of the sea, measure the immeasurable, rummage around in the bowels of the earth as if all of the important tasks had already been completed, and spend their lives with sophistries whose greatest value consists in preventing them from doing something worse" (S4:95). The "fourth class," then, was occupied by those "amiable people whom nature has given the happy disposition toward a harmonious temperament [*harmonischen Gemütsart*], a fine feeling for the beautiful, and noble inclinations toward the good" (S4:87).

This was all well and good for those who were born with such a "happy disposition"—or lacking that, at least with a sizable inheritance that granted them the leisure to cultivate whatever qualities nature had unfairly neglected to bestow on them. But what was to be done for those who had not been so favorably smiled upon by fortune? Shaftesbury's aristocratic disdain, or simple disregard, for the multitudes had caused him to pass fairly quickly over this question, and none of his British followers had seen it worth his while to raise it again. Since Wieland himself lacked noble parentage, however, he found himself forced to confront many of the unpleasant realities his idol had been able to ignore. Like all moral philosophers of his day, Wieland also recognized the need to establish or discover "a few simple laws that are based on an infallible authority, that contain their reward in themselves, and that rest on principles that ensure us the highest degree of happiness" (S4:98). Not wishing to abandon entirely his beloved philosophy for some more egalitarian but pedestrian ideal, Wieland tried to find a way to mediate between the dictates imposed by the lofty ideal of moral beauty and the somewhat less exalted needs of a middle-class reading public.

Besides, Wieland's early religious training had instilled in him too great a confidence in the powers of the individual to govern and legislate the affective life for him simply to consign the mass of humanity to perpetual inner servitude to vice. The Pietistic penchant for a pragmatic approach to spiritual concerns led him to think about constructive means of attaining his goal of promoting virtue that went beyond the mere exhortation, favored especially by philosophers, to exercise one's reason and to rely on common sense. Wieland—a realist even in this, his most idealistic period—particularly doubted that learned treatises, or even stern sermons, could themselves bring about genuine morality. As he wrote in the "Platonische Betrachtungen," and making another sideswipe at merely abstract or speculative solutions: "If it is true that living examples and speaking portraits are of greater use to virtue than moral or metaphysical dissertations, then this small number of active, wise people, of both sexes, contributes more to the true advantage of humanity than the entire, vast world of speculative scholars" (S4:88). It is no surprise that this sounds remarkably similar to Spener's injunction that "the reality of our religion consists not of words but of deeds."[14] The difficulty, of course, still remained in finding the "living examples" Wieland mentioned who possessed the ability—that is to say, the resolve and the strength of will—to transform these words into deeds. Wieland had undertaken his duties as a tutor and assumed the role of spiritual mentor to his female friends partly in the idealistic hope of joining—or failing that, of creating—a society of such people. Inevitably he was disappointed; but in the wake of his disappointment he came to realize that in the absence of a convenient number of suitable candidates who could act as living examples of virtue, some sort of "speaking portraits"—drawn, if need be, by his own pen—would have to do.

In yet another essay written for the Tuesday Society, called "Theages, oder Unterredungen von Schönheit und Liebe" (Theages, or conversations about beauty and love), which first appeared in 1758, Wieland explicitly stated for the first time his own conception of the role that art can and should play in promoting the ideal of virtue he espoused. Using the contrivance of a letter addressed to a certain "Herr P.," Wieland began the essay by introducing a figure by the name of Nicias, who is described as a "Platonic hermit" and, for additional emphasis, is called a "virtuoso in Shaftesbury's

14. Philip Jacob Spener, *Pia Desideria*, trans. and ed. Theodore G. Tappert (Philadelphia: Fortress Press, 1964), 104. In this context, one might think as well of Francke, who wrote in his *Verbesserte Methode des Pädagogiums*: "True godliness is best imparted to tender youth by the godly example of the teacher himself." Cited in F. Ernst Stoeffler, *German Pietism during the Eighteenth Century*, Studies in the History of Religions, vol. 24 (Leiden: E. J. Brill, 1973), 27.

sense."[15] Recounting his visits to the portrait gallery owned by a woman named Aspasia, Nicias soon enters into a general disquisition about the relative effect of both poetry and painting, and he issues the following account of their function:

> To please should never be the main purpose, and certainly not the only one. To be useful in a pleasant way, that is the general law of the arts. No one doubts the good effects of a poem in which virtue becomes visible in examples. A painting that represents such an example has to have similar effects. When I am in Aspasia's gallery, I imagine that I am at a majestic assembly of the most virtuous people; their images make the same impressions, except weaker, that their living presence would make. And by pausing in the contemplation of a single work, a number of sensations and thoughts develop that supplement the notion of the painter, and, taken together, create a stronger effect than any work of poetry alone would be able to have. I think that an ethics in allegorical paintings, according to the idea that Shaftesbury sets forth in his letter about the choice of Hercules, would be an excellent means of forming [*bilden*] the taste and the hearts of young people. (3:178–79)[16]

This last line provides at the very least a linguistic bridge to another work Wieland wrote in the same year and which we have already examined in some detail: his "Plan einer Akademie zu Bildung des Verstandes und des Herzens junger Leute." As he had also set forth in that essay, during this epoch of Wieland's life, the word "education" (*Bildung*) meant cultivation toward the very specific goal of *kalokagathia*, however idiosyncratic his own understanding of the concept may have been. And here, in the words of Nicias, Wieland expressly held out the possibility of putting works of art in the service of attaining that greater goal. But by having Nicias say that setting "ethics in allegorical paintings" would be a suitable way to achieve that end, Wieland also indicated what formal structure he thought was most appropriate to realizing his intention.[17] *Bildung*, that is, might be most effectively promoted through the judicious use of allegorical images, or

15. Wieland, "Theages," in *Werke*, 3:169.
16. See the remarks by Klaus Bäppler, *Der philosophische Wieland. Stufen und Prägungen seines Denkens* (Bern: Francke, 1974), 13–29, who devotes an entire chapter to this essay.
17. Although Nicias was indeed speaking of "paintings" (*Gemälde*) in the literal sense, this word was often used metaphorically at the time, and especially in Zurich, to refer to *literary* "scenes" or "portraits" that had, moreover, a specifically moral purpose. In fact, in collaboration with his friend and colleague, Johann Jakob Breitinger, Bodmer had founded a "moral weekly" that was inspired by the English *Spectator* called *Discourse der Mahlern* (Discourses of the painters), which appeared in 1721–23, and was reissued in 1748 as *Der Mahler der Sitten* (The painter of morals). This habit of comparing poetic images to pictorial ones (which Lessing famously and successfully objected to in his *Laokoon*) is further demonstrated by another of Bodmer's works, *Betrachtungen über die Poetischen Gemählde der Dichter* (Observations on the poetic paintings of writers), published in 1741.

Bilder, which engage the reader's imagination and move him or her to practical action. Wieland's novel *Geschichte des Agathon*—which was, he explained, "the first book of mine written for the world at large, all the earlier things being written only for myself and a few friends of both sexes"[18]—grew immediately out of this complex bundle of ideas about the relationship between the effect, function, and form of art in the interest of advancing a particular moral program.

Ever since Aristotle had defined the effect of tragedy as consisting in the arousal of pity and fear leading to a purification of the emotions, artists and philosophers had both recognized and sought to exploit the sensible appeal of literary art. But the eighteenth century lacked a conception of literature, and of art in general, that existed purely for the sake of inducing some sort of emotional response in the observer—or to restate the matter, that had no recognizable end outside itself. Still very much under the sway of seventeenth-century neoclassical poetics, most Enlightenment writers accordingly conceived of their craft as having a "useful," which mainly meant an explicitly moral, purpose. In close conformity with the ancient rhetorical tradition descending from Aristotle, Cicero, and Quintilian, Wieland had thus likewise let Nicias describe the artistic task as one in which the goal of *persuasio* was achieved by combining *docere* and *movere*, or, as the Horatian dictum stipulated it, by joining *prodesse* with *delectare* and making poems both "useful" (*utile*) as well as "sweet" (*dulce*).[19] Not surprisingly, contemporary readers of Wieland's *Agathon* saw the work primarily from this perspective as well, and an anonymous critic for the *Allgemeine Deutsche Bibliothek*, for instance, remarked in 1768 that the novel offered a "series of psychological observations and moral portraits, which can provide an endless amount of pleasure [*Vergnügen*] and profit [*Nuzen*] for the philosopher, the statesman, and every thinking person." In order to prevent anyone from misconstruing this fairly tepid praise as an unqualified endorsement, however, the reviewer still thought it was necessary to remind the public that "the form of a novel is the least appropriate and the most dangerous means of presenting a useful example [*utile exemplar*] to people."[20]

Wieland himself clearly thought that the tradition of moral beauty, considered both as a philosophical and ethical ideal, but also as a social pro-

18. To Geßner, 28 April 1763, *Briefe*, 3:163. Cited in Michael Beddow, *The Fiction of Humanity: Studies in the Bildungsroman from Wieland to Thomas Mann* (Cambridge: Cambridge University Press, 1982), 60.

19. The best introduction to the influence of classical rhetorical categories on eighteenth-century aesthetic theories remains Klaus Dockhorn, *Macht und Wirkung der Rhetorik. Vier Aufsätze zur Ideengeschichte der Vormoderne* (Bad Homburg: Gehlen, 1968), especially the essay "Die Rhetorik als Quelle des vorromantischen Irrationalismus in der Literatur- und Geistesgeschichte," 46–95. Wieland's indebtedness to the classical rhetorical tradition has also been studied by John A. McCarthy, "Wieland as Essayist," *Lessing Yearbook* 8 (1976): 125–39.

20. Cited from Hans-Jürgen Gaycken, *Christoph Martin Wieland: Kritik seiner Werke in Aufklärung, Romantik und Moderne* (Frankfurt am Main: Peter Lang, 1982), 22–23.

gram, could be aligned with this understanding of poetry. Beauty of soul, as we have seen, was generally thought to exert an irresistible attraction on those fortunate enough to have it fall within their purview, and the pleasure we experienced in the presence of such perfect virtue was deemed so compelling that we would subsequently seek to prolong the experience by reproducing that same condition in ourselves. But as was all too obvious, and as Wieland had also admitted, few if any such "living examples" of moral beauty could be found, certainly not enough for the characteristics of beauty of soul to be formalized—or mass-produced. Given contemporary assumptions about the potential affective power of poetry, however, it seemed only a small step to join the qualities then thought to be inherent in literature with this philosophical construction. Wieland thus tried to give palpable persuasiveness to the theory of moral beauty by enclosing its precepts within the characters of a novel. For the novel could not only exhibit such exalted beings, it could also and more generally, as a literary work, bring about the same emotional effect in the reader as "real" beauty of soul was thought to produce on those who beheld it. Wieland thus sought to exploit the resources theoretically present in the novel as a literary form in order to achieve his pedagogical and social aims: to give pleasure and to trigger the emulation of the conditions that give rise to this pleasure—namely, virtue— in his readers.

Not that Wieland was the first person to establish the link between literature and this particular ethical ideal. To name only one: Klopstock, Wieland's predecessor in the enjoyment of Bodmer's benefactions, had apodictically written in an essay of 1759 that "the final purpose of higher poetry, and at the same time the true mark of its value, is moral beauty."[21] But Wieland was among the first to realize the possibilities for *promoting*, and not just for depicting, moral beauty that were latent in the contemporary conception of the effect that literature was supposed to produce. Although the discourse concerning beauty of soul had already reached a fairly high level of sophistication by the mid-1750s, few had considered using literature, and certainly not novels, in this eminently instrumental fashion in order to further this commonly acknowledged goal.[22] Wieland therefore set out into

21. Friedrich Gottlieb Klopstock, "Gedanken über die Natur der Poesie," in *Ausgewählte Werke* (Munich: Carl Hanser, 1962), 1001.
22. That philosophy could propagate morality with the help of literary devices had been envisioned most recently by David Hume (who also, incidentally, made explicit use of the metaphorical meaning of "painting" discussed earlier); but Hume did not seem to think that literature alone could perform this task. See his *Enquiries concerning Human Understanding and concerning the Principles of Morals*, ed. L. A. Selby-Bigge, 3d ed., rev. P. H. Nidditch (Oxford: Oxford University Press, 1975), 5–6: "As virtue, of all objects, is allowed to be the most valuable, [certain] philosophers paint her in the most amiable colours; borrowing all helps from poetry and eloquence, and treating their subject in any easy and obvious manner, and such as is best fitted to please the imagination, and engage the affections. They select the most striking observations and instances from common life; place opposite char-

largely unchartered waters when he sent about pursuing his plan. Indeed, in order to satisfy the multifarious requirements he had established regarding the role of art in the "education" [*Bildung*] of his readers, he found it necessary to create an entirely new genre of literature. His solution to this literary and pedagogical problem was his novel *Agathon*, which came to be seen as the prototype of that typically (if obscurely) German phenomenon: the bildungsroman.[23]

This term has most often been taken in a narrow sense to refer to the internal depiction of the protagonist's own *Bildung*, or to the portrayal within the novel of the gradual development and maturation that ultimately forms the finished character of the hero.[24] Although the narration of events leading to the completion of the central figure's personality is certainly crucial to every bildungsroman, this represents only one part of its intended overall design. The bildungsroman, that is, as Wieland conceived it (though the word itself did not yet exist), was supposed to shape, to form, to cultivate the reader as well. Not simply a literary category, the bildungsroman finds its fullest and most important realization in its formative influence on the reader.

It is telling that the first person to name and describe the bildungsroman also recognized this double agency. Although Dilthey has long been credited for having first coined the word, it actually came into existence during the second decade of the nineteenth century, when an otherwise undistinguished and now forgotten critic by the name of Karl Morgenstern gave a series of lectures "Ueber das Wesen des Bildungsromans" (On the essence of the bildungsroman).[25] Despite his patent limitations as a literary theorist or philosopher, Morgenstern deserves recognition for more than simply hav-

---

acters in a proper contrast; and alluring us into the paths of virtue by the views of glory and happiness, direct our steps in these paths by the soundest precepts and most illustrious examples. They make us *feel* the difference between vice and virtue."

23. Despite the specificity of its national origins, the term has gained widespread acceptance, as is evidenced, for instance, by the recent doctoral thesis by Wangari Muringi Waigwa-Stone, "The Liminal Novel: Studies in the French-African Bildungsroman of the 1950s" (Ph.D. diss, University of Utah, 1989).

24. See the classic statement in Wilhelm Dilthey, *Poetry and Experience*, in *Selected Works*, ed. Rudolf A. Makkreel and Frithjof Rodi, vol. 5 (Princeton: Princeton University Press, 1985), 336: "A lawlike development is discerned in the individual's life; each of its levels has intrinsic value and is at the same time the basis for a higher level. Life's dissonances and conflicts appear as necessary transitions to be withstood by the individual on his way towards maturity and harmony." In one of the later and influential books on the subject, the study by E. L. Stahl, *Die religiöse und die humanitätsphilosophische Bildungsidee und die Entstehung des deutschen Bildungsromans im 18. Jahrhundert* (Bern: Paul Haupt, 1934), the focus remains exclusively on the representation of the hero's *Bildung* within the novel. See also "The Bildungsroman as a Genre," in Martin Swales, *The German Bildungsroman from Wieland to Hesse* (Princeton: Princeton University Press, 1978), 9–37.

25. Morgenstern's claim to priority was first brought to general attention in an article by Fritz Martini, "Der Bildungsroman: Zur Geschichte des Wortes und der Theorie," *Deutsche Vierteljahrsschrift* 35 (1961): 44–63.

ing introduced a new word into our critical vocabulary. For not only was he the first to use the word "bildungsroman" to designate the class of novels we still recognize today by that name, he was also probably the last to use it in its original, eighteenth-century sense. Morgenstern specified that a novel "may be called a bildungsroman first and foremost because of its subject, because it represents the *Bildung* of the hero from its beginning, through its continuation, and up to a certain stage of completion." That statement, as general and vague as it is, still largely conforms to our current definition of the form. But he then went on to say that the bildungsroman earned its name "secondly because precisely through this representation it promotes the reader's *Bildung* to a greater degree than any other kind of novel."[26] Morgenstern had thus stipulated that to qualify as a bildungsroman, a novel had to demonstrate both internal and external significance. A true representative of the form not only depicted an individual human being undergoing the process of *Bildung*, it also aimed at stimulating the same activity in the reader.[27] Although he never indicated precisely what he thought the final result of such a *Bildung* in the reader should be, Morgenstern nevertheless insisted—repeatedly—that the name he had given to the new genre referred as much to its effect as to the form itself. It was also not accidental that Morgenstern elaborated his nomenclature with very particular works in mind, and at one point he singled out

the unforgettable Wieland's . . . *Agathon*, which is in my opinion one of the most excellent of all the works in this genre, aspiring to the beautiful ideal of Greek *kalokagathia* all the more successfully since its author, who possessed a great deal in the way of a beautiful Athenian soul, deposited in the novel the treasure of his own inner *Bildung* toward that wisdom which he so happily practiced before our eyes in a long and cheerful life.[28]

26. Karl Morgenstern, "Ueber das Wesen des Bildungsromans," in *Zur Geschichte des deutschen Bildungsromans*, ed. Rolf Selbmann (Darmstadt: Wissenschaftliche Buchgesellschaft, 1988), 64. Morgenstern conceived of this second aspect of the Bildungsroman very much in moral terms. Following the passage just cited, he claimed that the author has two main responsibilities: one is properly aesthetic, the other ethical, and he argued that the "novelist will wisely unite the end of art, namely to occasion pleasure and enjoyment through beauty, with the purely human goal of being useful, of instructing, and of improving others—in a word, of cultivating them [*bilden*], and here again the old Horatian rule will apply: 'Omne tulit punctum, qui miscuit utile dulci.' "
27. In a recent article by Dennis F. Mahoney, "Hölderlins 'Hyperion' und der Bildungsroman: Zur Umbildung eines Begriffs," in *Verlorene Klassik? Ein Symposium*, ed. Wolfgang Wittkowski (Tübingen: Max Niemeyer, 1986), 224–32, Mahoney also argues for a definition of the genre based not solely on its content, but on its effect on the reader as well. Although he acknowledges that Morgenstern had already proposed this point of view, Mahoney dismisses his predecessor's argument as "rather home-baked reflections."
28. Morgenstern, "Ueber das Wesen des Bildungsromans," 65. In making this biographical parallel, Morgenstern may have been thinking about the letter Wieland addressed to Zimmermann on 5 January 1762, in Christoph Martin Wieland, *Ausgewählte Briefe* (Zurich:

As a comment on the general aim and inspiration of the novel itself, Morgenstern's characterization of *Agathon* is remarkably perceptive. But commentators have often been mislead by the same wish to see biographical parallels to Wieland's life in the novel and have imagined that it is, at some basic level, a realistic evocation of the author's own inner state at the time of its writing.[29] But although Wieland arguably succeeded in providing a psychologically sensitive delineation of personality in the book, it would be not just difficult, but even absurd to claim that *Agathon* is a "realistic" work in the sense normally reserved for novels written during the modern period.[30] Many factors contribute to its general lack of realism: the setting of the novel in a patently idealized ancient Greece that makes little pretense to historical accuracy; the improbable claim that we are reading a recently discovered manuscript (a claim that the "editor," even as he makes it, says he doubts his readers will believe); and the long, digressive passages devoted to discussions of philosophical concerns all inhibit, if not actually destroy, the verisimilar texture of the novel. As an alternative to placing the work in the tradition of Richardson and Fielding, I thus propose instead that Wieland wrote *Agathon* quite deliberately as an *allegorical* novel, and specifically as an allegory in which the ideas that informed contemporary ethical thought assume distinct personalities as characters in the book, with the beautiful soul residing at the center of the design.

As a legitimate art form, allegorical fiction has been out of vogue for more than two hundred years, and it is thus hardly astonishing that commentators have not been anxious to identify *Agathon* as an allegory.[31] Until very recently, the romantically inspired distaste for allegory in favor of symbolic modes

---

Geßnersche Buchhandlung, 1815), 2:164, in which Wieland announced for the first time that he was working on a novel to be titled *Agathon*. "In it," he confessed, "I portray myself as I imagine having been in Agathon's circumstances, and at the end I make him as happy as I hoped to be." Careful attention to Wieland's words will reveal, however, that he was much more ambiguous about his own attainment of happiness and wisdom than Morgenstern imagined—or wished—him to be.

29. See Henry Hatfield, *Aesthetic Paganism in German Literature: From Winckelmann to the Death of Goethe* (Cambridge: Harvard University Press, 1964), 37, who writes: "To a great extent, Agathon represents Wieland himself." Sengle, *Wieland*, 190, also states that the novel is distinguished in two primary ways: "in this autobiographical turn and in the concentration on the individual human being that is connected with that tendency." The entire premise of the book by Wolfgang Paulsen, *Christoph Martin Wieland. Der Mensch und sein Werk in Psychologischen Perspektiven* (Bern: Francke, 1975), also rests on this assumption.

30. See the classic statement in Ian Watt, *The Rise of the Novel: Studies in Defoe, Richardson, and Fielding* (Berkeley and Los Angeles: University of California Press, 1959), esp. 9–34.

31. Sengle, *Wieland*, 187, for example, goes to great lengths to argue that Wieland wanted "to advance to a realistic image of humanity" and that the novel is symbolic, or as he puts it, "In *Agathon* antiquity is a symbolic world, not a mere masquerade" (191), the latter phrase a pejorative evocation of allegory's ostensible lack of serious artistic quality. The only exception I have found to this general tendency is the article by Horst Thomé, "Menschliche Natur und Allegorie sozialer Verhältnisse: Zur politischen Funktion philosophischer Konzeptionen in Wielands 'Geschichte des Agathon,'" *Jahrbuch der deutschen Schillergesellschaft* 22 (1978): esp. 219.

of writing sustained the lingering suspicion that allegory was, if not completely devoid of any aesthetic merit, then somehow simply too mechanical or superficially transparent to generate genuine emotional interest.[32] Yet writers during most of the eighteenth century thought differently about the matter. Winckelmann endorsed the mode in 1766 in his *Versuch einer Allegorie* (Essay on allegory), in which he defined and defended the form as a way of "indicating concepts through images [*Bilder*] . . . that is, it should personalize ideas in figures."[33] And, as we saw in "Theages," Wieland himself was fully prepared to think of art in allegorical terms. The obvious efficacy of allegory to convey abstract thought in terms one can more readily grasp had of course long been the primary justification for its use. The Platonic doctrine that certain objects in the visible realm, and most especially the phenomena of physical beauty, corresponded to, or could put us in mind of, the invisible sphere of ideas lent the form a philosophical legitimacy that must have appealed to Wieland. That allegory had also historically been a favored method of conveying, in particular, religious and moral ideas could only have made it all the more attractive to him as a means to address the issues he had formulated for himself. And it is the insistent reference to such a well defined and readily identifiable set of ideas that sets the allegorically structured *Agathon* apart from those novels of the time more properly called realistic. This difference is especially apparent when Wieland's work is actually compared to, say, Henry Fielding's *Tom Jones*, which literary historians have improbably yet repeatedly claimed is a close relative of Wieland's work, but which lacks any similarly coherent abstract focus.[34] Describing *Agathon* as an allegorical work in no way conflicts with the assertion that it is a true— and perhaps the first true—bildungsroman.[35] On the contrary, the two generic forms complement one another in a productive and positive manner, and in this particular instance their interaction is in fact crucial for an understanding of the novel's most general aim.

Agathon follows so closely an almost archetypical pattern of allegorical

32. The most famous recent attempt to reverse the traditional hierarchy of values is by Paul de Man, "The Rhetoric of Temporality," in *Blindness and Insight: Essays in the Rhetoric of Contemporary Criticism*, intro. Wlad Godzich, 2d ed. (Minneapolis: University of Minnesota Press, 1983), 187–228. See also "Rehabilitation of Allegory," in Hans-Georg Gadamer, *Truth and Method*, ed. Garrett Bareden and John Cumming (London: Sheed & Ward, 1975), esp. 63–73.

33. Johann Joachim Winckelmann, *Versuch einer Allegorie besonders für die Kunst* (Dresden: Walther, 1766), 2. Characteristically, Winckelmann defended the historical priority of allegory and claimed that "painting thoughts is indisputably older than writing them, as we know from the history of the peoples in the old and new worlds" (3).

34. In his perceptive book, *The Fiction of Humanity*, Michael Beddow also points out the differences between Fielding and Wieland. See 21–23.

35. I therefore disagree with Thomé, "Menschliche Natur und Allegorie sozialer Verhältnisse," 219, who writes that "Wieland's treatment of contemporary social relationships [can] be described as allegorical. He thus stands in opposition to the early forms of the symbolic bildungsroman."

fiction that only the relative unpopularity of both Wieland and allegory itself can explain why *Agathon*'s allegorical character has been overlooked.[36] But the evidence of its formal inspiration is everywhere. Like many allegorical works, *Agathon* begins with a hero in severe distress who embarks on a long and difficult journey: lost in the middle of the woods, Agathon—who through an ill turn of fate had lost his fortune, his friends, and even his fatherland only a few days before—tries to find his bearings by scaling a nearby mountain. But the closer he seems to come to its summit, the more his goal appears to recede. As night approaches, Agathon has only reached the middle of the slope, and unable to continue because of the growing darkness, he falls exhausted to the ground and quickly goes to sleep.[37] Several chords in an allegorical key are struck in this very first scene.[38] Suddenly forced from the peak of happiness, Agathon must now set out on a search to regain, if possible, what he has unfairly lost, and in the progress of his quest, which is at the same time the enactment of his moral education, he will encounter several guides who will either aid him or lead him astray.[39] The opening image thus stands as a cipher for his subsequent adventures; that he ascends only halfway up the mountain can likewise be taken as an early indication of where the novel, in ideational terms, will end.

36. Only occasionally, and mostly in asides, have critics considered the possibility that Wieland wrote in the allegorical mode. In his postscript to *Agathon*, Fritz Martini briefly addresses the issue of the setting of the novel in Greece, and writes that "Wieland was not concerned with providing a mimetic realism, as was befitting the genre, but rather he depicted the portrayed world from the almost allegorical function it acquired within the context of the novel" (951). But Martini does not consider that the entire work is allegorical. Hermann Müller-Solger, *Der Dichtertraum: Studien zur Entwicklung der dichterischen Phantasie im Werk Christoph Martin Wielands* (Göttingen: Vandenhoeck & Ruprecht, 1970), 296, writes that Wieland's verse epic, *Oberon*, which appeared in 1780, is an "allegory of the idea of the reconciliation between love and law."

37. See Edwin Honig, *Dark Conceit: The Making of Allegory* (Providence: Brown University Press, 1972), 74: "Generally the hero . . . starts out in despair to face an unprecedented ordeal. The progress of the ordeal provides the whole sequence of action for the ensuing allegory." See also 76–78, and Angus Fletcher, *Allegory: The Theory of a Symbolic Mode* (Ithaca: Cornell University Press, 1964), 349, on the importance of sleep and dreaming in allegories.

38. In fact, many more than I have mentioned. The novel begins with the following disclaimer: "The editor of the present story sees so little probability of convincing the public that it has actually been taken from an old Greek manuscript that he believes that it is best to say nothing concerning this subject and to leave it to the reader to think what he will of it." The ironic tone of this passage is sustained throughout much of the novel, and the narrator/editor often intrudes to make general comments on the hero and his predicament. Irony is a mode of expression clearly related to the allegory. Both are "saying something else" than what appears on the surface, and thus they have long been associated. See Honig, *Dark Conceit*, 15, 54, and 129–37; and Fletcher, *Allegory*, 84 and 229. See also the remarks on Wieland's irony in John A. McCarthy, *Fantasy and Reality: An Epistemological Approach to Wieland* (Frankfurt am Main: Peter Lang, 1974), 73–76. Swales, *German Bildungsroman*, 39, cites this passage and has fine remarks on the rather vertiginous qualities of its irony.

39. See Honig, *Dark Conceit*, 74; and Maureen Quilligan, *The Language of Allegory. Defining the Genre* (Ithaca: Cornell University Press, 1979), 133.

Even how its eponymous hero is handled betrays a tendency to exploit familiar allegorical conceits that is too striking, in fact almost too obvious, to be merely coincidental. Fortuitously called "Agathon" (good), he is also said by the narrator to have been of "such wonderful beauty" that the renowned Athenian sculptors Zeuxis and Alcamenes frequently employed him as a model in their portrayals of Apollo or the young Bacchus.[40] The beautiful (*kalos*) young man "Agathon" represents, that is, the very embodiment—or in the phraseology of allegorical interpretation, the personification—of the ideal of *kalokagathia*.[41] Indeed, *Agathon* itself as a whole is, as we will see, an allegorical fable "about" that most attractive proposal of modern moral philosophy which Wieland himself had helped to revive from ancient Greek thought. It is a work, that is, in which the ideas from the contemporary debate about the possibility of an ethical code based on the assumption of inner beauty do not just gain fictional human form in the figure of the protagonist—but also structural shape through the allegorical construction of the entire novel.

Naturally, it has not remained hidden from previous critics that even allowing for the requisite vicissitudes of its lengthy plot, the novel possesses a remarkably simple and even transparent conceptual structure. Everyone has recognized that the novel is basically concerned with the protagonist's efforts to reconcile the conflicting demands made by the emotional and rational sides of human nature.[42] But we have seen that it was precisely this dichotomy that characterized the central problem of eighteenth-century ethical philosophy, namely, the issue of how we can and do make moral decisions: do we somehow "feel" what is right and wrong, or is it the rational mind alone that can inform us of our duty? As Agathon himself asks one of the characters in the novel: "On what do you base your virtue?" (1.1.93). This was the central issue of mid-eighteenth-century ethical philosophy, for it was, as we know, a time in which the traditional answers to this question had lost their immediate and comfortable certainty. Much of the novel accordingly centers on this fundamental problem, and it tries to determine

40. Wieland, *Geschichte des Agathon*, in *Sämmtliche Werke*, 1.1.31. Henceforth cited parenthetically in the text as "*Agathon*" by volume, book, and page number. Wieland's novel went through three editions during his lifetime, the first appearing in 1766–67, the second in 1773, with the third being the present one. Many, if not most, critics have asserted that the first edition, even though it was unfinished and thus remained a fragment, is the most successful artistically; see, for example, Sengle, *Wieland*, 202. But, as pointed out by Melitta Gerhard, *Der deutsche Entwicklungsroman bis zu Goethes "Wilhelm Meister"* (Halle: Niemeyer, 1926), 102, this last edition, which alone contains the elaboration of Archytas's philosophy at the end, fulfills, not changes, Wieland's original plan for the novel.
41. In Quilligan, *Language of Allegory*, 42, we read that this sort of wordplay is "one of the most trustworthy signals of allegory."
42. See Swales, *German Bildungsroman*, 44, and "Idealism versus Materialism," in McCarthy, *Fantasy and Reality*, 71–106.

what the role of custom and example might be in forming moral character, or to what extent our moral makeup is "natural" or the result of external influence. Most important in psychological terms, it seeks to establish what the respective contributions of the senses and of the reflective faculties are in the administration of practical life.

There is a well defined, if somewhat unconventional, progression of plot in the novel that as illogical and inconsistent as it has seemed to some observers, makes eminent sense if considered as conforming to the contingencies of allegory. The novel is fairly evenly divided into three volumes, or "parts," and even though these parts do not follow a straightforward chronological sequence (the book begins, as we have discovered, in medias res, and only in the second segment does Agathon tell the story of his childhood and early education), the narrated order of events nevertheless exhibits a fundamental unity concerning the ideational, or allegorical, referent. The first part chronicles how Agathon, awakened from his slumbers on the mountain, narrowly escapes being dismembered à la Orpheus by a passing troupe of Maenads, only to be enslaved by roving pirates and then sold to a sophist by the name of Hippias—his first "guide"—who takes Agathon into service at his home in Smyrna. (Just in case we might still have some difficulty in discovering our hero's true identity, Wieland had Hippias rename his new servant "Kallias," thus nominally joining the two halves of his allegorical identity.) Hippias, a skeptical and pleasure-loving sophistic materialist, soon discovers with some amused surprise that his new factotum is an accomplished student of philosophy, and in fact a disciple of Plato. Agathon reveals that he spends his time thinking, as he tells his new master, "how happy the condition of the spirits must be who have cast off their coarse animal body and live through millennia contemplating the truly Beautiful, the Immortal, the Eternal, and Divine" (1:1.85). Charmed but unconvinced by Kallias's *alias* Agathon's idealistic ruminations, Hippias responds at first by agreeing that human beings are indeed united in their common attempts to attain the greatest degree of happiness. But his own categorical imperative celebrates not the sort of intellectual contentment advocated by Plato, or even by Locke and Wolff; rather, he advocates *volupté*, pure sensual self-indulgence, unimpeded physical pleasure. "Satisfy your needs," Hippias exhorts his captive audience, "gratify all of your senses; and, as far as you are able to do so, spare yourself all painful sensations" (1.1.114). This sounds very much like a Hobbesian conception of moral good: what one desires is by definition good, and our actions are determined only by such material wishes and not by abstract principles or laws. Being a consistent epicurean, Hippias mistrusts the power of rational arguments alone to convince Agathon of what he thinks is the chimerical and even hypocritical nature of Agathon's moral musings. Hippias therefore enlists the aid of Sensuality itself in the form of Danae, a beautiful courtesan, whom he engages to seduce his idealistic young retainer into accepting his doctrine. After much staunch and noble resistance, Agathon (who is unaware of Danae's professional skills) eventually succumbs to the physical charms of his attractive new companion and allows himself to experience the pleasures of his "coarse animal body."

This first segment, or part, of the novel is thus dominated by Agathon's encounters with what are, in essence, the allegorical embodiments of Sensation, understood in both its epistemological as well as its more elemental meanings, with the philosophically agile Hippias providing the theoretical framework, one might say, for Danae's practical demonstrations. The narrative order of sequence here is important, since it does not correspond to the chronological development of the protagonist (which would make more sense if Wieland's aim had been merely to document the gradual education of his fictional hero). The plot corresponds, instead, to the abstract plan determined by the nature of the allegorical referent itself. Almost every eighteenth-century philosophical treatise, best exemplified by Locke's and Condillac's "essays," began with a consideration of sensation, that first, most certain realm of experience, before advancing to the less tangible phenomena of the mind. As Rousseau himself also wrote, in that famous section of *Émile* "The Creed of the Savoyard Priest": "I exist, and I have senses through which I receive impressions. This is the first truth that strikes me and I am forced to accept it."[43] Here Wieland similarly began with the brute facticity and material solidity of sense, which is no less vital to the formation of moral judgment than to the development of any other kind of mental activity. Since the reflective powers of the mind that exist independently of any contribution of the senses have not yet entered into the equation, virtually no mention has yet been made made of moral beauty—the allegorical frame of reference for *Agathon* as a whole—during this entire first section of the novel.

The second part serves, then, as a counterpoint and complement to the first. Here the narrator steps back and lets Agathon tell Danae in his own voice the story of his sheltered youth at Delphi, his early and chaste love of Psyche (which managed to remain a completely platonic affair—and fortunately so, as it turns out, for Psyche later proves to be his sister), and his training at Plato's Academy in Athens. Agathon relates how, in the artificial isolation of Delphi, he was taught to value only "the beauty and purity of the soul, abstraction from the objects of sense, the love of immortal and eternal things" (1.2.14). By its very remoteness, as well as by the lessons imparted

43. Jean-Jacques Rousseau, *Émile*, trans. Barbara Foxley (London: J. M. Dent & Sons, 1938), 232. See also Rousseau, *Sur l'origine de l'inégalité*, in *Oeuvres complètes*, 3:164: "The first feeling [*sentiment*] of a human being is that of one's existence."

there, Delphi is thus the emblematic home of pure Reason or Reflection, and Agathon's moral conceptions during this period reflect the abstract, disembodied refinement of their origin. Agathon also tells how he tested himself in the political arena: after a failed effort in the republic of Athens (which had led to the banishment whose effects we witnessed in the opening scene), he retraced the steps of his great hero, Plato, and journeyed to Syracuse in an attempt to reform the tyrant Dionysus. Confronted by greed, corruption, and apathy, Agathon's hopes are shattered once again, and the citizens of Syracuse reward him for his efforts on their behalf by throwing him into jail. Besides underscoring the incapacity of his ideals to affect the world, this precipitous plunge into the realm of politics also represents the logical effort to extend Agathon's experience from his own individual fate to that of the collective whole. His sojourns in Athens and Syracuse, in other words, are the allegorical depiction of the attempt to create an entire society, and not just an individual citizen, on the basis of abstract ideals derived from Reflection alone. But it is clear from Agathon's experiences that like Sensation, Reflection by itself cannot provide us an adequate notion of the world and our duties in it. Only the deliberate union of these two spheres, of sensation *and* reflection, of the passions *and* reason, can lead us toward the equilibrium, or harmony, that was thought to characterize mature morality and, hence, social stability. Between these two extremes, then, is the path that is supposed to lead Agathon to his goal. As the narrator sententiously remarks at a certain significant juncture, "virtue (one tends to say after Aristotle or Horace) is the middle road between two detours, both of which one should take equal care to avoid" (1.2.256).

Appropriately, then, it is not until the third and concluding part of the *Geschichte des Agathon* that Wieland attempted to perform a synthesis of the first two sections of the book by joining its two allegorical halves. As if performing a coda-like reprise, Wieland began this final part by depicting Agathon having lost his way once again in a forest, only this time he is not alone, but accompanied by his brother, Kritolaos. By thus thematically linking this episode with the opening scene, Wieland obviously wished to emphasize its importance. A storm ensues, and the two brothers, seeking shelter, stumble upon an isolated estate, which—coincidentally—belongs to Danae, whom Agathon had abandoned upon learning that she was actually a prostitute and who had subsequently retired to this house "to devote herself to virtue" (1.3.225). While he waits for the lady of the manor to appear (whose identity, however, is still unknown), Agathon busies himself with the inspection of several paintings that hang in a large hall of the house. The title of this chapter, "Ein Studium für die Seelenmahler" (A study for painters of Souls) recalls Wieland's earlier essay, "Theages," and the episode concerning Aspasia's allegorical picture gallery. Portentously, it is here, too, and in reference to the reformed Danae, that the phrase "beautiful soul" occurs for the first time in the novel.

It has often puzzled critics that the first and only explicit instance of a beautiful soul in the novel is none other than Danae herself. Why, many have wondered, did he decide to portray the paragon of human virtue as a former, though reassuringly repentant prostitute? Was this, they asked, Wieland's not so subtle attempt to undermine that very ideal? Or was there some other, hidden message that virtue, if not innately present in one's bosom, could at least be learned and that even a secular morality had room for the cleansing act of contrition? These questions are raised and partially addressed in a short essay that Wilhelm von Humboldt composed about fifteen years after *Agathon* appeared, titled simply "Über Religion" (On Religion).[44] In it, Humboldt portrayed human nature, fairly conventionally, as a complex mixture of sensual and intellectual, or physical and spiritual, constituents and that "virtue rests on the correct equilibrium of all of the faculties of the soul."[45] Yet Humboldt realized that explaining how we move from the one sphere to the other—that is from unreflected sensual experience to the abstract perfection of virtue—was something of a problem. He proposed that the distance one had to travel from "the raw, uncultivated savage, who knows only sensual desire and sensual pleasure . . . to moral cultivation [*moralische Bildung*] is an unbridgeable chasm over which only aesthetic cultivation can prepare the way for the transition" (1:17). In fact, Humboldt went on to argue, not only was the step from physical pleasure to intellectual delight necessary to the development of culture at large, the achievement of true moral cultivation inevitably disinclined us against unmitigated sensual lust and reinforced our enjoyment of noncarnal satisfactions. "The transition from the merely sensual pleasure to the feeling of the sensually beautiful," Humboldt explained, "finally makes the former distasteful to the soul and prepares the step toward the morally beautiful. I thus do not know whether the attempt of giving base sensuality a more charming form should deserve our thanks rather than our censure" (1:18). Humboldt argued, in other words, that we needed a surfeit of sensual pleasure precisely in order to wean ourselves from the desire for it, and only in this way could we advance to the stage of "the morally beautiful." To underscore this greater cultural profit in the experience of undiluted animal pleasure, transitory though the usefulness of the instrument may be, Humboldt then added a remarkable footnote to this last sentence, saying: "May not this reflection give a different direction to the peculiar controversy about the expression

44. Wieland did not add the story of Danae to the novel until the second edition in 1774.
45. Wilhelm von Humboldt, "Über Religion," in *Werke*, and Andreas Flitner and Klaus Giel (Darmstadt: Wissenschaftliche Buchgesellschaft, 1960–81), 1:15.

Freudenmädchen?" (1:18).[46] The German word that Humboldt used here, *Freudenmädchen*, literally means "girl of joy" or "pleasure," or, in a word, "prostitute."[47] Because—or so Humboldt seems to be saying—frequent patronage of a prostitute would eventually gall purely sensual pleasure, she deserved our esteem (and, presumably, one's business) since she ultimately served the cause of advancing the most perfect morality, indeed of promoting the progress of civilization itself. In a perverse extension of Plato's conception of *eros*, Humboldt thus seemed to view the prostitute as the mediator between sense and mind, as a privileged means, no less, of making the transition to moral beauty. It appears that one could take a shortcut to becoming a beautiful soul by buying one's way into the intimate society; but only on the condition, of course, that someone else was willing to sell.

Understandably, perhaps, Humboldt never published this essay, but even if Wieland had been able to read it, he would probably not have been prepared to adopt this view entirely, even though he took a far more liberal view of such matters than the majority of his readers found acceptable. But Danae occupies at least indirectly a structural category similar to the one Humboldt assigned to his philosophical *Freudenmädchen*. Having experienced, no doubt even more intensely than Agathon himself, the extremes of sensible and spiritual life, Danae is presumably in a unique position to be able to harmonize, or at any rate to negotiate between, their opposing demands. She is thus the nexus, the central point of convergence, for the ideational strands of the novel, and thus the central symbol of its ethical system. Yet given her previous experiences, Wieland's suggestion that Danae represented the very incarnation of virtue (she is, after all, the only character explicitly called a *schöne Seele*), this identification of prostitution with moral goodness seemed to affront his readers—and to confirm their suspicions about novels in general. What is it, then, that qualifies Danae to serve in this crucial capacity? What enables her to perform her role as the model of moral probity? What, in short, makes her a beautiful soul? Instead of confronting this issue directly, however, Wieland fled from the potentially

46. Humboldt did not just theorize about prostitutes: he regularly sought out their services. During his extended trips to France and Switzerland in 1789, for instance, he carefully recorded all of his travel expenses in his diary, including the following noteworthy entry: "27 July in Spa, 1 crown to a whore [*Hure*]; 30 July in Brussels, 7 sous to a whore; 6 August in Paris, ½ crown to a whore; 10 August, same place, 1 carolin for 'fleshly pleasure'; 14 August, same place, 2 crowns 24 sous for 'sensual pleasure'; 17 August, same place, 2 crowns 24 sous for 'sensual pleasure'; 19 August, same place, 2 crowns 12 sous to 'sensual pleasure'; 25 August, same place, 2½ crowns 12 sous for 'sensual pleasure'." Cited from Peter Berglar, *Wilhelm von Humboldt* (Hamburg: Rowohlt, 1970), 39.

47. The "controversy" to which Humboldt referred had begun in September 1787, when an anonymous essay appeared "Über den Ausdruck Freudenmädchen," in which several alternative words for "prostitute" were advanced. This article was answered a year later by Johann Timotheus Hermes, who suggested the phrases "Tochter des Leids" (daughter of suffering) and "Jammermädchen" (girl of sorrow). See Humboldt, *Werke*, 5:296.

uncomfortable questions that Danae's identity raised by making the uncon-
vincing assertion that her qualities were simply somehow natural. "A beautiful soul," the narrator offers by way of explanation, "into which nature has
engraved the lineaments of virtue (as Cicero says), which is gifted with the
most tender sensibility for the Beautiful and the Good and with an innate
facility for performing every social virtue, can be hindered in its development by a confluence of unfavorable occurrences, or its original form [*Bildung*] can be disfigured." However, "the principal features of the soul remain incorruptible. A beautiful soul can go astray, it can be deceived by
delusions and lies: but it cannot cease to be a beautiful soul" (*Agathon*,
1.3.242–43). Danae may have polluted her body, but she never compromised her essential purity.

But this is a serious corruption of the very demanding traditional conception of moral beauty, which Shaftesbury and his disciples had always portrayed as the product of constant, active effort, as the final result of a highly
conscious and deliberate shaping of character, but not as an innate quality
that, once possessed, could never be lost. Wieland certainly knew all of that,
just as he knew of the supreme ethical importance attached to the concept
itself, yet nowhere did he provide an account of the quality itself, either in
Danae or in anyone else. At the same time, there is no doubt about her
function within the novel. As the narrator declares: "The love of virtue, the
desire to re-form [*umbilden*] oneself after this divine ideal of moral beauty,
takes possession of all our inclinations; it becomes a passion" (1.3.244). As a
"beautiful soul," Danae is now not only seized by this passion, she also
inspires it in others, who thus try—like Agathon—to assimilate themselves
to the "divine ideal of moral beauty" by bringing the entire store of their
feelings and thoughts into some sort of equitable balance. But even though
this conclusion represented both the conceptual and compositional aim of
the novel, Wieland was not able to specify precisely how this union was to be
achieved.

It is not until the final two chapters of the last edition of the novel, which
appeared in 1794, that Wieland attempted to resolve the central conflicts of
Agathon in the figure of the philosopher Archytas who presides over the
utopian republic of Tarentum. Archytas dispenses his sage advice in general
reflections on the nature of humanity, which he also views as being composed of "two different and mutually exclusive natures"—namely, the "animal" one and the "intellectual" one—which are in constant conflict with
one another and which must be reconciled if happiness is ever to be
achieved (1.3.392). More explicitly than ever before, Wieland thus tried to
force a resolution to the two allegorical elements that had stood in similar
conflict throughout the novel and that had found an ambiguous union in
Danae. It is at the very least indicative of the difficulties of this enterprise
that Wieland apparently did not feel ready to confront, let alone resolve, this

problem until almost twenty years after the original publication of the novel. Many critics who prefer the fragmentary first edition of 1766–67 have expressed dissatisfaction with the rather arbitrary syncretism of the conclusion Wieland eventually added. Yet as disappointing as it may be, it was the necessary culmination to the work, one demanded not only by the internal requirements of the allegorical meaning he had systematically elaborated, but, maybe even more significant, by the conception Wieland had about the external effect that such a work of art was supposed to have on his reader.[48] In other words, Wieland's efforts to unify the various strands of his narrative in a "harmonious" conclusion is thus a further sign of the complicity between the formal and thematic aspects of the book. The ideal of moral existence advocated by the novel was supposed to be pleasant and thus stimulate our desire to emulate it only by virtue of embodying the classical attributes of beauty, and *Agathon* itself could achieve its intended effect as a bildungsroman in both senses of the term only if the entire book reflected those qualities as well. Wieland encrypted *Agathon* as an allegorical evocation of the abstract concept of the beautiful soul, but he also wanted to lend it, as it were, a beautiful soul of its own.

That he failed to do so tells us as much about the ideas the book claims to advocate as about the artistic success of the work itself. For, in the end, Archytas leads Agathon to the realization that he can achieve only a relative stage of perfection, moral or otherwise. Just as Agathon, in the opening scene of the novel, manages to climb no more than halfway up the mountain, Archytas teaches him that human beings can indeed rise above the dense immediacy of simple sensation to which mere animals remain forever bound, but that they cannot attain the summit of pure, unobstructed rational vision that God alone can command. In the end, Agathon learns to see "that *true Enlightenment toward moral improvement* is the only thing on which the hope is founded for better times, that is, for better human beings" (1.3.419–20). Representing neither victory nor defeat, the compromise suggested by Agathon's final insight, which promises constant progress but implicitly denies the attainability of his original goal, allows the novel to end in a draw. But the dissonances remain largely hidden, or are rather glossed over, in the *Geschichte des Agathon*, and that was to a certain extent what Wieland intended. They become much more obvious, and this time contrary to the author's wishes, in the work of Wieland's French colleague, Jean-Jacques Rousseau.

48. Even though this section did not appear until the third edition came out in 1794, Wieland had already planned to write it immediately after finishing the first edition. In a letter to Geßner on 21 December 1767, he wrote that "in the next few years Agathon should receive a third part. This part will have the special title: 'Archytas' and contain speculative conversations between this wise old man and our Agathon." Cited in Gerhard, *Der deutsche Entwicklungsroman*, 102n.

Rousseau and the Society of "Belles Âmes"

Whereas Wieland's reputation languishes in the shadows of an almost irretrievable past, with even his name now known only to a mere handful of devoted, but slightly defensive scholars, Rousseau has of course become common property of the educated world. The imprint of his mind is deeply drawn on almost every page of our culture: entire revolutions—social, political, educational, artistic, and even sexual upheavals and transformations—have been variously attributed to (or blamed on) the force and effect of his ideas. One of the most vehement critics of civilization and its ostensible advances, he is widely given credit for having helped to institute the major modern forms of progressive thought. And, more broadly, Rousseau is recognized as one of the most influential political philosophers to have ever lived, and certainly as the single most important opponent of Hobbes and the most perspicacious precursor of Karl Marx. Not everyone approves of Rousseau, naturally, and much of his thought continues to arouse vigorous dissent. It cannot be denied that there are many disquieting aspects to his philosophy, and he has been repeatedly attacked for the apparent, as well as for the more submerged, totalitarian tendencies of his thinking. Above all, he has always been criticized for the jarring contradictions that abound in his writings. But these tensions constitute a large part of his power: from the very beginning of his career Rousseau provoked extreme responses, often attracting hostile and sometimes profoundly bitter criticism (from his enemies and former friends alike) while at the same time winning among the mass of his readers equally passionate and loyal devotion. Wieland likewise enjoyed considerable popular acclaim, even as he suffered occasional opprobrium from his peers. Yet the reaction his works elicited never approached the pitch excited by the person and thought of the extraordinary "Citizen of Geneva."

As if reflective of this marked disparity between them, Rousseau's only major work of fiction, *Julie, ou la Nouvelle Héloïse*, appears at first glance to differ in so many ways in both form and effect from the work of his German counterpart that it might initially seem unfruitful to compare the two novels at all. Rather than taking place in an artificially "classical" past that was highly stylized and thus emotionally alienating, the events described in Rousseau's novel were virtually contemporary with its appearance.[49] In addition, the ironic narrative distance that Wieland placed between himself and his subject also has no counterpart in Rousseau, who was inspired by the success of Crébillon and Richardson to employ the more immediate, inti-

---

49. See the "chronologie" in Jean-Jacques Rousseau, *Julie, ou la Nouvelle Héloïse*, in *Oeuvres complètes*, 2:1826–29, in which the editors determine that the novel opens in the autumn of 1732 and concludes at the end of 1745.

mate medium of the epistolary form, giving us the sense of having direct access to the innermost thoughts and feelings of his characters. In Wieland's *Agathon*, by contrast, the reader merely eavesdrops on the learned dialogues that ensue between the main protagonist and his various companions. But in reading *Julie* we might well forget that the passionate letters the characters exchange are not somehow addressed to us. Rousseau wielded the epistolary form with such eloquent virtuosity, in fact, that many of his readers responded with letters of their own to the author. "I have devoured the six volumes," one such enthusiast wrote to Rousseau with typical exuberance, "I am rereading them with rapture. This book should never come to an end. I have shed delicious tears."[50] Wieland also had many sympathetic readers, but it is doubtful that anyone bedewed the pages of his works so emotionally—or, for that matter, that he wished for such a reaction to occur. A certain Johann Georg Meusel, for instance, who wrote a review of Wieland's novel in 1768, found on the whole that it undoubtedly had many sterling qualities, but he also confessed that on occasion he had trouble stifling a "yawn" [*Gähnen*].[51] The publication history of the two books tells the story, in any case, with the brutal objectivity of numbers: whereas Rousseau's novel created an international sensation, selling out almost overnight when it first appeared and giving rise to no fewer than seventy-two editions before the end of the century, the sales of Wieland's *Agathon*, although not inconsequential, remained distinctly more modest, making only three editions necessary in his lifetime.

Nevertheless, as real as these and other differences are, there exist even deeper correspondences between *Julie* and *Agathon* that emerge on closer inspection. One of the most notable similarities between Rousseau and Wieland is their shared concern to use their literary works to achieve significant change, and specifically to encourage moral betterment, in their readers. Rousseau, no less than Wieland, possessed a working familiarity with the rhetorical tradition of antiquity, and he also mainly subscribed to the Horatian conception of poetry. Here too, however, the means they both employed, and their respective faith in the efficacy of those means, diverge in important ways. Unlike most modern moralists—including those who subscribed to the Christian doctrine of original sin and those, such as Hobbes, who had other reasons to believe in human baseness—Rousseau felt that human nature, in its original state, was basically and intrinsically good. The qualification of "original" is crucial: for Rousseau believed that although we began in blissful innocence, somewhere in our collective development

50. Cited in Lester G. Crocker, *Jean-Jacques Rousseau* (New York: Macmillan, 1968–73), 2:101.
51. See Lieselotte E. Kurth-Voigt, "Wielands 'Geschichte des Agathon': Zur journalistischen Rezeption des Romans," *Wieland-Studien* 1 (1991): 13–14

something had gone terribly wrong. "Human beings are evil," he thus proclaimed in the second *Discours sur l'inégalité* of 1755, even though "humankind is by nature good" (3:202). Rousseau refused to imagine that the evil so much in evidence in the world expressed our real inner constitution, and he preferred to think that our current malaise represented an aberration from our true being. He attempted to isolate several causes for the corruption he felt afflicted modern society, and his two *Discours* are essentially given over to his analyses of the various roots of all evil. But at bottom the primary reason for the decadence that Rousseau thought characterized the modern world was that humanity had gradually distanced itself from the simple virtues supposedly present in the untutored breasts of our first forebears, and that this so-called progress itself was to blame. As he put it in the first *Discours*, "Our souls have been corrupted in the same degree to which our sciences and arts have advanced toward perfection" (3:9). The task Rousseau modestly set for himself was to put us in mind, and with *Julie* actually to move us toward the recovery, of that original state of moral innocence which we had all lost long ago.

Given his extreme reservations regarding the value of the sciences and the arts, it seems paradoxical that Rousseau would have believed that such a clearly compromised medium as the novel could help reform the very condition he had more than indirectly accused it of creating. In the Second Preface to *Julie*, in fact, Rousseau took up this issue directly. The preface is constructed as a dialogue between an otherwise unidentified "N." and an equally unnamed "R." (although the latter is finally revealed to be none other than Rousseau himself). At a certain juncture, N. says that he thinks that the novel, despite its division into six "parts," falls evenly into two distinct, and distinctly conflicting, halves, and he thus wonders how or if they can be reconciled. N. asks in particular how the less than virtuous tale beginning the novel—namely, the illicit love affair between Julie d'Etange, the only daughter of a noble and wealthy Swiss family, and Saint-Preux, a young man without visible means who was hired as a private tutor to finish her education and instead seduces her—could be seen as being uniform with the second half. For here the fallen Julie (much like Danae in *Agathon*) has redeemed herself through honest penitence and her resolve to devote herself to the conduct of a virtuous life with her husband, Monsieur de Wolmar, at their estate at Clarens. "The end of the story makes the beginning all the more reprehensible," N. not unreasonably argues. "The children's games that precede the lessons of wisdom prevent us from waiting for them; the evil scandalizes before the good can edify; in a word, the indignant reader is repulsed and puts down the book at the moment he might profit from it." With irrefutable logic and even more irresistible cunning, R. makes this very circumstance—the truth of which he not only does not dispute, but even readily confirms—part of his counterargument. R. acknowledges that the book may produce precisely the reaction that N. describes, but that the novel was not written for such people anyway. "I think," R. responds, "that the end of the story would be superfluous to the readers who are repulsed by the beginning, and the same beginning ought to be agreeable to those for whom the end can be useful [*utile*]. . . . In order to make what one wants to say useful, it is first necessary to make oneself heard by those who should make use of it" (17). That one would actually read— and, moreover, *finish*—the novel was in itself therefore an incontrovertible sign that one was badly in need of the instruction it promised to provide. Thus, seen from a wider perspective, the very success of *Julie* was proof positive of the almost boundless depravity of society at large and the great necessity of the moral model that the story purports to contain.

There is no doubt that Rousseau meant for *Julie*, or at least its second half, to act as such a "useful" model for its readers to follow, thus leading them out of the moral debasement which their perusal of the book made plain. It is in that particular sense, or more specifically in the sense that Karl Morgenstern first advanced, that *Julie*, like *Agathon*, is also very self-consciously a bildungsroman.[52] As R. himself phrased it in the preface, "I like to imagine husband and wife reading this tale together, drawing from it new courage to endure their common labors and, perhaps, new insights for making them useful. How could they contemplate in it the image of a happy household without wanting to imitate such a pleasant [*doux*] model?" (23). It is not necessary to speculate about how this conception of the novel's intended effect conforms to Rousseau's theories concerning the inevitable formative influence wrought on us by our intellectual and physical environments.[53] A scrupulous and accomplished stylist, Rousseau confidently put a tempered but unfaltering faith in the power of rhetoric to help achieve his pedagogical purposes. Yet as we will presently see, it is the very ambiguity of the model that Rousseau put forward, or at least of how that model can or ought to be understood, that imperils Rousseau's entire enterprise.

From the very first letter of the novel Rousseau seemed to want to leave no room for uncertainty about the nature of Julie's moral constitution. Enumerating the reasons why he has fallen in love with Julie, his unsuspecting and innocent charge, Saint-Preux explains to her that "it is that touching combination of a lively sensibility and an invariably sweet disposition, it is that tender pity for all the misfortunes of others, it is that justness of spirit

---

52. Morgenstern himself, in fact, viewed *Julie* as an exemplar of the genre; see Morgenstern, "Zur Geschichte des Bildungsromans," in Selbmann, *Zur Geschichte des deutschen Bildungsromans*, 82.

53. See H. Gaston Hall, "The Concept of Virtue in *La Nouvelle Heloise*," *Yale French Studies* 28 (1961–62): 25.

and that exquisite taste which derive their excellence from the purity of your soul."[54] Or in other words, as Saint-Preux expresses it not much later, Julie is a "beautiful soul" (*belle âme*) (1.10.52 [45]). Julie herself is accustomed to speaking of her fellows in similar terms, and she also remarks that whenever, as a young woman, she had felt the desire to love (and, it ought to go without saying, to marry) someone, "I did not ask Heaven to unite me to a charming man but to a man who had a beautiful soul" (1.13.62 [51]). And, indeed, despite their eventual transgressions both Julie and Saint-Preux themselves are described by others in just this way as well, as for example when their friend and would-be benefactor, the compassionate English nobleman, Lord Bomston, writes about them in a letter to Julie's friend, Claire: "These two beautiful souls left nature's hand made for each other" (2.2.193 [163]). Lord Bomston himself also falls under this generous rubric, and in a letter that Julie writes to him she mentions that "people say, my Lord, that you have a beautiful soul and a sensitive heart" (1.58.161 [131]). (Curiously, later in the novel Bomston falls in love with a prostitute he encounters in Italy; it seems that he wished to establish permanent residence on Humboldt's bridge spanning the gulf between bare sensual delight and moral perfection.)

Almost everyone in this novel, then, can apparently lay rightful claim to the title that was otherwise the exclusive designation of a small minority.[55] But what is the real nature of these "beautiful souls" who people the pages of *Julie* in such abundance? We already know that as seemingly virtuous as Julie herself may later become under the watchful guidance of her husband, Wolmar, she is a woman with a less than wholesome past. Unlike Wieland's Danae in *Agathon*, she was, of course, no courtesan; but according to contemporary codes of behavior the difference was merely relative, or rather it was not the absolute one that existed between her compromised state and the unsullied purity of virginity. Nor can Saint-Preux be seen as supplying the pattern after which we, as readers, should be expected to model our lives. He is an insistent suitor and Julie's eventual seducer, an unstable egotist who bounds from one emotional extreme to another and who consistently fails to fulfill (or, to put it more kindly, rebels against) his personal and civic responsibilities. Even if one is willing to grant that as Lord Bomston

54. Jean Jacques Rousseau, *La nouvelle Héloïse: Julie, or the New Eloise*, trans. and abr. Judith H. McDowell (University Park: Pennsylvania State University Press, 1968), 1.1.32 (26). Wherever possible, I have used the (abridged) translation of the novel and included the page number in brackets after the reference to the French edition. Pity, or compassion (*pitié*), is in fact the cardinal virtue according to Rousseau and the only one that he thought was totally "natural" and thus uncorrupted; see *Sur l'inégalité*, in *Oeuvres complètes*, 3:154–56.

55. See the interesting and highly critical comments on the "beautiful soul" in Irving Babbitt, *Rousseau and Romanticism* (Boston: Houghton Mifflin, 1919), 130–40, and passim.

declares, Julie and Saint-Preux "are so extraordinary that they cannot be judged by common rules" (1.60.165 [135]),[56] the discrepancy between the high ideal of moral beauty and their actual, ignoble actions causes one to wonder whether it might not be appropriate to look elsewhere for the model that Rousseau had promised.

It has been recognized for some time that the social order at Clarens, the small community created by Wolmar for himself, his wife, and their numerous domestic servants, constitutes an important part of Rousseau's vision of the ideal society, which he later more fully and systematically described in his *Contrat Social.* Clarens is supposed to represent, with experimental purity, the possibilities that are open to all who are willing to devote themselves to the realization of what Rousseau regarded as the highest human goal: to recover from the ills of civilization and regain our original state. Clarens is to be a refuge from the trivial temptations and empty pursuits of the corrupt external world (for which Paris is most often named as the prime exemplar) and, among other things, it is clearly intended to work as a cure for the dangerous passions that had so violently upset Julie's inner equilibrium. As Jean Starobinski has cogently argued, the evocation of the estate at Clarens falls in line with the structure that governed virtually the entirety of Rousseau's thought. In all of his works, Rousseau always presented himself as attempting to tear away the "veil" of false conventions, hypocrisy, and lies, all of which masked our true feelings, thoughts, and desires. Rousseau wanted to supplant the "obstruction" of artificial civilized behavior with the "transparency" of untrammeled nature and truth.[57] Clarens, then, is that place in *Julie* where human beings are given the opportunity to regain the simplicity and wholeness of nature that had been forfeited in the name of its opposite.

When Saint-Preux returns to Europe after several years' absence, during which he had journeyed around the world in the attempt to rid himself of his own destructive emotions, he soon travels to Clarens, where he meets M. de Wolmar. This meeting—in which Julie and Saint-Preux tenderly but chastely embrace after their long separation, whereupon she guides her former lover by the hand into the open arms of her husband—this scene of apparent forgiveness and reconciliation provided the motif for an engraving that illustrated the second edition of the novel and whose caption momentously reads: "La confiance des belles âmes" ("The Trust of Beautiful Souls").[58] Such complete "trust" is not just supposed to be one of the main

---

56. Claire repeats this view in a subsequent letter to Julie, saying that she "is beginning to perceive from all she sees how much your two hearts are above ordinary rules" (3.4.313 [233]).

57. Jean Starobinski, *Jean-Jacques Rousseau: Transparency and Obstruction,* trans. Arthur Goldhammer, intro. Robert J. Morrissey (Chicago: University of Chicago Press, 1988).

58. See plate 7; the engravings were made by Pierre-Philippe Choffard after originals by Hubert-François Gravelot for the Duchesne edition of 1761.

qualities of the beautiful souls that inhabit Clarens, it is said to express itself in all that takes place there. Immediately following this reunion, for instance, M. de Wolmar excuses himself and leaves the room to attend to some business, whereupon Julie begins to give an account of her behavior before and after Saint-Preux's departure. Saint-Preux is astounded to see that, when Wolmar unexpectedly reenters the room a few moments later, "she continued it in his presence exactly as if he had not been there." Wolmar notices this astonishment and says: "You have seen an example of the openness which prevails here. If you sincerely wish to be virtuous, learn to imitate it" (4.6.424 [290]). Wolmar then pronounces what could probably be considered the categorical imperative of Clarens: "The first step toward vice is to shroud innocent actions in mystery, and whoever likes to conceal something sooner or later has reason to conceal it. A single moral precept can take the place of all the others. It is this one: never do or say anything you do not want the whole world to see and hear" (4.6.424 [291]). Wolmar thus wants Saint-Preux—just as Rousseau wished for us—to believe that the regulation of the moral economy at Clarens is based on observing this single principle of practicing openness in one's actions, thoughts, and wishes. Clarity of mind and heart, honesty with oneself coupled with trust ("confidence") in others, form the stable foundation meant to support the moral order within this intimate community. It is a finely balanced enclave, in short, designed to promote the cultivation, or *Bildung,* of beautiful souls.[59]

But the more one learns about the actual management of Clarens and the methods M. de Wolmar employs to ensure that his directives are obeyed, the less that practice appears to coincide with theory. Instead of complete openness and transparent sincerity, we discover, on the contrary, that deceit, dissimulation, and even manipulative disregard for the freedom and autonomy of others are the true instruments of maintaining social stability in this experimental microcosm. The most striking aspect of the communal arrangement is its basic inequity: Rousseau, the great champion of human equality, gave us an organization that not only allowed, but virtually required the replication of autocratic forms of rule, with Wolmar presiding as the sole arbiter of justice and law. Even the arrangement of its social hierarchy presupposes an elite as well as a subservient working class, and the servants are all subject to Wolmar's efforts (both subtle and more overt) to mold their behavior and minds.[60] In a letter that Saint-Preux writes to his friend Lord Bomston, he says that at Clarens the male and female domestics are prevented from having much contact with one another, for—as he adds with no apparent sense of self-irony—"liaisons that are too intimate between

59. See the acute remarks by Starobinski, *Jean-Jacques Rousseau,* 101.
60. This is also the main criticism in the book by Crocker, *Jean-Jacques Rousseau,* 2:67–98.

the two sexes never produce anything but evil" (4.10.449). Saint-Preux goes on to explain, again apparently aware of the violent contradiction inherent in his very words, that "the great art by which the master and mistress make their servants such as they desire them to be is to appear to their people such as they are. Their conduct is always frank and open because they have no fear that their actions may belie their words. . . . Artlessly, they say what they think on every subject" (4.10.468 [302]).

But that is most emphatically what does not occur at Clarens. One particularly noteworthy example of the degree to which they dissimulate their beliefs and motives in order to achieve a desired effect is Wolmar's stance toward religion. As he at one point admits, he does not believe in God, but he nevertheless goes to church every Sunday in order to set a good example for his inferiors, thus plainly giving the lie to Saint-Preux's comments.[61] Wolmar even asks the domestics to eavesdrop on one another and to report what they hear to him. The ostensible reason for this mutual surveillance, as Wolmar says, is to allow him to anticipate and satisfy the wishes of his staff. In reality, he has in effect organized a network of spies, which is a de-humanizing, yet (as several totalitarian states during our own century have demonstrated) highly efficient means of social control.[62] But this sort of deception—both of oneself and of others—is not just confined to the control of lusty or recalcitrant servants: Julie also refrained from ever informing her husband of her ill-fated affair with Saint-Preux, and Wolmar, although he in fact knows of the incident, has never revealed his knowledge to his wife, thus compromising from the start the vaunted honesty and openness of their relationship. As Starobinski succinctly and accurately states it, "The belle âme has become a hypocrite."[63]

There is a famous moment in the novel in which this inner tension, this vibrating field of contradictory forces, crystallizes into a single, yet profoundly unstable image. It is the introduction of Julie's garden, her "Elysium," her refuge within an already tightly encircled space, the private retreat that as Wolmar warns Saint-Preux in the peculiarly overdetermined language spoken at Clarens, "has been planted by virtuous hands" (4.11.485 [313]). Saint-Preux is surprised at first to hear of its existence, for the garden is imperceptible to the eye from the outside because of the "dense foliage which surrounds it" (4.11.485 [313]); in addition, the gate leading into it is "always carefully locked" (4.11.471 [304–5]). Here, then, at the very heart of the realm that is said to rest on absolute candor and clarity is a mysteriously closed and concealed sphere. Upon first stepping into this

61. See ibid., 84
62. See the comments on the "spy system" at Clarens by James F. Jones, *La Nouvelle Héloïse: Rousseau and Utopia* (Geneva: Droz, 1978), 68.
63. Starobinski, *Jean-Jacques Rousseau,* 116.

forbidden spot, Saint-Preux is struck by what he thinks is a completely unspoiled wilderness, and he thinks he sees nothing but the signs of the unfettered course of nature. "This place is charming, it is true, but uncultivated and wild. I see no marks of human work" (4.11.472 [305]). But again, as in the case of Wolmar's surreptitious guidance of his staff, Saint-Preux has fallen prey to a carefully executed deception. Julie responds that he is right in thinking "that nature has done everything, but under my direction, and there is nothing here which I have not ordered" (4.11.472 [305]). When Saint-Preux expresses his amazement at the total lack of any apparent indications of artifice, Wolmar answers even more astonishingly with his own inimitable brand of disingenuous frankness that "it is because we have taken great pains to efface them. I have often been witness to, sometimes the accomplice of, this roguery" (4.11.479 [311]). He goes on to explain, unaware that he is symbolically undermining the avowed principles on which Clarens is supposed to be based, that the two sides of the garden "were closed in by walls. The walls have been hidden, not by trellises, but by thick shrubby trees which make the boundaries of the place seem to be the beginning of a wood" (4.11.479 [311]). Artificial nature, stylized innocence, constrained freedom: the head spins in the face of this swirling vortex of deliberate contrivance.

As an instance of enlightenment, Julie's garden is obscure indeed. Yet for all of its vertiginous qualities, it acts as a focus for the antagonistic forces that reside at the literal center of Clarens and thus of the novel as a whole. Moreover, it thematizes in a concentrated fashion the fundamental problem of the book: the question about the possibility of the existence of the beautiful soul. At once open to view and hidden from sight, a secret, self-enclosed space in the middle of a social organization that equated any kind of concealment with vice, a realm that falsely pretends to be something that by definition it can never be, Julie's garden tells us a great deal, probably more than even Rousseau wanted us to know. Paul de Man, still one of *Julie's* most perceptive readers, already recognized the preeminent significance of her garden, which he called "the central emblem" of the novel. De Man especially emphasized its formal and thematic implications: "On the allegorical level the garden functions as the landscape representative of the 'beautiful soul.' "[64] The garden, as a literary topos, has forever stood as the symbol of heightened and perfected being: from Eden to the secular *locus amoenus*, Paradise itself—derived from the Persian word for "park"—had always been conceived as place of natural beauty and calm, a restful space that both

64. See de Man, "The Rhetoric of Temporality," in *Blindness and Insight*, 201. In another essay, de Man developed his (highly idiosyncratic) views of the allegorical qualities inherent in the book; see "Allegory (*Julie*)," in Paul de Man, *Allegories of Reading: Figural Language in Rousseau, Nietzsche, Rilke, and Proust* (New Haven: Yale University Press, 1979), 188–220.

reflected and enhanced the inner state of those who were fortunate enough to reside there.[65] With Rousseau, however, the garden becomes the incarnation of a very specific ethical ideal, one that also relies essentially on the qualities of quiet harmony and unified balance, and the degree to which these aspects are implicitly negated in its literary realization tell us as much about that ideal itself as it does about its specific expression.

It is certainly true that he designed Julie's garden, the central allegorical sign of the beautiful soul in the novel, to afford us privileged insight into the inner being of the person who created it.[66] This is at least how Saint-Preux, for one, understands the garden and the name it was given, and at the end of his lengthy letter to Lord Bomston he muses that the "name Elysium was a symbol in some way of the soul of the one who had chosen it. I reflected that with a disturbed conscience she would not have selected that name. I said to myself that peace prevails in her inmost heart just as in the refuge she has named" (4.11.487 [315]).[67] But it is clear by now that the metaphysical reality of the garden, as it were, gives the lie to Saint-Preux's hopeful perceptions. Even at a purely formal level one may observe the effects of the fundamental incongruence that the garden exemplifies. For by employing a formal device that by its very nature relies on concrete images to embody abstract ideas and must therefore insistently point away from itself in order, paradoxically, to reveal its "true" identity, Rousseau reproduced the same familiar pattern of dissimulation in the literary means, the very structure itself, he had chosen to communicate the central "truth" of the book.

Like Saint-Preux, we, the readers of *Julie*, are of course not supposed to notice this conceit; we might otherwise become distracted from the depictions of virtue and morality that Rousseau had so painstakingly prepared in order to promote our collective edification. In another admiring passage about the skill with which Wolmar secretly directs the lives of those who depend on him, Saint-Preux writes that "the whole art of the master is to hide that constraint under a veil of pleasure or interest in such a way that they think they want everything that one obliges them to do" (4.10.453).[68] This description of Wolmar's techniques and intentions could serve just as

65. In his splendid book, *The Earthly Paradise and the Renaissance Epic* (Princeton: Princeton University Press, 1966), 11, A. Bartlett Giamatti shows that "the place of perfect repose and inner harmony is always remembered as a garden."

66. J. H. Broome, *Rousseau: A Study of His Thought* (London: Edward Arnold, 1963), 138, also recognized that "the *Nouvelle Héloïse* is more a philosophical allegory than it is a novel," but Broome wanted to defend Clarens, and the novel as a whole, as a positive or non-problematic political allegory.

67. I find it very difficult, however, to accept the thesis put forward by André Blanc, "Le Jardin de Julie," *Dix-huitième Siècle* 14 (1982): 357–76, who claims that the "garden" is an extended metaphor for Julie's "sexe."

68. See also Carol Blum, *Rousseau and the Republic of Virtue: The Language of Politics in the French Revolution* (Ithaca: Cornell University Press, 1986), 66–67, who discusses the novel as exemplifying "one of Rousseau's most characteristic imperatives: leading someone to virtue in a covert way."

well to define those of his author. Neither did Rousseau intend for us to notice the work of human hands in the construction of the novel, nor are we supposed to become aware of his roguery. And the response that *Julie* provoked from most of its contemporary admirers indicates that Rousseau's abilities were at least comparable to the talents of his fictional counterpart. The novel is meant to be *our* Clarens: as the Preface had insidiously argued, to have read this far is proof that we were more than in need of such guidance. And at the end of our stay—during which Rousseau seduces us with "pleasure" and "interest" so that we also become initiates in this secret society of beautiful souls—we are to go out into the world and, following the insensible dictates of its creator, model our lives after the lessons we absorbed in their midst.

As the example of Julie's garden showed with unintended forcefulness, however, that model itself only exists—or since existence is precisely what it lacks, it is only imaginable—by denying the principles on which it is based. As soon as we become conscious, for example, of the duplicity necessary to maintain the illusion of nature, the manipulation of thought required to produce the appearance of freedom of will, or the constant acts of repression (in both the psychological and political sense) needed to maintain the external semblance of virtue, Rousseau's surreptitious seduction, and his utopian hopes, come to a premature end. The beautiful soul—the unstable center of Rousseau's fictional dream—is finally prevented from being realized by all of the very conditions it simultaneously had to fulfill. Ultimately paralyzed by this irreconcilable set of conflicting demands, immobilized by the impossible impulse to satisfy so many opposing desires at once, the "belles âmes" at Clarens remained captives to the incompatible forces that had first inspired them.

To be sure, most of Rousseau's eighteenth-century readers took a much more forgiving view of these matters. They did not just think it possible that Julie and the beautiful souls of her acquaintance could be living among us; they were convinced that they actually did. Speaking in a representative voice, Adrien Cuyret, seigneur de Margency, avowed in a letter to Rousseau: "I believe that your charming Julie actually exists and I believe it for the honor of the humanity which I love. I believe that such a perfect character is not often found in society, but it is enough that there is one in nature."[69] Considering the tide of enthusiasm that swept over Europe in the wake of *Julie*, it seems almost natural that there were many other equally convinced, if no better founded, sightings of "beautiful souls" in the decades that followed.

69. Cited in Maurice Cranston, *The Noble Savage: Jean-Jacques Rousseau, 1754–1762* (Chicago: University of Chicago Press, 1991), 255.

5

The Cult of Physiognomy:
Physical Beauty as the
Cipher of Moral Excellence

For what's true beauty, but fair virtue's face,
Virtue made visible in outward grace?
—Edward Young

In 1775 Johann Caspar Lavater, a zealous Swiss pastor and a tirelessly prolific pamphleteer, published the first volume of his major work, the *Physiognomische Fragmente*. It was an event that almost instantaneously transformed Lavater into one of the most celebrated writers in Europe. By the end of the century, dozens of legitimate and almost as many pirated editions had appeared, and the work had been translated into virtually every major European language. This extraordinary success, welcome though it unquestionably was to Lavater, was not, however, altogether accidental. Many years after the publication of the *Fragmente*, Goethe—one of Lavater's friends and early collaborators—revealed that "not many people have more eagerly sought recognition than he did."[1] This consuming need for attention and self-promotion is visible in almost every aspect of Lavater's enterprise. As befits a work on physiognomy, even the physical appearance of his book was shrewdly designed to provoke the liveliest sort of interest about its contents. All four volumes of the *Fragmente* were massive royal folio editions, measuring almost two feet from top to bottom; they contained hundreds of painstakingly executed illustrations by some of the most talented engravers of the time; and—in cunning observance of the venerable principle that high prices command automatic respect—the set cost a small fortune. "It was by no means written for the vulgar multitude," Lavater rather grandly and probably disingenuously offered in explanation for the princely price of the book; "it is

---

1. Johann Wolfgang von Goethe, *From My Life: Poetry and Truth*, part 4, *Campaign in France 1792, Siege of Mainz*, ed. Thomas P. Saine and Jeffrey L. Sammons, trans. Robert R. Heitner and Thomas P. Saine, in *Collected Works* (New York: Suhrkamp, 1987), 5:582.

supposed to be neither read nor bought by the common man."[2] And heightening the allure of its overwrought exterior, the entire work was also written in
what was then the most modern, even fashionable, style of German prose.
Self-consciously playing with, or between, the conventions of both literary and
philosophical language, Lavater wrote in the jerky, breathless, colloquial style
affected by the so-called Stürmer und Dränger of the 1770s. Ellipses, dashes,
exclamation marks, even the title (which was a deliberate allusion to Herder's
fashionable new book, *Ueber die neuere Deutsche Litteratur*) all signal Lavater's
carefully calculated efforts to stimulate and hold the curiosity of an increasingly well informed and discriminating audience.

Yet all of these attention-grabbing ploys ultimately amounted to little
more than an early instance of clever marketing. The greatest attraction of
the *Physiognomische Fragmente* arose naturally from the intrinsic appeal of the
subject itself: the practice of discerning a person's true character on the
evidence presented by external appearance alone, and above all by the face.
Lavater explicitly promised that by studying his book and committing its
accompanying illustrative plates to memory, his readers would learn to decipher their neighbors' inner beings by scrutinizing their outer shells. Like a
glove that first shows its true shape when worn on a hand, the human body,
he thought, echoes in perceptible guise the very contours of the soul. It is a
seductive thesis, one that we would perhaps strongly like to believe, given the
uncertainty produced by even our most banal daily encounters with people
we may not otherwise know. And many, not only in German-speaking countries, but in France and England as well, did believe it: when Lavater died in
1801, a eulogy in *The Gentleman's Magazine* reported that the influence of his
books was so pervasive, and their prestige so high, that "they were thought as
necessary in every family as even the Bible itself. A servant would, at one
time, scarcely be hired till the descriptions and engravings of Lavater had
been consulted, in *careful* comparison with the lines and features of the
young man's or woman's countenance."[3]

The enormous success that Lavater enjoyed with his physiognomical investigations led some of his readers not only to forget, or to suppress, its
questionable aspects, but also to believe that the Swiss preacher had invented the procedure himself. In reality, physiognomy was an ancient exercise, and it is possible to find mention of its use in some of the earliest
documents of recorded history. Although physiognomy thus undoubtedly
existed—in fact, if not yet in name—long before Aristotle was born, it is his

2. Johann Caspar Lavater, *Physiognomische Fragmente zur Beförderung der Menschenkenntnis und
Menschenliebe* (Leipzig and Winterthur: Weidmanns, 1775; reprint, Zurich: Orell Füssli,
1968–69), preface to vol. 1, unpaginated. Henceforth cited parenthetically in the text as
"*Phys. Frag.*" by volume and page number.
3. See John Graham, *Lavater's Essays on Physiognomy: A Study in the History of Ideas* (Frankfurt
am Main: Peter Lang, 1979), 61.

apocryphal *Physiognomonica* that remains the first extant treatise on the art of reading human character on the basis of external signs. And although the *Physiognomonica* can no longer be confidently attributed to Aristotle, he was thought to have been its author for more than a thousand years, and his reputation guaranteed that this minor, somewhat muddled essay provided the theoretical starting point (and generally most of the explanatory descriptions of individual physical traits) for virtually every work devoted to the subject thereafter.[4] Yet despite the uninterrupted popularity of physiognomy, from around the death of Galen in A.D. 199 to the end of the seventeenth century it always remained closely, and dangerously, associated with the black arts of divination, astrology, and magic.[5] An act of Parliament in 1598 under Elizabeth I, for instance, underscored the real risks still attending the practice. The edict declared with graphic clarity that "all persons fayning to have knowledge of Phisiognomie or like Fantasticall Ymaginacions" were to "be stripped naked from the middle upwards and openly whipped until his body be bloudye."[6]

In light of this past, it was understandable that Lavater would want to insist that he offered something genuinely, demonstrably new. Supremely sensitive to the disreputable odor that physiognomy had never quite lost, Lavater claimed that he had placed it for the first time on the stable foundations of exact science. Finely attuned to the methodological temper of his time, Lavater categorically announced that "physiognomy can become a science [*Wissenschaft*] just as well as all other nonmathematical sciences" (*Phys. Frag.*, 1:52). Throughout all four volumes, Lavater thus repeatedly expressed his confidence—without ever offering convincing proof—that

4. For a good overview of the early history of physiognomy, see Graeme Tytler, *Physiognomy in the European Novel: Faces and Fortunes* (Princeton: Princeton University Press, 1982), esp. chaps. 1 and 2. See also the thorough and evenhanded summary by Georg Gustav Fülleborn, *Abriss einer Geschichte und Litteratur der Physiognomik*, in *Beyträge zur Geschichte der Philosophie* (Züllichau and Freystadt: Friedrich Frommann Verlag, 1797), vol. 3, part 8, pp. 1–188.
5. See Mary Cowling, *The Artist as Anthropologist: The Representation of Type and Character in Victorian Art* (Cambridge: Cambridge University Press, 1989), 15.
6. *Encyclopaedia Brittanica*, 11th ed., s.v. "physiognomy." Although physiognomy did not attract such drastic forms of punishment in the early eighteenth century, it was still regarded with a great deal of suspicion. In the 8 June 1711 installment of *The Spectator*, for example, Addison warned against this form of "prejudice" and even explicitly identified it as a moral failing: "A wise Man should be particularly cautious how he gives Credit to a Man's outward Appearance. It is an irreparable Injustice we are guilty of towards one another, when we are prejudiced by the Looks and Features of those whom we do not know. How often do we conceive Hatred against a Person of Worth, or fancy a Man to be proud and ill-natured by his Aspect, whom we think we cannot esteem too much when we are acquainted with his real Character? Dr. *Moore*, in his admirable System of Ethicks, reckons this particular Inclination, to take a Prejudice against a Man for his Looks, among the smaller Vices in Morality, and, if I remember, gives it the Name of a *Prosopolepsia.*" See no. 86 in Joseph Addison, *The Spectator*, ed. Donald F. Bond (Oxford: Oxford University Press, 1965), 1:368–69.

physiognomy could achieve the precision that other disciplines were also said to have already reached.[7] Imitating the fastidious manner of a professor of philosophy who must define all of the terms under discussion before proceeding to the next stage of an argument, Lavater sought to give the impression that physiognomy satisfied in particular the criteria of the analytic method.[8] "Observation, or perception accompanied by distinguishing, is the soul of physiognomy; . . . Observation is attentiveness; . . . Attentiveness is viewing something in particular by setting aside everything else, and by analyzing [*zergliedern*] its distinctive marks and peculiarities, and thus it means to distinguish" (*Phys. Frag.*, 1:173). Analysis, then, or the decompositive method, ostensibly provided the intellectual tools to perform a philosophical dissection, an abstract anatomical dismemberment, permitting the physiognomist to reveal the sustaining structure of the psyche itself.[9]

It is at this point that some of the underlying reasons begin to emerge for the overwhelmingly enthusiastic reception Lavater's work had enjoyed, which seems to have been remarkably positive for what was otherwise such a skeptical age. The middle of the eighteenth century was especially marked, as we have seen, by numerous attempts to legitimate certain fields of inquiry that had previously been banished to the fringes of recognized endeavor. The only way to make these disciplines presentable on the stage of rational discourse was to demonstrate how they could be brought into conformity with modern conceptions of proper scientific procedure. The prize contest posted by the Berlin academy a little more than a decade before Lavater's *Physiognomische Fragmente* was published, to name only the most visible example, had been an immediate response to recent efforts to systematize and rationalize natural theology and moral philosophy.[10] And by performing the

7. Apparently Lavater never lost this faith. Wilhelm von Humboldt visited him in Zurich in October 1789 and remarked that "he still maintains that all physiognomical rules will one day be proven mathematically." Humboldt, *Werke*, ed. Andreas Flitner and Klaus Giel (Darmstadt: Wissenschaftliche Buchgesellschaft, 1960–81), 5:25.

8. See also Cowling, *Artist as Anthropologist*, 10, who notes in general that "the physiognomical approach was often quoted as synonymous with scientific observation, and as demonstrating the application of the Baconian method to human nature: a method by which inductions were to be formed only on the basis of painstaking observation."

9. See the interesting parallels between physiognomy and dissection drawn by Barbara Maria Stafford, *Body Criticism: Imaging the Unseen in Enlightenment Art and Medicine* (Cambridge: The MIT Press, 1991).

10. There had also been a controversy within the Berlin Academy about physiognomy, thus indirectly conferring on it more visibility and legitimacy than it probably otherwise would have enjoyed. Henri de Catt read three papers before the academy from 1768 to 1770 attacking it. In response, Antoine Joseph Pernety also read three (rather repetitive and confused) essays defending the practice. Pernety also played a decisive role in the life of another contemporary, for he was the man whom Frederick II, confusing him with his more accomplished uncle Jacques, appointed as the Royal Librarian over Lessing. Pernety soon went mad and journeyed to Spain in search of the philosopher's stone.

same gesture Alexander Baumgarten had almost single-handedly created a philosophical discipline out of what had previously been the reserve primarily of cultivated dilettantes. In its nascent form, aesthetics had consisted of occasional essays, treatises, and dialogues, but not sober philosophical works that measured up to, or even aspired to, the rigorous test of truth; and Baumgarten had elevated aesthetics into that sphere by trying to force it into a consistent methodological form. When Lavater proleptically sought to counter one of the many arguments he imagined would (and later did) arise against his theory—namely, that "even if there really should be some truth in it, physiognomy will never become a *science*"—it was therefore not an accidental choice of comparative terms when he added in a footnote: "At least I won't have to fear this objection from the philosophers of the Baumgarten school. His idealistic definition of *scientia* is well known, and he still has no reservations about placing *semiotics* among the sciences" (*Phys. Frag.*, 1:52). Similarly, in a section of the *Fragmente* titled "The Physiognomist," there appears to be a specific allusion to Baumgarten's definition of aesthetics as the study of sensate perception in analogy to the higher-order functions of logic when Lavater insists that "physiognomy is the greatest exercise of the understanding, the logic of physical differences!" (1:174). If Baumgarten had been able to make aesthetics acceptable as a science, then why could he, Lavater, not do the same for physiognomy?

Yet Lavater's *Physiognomische Fragmente* would not have become the tremendous social and cultural success that it did if it had not answered a greater and more immediate need than the demand for abstract coherence and methodological rigor. Soundness of method might have satisfied the philosophers, but it meant less to the common reader. Lavater's popularity was rooted, instead, in a kind of quick, nervous attunement to the complex religious, moral, and artistic currents of his day. Goethe keenly observed this responsiveness as well, and he reported that "no one has written like him for and about his own time. His writings are true daily bulletins and require the most factual annotation from the history of the era. They are written in the language of the coterie, with which one must be familiar in order to do them justice."[11] A generalist in the widest—and often the worst—sense of the word, Lavater absorbed the most eclectic strains of both high and popular contemporary culture, mixing together theology, metaphysics, and classical archaeology with superstition, folktale, and that particularly insidious brand of parochial prejudice so often known as "common sense." A fervently committed Christian, he was one of the leading figures of late-eighteenth-century neo-Pietism, and the majority of his other writings, most famously

11. Goethe, *Poetry and Truth*, in *Collected Works*, 4:582.

his *Aussichten in die Ewigkeit* (Vistas of eternity), dealt directly and at length with religious issues.[12] Not subscribing to the anti-intellectual tendencies of some reborn Pietists, he also read broadly, albeit unsystematically, in philosophy and metaphysics, appearing to be sufficiently acquainted—as we just saw—with the German institutional tradition descending from Leibniz, Wolff, and Baumgarten; and he also betrayed a familiarity with the works of the main French and English thinkers, many of whom he quoted extensively throughout the *Fragmente*. And living in the wake of Winckelmann, he shared the general enthrallment with classical Greece that had taken hold of the German imagination. One thus finds Lavater repeating at one point, as if it were the most unshakable certainty, the prevalent belief "that Art has not yet invented or elaborated anything more majestic, pure, and noble than the ancient Greek statues from the best time" (*Phys. Frag.*, 3:40).

But at the center of all of his preoccupations, the constant point of reference for the whole of his physiognomical science, was the most famous figure of the 1770s, made popular in the previous decade by the novels of Wieland, Rousseau, and countless other, lesser writers. In accordance with the governing precept of physiognomy, in which it was postulated that there was a necessary and demonstrable connection between inner constitution and outer form, Lavater wrote in the conviction that physical perfection gave nothing but visible expression to the spiritual personification of moral excellence. After citing Winckelmann's description of the Belvedere Apollo, in which Winckelmann had referred in passing to "the realm of noncorporeal beauties," Lavater sniffed in a footnote: "Winckelmannian enthusiasm. Noncorporeal beauties! Almost as much of an absurdity as mindless animation. Wisdom, virtue, force are never abstract, exist nowhere than in wise, virtuous, powerful substances! Nowhere else than in visible, tangible beings that are perceptible by means of corporeal instruments, or at least not without them" (1:132). No longer simply the subject of abstract fancy or fictional narratives alone, the beautiful soul silently assumed in Lavater's mind a substantial, material body. Lavater did not just hope, he expressly argued as a (God-)given fact that beautiful souls not only actually existed and moved among us, but, moreover, that they naturally resided in beautiful bodies. With his physiognomical theory, then, Lavater came the closest yet to revealing the incarnation, the true embodiment in flesh and bone (favorably shaped, of course) of the beautiful soul.

12. On Lavater's Pietism, see F. Ernest Stoeffler, *German Pietism during the Eighteenth Century*, Studies in the History of Religions, vol. 24 (Leiden: E. J. Brill, 1973), 253–57; and Horst Weigelt, *Lavater und die Stillen im Lande: Distanz und Nähe. Die Beziehungen Lavaters zu Frömmigkeitsbewegungen im 18. Jahrhundert* (Göttingen: Vandenhoeck & Ruprecht, 1988). See also the unusually positive comments on Lavater in Albrecht Ritschl, *Geschichte des Pietismus* (Bonn: Adolph Marcus, 1880–86), 1:501–23.

The entrance of the beautiful soul into the world of tangible reality represented a necessary, even inevitable, step in the internal teleology of the concept itself. We have already seen it traverse the boundaries that separated both philosophical speculation and religious fervor from literary practice, which had resulted in a metamorphosis that lent the idea an ever greater density of ontological weight. Putting perhaps too much naive trust in the mimetic basis of literature (and for that matter, of all art in general), Lavater made the further conclusion that the *schöne Seelen* or *belles âmes* that he had read about must have been modeled on real antecedents in nature. It was a mistake made by many, as witnessed by the hundreds of concerned or merely inquisitive letters to Richardson and Rousseau about the further particulars of the fates of Pamela, Clarissa, or Julie. In fact, of course, beautiful souls did not predate their literary existence at all; something of the reverse actually held true. Moral beauty had always been an intuitive ideal, an imaginative goal that it was thought everyone was supposed to strive to attain, a transcendental model according to which one should seek to tailor one's self. But its source and inspiration had always been located in that abstract domain itself—whether it was the Platonic sphere of Forms, the Divine Beauty of God, or the more formalized philosophical notion of perfection—but most certainly not in fallen reality. The two novels we examined had tried to bring this ideal closer still; yet as their allegorical structure revealed, they too derived their content from the intangible realm of ideas (and other texts), not from life itself. By mistaking, or in any case inverting, this relation, Lavater tried in effect to force nature to imitate art: he wanted some graspable certainty, an objective correlative, to confirm in three-dimensional form the hypothesis supporting moral beauty. The inner movement of this process thus amounted very literally to the gradual hypostatization of an ideal. Just as Socrates had humanized moral philosophy by removing it from the sphere of the gods, Lavater sought to perform the final gesture of pulling the beautiful soul down from the heavens—or rather, out of novels—and placing it within our very midst.

Since Lavater's many undeniable gifts did not include originality, it should cause no great wonder that he was also not the first to construe this intimate relation between external and internal beauty. Plato himself had already provided a compelling and nuanced account of the possible correspondence between physical comeliness and exquisite virtue. In the third book of the *Republic*, for instance, Plato proposed that "when there is a coincidence of a beautiful disposition in the soul and corresponding and harmonious beauties of the same type in the bodily form—is not this the fairest spectacle for one who is capable of its contemplation?" (402d). But as the example of Socrates famously showed, Plato did not believe that this correspondence universally held. St. Bernard of Clairvaux, too, although from a different perspective and with a different purpose in view, thought that

> when this beauty and brightness has filled the inmost part of the heart, it must become outwardly visible, and not be like a lamp hidden under a bushel, but be a light shining in darkness, which cannot be hidden. . . . So when the movements of the limbs and sense, its gestures and habits, are seen to be resolute, pure, restrained, free from all presumption and licence, with no sign of triviality and idleness, but given just dealing, zealous in piety, then the beauty of the soul will be seen openly.[13]

In the modern period, Francis Bacon was possibly the first to treat the question primarily in terms of the presumed connection between physical beauty and morality in one of his *Essays* of 1625.[14] Predictably, as if to underscore the intrinsic mutual dependency of the external and internal spheres, Bacon also advocated—while, it is true, voicing certain restrictions on—the practice of physiognomy, which he broadly defined as "discovering the dispositions of the mind by the lineaments of the body."[15] In the eighteenth century, Francis Hutcheson, in the second half of his *Inquiry into the Original of Our Ideas of Beauty and Virtue*, likewise considered "the External Beauty of Persons" as a probable, though by no means infallible, sign of moral excellence. Hutcheson explained the attraction of this variety of beauty as residing in a merely supposed but not proven or assured association with goodness: "Now it is some apprehended *Morality*," he prudently wrote, "some natural or imagin'd Indication of *concomitant Virtue*, which gives it this powerful Charm above all other kinds of *Beauty*."[16] But Hutcheson's restraint in insisting on an actual concurrence of both types of beauty did dnot prevent him in the end from indulging in a utopian vision of a society filled with "good-and-beautiful" people, once again illustrating the almost irresistibly seductive pull of the idea itself on even the most judicious minds:

> Beauty gives a favourable Presumption of *good moral Dispositions,* and *Acquaintance* confirms this into a *real Love* of *Esteem,* or begets it, where there is little

13. Bernard of Clairvaux, *On the Song of Songs*, vol. 4, trans. Irene Edmonds, intro. Jean Leclerq (Kalamazoo, Mich.: Cistercian Publications, 1980), Sermon 85, sec. iv, § 11, 207.
14. See Francis Bacon, "Of Beauty," in *The Essayes or Counsels, Civill and Morall*, ed. Michael Kiernan (Cambridge: Harvard University Press, 1985), 132–33. On the essay itself, see the very illuminating article by A. Philip McMahon, "Francis Bacon's Essay of *Beauty*," *PMLA* 60 (1945): 716–59.
15. See Francis Bacon, *De Augmentis*, in *Works*, ed. James Spedding, Robert Leslie Ellis, and Douglas Denon Heath, 2d ed. (London: Longmans, 1887–1901), 4:375.
16. Francis Hutcheson, *An Inquiry into the Original of Our Ideas of Beauty and Virtue*, 2d ed. (London, 1726; reprint, New York: Garland, 1971), 250.

Beauty. This raises an expectation of the greatest *moral Pleasures* along with the *sensible,* and a thousand tender Sentiments of *Humanity* and *Generosity;* and makes us impatient for a *Society* which we imagine big and unspeakable *moral Pleasures:* where nothing is indifferent, and every trifling Service, being an Evidence of *this strong Love* of *Esteem,* is mutually receiv'd with the Rapture and Gratitude of the greatest Benefit, and of the most substantial Obligation. And where *Prudence* and *Good-nature* influence both sides, this *Society* may answer all their Expectations. (256)

For whatever reason, however, Hutcheson never went beyond expressions indicating the mere probability of this agreement.

John Gilbert Cooper, finally, in his *Life of Socrates* of 1750, explicitly linked the modern concept of moral beauty and its concomitant physical manifestation with the ancient Greek notion of *kalokagathia.* Cooper wrote (less with complete historical accuracy than with a conviction born of his own times) that Socrates accepted the unity of beauty and goodness expressed in this word, and "being thus accustomed to the *good* and *beautiful* in Morals, he was led by an amicable Intercourse of Ideas, to look upon the Comeliness of a handsome Person as the external Mark of inward Goodness, which made itself thus visible to the Sight by the correspondent features of an amiable Countenance."[17] Cooper's testimony is crucial here, not only for its clarity and concision, but also because his book played a decisive role in shaping the image of antiquity, and naturally of Socrates in particular, that many German thinkers came to hold, including Mendelssohn and Hamann, who were in turn instrumental in influencing Lavater's views on the same subject.[18]

Although Lavater therefore remained fundamentally indebted to his numerous predecessors for the actual substance of his ideas about physiog-

17. John Gilbert Cooper, *The Life of Socrates,* 3d ed. (London: Dodsley, 1750), 67. See also 66 n. 27, in which Cooper explains: "This Analogy between the Perfection in Nature and that in Morals, *Socrates* constantly had in View in all his Discourses, which his Disciples express'd in the compound Word *kalokagathia,* for a proper Regulation of our Passions, or an exact Performance of those Duties which are required from the respective Station of Life we act in, to Society, answers in the Moral World to that Symmetry and Proportion which is constituted by the Agreement of particular Parts in the Natural; so that Good and Beauty may be used indiscriminately as a proper Expression for Excellence in either."
18. In his *Sokratische Denkwürdigkeiten,* in Johann Georg Hamann, *Sämmtliche Werke,* ed. Josef Nadler (Vienna: Herder, 1949–57), 2:65, Hamann did not have especially kind words to say about Cooper, calling his book "nothing but a school exercise that produces the disgust occasioned by an apology and polemic at once." Despite this equally polemical verdict, however, Hamann was in fact indebted to Cooper for a great deal of his information about Socrates. Mendelssohn was much more generous—and honest—when he wrote in the preface to his *Phaedon, oder über die Unsterblichkeit der Seele,* in *Schriften zur Philosophie, Aesthetik und Apologetik,* ed. Moritz Brasch (Leipzig, 1980; reprint, Hildesheim: Georg Olms, 1968), 1:133, that in delineating the character of Socrates, "Cooper's Life of Socrates served as my guide."

nomy, how he went about employing these inherited notions gave him whatever novelty he could legitimately claim as his own. It is revealing that what set Lavater apart from his forerunners, in fact, was, as he expressed it in one of his chapter or "fragment" headings, the absolute and unquestioned faith that he placed in the truth of "the Harmony of Moral and Corporeal Beauty" (*Phys. Frag.*, 1:57). In Lavater's eyes it was completely irrefutable that there was an intimate, inseparable bond uniting virtue, or moral beauty, with the visible corporeal kind. It is worth stressing that Lavater need not have taken this dogmatic stance. There were many thinkers who accepted the notion of moral beauty and who even wrote sympathetically about physiognomy in general but still questioned its reliability on specific details. And there were those who—like Hutcheson and Cooper—wisely hesitated at positing an uninterrupted communication between the beauty of body and that of soul, but considered it theoretically possible. In Christian Wolff's book on moral philosophy of 1720, for example, we read the much more circumspect assessment that "the art of recognizing people's characters from the form of their limbs and of their entire body (which one tends to call *physiognomy*) no doubt has good grounds; but I will leave aside for the moment—because this is not the place to treat this art—the question of whether people have so far been accurate when they wanted to make particular interpretations of this relationship between body and character."[19] There were others, of course, who impatiently dispensed with this sort of coy equivocation and completely denied that physiognomy in the strict sense possessed any legitimacy whatsoever. The chevalier de Jaucourt, who wrote the article "Physionomie" for the *Encyclopédie* sometime in the mid-1760s, categorically rejected its validity, typically calling it quite simply a "type of prejudice." To bolster his objection, he approvingly cited Buffon's opinion that a "poorly made body can contain a very beautiful soul [*une fort belle âme*], and one should not judge the natural good or evil of a person by the features of the face; for these traits have no connection with the nature of the soul."[20] As Buffon's choice of words indicates, one could therefore still accept the doctrine of the beautiful soul without subscribing to physiognomy itself. But Lavater remained unimpressed by either empirical evidence or other, similarly imposing pronouncements by the century's preeminent scientists and thinkers. If anything, criticism only stiffened his faith in the correctness of his theory: in the chapter of the *Physiognomische Fragmente* just mentioned, Lavater stated the matter with brutal bluntness: "The beauty

19. Christian Wolff, *Vernünfftige Gedancken von der Menschen Thun und Lassen, zu Beförderung ihrer Glückseeligkeit,* 4th ed. (Frankfurt and Leipzig, 1733; reprint, ed. Hans Werner Arndt, Hildesheim: Georg Olms, 1976), § 213, p. 137.
20. *Encyclopédie, ou Dictionnaire raisonné des sciences, des arts et des métiers, par une société de gens de lettres,* ed. Denis Diderot and Jean Le Rond d'Alembert (Paris, 1751–67), 12:538.

and the ugliness of a face has a correct and exact relationship to the beauty and ugliness of the moral constitution of a person." Or as he expressed it even more crudely: "The better one is morally, the more beautiful one is; the worse one is morally, the uglier" (1:63).

Given the skepticism that Lavater knew would greet his thesis, he realized that he had to provide proof, and not just simple assertions, for his contention that the physical body perfectly described the inner person.[21] One device he used to great effect was to raise predictable objections himself, often expressing slightly paternalistic impatience with the nature of the question—as if to say that he found it astonishing that anyone would believe that he, the great divinator, did not know that there are exceptions to every rule! Yet his main theoretical support, although present in the *Fragmente*, had been more fully elaborated in his somewhat earlier *Aussichten in die Ewigkeit*, which he had published in a series of "letters" beginning in 1768. In the sixteenth letter, written in 1772 and published in the following year, Lavater had envisioned a "language that would have all conceivable perfections and would render unnecessary all sounds that are even slightly arbitrary, that is, all merely figuratively imitative sounds."[22] Rehearsing the theory of "natural" and "arbitrary" signs that was the shared intellectual possession of virtually every Enlightenment thinker who reflected on language, Lavater thought that the body represented such a transparent "language" since it consisted of nothing but quite literally "natural" signs.[23] He thus thought that the absence of arbitrariness—the German word *unwillkürlich* better expresses the implied lack of volition, or even of conscious intention—in bodily movements, gestures, and facial expressions guaranteed the authenticity and truth of these "nonarbitrary," or natural, signs. He thought, in other words, that the signifying limb or eyebrow did not simply express, but was intimately bound up with

---

21. Goethe, *Poetry and Truth*, in *Collected Works*, 4:449, noted that Lavater "was greatly embarrassed when persons were present whose ugly appearance could not but stamp them indelibly as sworn enemies of his doctrine about the significance of forms. They would customarily employ their adequate common sense, and indeed other gifts and talents, in a passionately malevolent, pettily skeptical fashion to invalidate a doctrine that seemed to insult them personally. For there are not many people as magnanimous as Socrates, who would have interpreted his goatish exterior as proof that he had to *earn* his morality. The harsh obduracy of such opponents was a fearful thing to Lavater, but he was not without passion in combatting it, just as the fire in a forge must hiss at the resistant ore as if the latter were both tedious and hostile."

22. Johann Caspar Lavater, *Aussichten in die Ewigkeit*, in *Ausgewählte Werke*, ed. Ernst Staehelin (Zürich: Zwingli, 1943), 1:182.

23. See Andreas Käuser, "Die Physiognomik des 18. Jahrhunderts als Ursprung der modernen Geisteswissenschaft," *Germanisch-Romanische Monatsschrift* Neue Folge 41 (1991): esp. 134–40; and by Carsten Zelle, "Physiognomie des Schreckens im achtzehnten Jahrhundert: Zu Johann Caspar Lavater und Charles Lebrun," *Lessing Yearbook* 21 (1989): 90–91. An older treatment of this issue can be found in Eduard Spranger, *Wilhelm von Humboldt und die Humanitätsidee* (Berlin: Reuther & Reichard, 1909), esp. chap. 4, "Die Chiffreschrift der Natur," 153–82.

the signified emotion. This unimpeded commerce between sign and meaning is clearly not the case with words, or the arbitrary signs of linguistic communication, and from Locke onward, eighteenth-century thinkers had sought to contain and control the profligate imprecision of language. Thus the governing assumption of physiognomy was that unlike verbal or written discourse, body language spoke the truth.

But Lavater also subsumed this semiotic postulate under his more general religious views. Here again he took an idiosyncratic approach. Hamann, for example, had likewise literalized the metaphor of the "book of nature" in his *Aesthetica in nuce,* but he felt that in our fallen state, we had lost our ability to decipher that natural language. Lavater, however, retained an optimistic faith not only in the beneficent presence and continuing interest of the divine Author in his works, but also in our—or at any rate, in Lavater's own—ability to gain access to that meaningful presence. Indeed, the motto for the *Physiognomische Fragmente* reads "God created human beings in His image," and in the *Aussichten,* too, Lavater claimed that "as Christ is the most eloquent, most vital, most perfect image of the invisible God, an image in which everything has inexhaustible and infinite meaning . . . so is every human being (an image of God and Christ) in the same way completely expression, simultaneous, true, comprehensive, inexhaustible, ineffable, inimitable expression; every person is completely natural language [*Natursprache*]."[24] As far as Lavater was concerned, every person he encountered literally appeared to him as an open book written in the unambiguous hand of God.

Although he considerably softened such outbursts of religious fervor in the *Fragmente* itself, he never abandoned the fundamental notion that unlike the arbitrary signs of language, in which words and meanings may and often do widely diverge—the natural language of the body was the most reliable guarantor of certain knowledge because that "natural language" was the tangible expression of God's creative and unequivocal word. As he put it in the section assertively titled "On the Truth of Physiognomy": "Arbitrariness is the philosophy of fools, a contagion for the natural sciences, philosophy, and religion. To ban it everywhere is the work of the true scientist, the true philosopher, and the true theologian" (*Phys. Frag.,* 1:47). Physiognomy, for Lavater, provided living proof of the falsity of arbitrariness and of the truth of God's presence in the world. On the most general level, then, Lavater intended to transfer his priesterly role into the extra-ecclesiastical domain, and just as he interpreted the Holy Scripture for the faithful, he now offered his exegetic services in decoding the larger book of nature for the fallen.

Even though Lavater repeatedly professed his wish to establish physiog-

24. Lavater, *Aussichten in die Ewigkeit,* 183. See also Alice A. Kuzniar, "Signs of the Future: Reading (in) Lavater's *Aussichten,*" *Seminar* 22 (1986): 1–19.

nomy on the most stable scientific footing possible—which meant to transform it into a purely descriptive discipline that yielded empirically verifiable data—he also wanted to incorporate something approaching a prescriptive element, or more precisely a pedagogical one, into the final equation. He believed that a command of the physiognomic vocabulary would ultimately allow us not merely to recognize, but moreover to encourage, as he phrased it in unmistakably Wolffian accents, the "perfection of the inner person" (1:77). An insistently, though rather diffuse, moralistic tone is thus audible throughout the book (even its subtitle promised, after all, that the book would serve "the advancement of the knowledge of humanity and brotherly love"). And it is here that Lavater seemed to rejoin the main current of contemporary thought about the effect and purpose of moral beauty. Toward the end of the chapter "On the Use of Physiognomy"—which is itself less useful than the heading would lead one to expect—he speculated that an understanding of physiognomy "would be an active means of eliminating vice, or at least of limiting and lessening it" (1:161). If everyone were equally well versed in physiognomical exegesis, it would be a powerful impetus for all of us to improve our moral being in order that it be reflected in our outward form. "Even the most determined scoundrel," Lavater explained, "does not want to appear to be wicked, or at least to be called thus. How many people who are vicious merely coincidentally, merely out of foolishness and thoughtlessness, who do not cringe before God or the idea of God, would avoid the glance of a careful observer; would go into themselves and conquer their bad habits— in order to appear with a more virtuous face?" According to Lavater, the greatest benefit to be derived from this enterprise, would be therefore the "*cultivation [Bildung], guidance, and improvement of human hearts*" (1:161). In order, in other words, to avoid exposing oneself as being debauched or dishonest, everyone would strive to become as virtuous as possible so that this goodness would be duly reflected in the face.

Despite his desire to place his physiognomical science in the service of improving the moral condition of humanity, Lavater probably realized that certain basic logical problems arose from this argument and he thus quickly left the issue behind. The most serious contradiction, which Lavater could hardly have confronted, had to do with the primary proposition of physiognomy itself. As a "science," it would have depended on the universality and, moreover, the *immutability* of the laws that supposedly governed the relationship between the physical and spiritual realm. Indeed, in an inadvertently comical passage that later became the subject of some controversy and ridicule, Lavater elevated the nose to a level of special expressive importance because he thought it was the organ that was least susceptible of being affected by dissimulation. Unlike, say, the brow, whose shape and thus "meaning" changed as the hairline receded, the nose was—at least in those days—immutable (1:213).[25] But if this assumption held true, then it was obvious that any effort to better ourselves would forever fail in the face of such manifest and inalterable marks of either past or present depravity. Furthermore, if the main motivation for ethically good behavior were thus to spring from the fear of otherwise marring one's pretty visage, then modern moral philosophy, or rather the particular solutions proposed under the name of moral beauty, would have truly made no appreciable advance over Hobbes after all.

Yet Lavater, preferring simple declaration to analytic probing, generally avoided any searching questions that might lead to serious examination of the premises he glibly took for granted. Had it been possible to do so, he would probably have preferred to exclude language—that is, the arbitrary and therefore unreliable medium of artificial linguistic signs—from his book entirely and to let his engraved images alone do the talking. Significantly, Lavater explicitly stated this wish close to the end of the first volume, when he asked rhetorically: "Should there not also be a portrait of a thoroughly beautiful, thoroughly noble soul among the studies in this fragment? Indeed, would it not have been best to present nothing but portraits in the whole book instead of ideals so as to remove from all doubt the harmony of physical and moral beauty and vice?" (*Phys. Frag.*, 1:234). This section thus bears special weight since it is the first time that the phrase "beautiful soul"—which as we have seen signifies a specificity or concreteness lacking in the terms "moral beauty" or even "beauty of soul"—appears in the book. And, indeed, Lavater introduced (fittingly depicted by an accompanying portrait) a very real, actual person from his circle of acquaintances as the living instantiation of this noble ideal. The model he produced of such a "thoroughly beautiful soul" was not, however, an aristocratic woman with refined taste and pleasant manners, or an artistic genius with a Grecian profile, but a Swiss farmer with the unlikely name of Kleinjogg.

Kleinjogg, as a certain Jakob Gujer was familiarly known, had recently been made the subject of a book by Hans Kaspar Hirzel, who was at that time the eighteenth-century equivalent of the surgeon general of Zurich. In 1761 Hirzel had published *Die Wirthschaft eines philosophischen Bauers* (The economy of a philosophical farmer), in which he portrayed Kleinjogg as the very model of modern domestic wisdom and industry. Jakob Gujer *alias* Kleinjogg subsequently become something of a local celebrity, and he received visits from numerous curiosity seekers and foreign travelers, including the young Goethe. But even after achieving such fame he never deviated, it appears,

---

25. On the continuing primacy of the proboscis in physiognomic theory and practice, see Cowling, *Artist as Anthropologist*, 79–81 and 145–50.

from his path of rustic simplicity.[26] As in almost every other aspect of eighteenth-century life and manners, classical precedents immediately sprang to mind, and it was clear that in writing his book, Hirzel wished to play a latter-day Xenophon to Kleinjogg's Socrates. This connection became more explicit in the French and English translations of Hirzel's book that almost immediately appeared: *Le Socrate rustique, ou, Description de conduite économique et moral d'un paysan philosophe* and, in the rendition by his English translator, Arthur Young, *The rural Socrates; or, A description of the oeconomical and moral conduct of a country philosopher*. For Lavater, of course, the main issue was the degree to which Kleinjogg's Socratic countenance mirrored, as Hirzel himself had also described it, "the beauty of his soul" (*Phys. Frag.*, 1:237). Kleinjogg therefore acquired tremendous importance for Lavater as the true embodiment of human moral perfection, a significance that is, moreover, structurally and rhetorically enhanced by the placement of this section near the end of the first volume. One might reasonably expect that Lavater would have thus provided a characterization of Kleinjogg's outstanding moral and hence physical traits, or at least an explanation of why he occupied this exalted position relative to the common run of humanity. Here, finally, Lavater had the opportunity to *show* his readers, rather than rely on the uncertain instrument of language to describe, the quintessence of human virtue. But it is revealing that all Lavater could muster were vague, tautological generalities—conveyed, apparently, for added effect with all of the stylistic affectations of his broken, breezy manner—such as the following:

> This entire, true human figure before me! the entire human being a farmer! the entire farmer—human being!—So free of care! of effort! of calculation! A light without glare! warmth without heat! Such an intimate feeling of himself—without egotism! Such belief in himself without pride! Not a brilliant, not a deep understanding, yet—so healthy, so immune to the breath of prejudice. So incorruptible—so resistant to labyrinthine temptations! Always at work and rest! Full of noble industry and simple, moderate calm! So always in his circle! Such a sun in his world! (1:237)

As useless as this description is for any greater appreciation of either beauty of soul or its physical manifestation, the verbless repetition and halting syntax of Lavater's faltering, exclamatory account are eloquent in another, albeit unintended, way. As Rousseau's *La Nouvelle Héloïse* had demonstrated, such heightened moments of supposed revelation often disclose, in concentrated form, the otherwise widely dispersed contradictions that threaten the inner consistency of the narrative as a whole. Julie's garden, the allegorical summa-

26. See the description of Jakob Gujer in Wilhelm Bode, *Goethes Schweizer Reisen* (Leipzig: H. Haessel, 1922), 18–24.

tion of the novel's didactic aim, the "natural" equivalent of the beautiful soul, had dissolved in a *fata morgana* of irreconcilable tensions. In general terms, by both calling attention to themselves as containing special insight or meaning regarding the whole and at the same time disastrously failing to render that proffered meaning coherently, these ostensibly symbolic or emblematic moments endanger the very concept they are meant to celebrate. In Lavater's particular case, the evident inability to enumerate those qualities which constitute moral or even corporeal beauty in the philosophical farmer Kleinjogg thus strikes at the heart of his entire enterprise.

As the extraordinary popularity of his book attests, not everyone who read Lavater came to this conclusion; or when some did, the resultant dissension and dispute did not seriously affect his public stature. On the contrary: partly by virtue of its somewhat cloying accessibility, and partly because it appeared to confirm popular preconceptions about appearance and character "scientifically," his book helped to establish even more firmly in the common consciousness the notion, as well as the value, of the beautiful soul as a social and ethical ideal. But this outcome was in a more important sense the predictable result of the very manner in which the issue was discussed in the first place. Although there were numerous thinkers both in Germany and abroad who staunchly opposed the basic principles of physiognomy, and especially the claim that moral beauty inevitably and necessarily corresponded to its appropriate physical counterpart, virtually no one questioned the premises themselves on which this assertion rested. Even, in other words, as the validity of physiognomy was in some quarters vigorously denied, the idea that a soul could somehow be "beautiful" was not. The highly publicized, even bitter, controversy over Lavater's claim that a beautiful face bespoke an equally beautiful soul thus subtly reinforced general acceptance of the terms of the dispute itself.

Still, some of his contemporaries had, as we know, already calmly condoned not only the fundamental notions underlying the debate, but they had accepted the whole train of its implications as well. Johann Georg Sulzer was one such thinker who, besides being Swiss like Lavater, was also, it turns out, an acquaintance of Hirzel and hence undoubtedly at least knew of Kleinjogg. Sulzer is still remembered for having attained a noteworthy reputation as a philosopher at the Berlin academy, where he served as the director of the "speculative" class from 1775 until his death four years later.[27] His opinions thus have an air of official orthodoxy, which ensured their broad reception but also exposed him to the criticism of ambitious young writers who wanted to make their mark in time-honored fashion by revolting

27. On these and other biographical details, see the brief introductory sketch to the article by Friedrich Springorum, "Über das Sittliche in der Ästhetik Johann Georg Sulzers," *Archiv für die gesamte Psychologie* 72 (1929): 1–2.

against the Establishment.[28] Although Sulzer wrote many shorter articles and essays on various philosophical subjects, his *chef d'oeuvre* is the *Allgemeine Theorie der schönen Künste* (General theory of the fine arts), which appeared in two volumes published between 1771 and 1774. The title of the work is slightly deceptive, for rather than presenting a systematic "theory" of the conventional kind, Sulzer offered his thoughts in an encyclopedic form, with articles on every conceivable topic relating to the arts arranged in alphabetical order. Since Sulzer is usually described—which is to say dismissed —as a popularizer of the Leibniz-Wolffian school of philosophy, this arrangement of the work, which occurred in evident emulation of Diderot's and d'Alembert's *Encyclopédie*, should alert us to a more complex state of affairs.[29] For although Sulzer did adopt a good part of Baumgarten's theory of aesthetics, he borrowed no less liberally from the theories of the English and French thinkers whose works had played such a decisive role in the recent reorganization of the academy—and in the formulation of the ideal of moral beauty.

In the preface to the *Allgemeine Theorie*, Sulzer accordingly unfolded a view of art that looked primarily to its social or, more precisely, its pedagogical function. Above all else, he felt that art must have an overtly moral basis and purpose. This practical perspective on art, which we know was entirely typical of the time, often occasions derisive comment from present-day observers, who see it as a reactionary stance that Kant was finally to overcome with his conception of completely autonomous art, or of beauty free from all extraneous ends.[30] (Kant himself, however, though perhaps with a touch of gracious irony, more than once referred to him as the "excellent Sulzer.")[31] Unfortunately, the anachronistic judgment of Sulzer has obscured his general importance for aesthetics and his particular and substantial contribution to the development of the late-eighteenth-century conception of the beautiful soul. It has also prevented us from seeing how, along the way, his work, appearing only a few years before the *Fragmente*, lent tacit theoretical sup-

---

28. One such upstart was the twenty-three-year-old Goethe, who delivered a devastating critique of Sulzer in a review of the first volume of the *Allgemeine Theorie* for the *Frankfurter Gelehrte Anzeigen* in 1772. See Goethe, *Werke: Hamburger Ausgabe*, ed. Erich Trunz (Munich: C. H. Beck, 1981), 12:15–20.

29. The French, at least, recognized this affinity: Sulzer was an unwitting contributor to the *Supplément* for the *Encyclopédie* that began to appear in 1776, in which several articles from his *Allgemeine Theorie* had been translated into French and published without Sulzer's knowledge; cf. Lawrence Kerslake, "Johann Georg Sulzer and the supplement to the *Encyclopédie*," *Studies on Voltaire and the Eighteenth Century* 148 (1976): 225–47.

30. This is the tenor of the remarks on Sulzer by Armand Nivelle, *Kunst- und Dichtungstheorien zwischen Aufklärung und Klassik*, 2d exp. ed. (Berlin: Walter de Gruyter, 1971), 54–55.

31. See, for example, Immanuel Kant, *Foundations of the Metaphysics of Morals*, in *Critique of Practical Reason and Other Writings in Moral Philosophy*, trans. and ed. Lewis White Beck (Chicago: University of Chicago Press, 1949), 42.

port to Lavater's physiognomical endeavors by virtue of Sulzer's academic position and authority.

Sulzer began the preface to the *Allgemeine Theorie* by asserting that human beings possess two main intellectual faculties that although they appear to be independent of one another, are nevertheless both indispensible to the happiness of society, namely, our understanding and our "moral feeling" (*sittliches Gefühl*). If one is to enjoy the fruits of the understanding and be happy in the social fold, he argued, "then the feeling for the moral order, then all social virtues, then the feeling for the beautiful and the good have to be planted in everyone's mind."[32] So far Sulzer had mainly reiterated, if a little artlessly, no more than what the majority of educated Europeans also thought about the importance of morality to the maintenance of the social fabric. There was also an echo of a familiar complaint when Sulzer went on to protest that whereas a great deal had been accomplished in all of the areas in which the understanding alone is applied—that is, primarily in the sciences—not as many advances had been made with regard to the moral constitution of humanity. "Everywhere one looks," he observed, "there are great and valuable institutions for the maintenance of the understanding; but, in inverse proportion, the true care of moral feeling has been neglected." But Sulzer was convinced that the solution to this urgent concern lay more or less immediately at hand. "From a frequently repeated enjoyment of the pleasure arising from the good and beautiful grows the desire for the same, and from the unpleasant impression that the ugly and evil make on us arises the antipathy toward everything that runs counter to the moral order" (*AT*, 1:xiii).

Besides conforming to the equation of ugliness and evil (which is of course the obvious and necessary correlate to the identification of beauty with goodness), this brief passage demonstrates that Sulzer had completely absorbed, more thoroughly perhaps than even Wieland had done, the inner justification of the notion of moral beauty, thus believing that the arts could and, what is more, *should* be harnessed to achieve that specific goal within the percipient. Sulzer was not ashamed to treat art in this eminently instrumental way, and he stipulated that the primary task of the "fine arts" (the "schöne Künste" of the title) was to create or encourage "a lively feeling for the beautiful and the good, and a strong disinclination toward ugliness and evil" (1:xiii). Thus since the ultimate prosperity of society depends, according to Sulzer, on the full development—or as he wrote in the language he inherited from Wolff and Baumgarten, the "perfection"—of these essen-

---

32. See Johann Georg Sulzer, *Allgemeine Theorie der schönen Künste*, 2d exp. ed. (Leipzig, 1792; reprint, ed. Christian Friedrich von Blankenburg et al., intro. Giorgio Tonelli, Hildesheim: Georg Olms, 1967–70), 1:xii. Henceforth cited parenthetically in the text as "*AT*" by volume and page numbers.

tially immediate, nonreflective responses, the arts receive the greatest significance imaginable. They become the means by which humanity can be elevated to its highest and most proper station. Art, that is, ought to be designed to transfigure us all into beautiful souls.

Not that Sulzer ever stated this last conclusion so directly. But even though he never actually used the phrase "beautiful soul" in the *Allgemeine Theorie*, it is everywhere implied, and moreover, it is strictly necessary for the integrity of his theory. In one of the few studies dedicated to Sulzer's work, Friedrich Springorum perceptively recognized that something essential was lacking or left unspoken in Sulzer's elaboration of his theory. Because Springorum seemed to be unaware of the discourse of moral beauty that Sulzer himself took for granted, he could not answer the questions that he posed to himself, even though he realized that he had touched on some basic, but unexpressed, aspect of Sulzer's thought. Trying to come to terms with Sulzer's concept of beauty, he wrote:

> What, we must ask ourselves, does this new concept of higher beauty actually mean? It is supposed to emerge from the close union of (sensate) beauty, goodness, and perfection? Of what nature can this union be? Is it to be found in an object in which the three aesthetic powers are united? Or is it located in the mind of the observer as a psychological reality? Sulzer gives us no satisfactory answer to all of these questions. We stand here in the middle of Sulzer's intellectual world and precisely at this point, in which we would like to have the most detailed and clear information, Sulzer remains silent.[33]

The nature of "this union" of perfection, goodness, and beauty was, for Sulzer and for his entire generation, nothing other than the beautiful soul. But we have become accustomed to encountering such silence, actual or implicit, at the very moment when a full and adequate definition of the beautiful soul is most needed. Lavater had resorted to dumbly proffering engravings and, at best, had engaged in phatic stammering when confronted with the task of capturing it in conceptual terms. And here, too, at the center of Sulzer's theory, we are faced with a similar silence. Springorum, although again without establishing this crucial connection, went on to write that Sulzer appeared to feel that his notion of beauty could not be expressed in words or concepts, but could be grasped only through an image. "This image, this sensately graspable sign of a higher beauty is above all—according to Sulzer—the beauty of the human form."[34] Indeed, in what can be considered the most important article in the *Allgemeine Theorie*,

33. Springorum, "Über das Sittliche," 28.
34. Ibid., 29. It is telling that after working toward this insight, Springorum's argument also loses its momentum and then trails off into repetitive exegesis.

"Beauty" ("Schönheit"), Sulzer concentrated his discussion of beauty almost exclusively on the human body itself—which he considered "the most beautiful of all visible objects"—and specifically on its capacity to express the character of the soul it housed (*AT*, 4:319). Like Lavater and many others besides, Sulzer believed that the entirety of nature—and thus the human body as well—was nothing less than an expression of "the Highest Wisdom" and that nature therefore reflected the perfection, purposiveness, simplicity, and goodness of its maker.[35] Given this divine collateral, so to speak, Sulzer asked with mock incredulity how it could be possible that "someone may doubt that every beauty of form indicates something of inner perfection or goodness, or that every ugliness announces something of the opposite?" (*AT*, 4:321). Brushing such doubts aside, Sulzer underscored his faith in the coincidence of physical beauty and inner virtue by using Wolffian categories of ethical thought to describe the effect this symmetry must have on us. "Thus the external form can express the inner character of the person; and when it happens, then the pleasure [*Wohlgefallen*] that we experience while witnessing the inner worth of the person is the greatest cause of the pleasurable effect that the external form has on us. We value in the outer form what pleases us in the inner constitution. We see the soul in the body" (4:322).

Sulzer probably assumed that everyone would immediately know what he was talking about, and he thus graciously spared his readers the irritation or embarrassment of being told the obvious. Yet by neglecting to mention what resided at the very heart of his philosophy, Sulzer was not just tactfully inviting his readers to infer his meaning, he was also indirectly capitulating before the task of naming the qualities of soul that were supposed to be reflected so unproblematically by the body. In so doing, Sulzer had permitted a veil to descend over the center of his theory, thus inadvertently concealing what he most wanted to reveal. This dark spot, where Sulzer becomes strangely mute at the very moment he should have been the most articulate, marks that same fundamental conceptual opacity obscuring the beautiful soul which had presented such difficulties to his predecessors as well. The beautiful soul, obviously modest—or vain—about her appearance, had once more successfully evaded the ruder attempts to capture and clothe her in the clumsy garments of language.

We have lingered so long over Sulzer's compendious book not because he was himself an abundantly original thinker, but because he did come to exert a considerable influence on the thought of his time and, most important for us, on the aesthetic philosophy of Schiller. In many respects Sulzer's work merely embodied the prevalent midcentury beliefs about the power of art to effect real social and thus moral change. And by writing in a plain and

35. See the article "Natur," in Sulzer, *AT*, 4:507.

relatively direct German, he managed to synthesize accepted knowledge so skillfully and to express current aesthetic concerns so clearly that he was able to reach a wider and more receptive readership than many other previous writers on the subject had managed to do. (It should be remembered that the founder of philosophical aesthetics, Alexander Baumgarten, had chosen to write his *Aesthetica* of 1750–58 in the traditional academic language of Latin, which of course severely limited his potential audience.) And whether Sulzer would have approved of the association or not, the widespread effect of his *Allgemeine Theorie* also helped to generate a sympathetic climate of opinion about moral beauty and its physical extension. The book thus served as an authoritative, if unintentional, corroboration of the claims that Lavater made in his own physiognomical writings about the identity of physical perfection and inner virtue.

Two German-speaking writers who resisted the temptations of physiognomy were, curiously (or perhaps symptomatically), outsiders in a more general sense as well. Georg Christoph Lichtenberg, who possessed impeccable professional credentials as a physicist, astronomer, and mathematician at Göttingen, wrote one of the earliest, most brilliant, and consequently one of the most damaging critiques of Lavater's physiognomical theories to appear at the time. Moses Mendelssohn also, although unwillingly, became drawn into the physiognomical fray when he composed two shorter works that contain some of the most perceptive contemporary comments not just about physiognomy itself, but about the very idea of moral beauty. Owing to an assortment of considerations, however, Mendelssohn finally decided to keep his essays to himself, and his views never reached the broader public. But both of these men, as respected as they were in their day, gradually and for different reasons faded in significance for later generations. Toward the end of his life, Lichtenberg's reputation suffered from his oddly prolonged loyalty to the phlogiston theory of combustion and in his increasingly eccentric adherence to what many considered superseded literary tastes.[36] And although Mendelssohn was greatly, even fervently, admired by many intellectuals throughout Europe during his lifetime, prejudice began to obscure his memory soon after his death. In what was to become a far too typical incident, a plan to erect an obelisk decorated with portraits of Leibniz, Lambert, Sulzer, and Mendelssohn himself on the square facing the Berlin Opera ran into obstacles almost immediately after Mendelssohn died in 1786. The main barrier to the project appears to have been, quite simply, anti-Semitism. A Prussian general by the name of Johann Andreas von Scholten deplored the cowardice and bias that his fellow Berliners had thus

36. See Franz H. Mautner, *Lichtenberg: Geschichte seines Geistes* (Berlin: Walter de Gruyter, 1968), 4.

displayed, and in a letter to David Friedländer he feared that "even among our learned men there will perhaps be some who look askance because they cannot forgive our philosopher that he was circumcised and wore a beard."[37] It is still the case today that Mendelssohn is often relegated to that rank of dilettante thinkers to whom many German scholars like to refer, with contemptuous dismissal, as "popular philosophers."

In the autumn of 1777, Lichtenberg published the essay "Über Physiognomik" (On physiognomy) in an annual journal called the *Göttingsche Taschenkalender*, of which he had just assumed the general editorship. The vehemence and skill with which he rejected Lavater's arguments, a writer and a work that were then at the height of an almost idolatrous popularity, caused an enormous stir in German educated circles. Within months after it had first appeared, more than eight thousand copies of the issue containing the essay had been sold, making a reissue both necessary and desirable.[38] But as Lichtenberg wrote in the introduction to the second edition, which appeared in the following year, it was precisely the unthinking acceptance of Lavater's theories, and the frightening specter of their possible universal application, that caused him to risk the disfavor of the public by criticizing one of its darlings. In Lichtenberg's own acerbic words, which sardonically alluded to the subtitle of the *Fragmente*:

> I wanted to prevent people from practicing physiognomy for the advancement of brotherly love in the same way that, in earlier times, people scorched and burned for the advancement of the love of God. . . . I wanted to awaken distrust against that kind of transcendental ventriloquism which is employed to make many people think that something that is spoken on earth comes from heaven; I wanted to make certain, now that the most coarse superstition has been banned from the better circles, that a more refined one did not insinuate itself in its place—a superstition that, precisely because of the mask of reason it wears, becomes more dangerous than the coarse variety. . . . Now people wish to read the signs on our brow, whereas it used to be the signs in the heavens.[39]

It was a powerful blast. In his indignation at Lavater's presumptuous posturing (for Lavater always hinted that for whatever mysterious reasons, he was one of the chosen few capable of deciphering God's cryptic signs), in his wariness of how physiognomy seemed to reinforce entrenched prejudice

37. Cited from Alexander Altmann, *Moses Mendelssohn: A Biographical Study* (Philadelphia: Jewish Publication Society of America, 1973), 754–55.
38. See Mautner, *Lichtenberg*, 188.
39. Georg Christoph Lichtenberg, "Über Physiognomik; wider die Physiognomen," in *Aphorismen. Schriften. Briefe*, ed. Wolfgang Promies and Barbara Promies (Munich: Hanser, 1974), 269–70.

rather than reveal hidden and previously unsuspected truths, and in his efforts to foster tolerance rather than breed suspicion, Lichtenberg here validated his credentials as a confirmed and unfaltering *philosophe*. Indeed, by making passing reference to the Inquisition and to physiognomy's family resemblance to astrology, this passage contains the germ of Lichtenberg's general strategy for countering Lavater's claims. Simply by citing historical precedents and plain facts that contradicted Lavater's unfounded assertions —in other words, by applying the very standards of scientific procedure to physiognomy that Lavater himself spuriously claimed as his own— Lichtenberg was able to strike at one of the main supporting pillars of Lavater's theory, namely, that the laws of physiognomy were universal, regular, and unchanging. If Lichtenberg would simply produce a person who was both morally good and physically unattractive, Lavater's theory would instantly dissolve.

Perhaps in part because nature had not blessed Lichtenberg with a well-proportioned figure (he suffered from a severly hunched back), he seemed especially disturbed, even personally offended, by the centerpiece of Lavater's book: "the rash and devastating notion that the most beautiful soul inhabits the most beautiful body, and the ugliest soul occupies the ugliest body. . . . Great God! What does beauty of the body, whose entire measure was perhaps originally refined sensuous pleasure [*Lust*] . . . have to do with beauty of the soul, which battles so strenuously against this pleasure and stretches into eternity?" (282). Once again calling on common sense and everyday experience to erode confidence in Lavater's proposition, Lichtenberg implied that in positing this absolute harmony between a fair exterior and real virtue Lavater was naive, or disingenuous—or worse. With an audible bitterness that suggests more than a merely impartial devotion to intellectual probity, he observed:

> That such a principle, which has not been proven but merely exclaimed, and which will not and cannot be proven, could have found acceptance here and there is hardly conceivable, and only imaginable in the Germany of today. For are not all history books and all large cities full of beautiful villains? To be sure, whoever wishes to see beautiful rogues, smooth deceivers and charming orphan abusers cannot look for them behind hedges and in village jails. One has to go to where they eat from silver spoons, where they have a knowledge of faces and control over their muscles, where they make families wretched with a shrug of the shoulders, and destroy name and credit with a whisper, or stutter with affected indecision. (283)

The outrage Lichtenberg expressed here over the abuses lightly committed by the rich and powerful stands in marked contrast to Lavater's utopian

fantasies or his weakly placative promises that physiognomy could help improve his fellows and promote brotherly love—at least, that is, among those
wealthy enough to afford his lavishly embellished tomes. Coupled with his
pronounced criticism of the parochial state of German society (Berlin could
hardly compare in either size or cosmopolitan flair to London or Paris at the
time) is the suggestion that Lavater may have been using this collective lack
of sophistication to his own personal advantage. Lichtenberg appears to
have suspected Lavater not just of provincial credulity or of indulging in
unscientific wishful thinking, but, what is far worse, of somehow also being
hypocritically complicitous with the very forces of evil that he purported to
oppose.

Nonetheless, it is remarkable that even though the main tenets of Lavater's physiognomic theory aroused his gravest misgivings, Lichtenberg still
believed that beauty of soul itself did in some sense really exist. In fact, he
also believed that physiognomy, properly understood, was not entirely without merit either, but that Lavater had merely approached the matter wrong-
ly. Instead of insisting that every fixed part of the body, and particularly of
the face, infallibly corresponds to a single, identifiable character trait, Lichtenberg proposed concentrating on the appearance of fleeting emotions as
they are manifested above all in gestures and facial expressions. For this
alternative branch of study he coined the word—still used today in behav-
ioral sciences—"pathognomics." "Pathognomic signs," Lichtenberg averred,
"regularly repeated, do not all disappear again completely and thus leave
behind physiognomic impressions. Thus there occasionally arise the foolishness wrinkle, which comes from admiring everything and understanding
nothing; the hypocritical-deceiver wrinkle, those little dimples in the cheeks;
the stubborn wrinkle, and heaven knows what other kinds of wrinkles"
(293).[40] Lichtenberg even asserted that in so far as any occupation of this
sort can lay any claim to truth and prove beneficial to the promotion of
morality, the observation of such pathognomic signs will confirm the larger
maxim that *"virtue makes one more beautiful, vice more ugly."*[41]

---

40. Although Lichtenberg may have invented the word "pathognomy," he was by no means
the first to identify it as being strictly separate from physiognomy. See the comments by
Bacon, *De Augmentis*, in *Works*, 4:376: "Aristotle has very ingeniously and diligently handled
the structure of the body when at rest, but the structure of the body when in motion (that is
the gestures of the body) he has omitted; which nevertheless are equally within the observations of art, and of greater use and advantage. For the lineaments of the body disclose the
dispositions and inclinations of the mind in general; but the motions and gestures of
the countenance and parts do not only so, but disclose likewise the seasons of access, for the
present humour and state of the mind and will. For as your Majesty says most aptly and
elegantly, 'As the tongue speaketh to the ear so the gesture speaketh to the eye.' . . . [F]or
we all laugh and weep and frown and blush nearly in the same fashion; and so it is (for the
most part) in the more subtle motions."
41. Lichtenberg, "Über Physiognomik," 294.

The differences in both degree and kind between this statement and Lavater's claim that moral goodness inevitably and recognizably expressed itself as physical beauty are evident. Lichtenberg's emphasis on process and change, which are the essence of his definition of "pathognomy," reveals the concern of a true moralist, whereas Lavater too often betrays the rigidity of a demagogue. Yet it is no less plain that Lichtenberg was disinclined to relinquish the thought that a deeper, perhaps obscure, correspondence obtained between beauty and virtue. Skeptical scientist, even sophisticated critic of language though he was, Lichtenberg refused to allow himself to be awakened from the dream of the beautiful soul. Or maybe his distorted, hunched back, which had resulted from an early rachitic illness and plagued him with pain and humiliation for the rest of his life, led him secretly to harbor the hope that the beauty that had been denied to his mortal frame had at least been mercifully bestowed on that part of him which "stretches into eternity."

Whereas Lichtenberg sought to dismantle Lavater's work by using counterexamples drawn from history and his own experience, and even by employing the sharper polemical weapons of satire and ridicule, Lavater's other major contemporary critic, Mendelssohn, approached the problem from a slightly different perspective. More at home in the rigors of philosophical analysis than Lichtenberg, Mendelssohn tried to unravel the tangled web of unexamined assumptions that supplied the underpinnings of Lavater's text. Not surprisingly, he also concentrated on the crucial issue concerning the purported "harmony of internal and external beauty" and, although he likewise did not dismiss the notion entirely, he came to conclusions very different from those reached by Lavater about its possibility.

Mendelssohn's dealings with Lavater did not actually begin with his critical reflections on the *Physiognomische Fragmente*. In 1763 Lavater had stopped in Berlin during one of his proselytizing pilgrimages and was introduced to Mendelssohn, whom Lavater already knew by his published writings as "a brilliant metaphysician" and whom he was apparently anxious to meet.[42] Strangely, they seem to have skirted religious issues entirely and to have spoken primarily about literature and current events; but their conversation made a deep impression on the itinerant preacher. In the following year, while again in Berlin, Lavater visited Mendelssohn once more, and he collected the courage to broach the topic that had probably burned in his conscience throughout their first encounter: he asked Mendelssohn, a famous Jew, to state his views openly on Christianity. Specifically, Lavater wanted to know, given that Mendelssohn was such a gifted proponent of enlightened wisdom, why he did not convert to Christianity, which was—so

---

42. From a letter of 18 April 1763 from Lavater to J. J. Breitinger; see this letter and the description of their meeting in Altmann, *Moses Mendelssohn*, 201–5.

it seemed to Lavater—the only religion a truly philosophical mind could embrace. Although Mendelssohn showed warranted caution in revealing his views and repeatedly requested that they not be made public, he responded with grace and tact—yet also with resolution—by reaffirming his allegiance to Judaism.[43] But Mendelssohn's answer did not satisfy his visitor, who respected neither Mendelssohn's beliefs nor his wishes: a few years later, in 1769, Lavater publicly challenged Mendelssohn in a printed statement either to refute the correctness of Charles Bonnet's *La Palingénésie philosophique*, which employed modern conceptions of psychology and physiology in an attempt to undergird Christianity, or to renounce his faith and join the Christian fold.

It was a mean and disgraceful tactic, and Mendelssohn was appalled and worried at once. As a Jew living in Berlin, he was dependent on the precarious good will of the local authorities, and he could ill afford to become embroiled in a dispute that would inescapably pit him against the representatives of a government that already barely deigned to protect him. He had thus studiously avoided any controversy about religious matters, and now Lavater had tried to bully him into publicly airing his private convictions. After collecting himself, Mendelssohn composed a solicitous yet dignified response in which he explained that a detailed defense of his beliefs was both unnecessary and unwise. In a pointed remark that indicated how much Lavater's words had distressed him, Mendelssohn mentioned that he had hoped that such apologies would be superfluous, even inappropriate, among those who adhered to the principles of tolerance and basic human charity. "I have the fortune of calling many an excellent man my friend who is not of my faith," he wrote. "We genuinely love one another even though we suspect, in fact presuppose, that in religious matters we are of completely divergent opinions. I enjoy the pleasure of their company, which both improves and delights me. Never has my heart secretly called out to me: 'too bad for the beautiful soul [*schöne Seele*]'! Whoever believes that salvation cannot be found outside of his church must often feel such sighs rising in his breast" (7:13).

In spite of its potential for more embarrassing, not to say dangerous, revelations, the issue finally laid itself to rest in an atmosphere of relatively amicable accord after several subsequent exchanges of letters.[44] But it was not forgotten: the episode, or more precisely Mendelssohn's exemplary display of forbearance and fortitude, so impressed his friend Lessing that it

43. See Altmann, *Moses Mendelssohn*, 204. Mendelssohn related these events himself in his "Schreiben an den Herrn Diaconus Lavater zu Zürich," in *Gesammelte Schriften: Jubiläumsausgabe*, ed. Fritz Bamberger et al. (Sutttgart: Friedrich Frommann Verlag; Bad Cannstatt: Günter Holzboog, 1972–   ), 7:7–8.
44. See the meticulous and exhaustive account in Altmann, *Moses Mendelssohn*, 209–63.

served as the inspiration for the famous ring parable in his play *Nathan der Weise*.[45] Still, when Mendelssohn took up the matter of physiognomy eight years later, the unpleasant memory of his confrontation with Lavater must have prevented him from expressing his views as freely as he might have otherwise done. While making general remarks about Lavater's style, for example, Mendelssohn questioned Lavater's claims that physiognomy possessed scientific legitimacy, without neglecting to display his customary restraint: "The spirit of scientific observation demands cold-blooded reflection, at most moderate warmth, if it is to be refined. But in the face of Lavater's fiery imagination it evaporates all too quickly. . . . Enthusiasm generally makes us think that signs are more expressive than they really are. Such a disposition of the soul thus leads us to be inclined to read much more in physiognomies than they contain." In a magnanimous gesture, Mendelssohn went on to offer the suggestion that the failure to make physiognomy into a reliable science may not "lie alone with Lavater. It seems to me that our language and our psychology [*Seelenlehre*] are not yet developed enough for physiognomy."[46] There are, he explained, so many different gradations and kinds of both physical and moral qualities, which then combine to produce all manner of characters, talents, and aptitudes, that a true physiognomics could be possible only after every aspect of the human constitution had been examined and fully understood. Until then, Mendelssohn thought, any attempt—including Lavater's—to create a physiognomical theory would be a provisional effort at best.

As offensive as Lavater's pseudoscientific perorations were to Mendelssohn's own discriminating sensibilities, he nevertheless felt a powerful attraction to the idea of the beautiful soul (which was, as we just witnessed, an expression with which he was certainly familiar). Like virtually all of his contemporaries, Mendelssohn did not therefore call its viability as an ethical model—indeed as *the* expression of perfect virtue—into serious doubt. Or rather, he never did so explicitly. The second essay he wrote in the wake of the Lavater affair was prompted by Lichtenberg's attack on the *Fragmente* and titled "Ueber einige Einwürfe gegen die Physiognomik, und vorzüglich gegen die von Herrn Lavater behauptete Harmonie zwischen Schönheit

45. To his credit, Goethe, who was friendly with Lavater during this period, criticized Lavater's behavior in the affair; in *Poetry and Truth*, in *Collected Works*, 4:446, he wrote that Lavater "did not understand how anyone could live and breathe and not also be a Christian. My relationship to the Christian religion was only a matter of heart and mind, and I had not the slightest conception of that physical kinship toward which Lavater inclined. Consequently I was offended by the vehement importunity of this intelligent, sensitive man when he attacked me, as well as Mendelssohn and others, and declared that we must either join him as Christians, Christians of his type, or we must draw him over to *our* side and likewise convince *him* of the source of our consolation."
46. Moses Mendelssohn, "Zufällige Gedanken über die Harmonie der inneren und äusseren Schönheit," in *Gesammelte Schriften*, 3.1:328.

und Tugend" (On some objections to physiognomy, and especially to the harmony between beauty and virtue that Mr. Lavater claims). Here Mendelssohn adopted a position that would prove congenial to thinkers of a century hence. "I believe to have discovered," he wrote, "that this dispute, like many, and I might almost say most, disputes of the philosophers, amounts in the end to an ambiguity and uncertainty of expression, that is, to what is really a quarrel over words [*Wortstreit*]."[47] What was needed, he felt, was more scrupulous attention to the main terms of the disagreement. "If one were only to agree about the meaning of the words 'virtue, beauty, and harmony' and relate them to certain and distinct characteristics [*Merkmale*], then the dispute would be as good as ended and peace restored" (3.1:331). As Mendelssohn himself well knew, coming to such an agreement, however, would prove to be more difficult than it first appeared.

Mendelssohn had of course already formulated a good part of his definition of the meaning of these words in the prize essay he had written for the Berlin academy in 1763. The central maxim of human moral conduct, for him as for Baumgarten and Wolff, consisted in the ceaseless striving to make one's "internal and external state" as perfect as possible. Although beauty had figured as an important part of that earlier account, Mendelssohn had neglected to mention how he defined beauty itself. At the beginning of his first essay on Lavater's *Fragmente*, he therefore set forth that "beauty is nothing other than goodness [*Güte*] and fitness [*Tüchtigkeit*] that have become visible" (3.1:321). Yet he went on to argue that goodness is a more objective quality than beauty, since a thing will either be suitable to the task it has to perform or not; beauty, on the other hand, contains many subjective elements, causing different people to respond positively, some neutrally, and yet others with complete antipathy to one and the same ostensibly "beautiful" object. Mendelssohn's hopeful response to this apparently hopelessly relativistic situation was to claim that "Providence has seen to it that we can usually recognize inner fitness through external beauty and goodness through charm [*Annehmlichkeit*]" (3.1:322). With that seemingly careless comment that body and soul "usually" coincide, Mendelssohn had already reduced Lavater's grandiose certainties to mere probabilities.

Still, the question of human beauty itself intrigued Mendelssohn, and he devoted the rest of the essay to an exploration of this perennial problem. He began by differentiating between two ways in which beauty could manifest itself: one—which he called "dead beauty"—resided in the static realm of form; and form, although it can also be indicative of inner qualities, mainly refers to external attributes. The other and more interesting way beauty

47. Moses Mendelssohn, "Ueber einige Einwürfe gegen die Physiognomik, und vorzüglich gegen die von Herrn Lavater behauptete Harmonie zwischen Schönheit und Tugend," in *Gesammelte Schriften*, 3.1:329.

made its appearance was, according to Mendelssohn, through expression, which he termed "living beauty." This latter type existed in three primary gradations: the first, which he called "organic" beauty, was displayed by sensuous characteristics that naturally express inner perfections (for example, a ruddy glow on one's cheeks would be such a sign of health); next were so-called animal beauties, which we perceive through external signs that indicate the presence of the sort of basic consciousness that humans have in common with beasts, such as sensation, natural drives and so on; finally, there is the purely "human" or "intellectual" beauty, whereby reason, freedom of the will, sensitivity, morality, and so on, are expressed in a natural manner. "From the harmonious combination and union of all of these beauties," Mendelssohn explained, "springs the *beauty of humanity*" (3.1:323).

By thus distinguishing between "dead form" and "living expression" in his definition of human beauty, Mendelssohn not only dispensed with Lavater's simpleminded equation of the physical and moral being, he had also advanced to a more generous conception of the nature of inner beauty as a whole. Not just virtue, however it may be constituted, but all of the distinct possessions of the human mind, each developed according to individual capacity, now counted as essential components of the beautiful soul. In addition, Mendelssohn allowed for enormous variety in how this beauty might be composed and therefore brought forth. "Every subject has his own mixture of abilities and inclinations, which make up his genius and character. In this mixture, one quality will generally protrude, as it were, and become the main feature of his genius or character; the other qualities are then subordinated to this one." In view of the virtually infinite number of possible permutations in the construction of human character, Mendelssohn thus concluded that "there is no absolute ideal of beauty. Rather, every subject demands, according to the measure of his powers and abilities, his own ideal that corresponds to that measure. An absolute ideal would combine all of the previously mentioned beauties in the highest degree and in the most perfect harmony. This is as impossible as it is for a body to travel at the greatest possible speed or in all directions at once" (3.1:323). Thus even the inner—or as Mendelssohn preferred to put it, the "living" and thus "expressive"—beauties that combine to create our individual characters frustrate in their complexity any attempt to arrange them into something resembling systematic order. But if one would add the further complication of relating the external beauties of form to this varied array of inner qualities, then the situation becomes even more difficult to unravel. "Every one of these qualities has its own particular physiognomy that occasionally collides with the requirements of dead beauty. From this stem the different judgments of peoples and times with respect to beauty, the astonishing multiplicity of *taste*" (3.1:325). Among its many other shortcomings, Lavater's theory had also entirely neglected to take such historical and cultural diversity into account. For in the same manner of thinking, just as various cultures and historical periods have their own standards of beauty, so too will each expression of each quality that is perceived to be beautiful within those communities have its own specific physiognomical form. Quite apart from the accidental effects of age, illness, climate, and diet, these variables alone provide a sufficiently Protean set of correspondences between physical features and intellectual qualities that Lavater's fundamental conception is rendered uselessly vague and, ultimately, practically meaningless.

Although more subtle in his analysis and less aggressive in his approach, Mendelssohn had thus delivered a critique of Lavater's *Fragmente* that was, in its effect, every bit as devastating as Lichtenberg's passionate denunciation of Lavater's latent—or all too manifest—chauvinism. Although physiognomy continued to arouse a popular response, especially in France and England, that was largely fueled by a potent amalgam of fear and fascination, among German intellectuals in any case it never recovered its formerly fashionable reputability after Lichtenberg's assault. Throughout the 1780s and 1790s, whenever the larger philosophical question arose about the relation between body and soul, writers usually referred at least briefly to the practice, noting its uncertain foundations, its limitations, and—sometimes —its dangers. In Schiller's dissertation of 1780, for example, "Versuch über den Zusammenhang der tierischen Natur des Menschen mit seiner geistigen" ("Essay on the Relationship between the Animal and Intellectual Nature of the Human Being"), Schiller wrote that he agreed in principle, as had Lichtenberg, with the thesis that "every noble and benevolent [emotion] *beautifies* the body, which every ignoble and malicious one mutilates into *bestial* forms."[48] But at the same time Schiller doubted that anything approaching a fully developed physiognomy in Lavater's understanding of it would be, or could be, soon published (5:319).[49] Kant, too, seemed certain

---

48. See Friedrich Schiller, "Versuch über den Zusammenhang der tierischen Natur des Menschen mit seiner geistigen," in *Sämtliche Werke,* ed. Gerhard Fricke and Herbert G. Göpfert (Munich: Carl Hauser, 1958–59), 5:317.
49. Schiller also composed a satirical epitaph for Lavater, which he published in 1782— nineteen years before Lavater died:

"Grabschrift
eines gewissen Physiognomen"

Wes Geistes Kind im Kopf gesessen,
Konnt' er auf jeder Nase lesen:
Und doch - daß *er* es nicht gewesen,
Den Gott zu diesem Werk erlesen,
Konnt' er nicht auf der *seinen* lesen.

[Epitaph of a certain Physiognomist: He could read from every nose the spirit inside the head: And yet—he was unable to read from his *own* that *he* was not the one whom God had chosen for this task.] *Sämtliche Werke,* 1:72.

that, as he put it in the section dedicated to physiognomy in his *Anthropologie in pragmatischer Hinsicht* (Anthropology from a pragmatic point of view) of 1798, "there is a characterization by physiognomy, but it can never become a science."[50] And he also explicitly rejected Lavater's thesis that God would have "joined a beautiful body with a good soul in order to commend the person He created to other people"; such an assumption, Kant asserted, was simply "absurd" (160–61). Finally, in 1807 Hegel thought that the issue still merited enough attention to surrender a substantial portion of his *Phänomenologie des Geistes* (Phenomenology of spirit) to a discussion of why, in his opinion, physiognomy—as well as its sister-science phrenology—was "something which lacks both foundation and finality."[51] It was hard to argue with Hegel.

Yet even after these and other disavowals of its truth or, indeed, of its possibility, physiognomy and its various offspring by no means disappeared from the European stage. The theater, in fact, was one place where it continued to find a welcome home. Johann Jakob Engel, among other things an acquaintance and sometime collaborator of Mendelssohn, recognized the potential of pathognomic observation for the practical needs of actors and artists, and he developed his insights in the *Ideen zu einer Mimik* (Ideas toward a theory of mimicry), which appeared in 1785–86. It is an unfairly neglected work, for it not only presents a nuanced investigation of the various processes by which emotions are expressed, it also offers one of the first extended arguments for a new so-called natural method of acting that was, despite its name, based on a conscious or highly reflective command of the body and its movements. Although he realized that it seemed paradoxical, Engel explained that learning the hidden laws of gestures and facial expressions was crucial to their convincing, that is to say apparently unconscious, representation in the theater:

> Actors all speak of *emotion* and believe that they would certainly perform brilliantly if they would only follow the advice of Cahusac and merge with their material to the point of enthusiastic abandon. I know of only one actor (but still the best one I have ever known)—namely our Ekhof—who never relied on mere emotion with respect either to declamation or to acting itself. Rather, during the performance, he took care not to slip too far into an emotional state so that he would not lose his presence of mind, and thus act with less truth, expression, harmony, and composure.[52]

50. Immanuel Kant, *Anthropology from a Pragmatic Point of View*, trans. Mary J. Gregor (The Hague: Martinus Nijhoff, 1974), 161.
51. Georg Wilhelm Friedrich Hegel, *Phenomenology of Spirit*, trans. A. V. Miller (Oxford: Oxford University Press, 1977), 193.
52. Johann Jakob Engel, *Ideen zu einer Mimik*, in *Schriften* (Berlin: Mylius'sche Buchhandlung, 1844), 7:10. The actor Engel referred to was Hans Conrad Dietrich Ekhof

By insisting that the successful illusion of real emotion on the stage depended on its absence in the actor, who must therefore exercise the most precise and demanding self-control, Engel thus adumbrated the salient propositions of Diderot's much more famous *Paradoxe sur le comédien*, which, though written between 1769 and 1773, did not appear in print until 1830.[53] But Engel felt that even beyond the question of its immediate usefulness to actors in improving their craft, a knowledge of Lichtenberg's "pathognomy" did not actually need to be justified by constantly underscoring its potential pragmatic application. It deserved, Engel thought, to be treated like any other branch of inquiry. "After all," he reflected, "the theory of such an art form would still be a kind of knowledge, and moreover knowledge of humanity, which as such would have its own inner absolute value; a value that even without that relative worth, would have to make it estimable to the mind of every thinking man. Should not the moral human being be just as valuable to an observer as the polyp was to Trembley or the aphid to Bonnet?"[54] In the course of the next century, several other thinkers and scientists implicitly agreed with Engel's point of view. In 1806 Sir Charles Bell brought out his *Essay on the Anatomy of Expression*, and in 1872 Charles Darwin, toward the end of his long and controversial career, published his *Expression of the Emotions in Man and Animals*, which Darwin himself placed in the tradition of eighteenth-century efforts on the same subject.[55]

In his view that the study of the physical, or the purely organic, characteristics of human beings constituted a valuable field of study in its own right, Engel had therefore pointed in one of the directions that modern physiology would ultimately take. The most important step on this path was to abandon the chimerical hope that one could somehow divine the "true" nature of the soul from the constitution of its corporeal shell. By respecting this more narrowly limited range of expectations, it was even ventured that physiognomy itself might perhaps still deserve some consideration. Or so

(or Eckhof), who lived from 1720 to 1778, and might be considered the German equivalent of the great English actor David Garrick. Lessing (who, incidentally, mentioned Ekhof in very flattering terms as well in his *Hamburgische Dramaturgie*), was also an early proponent of the "natural" acting method, as opposed to the classical French declamatory style inherited from the previous century. There is a very good presentation of this transition in acting styles in Theodore Ziolkowski, "Language and Mimetic Action in Lessing's *Miss Sara Sampson*," *Germanic Review* 40 (1965): 261–76.

53. See the illuminating discussion of the essay and its significance by Arthur M. Wilson, *Diderot* (New York: Oxford University Press, 1972), 621–28.

54. Engel, *Ideen zu einer Mimik*, in *Schriften*, 7:14.

55. See Charles Darwin, *The Expression of the Emotions in Man and Animals* (Chicago: University of Chicago Press, 1965), 2–8. The most ambitious attempt to construct a modern theory of expression is by Wilhelm Wundt, *Völkerpsychologie: Eine Untersuchung der Entwicklungsgesetze von Sprache, Mythos und Sitte* (Leipzig: Engelmann, 1900–1928), who mentions Engel as his predecessor (1:93). Karl Bühler, *Ausdruckstheorie: Das System an der Geschichte aufgezeigt*, intro. Albert Wellek, 2d ed. (Stuttgart: G. Fischer, 1968), saw Engel as the father of modern gestural psychology.

thought one of Engel's most prominent students: Wilhelm von Humboldt.[56] In an essay Humboldt wrote while in Paris in 1799, *Musée des petits Augustins*, he acknowledged that physiognomy stood on unstable ground, but he also declared his reluctance to consign it entirely to the dustbin of history. "Physiognomy has become so questionable only because people have degraded it by using it as a means of reading the inner being of a person from the exterior, and thereby preempting the actual examination that requires time and opportunity. It is, to be sure, a strange proposal: to forego the reliable and distinct language of actions and even of speech in favor of the ambiguous and indistinct one of silhouettes that display outlines bent in this or that way" (*Werke* 1:520). Humboldt thus advocated, instead, a modified theory of physiognomy, one that dealt more or less exclusively with external appearance, a kind of comparative taxonomy of primarily facial features. As he put it, "the true purpose of physiognomy should thus be none other than the knowledge of human physiognomies, independent of all study of inner character" (*Werke* 1:522). But Humboldt, who always had trouble summoning the discipline or even the interest to execute all of the myriad plans he sketched out for himself, never expanded on the few brief comments he made in this essay about a "truer," if tailored down, physiognomy.

Despite the critical discussions taking place in Germany, Lavater's theories caught hold in France on the threshold of the Revolution, and their putative value in enabling the reliable interpretation of character allowed his ideas to enter into French revolutionary discourse about creating a "homme nouveau, républicain et vertueux."[57] But the potential in physiognomy for abuse—which Lichtenberg, for one, had keenly perceived—grew into a real and life-threatening danger as the Revolution degenerated from democratic idealism to autocratic carnage. The distance one had to travel from effusively praising the features thought to characterize a "true" republican to cutting off the head that bore the hateful marks of aristocracy was not as great as we would perhaps like to think. Yet there is reason to believe that this tendency toward violent excess lay inherent in the practice of physiognomy itself. On more than one occasion, Lavater himself uttered remarks that in light of Germany's own later history, give one pause indeed. In the pivotal section of the *Fragmente* "On the Harmony of Moral and Corporeal Beauty," Lavater considered the possible ways to improve the moral state of humanity as a whole. He proposed, apparently in deadly seriousness, that one should "take away from the ugliest people those children who really are the spitting image of their parents—remove them from their elders and raise them in a well-furnished and well-run public institution." So convinced was Lavater of his thesis that ugliness was the unmistakable sign of evil that he thus advised this primitive version of social engineering as a means of combatting both. Once these children have grown, he continued, they should be placed in circumstances that "will not too greatly tax their virtue and will not expose them to any extraordinary enticements to vice" (since these children had been born ugly and thus, so he believed, equipped with an innate propensity to viciousness, one could never take too many precautions). After these unfortunate creatures have reached maturity, they should also be forced to intermarry. "What increasingly beautiful people you will have by the fifth or sixth generation (as long as very untoward incidents do not intervene), and not just in their facial features, but in the fixed bone formation of the head, in the entire figure, in everything! For, in concert with the other virtues and with calmness of spirit, orderly industriousness, moderation, cleanliness—as well as some care for these things in education—really does produce beauty of flesh and color" (*Phys. Frag.*, 1:75–76).

It would be unfair, as well as unhistorical, to make Lavater himself distantly responsible for the subsequent rise of racist thinking in Germany, but his proposals necessarily sound more sinister in light of the experiences we have had during this century than they must have seemed to his own contemporaries. It remains, however, one of the strangest and saddest legacies of the eighteenth-century ideal of the beautiful soul, which had represented to its creators the very personification of moral goodness, that its fateful association with physiognomy allowed it, in our own time, to become entangled in a pernicious ideology that embodied just the opposite. For owing to its insistence on the absolute correspondence between inner character and external appearance, physiognomy could be exploited to foster not the "Brothery Love" promised by Lavater, but rather prejudice and hatred toward those who did not conform to the officially sanctioned canon of physical, and thus moral, beauty. And the question can probably never be answered whether this modern development represented a perversion or merely the most radical, though still strictly logical, extension of the original idea itself.

6

Kant and Schiller:
The Apotheosis of the Beautiful Soul

I slept, and dreamed that life was Beauty;
I woke, and found that life was Duty.
Was thy dream then a shadowy lie?
—Ellen Sturgis Hooper

By the end of the 1780s, particularly but by no means solely in the German-speaking states, the discourse generated by the concept of moral beauty had been completely absorbed, and largely accepted, by the learned and laymen alike. The "beautiful soul"—the "schöne Seele" and the "belle âme"—appeared in countless works and contexts: in philosophical essays and private letters, in novels, poems, and plays, and, if Lavater would have had his way, in the streets and salons of Europe as well. It was in every respect a remarkable phenomenon: in the relatively brief course of only seven or eight decades, beauty of soul had become nothing less than a cardinal ethical ideal of the Enlightenment, which in an age that remained convinced that there was nothing more important than morality meant a great deal indeed. But even more astonishing, perhaps, than the rapidity of its adoption was the apparent universality of its appeal. Traversing all other national, cultural, ideological, and even sexual boundaries, moral beauty emerged as one of the most important concepts defining and guiding the aspirations of countless educated men and women throughout the Western world to attain that supreme, if elusive, goal: the good life. During the late eighteenth century the beautiful soul literally embodied the ultimate achievement of human virtue, and virtue—as almost everyone agreed—was the one indisputably necessary condition of true and permanent happiness.

With these impressive gains came, of course, new challenges. The concept of moral beauty had, as we have seen, always had its detractors, including those (like Locke and Berkeley) who tended to scoff at the notion and those (such as Wolff and many of his followers) who simply avoided the matter entirely—whether out of conviction or convenience we will never know. But even among those who persisted in their belief that the beautiful soul represented the most profound expression of human moral existence, identifying exactly what moral beauty *was* had never been an easy task. In the final decade of the century this question, which had never been adequately answered or even, in fact, fully addressed before, had thus developed a pressing urgency, and some of the best minds of the day in Germany turned toward resolving it. Kant and Schiller were two such thinkers who were both captivated as well as beset by the problem of the beautiful soul—and it had indeed become a problem by then—and each sought to provide his own solution to the difficulties it raised. For the complications created by the very concept of the beautiful soul had by then already grown at least as great as the benefits it had once promised to bring.

It might be helpful, at this point, to recall briefly how and why the beautiful soul had been brought into existence in the first place. Moral beauty, as we have observed, had originally been born of the felt need to find an alternative to the traditional ethical system of the Christian religion. God was not yet dead, naturally, but many thinkers thought that it might be best to draw up some contingency plans just in case. Yet without that acknowledged transcendent source of the laws that governed (or more realistically, ought to govern) our behavior, many philosophers sought alternatives in the capacities that were inherent in human nature itself. Contrary to the popular perception of the Enlightenment, however, most of the participants in the debate did not necessarily place unqualified faith in the powers of reason—the Age of Reason could just as well be called the Age of Doubt. Yet they were forced to acknowledge that despite its limitations, reason nonetheless remained our most precious possession, and their propositions for a new ethical code reflected this cautious but determined optimism. It was perhaps only natural that the crisis that began in the seventeenth century and was caused by a renewed reliance on autonomous reason would be met by suggestions engendered by the same impulse: to enlarge the claims the rational mind made for itself. We thus witnessed Locke attempting to prove, as he expressed it in a pamphlet so titled, the reasonableness of Christianity, by showing that the dictates of the reasonable mind and divine revelation providentially concurred. Others, such as the Deists (and in Germany, once more, the indefatigable Wolff), tried to expand the role of reason even further and to dispense entirely with the cumbersome necessity of arguing for the convergence between rational judgment and the dictates of God. Human reason alone, they thought, should have sole legislative power over our will and actions. Although a belief in the Christian God continued to influence the lives and hopes of the majority of eighteenth-century Europeans, the structural place that the idea of God had previously occupied with respect to the regulation of human conduct had been ceded at that moment to yet another abstract principle: Humanity itself.

The rationalists' peculiar distrust in the infallibility of reason, and especially in its ability to administer the decisions we make in practical life, gave rise almost immediately to new scruples about the suitability of rational reflection to serve as the sole and absolute arbiter of moral comportment. In his *Enquiry*, Hume summarized this predicament in his characteristically graceful diction: "Extinguish all the warm feelings and prepossessions in favour of virtue, and all disgust or aversion to vice: render men totally indifferent towards these distinctions; and morality is no longer a practical study, nor has any tendency to regulate our lives and actions."[1] It was Shaftesbury who, borrowing his terms from ancient Greek authors to fashion a response to this modern dilemma, had had the good fortune to hit upon an idea that was both simple and attractive enough to allow it to disseminate among a large and varied audience, yet also refined enough to satisfy his more discerning readers. His conception of moral beauty was thus by no means original to him. But he ingeniously applied it to a new situation, and the result, the history of which we have traced in the preceding chapters, presents overwhelming evidence of its persuasiveness for contemporary minds.

The success of Shaftesbury's notion of moral beauty depended precisely on his attempt to achieve a balanced integration of both affective and rational elements in his conception of ethical knowledge and action, or to put it another way, on its capacity to combine the emotional and intellectual qualities of morality within a single, striking formulation. By equating virtue with beauty, or rather to argue that virtuous behavior exhibited the basic characteristics of beauty (namely, proportion, harmony, symmetry, and so on), Shaftesbury could also claim that they both elicited the same response, namely pleasure. Since it seemed self-evident that we would always choose pleasure over pain, the grounds of moral motivation appeared secure to Shaftesbury and his disciples. In order to stabilize and maximize the pleasure that accompanied whatever was morally beautiful, we would strive not only to form or cultivate ourselves according to this ideal model, but also to seek out the society of others of like mind and behavior. In this way, Shaftesbury had attempted to provide the rudimentary foundations of a social framework constructed according to the requirements of virtuous behavior alone.

Shaftesbury had always been careful to stress the significance of reason in the regulation of the affective life. What else, after all, are harmony, propor-

1. David Hume, *Enquiries concerning Human Understanding and concerning the Principles of Morals*, ed. L. A. Selby-Bigge, 3d ed., rev. P. H. Nidditch (Oxford: Oxford University Press, 1975), 172.

tion, and symmetry if not preeminently rational? But he also realized, as did Hume after him, that reason by itself did not suffice to move people to action. Moral beauty had the advantage of being based on simple, uniform, and universally valid norms—norms that at the same time appealed to our emotional needs in a way that Hume also regarded as necessary to prevent our indifference. Beauty of soul had thus also seemed to be an elegant bridge over the chasm separating mind and body, spanning a gulf that had troubled thinkers from Plato to Descartes. Shaftesbury's suggestion that we possessed a "moral sense" (although, as was already indicated, he rarely used this phrase himself), which allowed us to perceive such beauty, likewise revealed his attempt to perform a subtle negotiation between rigid rationalism and formless sensualism. For his use of the word "sense" did not imply that our moral faculty could be swayed by the vagaries of random, ever-changing sensate impressions, but that it simply acted very much like one of our physical organs of sense such as the eye, which had to be trained by and work in concert with a rational mind in order to "see" something like distance and three-dimensional space. He actually used the word "taste" more frequently to refer to the mechanism of our response to moral action, and here too the rational component was arguably the more important one. In the early eighteenth-century understanding of the term, "taste" was the result of the highly rational, self-conscious process of deliberate training. We are *not* born with taste, although we *are* born with the capacity to acquire it; taste is thus a product of education and cultivation—or, as the Germans would put it, of *Bildung*.

Complemented, expanded, and occasionally corrected by the moral philosophies of Shaftesbury's two most talented followers, principally Hutcheson and Hume himself, this idea of moral beauty, together with its many implications, entered and then conquered European moral consciousness during the first half of the century. In 1759, another one of the great Scottish moralists, Adam Smith, better known as the founder of modern free-market economic theory, gave this theory its midcentury stamp. Betraying even here a weakness for industry over ethics, Smith mixed mechanical metaphors with those of moral beauty when he asserted the following:

> That the tendency of virtue to promote, and of vice to disturb, the order of society, when we consider it coolly and philosophically, reflects a very great beauty upon the one, and a very great deformity upon the other, cannot, as I have observed upon a former occasion, be called in question. Human society, when we contemplate it in a certain abstract and philosophical light, appears like a great, and immense machine, whose regular and harmonious movements produce a thousand agreeable effects. As in any other beautiful and noble machine that was the production of human art, whatever tended

to render its movements more smooth and easy, would derive a beauty from this effect, and, on the contrary, whatever tended to obstruct them would displease upon that account; so virtue, which is, as it were the fine polish to the wheels of society, necessarily pleases; while vice, like the vile rust which makes them jar and grate upon one another, is as necessarily offensive.[2]

Once on the Continent, this agreeable constellation of ideas easily commingled with indigenous religious traditions, as well as with the Hellenic revival, thus taking the notion full circle, so to speak. As we have seen, within only a few years, the concept of moral beauty also assumed a position of preeminence not only in professional philosophy, but in popular thought as well. Such was its appeal that even those in Germany who had received their principal training within the dogmatic school of rationalist philosophy, such as Baumgarten, Mendelssohn, and Sulzer, found room in their theories to accommodate what Kant, in 1765, had also termed "this beautiful discovery of our times."[3] And as we have also discovered, Kant was prepared to consider moral beauty as a viable solution to certain problems confronting contemporary ethical philosophy during his own so-called pre-critical period.

In the course of his later development, Kant seems slowly, if inexorably, to have come to grasp the logical complexities of this "beautiful discovery." Over the next twenty years, marked especially by the "silent decade" in the 1770s during which he published almost nothing at all, he appears to have tried to circumvent the problem of morality, apparently unable to find a way to unravel its intricate entanglements. At the end of the prize essay that he had submitted to the Berlin academy in 1763, he had announced that "it is still a question to be settled whether it is simply the cognitive faculty or whether it is feeling . . . which decides the basic principles of practical philosophy."[4] It may be just a slight exaggeration to claim that the *Critique of Pure Reason* of 1781 stands as a monument to Kant's efforts to settle this fundamental issue and to secure the epistemological substructure on which his subsequent inquiry into the matter of morality could be based.

KANT AND MORAL BEAUTY

Like Locke, who undertook his *Essay* in order to determine "the Principles of morality and reveal'd Religion," Kant also set out, as he announced

2. Adam Smith, *The Theory of Moral Sentiments*, 12th ed. (Edinburgh, 1808), vol. 2, part 7, sec. 3, 310–11.
3. See Immanuel Kant, "Nachricht von der Einrichtung seiner Vorlesungen in dem Winterhalbenjahre von 1765–1766," in *Werkausgabe*, ed. Wilhelm Weischedel (Frankfurt am Main: Suhrkamp, 1968), 2:915.
4. Immanuel Kant, *Critique of Practical Reason and Other Writings in Moral Philosophy*, trans. and ed. Lewis White Beck (Chicago: University of Chicago Press, 1949), 285. Henceforth cited in text and notes as *WMP* by page number.

in the preface to the *Foundations of the Metaphysics of Morals* of 1785, to provide nothing less than the "establishment of the supreme principle of morality" (*WMP*, 54). Many of the most compelling accounts of ethics that had been put forth during the century prior to Kant's own attempt to deliver this "single principle" had, in one respect or another, featured moral beauty as the best way to describe the manifestation of perfect virtue. And at various intervals in Kant's own career the beautiful soul—that enticing, seductive embodiment of this ideal—had stood invitingly before his mind as well. After many years of meditating on its attractions, Kant finally, and no doubt reluctantly, decided that it was a temptation it was imperative to resist.

That Kant himself was intensely aware of the continued importance of the concept of moral beauty in contemporary ethical philosophy partially emerges from the very vehemence with which he tried to combat it. In the opening pages of the *Foundations*, in typical fashion, Kant spoke dismissively of "the essays on morality which that popular taste favors," in which one encountered any number of different motives for ethically good behavior: "sometimes perfection, and sometimes happiness, here moral feeling, there fear of God, a little of this and a little of that in a marvelous mixture" (69–70). As opposed to these eclectic traditions of moral thought, all of which nonetheless rested to some extent on the incitements promised by moral beauty (and which, although he did not admit it here, he had also himself previously endorsed), Kant now required in his critical phase the identification of a single, completely nonempirical determining ground for all moral conduct. He insisted repeatedly, and by now famously, that "all moral concepts have their seat and origin entirely a priori in reason." The degree to which Kant was committed to this unforgivingly rationalistic conception of how we are able to know how to act emerges from the following categorical pronouncement:

> For the pure conception of duty and of the moral law generally, with no admixture of empirical inducements, has an influence on the human heart so much more powerful than all other incentives which may be derived from the empirical field that reason, in the consciousness of its dignity, despises them and gradually becomes master over them. It has this influence only through reason, which thereby first realizes that it can of itself be practical. A mixed theory of morals which is put together both from incentives of feelings and inclinations and from rational concepts must, on the other hand, make the mind vacillate between motives which cannot be brought under any principle and which can lead only accidentally to the good and often to the bad. (70–71)

It was on the basis of these and similar statements that Kant became burdened with the reputation of having been a chilly and desiccated "rigorist," a severely puritanical thinker who seemed to wish to exclude everything that was human from his descriptions of humanity.[5] But Kant did not imagine that in order to be virtuous, we had to be unfeeling automatons to whom all material satisfactions were prohibited or, alternatively, that if we happened to enjoy performing a good deed, the act, because of that enjoyment, was tainted by emotion and therefore not a pure exercise of duty. Kant only wished to make clear that a desire for such pleasure (or for any other gain), innocent though it may in many instances be, could not supply the original, motivating reason for an action if that action were to qualify as being morally good. Moral conduct, Kant emphasized, always had to be totally disinterested. Virtue was valuable to the truly virtuous for its own sake, and not for any reward, no matter how "refined" such a reward might be (say, in the form of certain pleasant feelings or subjective leanings). Only a knowledge of our "duty," with complete indifference toward any subjective "inclination" that we may feel or hope to feel toward the object or result of our actions, could provide the stable foundation for a true morality. The rational mind —Kant never tired of writing—and the rational mind alone must therefore be the sole and stern determinant of virtue.

The numerous Platonic resonances within Kant's thought have not, of course, escaped previous notice, and this unbending equation of abstract, ascetic wisdom with virtue is not the least significant of these reverberations. Yet the main influence here, as in so many other instances in Kant's mature philosophy, is not of Greek, but of British extraction. Isaac Newton—or rather the symbolic figure known by that name and cherished by all Enlightenment philosophers—gave Kant his principal inspiration and model for his own philosophical enterprise. "Everything in nature works according to laws," Kant wrote as an observant Newtonian, and no other single sentence could better express the core of his assumptions about the functioning of both the intellectual and physical universe. Nothing occurred in heaven or on earth that was not governed by the unchanging, invariable laws of nature, and the workings of the human mind made no exception to this general and inflexible rule. To locate in the mind the one regulative principle that could serve as the guide for our practical lives would have thus been, in Kant's

5. For a clear discussion of this issue, see Karl Vorländer, "Der ethische Rigorismus," in *Kant. Schiller. Goethe*, 2d exp. ed. (Leipzig: Felix Meiner, 1923), 53–80. Schiller may have been the first to imply that Kant was a "rigorist" in this derogatory sense; see his "Über Anmut und Würde," in *Sämtliche Werke*, ed. Gerhard Fricke and Herbert G. Göpfert (Munich: Carl Hanser, 1958–59), 5:464. Schiller's "Über Anmut und Würde" is henceforth cited in text and notes by volume and page number from *Sämtliche Werke*. Kant appears to have been slightly touchy about the subject and in another work he defensively wrote: "Those who are partial to this strict mode of thinking are usually called *rigorists* (a name which is intended to carry reproach, but which actually praises)." See Immanuel Kant, *Religion within the Limits of Reason Alone*, trans. Theodore M. Green and Hoyt H. Hudson (Chicago: Open Court, 1934), 18.

view, the philosophical equivalent to Newton's discovery of the law of gravity. By laying special stress on this analogy, Kant saw himself as being able to grant the same objective, unerring necessity to the dictates of morality that the inexorable laws of Newtonian physics were thought to possess.

But there was a decisive difference between human beings and all other creatures or objects in nature. Unlike beasts or mere organic matter, human beings do not simply exist, they partake of the noumenal realm as well. We simultaneously inhabit, that is, the world of sense and the world of reason, which also means that we are often torn by their powerful, irreconcilable demands. Yet the cause of this conflict also delivered the solution for Kant. "Only a rational being has the capacity of acting according to the conception of laws, i.e. according to principles. This capacity is will" (*WMP*, 72). Out of this necessity thus comes virtue: the will constitutes our ability to choose what our reason recognizes as the right way to act. But, Kant realized, because our will is not always in complete accord with reason—since we are not perfect beings—we need some command that urges us to do what our reason demands. This was Kant's justification for the categorical imperative: "Imperatives are only formulas expressing the relation of objective laws of volition in general to the subjective imperfection of the will of this or that rational being, e.g. the human will" (73). The will thus mediates between the two realms of sensuous experience and rational thought; the will both *necessitates* (because of its association with human weakness), but also *enables* (because of its intrinsic relation to reason), our resolve to act according to laws that we prescribe to ourselves. Thanks to the possession of a free will, in other words, we are able to make up in conscious resolution what we lack in natural inclination.

And thanks to that qualification we have been alerted to one of the major weaknesses of Kant's ethical philosophy. Certainly, because we have a free will, we are *able to* choose what is right over what is wrong; but *why should we?* That we are rational creatures means that we *can* and, moreover, *ought* to abide by the moral law, but it does not mean that we shall. Kant recognized that we would not obey the moral law, self-imposed though it may be, unless we had some interest in doing so, and we call "the foundation in us of this interest . . . the moral feeling" (114). This seems to be a startling concession or retreat: here, at the very end of his book, Kant reintroduces the notion that he had tried to exorcise from his theory at the beginning. "In order to will that which reason alone prescribes to the sensuously affected rational being as that which he ought to will," he goes on to explain, "certainly there is required a power of reason to instill a feeling of pleasure or satisfaction in the fulfillment of duty" (114). Kant was absolutely certain that reason had to be the source and sole origin of the ideas of morality, and that freedom of will was the necessary condition for our ability to act in recognition of those ideas. But he was equally convinced, or perhaps he was resigned to admit, that "an explanation of how and why the universality of the maxim as law (and hence morality) interests us is completely impossible for us" (114).[6]

There is no reason to doubt that Kant had the idea of moral beauty in mind, however faintly, when he wrote this final paragraph. As strenuously as he had attempted to eliminate its role in the determination of moral conduct, the concept thus appears, almost in spite of those very endeavors, to have gained access to his theory at the critical juncture at which it became necessary to account for the reasons why we ought to be—as opposed to how we could be—virtuous.[7] (To explain the incentive to morality, Kant introduced the famous, and for many extremely arbitrary, attempt to ground motivation on a "feeling of respect" [Achtung] for the moral law, while at the same time insisting that this "feeling" was not really a feeling at all, but rather a consciousness of the moral law, thus trying to underscore the purely cognitive nature of this nonemotional, "non-feeling" of respect.)[8] The reemergence of the terminology of moral beauty at this point in Kant's mature ethical philosophy would seem in fact rather arbitrary to anyone unaware of the prominence of moral beauty in late eighteenth-century ethical philosophy. The formal coherence of his argument as it stands is not in fact seriously threatened by its presence, at least on the level on which Kant was actually working. As long as he always insisted that the grounds on which we do what is right are derived from the realm of reason alone and are thus in accord with a single objective standard, then it is irrelevant if, at the same time, we should also *incidentally* or *independently* have an interest, or pleasure, in performing our duty. But Kant also seemed to be stating that morally good conduct would not *fail* to interest us, and therefore by implication give us pleasure (however abstract), so that in purely practical terms it would actually be impossible to distinguish these two moments. Moreover, in the perfectly virtuous being, the rational recognition of and obedience to the moral law would finally (or so one hoped) merge with our subjective interest and desire to act according to it; ideally, duty in the end would coincide with inclination. Many years before Kant, Mendelssohn had also identified this union as the expression of accomplished virtue, the achievement of which he compared, interestingly enough, with artistic practice:

6. See also the largely sympathetic comments by Roger J. Sullivan, *Immanuel Kant's Moral Theory* (Cambridge: Cambridge University Press, 1989), 26–27 and 131–33.
7. There is a similar argument offered by Roman Gleissner, *Die Entstehung der ästhetischen Humanitätsidee in Deutschland* (Stuttgart: J. B. Metzler, 1988), 192–93. See also the comments on the conflict between reason and desire in Robert Paul Wolff, *The Autonomy of Reason: A Commentary on Kant's "Groundwork of the Metaphysic of Morals"* (New York: Harper & Row, 1973), esp. 117–38.
8. See the remarks by Lewis White Beck, *A Commentary on Kant's Critique of Practical Reason* (Chicago: University of Chicago Press, 1960), 221–23. It is evidence of his own difficulty in explaining this aspect of Kant's thought that Beck asserts about a related statement of Kant's that "he did not believe this even when he wrote this sentence" (222).

To be sure, virtue is a science and can be learned, but when it should be exercised, it demands not only scientific conviction, but also artful [*kunst-mässige*] practice and acquired skill. Indeed, whoever strives for the highest level of moral perfection, whoever strives for happiness by bringing the lower faculties of his soul into perfect harmony with the upper ones, has to proceed with the laws of nature in the same way an artist does with the rules of his art. He must continue to practice until he is no longer conscious of his rules through the constant exercise of them. He must persevere until his principles have turned into inclinations and his virtue seems to be more instinctive than rational.[9]

Although Kant probably would have agreed in principle with Mendelssohn's assessment, he was determined to establish the basis on which each of these elements rested before advancing to their fulfillment or realization in practice. He did not want to confuse the issue further, which was difficult enough to comprehend by itself, by discussing these two intrinsically related, but logically separate, matters in the same context—namely, the reason why we should choose to do what we knew to be good, and the subjective result in acting in conformity with that knowledge (namely, pleasure and the interest we take in such pleasure), which Kant thought must follow on such an action. Indeed, Kant appears to have capitulated before this task, and he quickly closed his study at this point by claiming that he had already reached "the supreme limit of all moral inquiry" (*WMP*, 116).

Yet the problem concerning the relation between beauty and goodness obviously continued to pursue Kant, for he again explicitly returned to it in the third, and last, of his great works of philosophy, the *Critique of Judgement* of 1790. Although the first half of the book is principally devoted to an examination of aesthetic judgment as a strictly independent cognitive activity, on several separate occasions in it he deals with the relationship between aesthetics and morality. Kant's theory of aesthetic judgment is notoriously difficult, and we will not need to rehearse its many complications here. But it is necessary to recall some of its primary characteristics in order to understand the basis on which Kant came to posit his view of the similarities between our appreciation of beauty and moral goodness.

Kant essentially defined the aesthetic judgment of beauty as the awareness of a particular sort of intellectual pleasure that he thought we necessarily experienced when we perceive certain objects. Such pleasure was caused, simply put, by what he called the harmonious "free play" of the mental faculties, without any interference by specific concepts, which meant that this pleasure was supposed to result from an entirely reflective or cognitive

9. Moses Mendelssohn, "Rhapsodie oder Zusätze zu den Briefen über die Empfindungen," in *Schriften zur Philosophie, Aesthetik und Apologetik*, ed. Moritz Brasch (Leipzig, 1880; reprint, Hildesheim: Georg Olms, 1968), 2:138.

operation that depended on the structure of the human mind itself and not on the necessarily contingent nature of the object being so perceived. In this way, Kant was able to argue that since aesthetic pleasure arose not from individual concepts (which can and usually do vary from person to person), but from the universally identical manner in which the mind functioned, aesthetic judgment was necessarily universal in nature and could potentially be shared by and communicated to anyone else. Kant also stipulated that for there to be a pure aesthetic judgment, there could not be any interest attached to the object deemed to be beautiful, for such an interest would imply that some specific concept was associated with that object, which would in turn restrict the free play of the faculties of the imagination and the understanding. It was on the basis of this argument, then, that Kant made the following comparison:

> We have a faculty of judgement which is merely aesthetic—a faculty of judging forms without the aid of concepts, and of finding, in the mere estimate of them, a delight that we at the same time make into a rule for every one, without this judgement being founded on an interest, or yet producing one.—On the other hand we have also a faculty of intellectual judgement for the mere forms of practical maxims (so far as they are of themselves qualified for universal legislation)—a faculty of determining an *a priori* delight, which we make into a law for every one, without our judgement being founded on any interest, *though here it produces one.* The pleasure or displeasure in the former judgment is called that of taste; the latter is called that of moral feeling.[10]

The points of intersection between the two cognitive operations are clearly apparent. But at this stage Kant was merely prepared to allow a formal analogy between aesthetic judgment and practical reason, or between taste and moral feeling. He did not say, that is, that beauty and virtue were in some obscure way dependent on, much less identical with, each other. In fact, there seemed to be every reason for him to reject that premise entirely: an awareness on the part of the perceiving subject of either the presence or lack of moral worthiness in an object of beauty would seem necessarily to elicit an active interest on the part of the percipient (it was after all Kant's great favorite, Hume, who had also said that "morality is a subject that interests us above all others").[11] And such an interest, as we have just witnessed, would appear to be antithetical to his definition of aesthetic judgment. Yet in a startling departure, in this same paragraph of the *Critique of*

10. Immanuel Kant, *The Critique of Judgement*, trans. James Creed Meredith (Oxford: Oxford University Press, 1952), §42. Henceforth cited parenthetically in the text as "*CJ*" by section.
11. David Hume, *A Treatise of Human Nature*, ed. L. A. Selby-Bigge, 2d ed., ed. P. H. Nidditch (Oxford: Oxford University Press, 1978), 455.

Judgement Kant made a further distinction between two types of interest we take in objects of beauty that, *expressis verbis*, was both prompted and necessitated by the concept of the beautiful soul.

Kant began by stating that some people "regarded it as a mark of a good moral character to take an interest in the beautiful generally." But, he added, others had found just the opposite to be true, and that these "*virtuosi* in matters of taste" were "not just often, but one might say as a general rule, vain, capricious, and addicted to injurious passions." To an impartial observer, it might appear, then, that "the feeling for the beautiful is specifically different from the moral feeling" (*CJ*, § 42). Kant wanted to demonstrate, however, that precisely the contrary held true, and that the crucial difference resided in the *kind* of beauty to which one was referring. In making this distinction, Kant felt that an interest in beauty as we find it in works of art signifies the latter, negative disposition, whereas an undiluted interest in the beauty of nature constituted for Kant a genuine mark of moral distinction. Such an interest coincides, he thought, "with the refined and well-grounded habits of thought of all people who have cultivated their moral feeling." To illustrate better what he meant, Kant gave the example of someone who forsook the frivolities of art in favor of the profundities of nature:

> If a man with taste enough to judge of works of fine art with the greatest correctness and refinement readily quits the room in which he meets with those beauties that minister to vanity or, at least, social joys, and betakes himself to the beautiful in nature, so that he may there find as it were a feast for his soul in a train of thought that he can never fully analyze, we will then view this his choice even with veneration and presuppose in him a beautiful soul [*eine schöne Seele*]. (§ 42)

To scorn art for the sake of nature was a sign, therefore, of moral beauty, indeed it bespoke a beautiful soul.

This is, as far as I can ascertain, the one and only time Kant ever used this phrase in his published writing, and its occurrence in the work of such a careful thinker should caution us against taking it too lightly. For it will emerge that the beautiful soul stood as the pivot on which his attempt turned to demonstrate how it was possible to take an interest in objects of beauty and yet still allow for a properly termed, or "pure," aesthetic judgment to take place.

Kant went on to explain how this apparent contradiction in our reaction to beauty in art and in nature was supposed to dissolve:

> Now, reason is further interested in ideas (for which in our moral feeling it brings about an immediate interest) having also objective reality. That is to

say, it is of interest to reason that nature should at least show a trace or give a hint that it contains in itself a ground for assuming a lawlike harmony of its products with our wholly disinterested delight (which we acknowledge *a priori* as a law for every one, without being able to ground it upon proofs). That being so, reason must take an interest in every manifestation on the part of nature of some such harmony. Hence the mind cannot reflect on the beauty of *nature* without at the same time finding its interest engaged. But this interest is akin to the moral. One, then, who takes such an interest in the beautiful in nature can only do so in so far as he has previously grounded his interest in the morally good. (§ 42)

This is a tenuous argument, and Kant knew it was shaky. He confessed that he imagined his readers would think that "this interpretation of aesthetic judgments in relation to moral feeling seems to be all too pedantic [*studiert*]," and he thus sought to defend it by anticipating this objection. But the success of his defensive maneuver is, to say the least, debatable. What Kant appeared to be claiming was that unlike art, which was often the product of contingent desires and interests (such as making money, achieving fame, and so on), the beauty of nature resulted from the agreement of natural objects with universal laws, which as Kant believed in faithful Newtonian fashion, uniformly governed everything in the universe, including, not incidentally, the criteria of beauty and moral goodness. Thus, Kant reasoned, when we perceive beauty in nature we are inevitably put in mind of the laws that guide moral behavior (provided, naturally, that we take cognizance of them) and we therefore take an interest in that beauty just as we are said to take an interest in morality. Here again, then, Kant had based his argument on the construction of an abstract analogy between our response to both beauty and goodness. We wish to see the real, physical analogue of what we otherwise can know only as abstract ideas. This desire, of course, had always provided the main justification for the beautiful soul itself, which in essence was supposed to serve as the sensate manifestation of the speculative idea of "moral beauty." But as one commentator has written about this section of Kant's *Critique of Judgement*, his conclusion is "indicative of some confusion. . . . An interest in the reality of an idea is not intrinsically moral, but is moral only if the idea is itself moral."[12] Kant had merely claimed that an

---

12. Paul Guyer, *Kant and the Claims of Taste* (Cambridge: Harvard University Press, 1979), 370. Guyer concludes that "Kant's argument thus involves at least one questionable premise, and does not appear to be sound." Similarly, on the following page, Guyer asks: "What about the demand for an intellectual interest in the beautiful itself? . . . Here too there are problems." Donald W. Crawford, *Kant's Aesthetic Theory* (Madison: University of Wisconsin Press, 1974), 148, also writes that "Kant's reasoning is somewhat obscure," and concludes: "It does not follow that an immediate interest in the beauties of nature implies a moral interest or the possession of moral feeling."

interest in the beauty of nature was "akin" to the interest we took in morality, but he had neglected to prove why this might have been so. Thus one of the logical pillars upholding the analogy Kant wanted to draw simply could not carry the weight he intended for it to bear.

Similarly, in the penultimate paragraph to the first half of the *Critique of Judgement*, Kant continued this earlier line of reasoning regarding the demonstration of the "reality" of ideas through analogy. Here he made the unprecedented and for many observers highly problematic claim that "the beautiful is the symbol of the morally good" (*CJ*, § 59).[13] By stating that beauty was *the* (and we should note that Kant specifically used the definite article and not the indefinite) symbol of morality, and by stipulating that a symbol was an indirect, or analogous, representation of something for which there is no physical correspondent—such as, for example, the cognitive operations involved in making aesthetic judgments or in activating practical reason—Kant sought to reestablish the link between these two spheres of beauty and morality that he had tried to forge earlier in the book. In Kant's view, as Paul Guyer puts it, one "thing may serve as the symbol of another only because the structure of reflection is similar in the two cases" (376). Indeed, Kant wanted to enlarge on the real significance of the exercise of aesthetic judgment, or taste, to an even greater degree: "Taste makes, as it were, the transition from the charm of sense to habitual moral interest possible without too violent a leap, for it represents the imagination, even in its freedom, as amenable to a purposeful determination for the understanding, and teaches us to find, even in sensuous objects, a free delight apart from any charm of sense" (*CJ*, § 59). But if as appears to be the case, the analogy itself on which this comparison was based in the first place is fatally flawed, then Kant's entire argument about the symbolic import of beauty is seriously compromised.[14]

The existence of these and other logical snarls, and Kant's evident cognizance of their existence, raises at least one question immediately: Why should Kant have deliberately endangered the theoretical coherence and integrity of a significant part of his critical enterprise by introducing an argument for which there was no apparent internal necessity and which

13. Also see Guyer, *Kant and the Claims of Taste*, 376.
14. The literature on this problem has grown in recent years. Salim Kemal, *Kant and Fine Art: An Essay on Kant and the Philosophy of Fine Art* (Oxford: Oxford University Press, 1986), and Kenneth F. Rogerson, *Kant's Aesthetics. The Roles of Form and Expression* (Lanham, Md.: University Press of America, 1986), argue for the necessary connection between morality and aesthetics in Kant's philosophy, and in his most recent book, Paul Guyer also changes his mind completely and now asserts that "the real heart of Kant's aesthetic theory and the underlying motivation for its creation is the connection to his moral theory." See Paul Guyer, *Kant and the Experience of Freedom: Essays on Aesthetics and Morality* (Cambridge: Cambridge University Press, 1993), 3. But it is one thing simply to make the assertion (as Kant does), and quite another to demonstrate its validity and consequences.

seemed, moreover, to present exactly that type of threat? Why, in other words, did he feel that he had to claim at all that beauty symbolized morality? It should be obvious by now that the only conceivable answer, but also the most convincing one, has to do with the pervasive, yet unfounded, belief at the time in the possibility and, more compelling, the desirability of moral beauty. Kant had tried to resist the idea of moral beauty and its attendant implications for much of his later philosophical life, but it so dominated contemporary ethical thinking that he could not, apparently, eliminate it entirely from his own. Although unacknowledged as such, the beautiful soul thus stood as the covert goal of Kant's aesthetic and hence his moral philosophy. Stoically resistant to the beautiful soul for so long, Kant appeared to heed its beckoning call in the end as well.

One reason for Kant's manifest inability—or unwillingness—to rid his moral theory of every vestige of the beautiful soul no doubt had to do with the very nature of the assumptions with which he unavoidably had to work as arguably the most representative philosopher of the Enlightenment. Standing at the culmination of a hundred-year development, Kant inherited, even as he transformed, the enormous framework of ideas that informed eighteenth-century epistemology and ethical thought. One way of describing his critical labors would be to compare his accomplishment with that of an architect who has assumed the task of constructing a small but durable edifice using the stones of an earlier building, which had been built on a precarious foundation. He explicitly stated, in the preface to the *Critique of Pure Reason* and elsewhere, that he would not and could not broaden the boundaries of philosophical investigation, and he instead announced his more modest ambition of putting what we already knew into some semblance of comprehensible and reliable order. Within the ethical superstructure of the eighteenth-century imagination, the idea of the beautiful soul was a foundation pier and could not be removed or replaced without risking the stability of the entire construction.

Yet the concept of moral beauty was not just a central aspect of Enlightened moral philosophy; it had helped to produce a large part of the discourse that constituted that very tradition. It was therefore virtually impossible to escape it, for simply by using the terms of contemporary moral philosophy, one could not refrain from simultaneously, even if unconsciously, employing the patterns of thought in which the idea of moral beauty was inextricably bound up. To transcend the strictures imposed by the beautiful soul would have meant to transcend Enlightenment philosophy itself, and that was something Kant was not ready, and probably not even able, to do. In order to overcome the ideology of moral beauty, a crisis of some sort had to occur. For just as the modern idea of moral beauty had arisen to fill the void left by the loss of faith in the theological ground of morality, so too would a new, yet similarly motivated, shift have to take place to cause the beautiful soul to vanish. Paradoxically, this reorientation which led to its disappearance was precipitated precisely by Kant's fulfillment of the inherent possibilities of eighteenth-century moral philosophy at large. But it was not for another decade or so that the consequences, and the potential resolutions, of this change were finally and fully realized.

SCHILLER'S "SCHÖNE SEELE"

If Kant struggled heroically, though ultimately in vain, to withstand the allure of moral beauty, then Friedrich Schiller willingly abandoned himself entirely to its charms. In his philosophical essays, poetry, and dramas, the beautiful soul found an attentive and devoted admirer who sacrificed his every energy to providing it with a richly appointed and comfortable abode. But the importance of moral beauty to Schiller's thought exceeded mere infatuation with an attractive ideal: during his most intensive involvement with the problems of aesthetic philosophy between the years 1788 and 1794, the beautiful soul became nothing less than the focal point of his theoretical endeavors. It is perhaps surprising to realize that although the beautiful soul had been, by the 1790s, part of the collective consciousness among educated Europeans for almost fifty years, it had never yet been made the object of an extended and independent philosophical investigation. In placing it so prominently at the center of his concerns, Schiller thus became the first to thematize the beautiful soul so explicitly and at such obsessive length. But his labors were rewarded by extremely equivocal results.

In many interpretations of Schiller's aesthetics there has been the tendency to concentrate almost exclusively on his relation to Kantian thought. Too often an examination of Schiller's ideas is thus confined to a comparative study of the respective arguments made by these two thinkers on any number of particular issues. This procedure usually results in the finding that Schiller had either "misunderstood" Kant or, conversely, that as a poet Schiller had been able to develop Kant's insights beyond the narrow horizons imposed by his mentor's academic focus.[15] But a more fruitful, as well as sounder, approach would be to see both Schiller and Kant as responding to the same complex field of historical forces, albeit in their own necessarily

15. For a critique of this tradition of exegesis, see the pugnacious first chapter in J. M. Ellis, *Schiller's "Kalliasbriefe" and the Study of His Aesthetic Theory* (The Hague: Mouton, 1969), esp. 15–16 and 32–33. R. D. Miller, *Schiller and the Ideal of Freedom. A Study of Schiller's Philosophical Works with Chapters on Kant* (Oxford: Oxford University Press, 1970), although praised in the foreword by Isaiah Berlin as "the clearest, most accurate, and intelligent account of the intellectual relationship between Kant and Schiller," is also a representative of the tradition with which Ellis finds fault.

idiosyncratic ways. This is not to deny that a clear and constant connection exists between Kant and Schiller. On every page of his aesthetic writings it is plain that Schiller read Kant carefully and admired what he read enormously. He used Kant's critical philosophy both as the starting point and as the conceptual frame of reference for many of his own arguments. Yet acknowledging this does not require us to weigh the works of Schiller and Kant against one another to the virtual exclusion of the greater cultural context in which both of them thought and wrote. The need for a more generous approach becomes especially acute if one wishes to evaluate the place of Schiller's treatment of the beautiful soul within the historical matrix that originally brought it forth.

One of the elements contributing to that broader design, and one that Kant and Schiller shared, came from what is by now a familiar quarter. Schiller was born and raised in the town of Marbach just north of Stuttgart in the Swabian state of Württemberg, which, it so happens, had provided an early and enthusiastic home to Pietism. Johann Arndt, the "father" of Pietism, enjoyed from the beginning a receptive readership in Württemberg, so much so that some members of the Swabian Lutheran orthodoxy tried, though with little success, to combat his influence as early as the 1620s. In 1662, even before he had begun to convene his *collegia pietatis* in Frankfurt, Spener was invited to stay for five months in Tübingen at the house of a law professor teaching at the university there, thus initiating what later became the more or less official theological orientation of that institution. Indeed, the famous foundation of the *Tübinger Stift*, which furnished so many later representatives of German idealist philosophy with their formal theological training (including, most notably, Hegel, Schelling, and Hölderlin), self-consciously promulgated Pietistic practices throughout the entire eighteenth century. And one of the most accomplished and respected theologians of the time, Johann Albrecht Bengel, who lived from 1687 to 1752 and has been called "the very soul of Swabian Pietism," exerted a profound effect on the religious and cultural life of Württemberg—and not only of Württemberg—for the rest of the century and into the next.[16] Schiller thus grew up in an atmosphere in which the habits of spiritual transformation and rebirth, precipitated by painful contrition and leading toward a purification of one's inner constitution, remained a central article of religious and moral behavior. The ethical impetus of Pietism, and most particularly its emphasis on achieving beauty of soul in the eyes of God, could not have failed to have had a formative influence on Schiller's youthful imagination.[17]

16. F. Ernest Stoeffler, *German Pietism during the Eighteenth Century*, Studies in the History of Religions, vol. 24 (Leiden: E. J. Brill, 1973), 90–94.
17. For a discussion of the importance of Bengel and more generally of Pietism in Schiller's early education, see Benno von Wiese, *Friedrich Schiller* (Stuttgart: J. B. Metzler, 1959), 57–

It is equally certain, however, that Pietism was not the only cultural force responsible for putting Schiller in mind of moral beauty. Like almost all of his compatriots, Schiller eventually fell under—or to put it more accurately, he compliantly prostrated himself before—the tyranny of Greece over the German imagination. As his elegiac poem "Die Götter Griechenlands" revealed, Schiller became unshakably convinced that the ancient Greeks enjoyed an unsurpassable superiority and he granted the Hellenic ideal of *kalokagathia* a predominant position in his private scale of moral and artistic values.[18] Although his participation in the cult of Greece did not really begin in earnest until the late 1780s (and even then was more emotional than truly antiquarian), one finds a somewhat immature but evocative instance of his later creed in a short essay of 1785 titled "Brief eines reisenden Dänen (Der Antikensaal zu Mannheim)" (Letter of a traveling Dane [The hall of antiquities at Mannheim]).[19] Most of the essay is derivative, mainly owing its rhetorical pathos, as well as its concrete examples of ancient art, to Winckelmann, and it thus need not detain us very long.[20] But at the end of the work, Schiller intones a paean to the Belvedere Torso in words that already render the faint, but discernible, outlines of his later preoccupations. Addressing his fictional correspondent, he exclaims: "Friend! This Torso tells me that two millennia ago there lived a great man who could create such a thing—that there lived a people that could give ideals to an artist who could produce such a work—that this people believed in truth and beauty because someone in their midst felt truth and beauty—that this people was noble because virtue and beauty are only sisters of the same mother."[21] After thus affirming the kinship of beauty and goodness that so many other Enlightenment thinkers had also borrowed from the Greeks and applied to their own immediate ends, Schiller concluded with a telling passage. Allowing the fictive mask of the Danish traveler to drop a bit, Schiller revealed an absorbing ambition that he, the celebrated though still young dramatist, must have felt as well: "To have created something that will not disappear, to live on when everything all around is being consumed— Oh, Friend, I cannot impose myself on the world to come through obelisks,

---

69. See also Lesley Sharpe, *Friedrich Schiller: Drama, Thought and Politics* (Cambridge: Cambridge University Press, 1991), 12–13, who also detects what she calls the "legacy of Pietism" in the ethical stance of Schiller's early plays.

18. Käte Hamburger, "Schillers Fragment 'Der Menschenfeind' und die Idee der Kalokagathie," in *Philosophie der Dichter: Novalis, Schiller, Rilke* (Stuttgart: W. Kohlhammer, 1966), 114, amusingly refers to Schiller as the "dogmatician of the kalokagathia idea."

19. On Schiller's relationship to antiquity, see Gerhard Storz, "Schiller und die Antike," *Jahrbuch der deutschen Schillergesellschaft* 10 (1966): 189–204.

20. See Henry Hatfield, *Aesthetic Paganism in German Literature: From Winckelmann to the Death of Goethe* (Cambridge: Harvard University Press, 1964), 120–21.

21. Friedrich Schiller, "Brief eines reisenden Dänen (Der Antikensaal zu Mannheim)," in *Sämtliche Werke*, 5:883–84.

conquered lands, discovered continents—I cannot make it remember me through a masterpiece—I cannot create a head for this Torso, but perhaps I can do a beautiful deed without any witnesses!" (5:884). To perform a virtuous action unobserved by anyone else constituted the essence of the Enlightenment goal of achieving an autonomous morality; it represented moral behavior that would bind for its own sake, irrespective of any potential reward or punishment. That Schiller should have placed the enactment of such a "beautiful deed" on an equivalent level with some of the greatest human achievements also signaled a precocious commitment to moral issues that although not unusual as such in the eighteenth century, nevertheless remained forever after a defining characteristic of his mature thought.

But Schiller did not sequester his mind either in religious reveries or in nostalgic longing for a distant and irretrievable past. His almost casual use of the phraseology of moral beauty should at least alert us that he was also very much a participant in, or at any rate keenly aware of, the intellectual debates taking place in his own time. He was certainly sensitive to the overriding importance of one's methodological orientation, and he once wrote in a letter to Goethe that "I can attest that in my speculations I have been as true to nature as is compatible with the concept of analysis; indeed, perhaps more loyal than our Kantians think permissible or even possible."[22] And concerning the development of aesthetic and ethical philosophy in particular he showed an impressive familiarity with most of the major works produced in Germany and abroad.[23] In 1788, for instance, he mentioned in a letter from the end of November to Caroline von Beulwitz that he planned to read Shaftesbury during the following summer and less than four years later he reported to Gottfried Körner his intention to tackle, among others, the works of Baumgarten and Sulzer.[24] In addition, he knew Henry Home's *Elements of Criticism*, Burke's *Inquiry*, most of Mendelssohn's published writings, and of course the critical philosophy of Kant. Schiller was also befriended and worked closely with Wieland during this period, and the older, pleasantly avuncular poet (who was, we recall, a fellow Swabian) had a demonstrable, though often underappreciated, influence on Schiller's thinking.[25] And it was during these years, in which there was a marked

22. Letter of 7 January 1795, Friedrich Schiller, *Briefe*, ed. Fritz Jonas (Stuttgart: Deutsche Verlags-Anstalt, 1892–96), 4:96. Henceforth cited in text and notes as "*Briefe*" by volume and page number.
23. See Heinz Otto Burger, "Europäisches Adelsideal und deutsche Klassik," in *Begriffsbestimmung der Klassik und des Klassischen*, ed. Heinz Otto Burger (Darmstadt: Wissenschaftliche Buchgesellschaft, 1972), 177–202.
24. See the letters from 27 November 1788 and 25 May 1792, in Schiller, *Briefe*, 2:163 and 3:201. See also Ernst Cassirer, "Schiller and Shaftesbury," *Publications of the English Goethe Society* 11 (1935): 37–59.
25. See the study of this relationship by Walter Hinderer, "Beiträge Wielands zu Schillers ästhetischer Erziehung," *Jahrbuch der deutschen Schillergesellschaft* 18 (1974): 348–87.

hiatus between his poetic production and his philosophical studies, that Schiller turned with increasing determination to one of the primary problems he saw confronting himself and his age, namely, "the difficulty of objectively advancing a concept of beauty."[26] His first extended attempt to do just that, which Schiller delivered in a series of letters, now referred to as the *Kalliasbriefe*, addressed to his friend and future patron Christian Gottfried Körner in preparation for a work that never materialized, led directly —and inescapably—into the same set of aporias that had threatened the consistency of Kant's moral and aesthetic thought as well.

It is of immediate and decisive consequence for an appreciation of these letters to understand that the word *kallias*, or "beauty," has nothing to do in the first place with art—understood in the modern, more restrictive sense of "fine art"—as some commentators seem to have imagined. Rather, in keeping with the tradition of thought against which he formulated his own ideas, Schiller conceived of beauty in the broadest possible manner, and even of "art" in the sense of some deliberate human agency as opposed to blind natural force. In his first letter to Körner on the subject, dated 25 January 1793, Schiller established the parameters that would circumscribe his investigation and categorically announced that he, for one, was "convinced that beauty is only the form of a form, and that that which one calls its material simply has to be a formed material. Perfection is the form of a material, whereas beauty is the form of this perfection" ("Kallias," 5:395).

Reminiscent of Shaftesbury's Neoplatonic distinction between the rational activity of a mind imposing a form or shape on a substance and the phenomenon that resulted from such an effort, Schiller's attempt to formulate a definition of beauty remained, at this stage, highly abstract. But besides confirming a Platonizing predilection on Schiller's part, this passage already indicates his fateful reliance on either received opinion or personal conviction to advance his own philosophical views.[27] We notice that he does not actually demonstrate, or even argue for, his belief that beauty is a "form of a form," but merely states it as established fact. And this pattern of assertion in place of argument will prove, as we will shortly see, a serious obstacle to the success of his theory—and, more generally, to the continued existence of the beautiful soul itself.

If we set aside for the moment the admittedly critical question of its validity, we can trace at least the internal progression of his reasoning as it

26. Friedrich Schiller, "Kallias oder über die Schönheit," in *Sämtliche Werke*, 5:394. Henceforth cited parenthetically in the text as "'Kallias'" by volume and page number from *Sämtliche Werke*.

27. I thus take issue with the uncritical statement about this particular passage made by S. S. Kerry, *Schiller's Writings on Aesthetics* (Manchester: Manchester University Press, 1961), 33, namely that "Schiller announces a doctrine of great originality and subtlety." This assertion, like the theory to which it refers, is never convincingly argued.

was continued in the next letter to Körner, dated 8 February 1793, for it was in this letter that he made a series of claims on which he tried to base many of his later ideas. Although the first letter contains no indication that he intended to address moral issues per se, it quickly became apparent to him that his approach demanded a consideration not only of "theoretical reason," but also of "practical reason." Building on his earlier remarks, and speaking now in recognizably Kantian accents, Schiller explained that the "*form* of practical reason is an immediate connection of the will with representations of reason, and thus the *exclusion of every external* ground of determination; for a will that is not determined by the mere form of practical reason is determined from without, with respect to material or heteronomous factors" ("Kallias," 5:398). Schiller thought that we ascribe freedom to human beings who thus demonstrate such "pure self-determination," but since freedom is something that can not be presented to the senses as such, what we see is merely the appearance, or manifestation, of freedom through the activity of the will. It is obvious that Schiller was operating here with argumentative mechanisms he had inherited from Kant about our need to observe tangible analogues to abstract ideas. For, Schiller continued, when actions, or the perceptible expressions of the instantiation of a will, are in fact manifestations of an absolutely free exercise of the will, these actions assume a particular perceptible characteristic. As he concluded, the "conformity of an action with the form of pure will is *morality*. The analogy of an appearance with the form of pure will, or of freedom, is *beauty* (in its widest significance)." Then, in his most memorable yet enigmatic line, Schiller proclaimed: "Beauty is therefore nothing other than freedom in appearance" (5:400).

Schiller leaves many questions unanswered here. If, as he seems to imply, beauty is indeed the sensuous manifestation of freedom, which otherwise has no corresponding physical expression, then one would first of all wish to know what the sensible attributes of beauty itself are. Schiller remained stubbornly silent on this vital topic, and at most he addressed it only negatively. "Purpose, order, proportion, perfection," he wrote in a later missive to Körner, "those qualities in which one had so long thought to have found beauty, have nothing whatsoever to do with it" (5:419). Yet he never revealed what perceptible qualities *do* have something to do with beauty, and without some indication of what they are, the rest of his argument necessarily rests on extremely unsteady ground.

Although it may never be possible to decide finally what the statement that "beauty is freedom in appearance" might mean, it is evident that Schiller, like Kant in effect though not in purpose, was seeking to link the ethical and aesthetic spheres in a union of mutual dependency. Schiller stated this aim even more emphatically in the next letter, dated 18 February. His friend

Körner had queried him on some points in his original formulations, and most of this letter consists of Schiller's efforts to elucidate in greater detail what he had previously put forward *in nuce*. Almost in a tone of defensive justification, he tried to persuade his skeptical correspondent that, "nevertheless, the concept of beauty is also applied in the figurative sense to morality, and this application is anything but empty. Although beauty adheres only to appearance, so too *moral beauty* is still a concept to which something corresponds in experience" (5:404). The logic of the second sentence is palpably tortured, but the passage is useful as a summary of Schiller's entire thesis—and of his quandary. If as Schiller himself had just maintained, beauty could only be experienced as something that was available to the senses, or that it "adhered only to appearance," then it was strictly speaking impossible for there to be anything like a "moral beauty," which— one has to assume—cannot have any corresponding sensuous characteristics.[28] The final clause of Schiller's statement expresses a desire rather than an actual state of being, and in it he attempts to perform by brute linguistic force what he could not, or in any case simply did not, accomplish by rational demonstration. Schiller seems to have sensed the danger to his enterprise, and hard on this scrambled account he told Körner that to make his meaning clearer, he would tell him a story.

The story itself—about a man who is robbed, wounded, stripped of his clothes, and left exposed to the elements to die until a secular Samaritan finally comes along to help him without pausing to consider whether his action would benefit himself or not, which Schiller then described as a "beautiful" deed in a technical sense—is relatively insignificant. What is absolutely crucial, however, is his telling of it. For by telling a story ostensibly to explain more effectively than he can in theoretical terms what he means by "beautiful action," Schiller had not only demonstrated his favored method of treating abstract thought, he had also, albeit unconsciously, repeated the gesture made by earlier advocates of moral beauty whenever they were confronted with the task of producing a beautiful soul. Since few were fortunate enough to have a Kleinjogg in their midst whom they could dumbly proffer, they instead told a story—say, in the form of a novel—and preferably an allegorical one. This issue requires closer attention, which we shall give it momentarily. Suffice it to say at this point that Schiller laid extraordinary stress on this simple tale, for after telling it he came to what is perhaps the most important conclusion of all of the *Kalliasbriefe*: "Thus a moral action would only then be a beautiful action when it looks as if nature were

28. This argument mirrors part of the critique presented by Hamburger, "Schillers Fragment 'Der Menschenfeind' und die Idee der Kalokagathie," esp. 92 and 103–4. For an intelligent response to this criticism, see Eva Schaper, "Friedrich Schiller: Adventures of a Kantian," *British Journal of Aesthetics* 4 (1964): 360–61.

working according to its own laws. In a word: a free action is a beautiful action when the autonomy of the mind and autonomy in appearance coincide." Once again leaving aside the matter of its internal coherence (which we already know to be in serious jeopardy), this statement then allowed Schiller to express the governing, although previously unarticulated, idea of the whole treatise. "For this reason," he concluded, "the maximum of perfection in the character of a human being is moral beauty, for it only then occurs *when duty has become a part of that person's nature*" ("Kallias," 5:407). The moment when the rational moral law, or "duty," merges with our subjective proclivities, or our "nature," is the instant in which we attain human perfection—or in other words, when we achieve moral beauty.

Here Schiller was trying to combine the modern terminological apparatus of Kantian philosophy with the older, inherited discourse of the beautiful soul, which Kant himself had tried to avoid, but toward which his thought eventually, and perhaps inexorably, tended. But it was an effort that was bound to result in the same perplexities that we had encountered in Kant's philosophy. Kant, we remember, had faltered primarily in his rendering of the function of interest in motivating morally good behavior. This interest, in its "purest" form, usually took the shape of the pleasure experienced by the agent in performing a "good deed." But in Kant's account it had remained unclear to what extent the interest in such pleasure was involved in the actual motivation of action. It was true that such an interest could not provide the *principle* of morality; only reason could perform that office if the autonomy and purity of morality were to be preserved. Yet interest did seem to play a prominent, though inadequately defined, role in putting that principle into real practice. The question of interest had likewise occupied an ambivalent position in Kant's aesthetic theory. On the one hand, Kant excluded interest from pure aesthetic judgments. But on the other, he allowed it to reenter when he sought to demonstrate the analogy between our experience of beauty (or to be more specific, the beauty of nature) and morality. Schiller similarly raised the issue of pleasure, while skirting the question of interest, when he wrote in the letter to Körner dated 23 February: "I have to prove that freedom in appearance necessarily brings about an effect on our faculty of feeling that is completely identical with the one that we find is associated with the representation of beauty" ("Kallias," 5:408).[29] And that "effect," of course, was pleasure.

To someone unfamiliar with the tradition of moral beauty, from which this self-imposed demand was implicitly derived, Schiller's vision of what he "had to prove" might very well seem, as it did to J. M. Ellis, to contain "some

29. In the same paragraph, Schiller went on to specify the nature of this "feeling": he intended, he wrote, to show "that from the compounded concept of freedom and appearance, or of sensuality harmonized with reason, there has to emerge a feeling of pleasure [*Lust*] that is identical to the delight that tends to accompany the representation of beauty."

very strange features."[30] Within that field of assumptions which enabled Schiller to formulate this criterion in the first place, however, it is not at all "strange" that he felt that he had to prove that our feeling is engaged in a completely identical manner by the phenomena of moral goodness and beauty. Moral beauty possesses its effective power to govern behavior by the very virtue of its ability to arouse the feeling of pleasure (abstract and intellectualized though it may be) in those who either perceive it in others or are able to produce it in themselves. To explain how this pleasure comes about, and what part it plays in enjoining us to act in one way or another, was thus absolutely vital to the theory itself—just as its absence was thoroughly damaging.

It therefore confirmed all the more irresistibly the profound and perhaps irresolvable difficulties Schiller faced that he never provided the promised proof. Instead, he simply abandoned the topic of pleasure altogether, either forgetting he had raised it or (perhaps) hoping that everyone else would. But he did not forget the central issue. Even though, as he wrote in the first letter to Körner, his attempt to generate and stabilize "a deduction of my concept of beauty" had not proved to be easy, or even possible, he nevertheless held on to the hope of defending the beautiful soul itself ("Kallias," 5:395). The main document of this effort, which had thus naturally grown out of his correspondence with Körner, is the essay "Über Anmut und Würde" (On grace and dignity).

Written with remarkable speed, "Über Anmut und Würde" was "completed," as Schiller noted on 20 June 1793 in another letter to his friend, "in not quite six weeks" (*Briefe*, 3:317). It is also one of the most accomplished literary performances Schiller delivered during his six-year involvement with philosophy. Rhetorically polished, finely balanced, evenly modulated in tone, and carried by an almost stately self-confidence, "Über Anmut und Würde" seems to embody the very qualities it describes. There is more than a little evidence that this impression was not wholly unintended. In a letter he sent in March of the same year to a poet, now obscure, by the name of Johann Heinrich Ramberg, Schiller explained that Kant's *Critique of Judgement* had stimulated him to search for his own definition of the concept of beauty. But, he allowed, being a poet himself, he had always felt it necessary, or at any rate appropriate, to approach such philosophical problems as a poet would. And "since the philosophy of the beautiful is, as it were, the point at which philosophers, artists, and poets meet, and because beauty itself would not excuse us if we would plead its case in some foreign territory, I have therefore also attempted to give my theoretical investigations an artistic clothing [*kunstmäßige Einkleidung*]" (3:300–301).

This was not the first or the last time that Schiller proposed discussing his

30. Ellis, *Schiller's "Kalliasbriefe"*, 54.

conception of beauty in terms that were themselves "beautiful," with the express purpose of making recondite philosophical notions more accessible to the popular mind. Schiller's long, meditative poem "Die Künstler" (The artists), for example, which he wrote at the end of 1788, has frequently been seen as marking his initiation into the philosophical issues that would remain with him for the next six years.[31] After he had finished the poem, Schiller wrote to Körner that in it he had "made the veiling of truth and morality in beauty the governing idea of the whole" poem (*Briefe*, 2:225). In suggesting that philosophical ideas could, or even should, be communicated in this fashion, Schiller may have even had the words of at least one admired predecessor in mind. In his *Foundations of the Metaphysics of Morals*, Kant himself had also held out the possibility of "clothing" philosophy in more generally comprehensible language—provided, that is, that certain conditions were first observed. "This condescension to popular notions," Kant rather condescendingly wrote, "is certainly very commendable once the ascent to the principles of pure reason has been satisfactorily accomplished. That would mean the prior establishment of the doctrine of morals on metaphysics and then, when it is established, to procure a hearing for it through popularization" (*WMP*, 69).[32] It is conceivable that Schiller imagined that Kant had already fulfilled these initial provisions himself and that the poet accordingly saw himself as having been no more (or no less) than the "popularizer of Kant."[33] But the issue at stake here exceeds the relatively narrow compass outlining the relationship between Kant and Schiller and embraces the very essence of the beautiful soul—or rather, since "essence" is just what it lacks, by pressing this particular issue we may be able to lift the veil suggesting its form.

Whether it was uncanny coincidence or a sign of his brilliantly conscious control over the tradition on which he was drawing, Schiller began "Über Anmut und Würde" with what he specifically called an allegory. Moreover, it was an allegory whose elements he derived from ancient Greek mythology. "In Greek fables," Schiller proposed, "the Goddess of Beauty is adorned with

31. The phrase "schöne Seele" also occurs three times in this poem, though not with anything like the systematic significance it later acquired for Schiller. See "Die Künstler," in *Sämtliche Werke*, 1:176, 178, and 187 (lines 115, 180, and 464).
32. This distinction between a "popular" and "rigorous" style in philosophy is also the subject of the first chapter in Hume, *Enquiry concerning Human Understanding*, 5–16.
33. See Todd Curtis Kontje, *Constructing Reality: A Rhetorical Analysis of Friedrich Schiller's Letters on the Aesthetic Education of Man* (New York: Peter Lang, 1987), 26. In a letter Schiller wrote to Kant on 13 June 1794, Schiller made an even more explicit statement about his popularizing intentions: "It was merely the intensity of my desire to make the results of the ethical theory you have founded palatable to a portion of the public that even now still seems to flee from it, together with the sincere wish of reconciling a no less worthy part of humanity to the severity of your system, that could have momentarily given me the appearance of being your opponent, for which I do indeed have very little ability and even less inclination." See Schiller, *Briefe*, 3:455.

a belt that possesses the power of granting *grace* to anyone who wears it."[34] The point of the "allegory," which Schiller helpfully explicated for us, was to show that "grace"—the quality being addressed in the first half of the essay—belongs to beauty. But since grace is likened to a belt that can be removed at will and lent to others, it is not the *exclusive* or defining "prerogative" of beauty. Even though, that is, grace is most often found paired with beauty, it can sometimes be found where no physical beauty seems to exist. And the rest of this section of the essay is devoted to an elaboration of this state of affairs and thus of what grace itself "really" is. But we notice that Schiller has already given us a demonstration of his poetic-philosophical method, and it thus mirrors his procedure in the *Kalliasbriefe* of telling a story to make a philosophical point. The introductory allegorical example is designed to give his readers a concrete image they can hold on to before plunging into a more technical discussion of its implications. Not sharing the later romantic antipathy toward allegory, Schiller seemed perfectly comfortable with using the term to describe his own art as well. In the letter to Körner in which he described his philosophical poem "Die Künstler" as "veiling" the idea of morality in beauty, Schiller claimed that "it is a *single* allegory that goes through the whole, only varying in perspective; one that I show the reader from all sides" (*Briefe*, 2:225).[35]

Allegory, as we know, had always been a distinguishing hallmark of treatments of the beautiful soul: Wieland's novel was an extended use of the device, whereas Rousseau's *Julie* contained only a few, though highly charged, allegorical moments. And in each case, the reliance on this brittle compositional mode, which both authors employed in order to give tangible credibility to an abstract notion, in the end only widened the gulf between physical reality and the insubstantial realm of ideas that the allegory was meant to close. There was, to be sure, a significant difference in their respective uses of the form: whereas Wieland and Rousseau had sought to use it to animate a philosophical idea in the fictional sphere, Schiller employed this literary

---

34. Schiller, "Über Anmut und Würde," 5:433. Herman Meyer, "Schillers philosophische Rhetorik," *Euphorion* 53 (1959): 326–27, points out that Schiller was significantly indebted to Sulzer for his concept of grace, or "Anmut," and in a footnote indicates that Schiller's definition of "Anmut" has similarities to Sulzer's entry under "Reiz." This is true, but at even a deeper level than Meyer assumed. We have seen that the dominant, though never explicitly announced, figure of the *Allgemeine Theorie* was none other than the beautiful soul, and Sulzer's description of "grace" as "a certain quality of the beautiful to express itself in visible forms" fits well within the physiognomical framework of this crypto-theory. See Johann Georg Sulzer, *Allgemeine Theorie der schönen Künste*, 2d exp. ed. (Leipzig, 1792; reprint, ed. Christian Friedrich von Blankenburg et al., intro. Giorgio Tonelli, Hildesheim: Georg Olms, 1967–70), 4:88.

35. The allegorical referent of the poem may be inferred from the last strophe, where we read: "Was schöne Seelen schön empfunden, / Muß trefflich und vollkommen sein" [What beautiful souls have felt to be beautiful / Must be excellent and perfect]. See Schiller, "Die Künstler," in *Sämtliche Werke*, 1:187.

technique within a philosophical tract. But by subsequently attempting to build his argument on the ground prepared by this allegorical tale, Schiller was (even if unwittingly) not only following a discursive pattern that had been a constitutive part of the tradition informing the notion of the beautiful soul, he was also simultaneously and inevitably committing his own attempt to reconcile its complexities to a course blocked by the same predictable conceptual impasses.

Schiller obviously could not have written all of "Über Anmut und Würde" in the allegorical style, and after the first few pages he dropped the contrivance, never again to return to the opening myth. But the transition from image to argument, although somewhat abrupt, is extremely important. Here Schiller displays his habit of casually, almost invisibly, inserting the main elements of his "proof," as if to divert attention from their initial appearance, only to rely substantially on them at a later and pivotal stage. Thus while still speaking of the Greeks and their myths, Schiller writes that "they never allow sensuality to appear without a soul," which seems to be a fairly innocuous although rather compact statement that may or may not be correct (5:436). But then he adds: "For that reason, they also saw grace as nothing other than such a beautiful expression of the soul in deliberate movements. Therefore, where grace occurs is where the soul is the motivating [literally "moving," *bewegende*] principle, and *therein* is contained the ground of the beauty of motion" (5:437). By defining grace as a beauty of motion, and this motion as being the perceptible result (or expression) of an activity of the soul, Schiller sets up the prerequisites of his theory. In a manner best described as arbitrary, Schiller has tried to make it *seem* that what is actually an unsupported declaration follows naturally from his original premise.[36] Yet nothing in the introductory allegory of Venus referred either to the phenomenon of motion or to any expression of inner states of being. Only the unstudied, but actually irrelevant, allusion to ancient Greek beliefs about the soul, which seemed appropriate solely because of the cultural source of the myth, established this crucial connection.

It is worth emphasizing how skillfully Schiller strove to envelop this hazy logic in elegant, pellucid prose—that was, after all, partially his aim. Throughout the essay, he deliberately tries, as he admits, to "clothe" the bare bones of philosophy in an attractive, and thus more palatable, exterior.[37] But, in so

36. Henry Home (Lord Kames), *Elements of Criticism* (New York: Campbell, 1823), 1:286, in the chapter "Dignity and Grace" also writes, although similarly neglecting to prove his argument, that grace "is undoubtedly connected with motion; for when the most graceful person is at rest, neither moving nor speaking, we lose sight of that quality as much as of colour in the dark." Schiller acknowledged his debt to Kames's work, which first appeared in 1762.

37. Again, this was an idea much in circulation at the time. In Wilhelm von Humboldt's essay "Über Religion," in *Werke*, ed. Andreas Flitner and Klaus Giel (Darmstadt: Wissen-

doing, Schiller necessarily had to assume that the ideas he sought to drape in such beautiful verbal garments were sturdy enough to carry the load he wanted to place on them. That much of the conceptual apparatus with which he operated lacked such stability clearly did not bode well. Yet there was another related and even more subtle correspondence between Schiller's method of composition and the very phenomenon he was describing. By claiming that grace consisted in "beauty in motion," and that the agent responsible for that motion was a soul that corresponded to that manifestation in kind, Schiller was clearly trying to argue that grace was somehow an external attribute of a specific inner constitution. Just as Schiller saw grace as the engaging expression of an immaterial being, so too he tried to enfold the immaterial truths of abstract thought in the pleasing form of his own rhetorical style, which expressed its truth, in turn, in the act of communication. Thus at its most extreme, his own graceful language was supposed to become the fair embodiment of the very ideal he was theoretically describing. The essay "Über Anmut und Würde," in other words, is supposed to *be* what it purports to portray, and Schiller must have imagined (or at least wished) that this identity would extend to the essay's *effect* as well.[38]

It is hardly astonishing that in order to explain how an outer form could so well express an inward state, Schiller resorted at this point in "Über Anmut und Würde" to the most familiar contemporary account of this union of body and soul. "Grace can only be found in *motion*," Schiller asserted, "for, in the world of sense, mental changes can only be manifested as motion. But this does not prevent fixed and static features from also exhibiting grace. These fixed features were originally nothing other than motions that, after repeated occurrence, finally became habitual and left permanent

schaftliche Buchgesellschaft, 1960–81), 1:31–32, which he wrote in 1788–89 and which Schiller surely knew, we read: "No one stands on such a low stage of culture that he would be incapable of reaching a higher one; and even if the more enlightened religious and philosophical ideas are not able to be immediately communicated to a large portion of the citizens, then, in order to conform to their own ideas, one should present the truth to this class of people in a different garment than one would otherwise choose if it were thus necessary to speak more to their imagination and their heart than to their cold reason."
38. Kontje, *Constructing Reality*, 13, has also, though less critically, seen the relation between Schiller's essays and his conception of style in helping to bring about what he theoretically set forth: "Beauty itself is described in a beautiful style (*die schöne Schreibart*) which is to produce beautiful souls (*schöne Seelen*) for the aesthetic state (*der ästhetische Staat*). The *Aesthetic Education* is an aesthetic object, an ethical act, and a political event, an example of what it depicts." Robert Markley, "Style as Philosophical Structure: The Contexts of Shaftesbury's *Characteristics*," in *The Philosopher as Writer. The Eighteenth Century*, ed. Robert Ginsberg (Selinsgrove: Susquehanna University Press, 1987), 147, notes that Shaftesbury had a similar notion of style in mind: "Throughout his writings, Shaftesbury insists on the power of forms to affect the reader. . . . Style, then, is an affective process as well as a reflection of a writer's values; it polishes the reader's manners as it incites the reader to virtuous actions. . . . Language, in other words, embodies and deploys a system of values; it does not passively reflect a moral or aesthetic order but attempts to define and shape what 'order' itself may be."

traces" (5:446). Schiller, in other words, borrowed the theoretical tools to describe this relation between internal and external nature from the pseudoscience of physiognomy, which was then still in vogue. It was not an auspicious decision, even if it seemed to be one close to hand. For although physiognomy also heavily relied on the discourse of moral beauty and thus lent itself naturally to Schiller's argument here, its legitimacy was not uncontested. At an important juncture in the development of his reasoning, therefore, Schiller resorted yet again to an external body of evidence to support his own conclusions. And once more that evidence simply could not carry the burden of proof that Schiller wanted, and in fact needed, it to.[39]

But to be fair to Schiller, as well as more exact, he did not simply adopt Lavater's vulgar equation of physical ugliness and moral vice, but he seemed instead to adhere to something more like Lichtenberg's or Engel's conception of pathognomy, in which gestures, for example, could be read as fairly reliable indications of certain kinds of emotional activity.[40] Schiller similarly believed that "when people speak we simultaneously see their glances, their facial features, their hands, indeed often their entire bodies *speak along*, and the *gestural* [*mimische*] part of conversation is frequently deemed to be the most eloquent" ("Über Anmut und Würde," 5:448). Building on this observation, Schiller went on to differentiate between nonsignifying, or "silent," parts of the body, and those that signify, or are "expressive" [*sprechend*]. "I call every appearance of the body expressive (in the broadest sense) which accompanies and expresses a mental state" (5:453).[41] This axiom is easy enough to accept, and it applies equally well to animals and human beings: sexual desire and hunger, for instance, are expressed in immediate ways that are common to both humans and beasts. The difference results from the uniquely human possession of a will: "It is true that nature *gives* man his purpose [*Bestimmung*], but it *places in his will* the fulfillment of it, therefore the present relationship of his condition to his purpose is not the product of nature, but must be his own work. The expression of this relationship in his

39. It is a sign of the myopic focus on Schiller's relationship to Kant (and of the desire to "save" Schiller from the taint of pre-critical or popular philosophy) that his indebtedness to physiognomical thought, and the consequences of this connection, have been all but overlooked. Von Wiese, *Schiller*, 104, briefly mentions Lavater in this context, but he leaves the issue of physiognomy aside in his discussion of the essay. Otherwise, I know of no study devoted to the relationship between Lavater and Schiller.

40. In the last of the *Kalliasbriefe*, dated 28 February 1793, Schiller wrote enthusiastically about the superlative acting abilities of Ekhof, about whom Engel had also written in similar terms in his *Ideen zu einer Mimik*. Since Ekhof died in 1778, Schiller probably never saw him perform, thus suggesting that a literary text, and perhaps Engel himself, was the source of his information. See Schiller, "Kallias," 5:430.

41. In a later passage in "Über Anmut und Würde," however, Schiller seemed to lend his unqualified faith to physiognomy: "For the physiognomist these silent features are not at all meaningless because the physiognomist does not merely want to know what people have made of themselves, but also what nature has done both for and against them" (5:455).

form [*Bildung*] thus does not belong to nature, but to himself, that is, it is an expression of the person" (5:454). Our behavior, therefore, unlike that of animals, is (or ought to be) the product of a conscious effort of will and, as such, must be judged as the expression of a rational mind.

We see that Schiller has set forth his propositions with great patience and skill; he has, it seems, merely articulated suggestions that, in themselves, appear reasonable enough and to which we can unhesitatingly assent. But then, picking up this last line of thought, he asserted so unobtrusively that we nearly miss it that "if we think of [someone] as a moral person, then we are justified to expect an expression of that moral person in his figure [*Gestalt*]" (5:457). The only reason we are "justified" in having this expectation is derived from Schiller's physiognomical assumptions, which we know to be questionable at best. But Schiller, undeterred by such scruples, went on to make the additional and equally unfounded claim that "an expressive form is thus demanded of a person as soon as one is conscious of his moral purpose." We expect, that is, some recognizable correspondence between outer behavior and inner constitution; if we observe virtuous acts and graceful actions, we assume the character of the person in question to reflect those qualities. Alternatively, once we gain an impression of someone's moral character (which can only occur, according to Schiller, through the agency of perceptible phenomena such as the actions or deeds just named), then we automatically assume that the external form will somehow be in harmony with the soul. On the doubtful strength of this conclusion, Schiller then performed one of the more momentous, and logically one of the most disastrous, speculative leaps of the essay:

> Wherever *moral* feeling finds satisfaction, *aesthetic* feeling does not want to come up short, and the correspondence with an idea in appearance should not come at a sacrifice. Therefore, just as strictly as reason demands an expression of morality, the eye demands beauty with equal insistence. Since both of these demands are directed toward the same object, although based on different authorities of judgment, then one and the same cause for the satisfaction of both must be provided. That intellectual disposition of man which most enables him to fulfill his purpose as a moral person must be allowed such an expression that is also, as mere appearance, the most advantageous. In other words: his moral capacity must be revealed through grace. (5:458–59)

The insistent, almost desperate use of the verb "must" throughout this passage in place of actual argument reveals with unforgiving clarity the breakdown of Schiller's logic. There is simply no reason given for this confluence of moral and aesthetic qualities—nor is one possible. Like Kant at a similar point in his own attempt to grapple with the supposed affinity between moral and aesthetic judgment, Schiller himself also saw the problem in his own thinking, and he admitted a few lines later that "here, then, is where a great difficulty presents itself." But the difficulty was even greater than Schiller imagined, and it resided at a deeper conceptual level than he could have afforded to acknowledge. Unable to remove this obstruction, he tried to circumvent it by issuing his own version of a categorical imperative: "In order to resolve this contradiction, one must assume 'that the moral cause in the mind that serves as the basis of grace necessarily produces in that sensuality which depends on that cause precisely that state [*Zustand*] which contains within itself the *natural conditions* [*Bedingungen*] of beauty'" (5:459). The quotation marks here are unexplained, but they are apparently designed to invoke the aura of an objective legislative pronouncement which one "must assume" and accordingly accept without question. In producing an impression of authority, these quotation marks are yet another instance of Schiller's manipulation of rhetorical devices in the absence of substantive argument. For what Schiller actually asserted, in purely circular reasoning, was that grace manifests itself as visible beauty because the expression of the soul that produces this phenomenon happens to coincide with the laws of physical beauty. The yawning emptiness of this assertion is exceeded only by the dizzying, and perhaps deliberately diversionary, complexity of its syntax.

Undeterred, Schiller pressed on to the next, and most important, stage of his exposition. If, as he had hoped to show, grace was indeed the external manifestation of an inner state, and since he adhered to the physiognomical faith in a correspondence *in kind* between these two realms, then he was now obliged to report on the nature of the soul that was responsible for actually producing such grace. Specifically, he had to show "what kind of moral sentiments are most compatible with the expression of beauty" (5:461). Here Schiller again returned to Kantian categories, and he portrayed human moral agency as a struggle in which people either sought to obey the dictates of rational duty, or succumbed to the temptations of sensual inclination. Schiller envisioned a third way, however (and one that Kant and Mendelssohn before him had also thought possible), in which "the drives of the latter are set in harmony with the laws of the former, and human beings are unified with themselves" (5:461).[42] Ideally, that is, we desire to do what our reason says we ought to do. In a phrase that characteristically enough for Schiller, appeals more to our optimistic sense of self-worth than to our more soberly realistic logical faculties, he objected to Kant's categorical conclusion that the greatest moral accomplishments would be always in conflict

42. There seems to be no work on the influence of Mendelssohn on Schiller, although Schiller mentioned him frequently here and elsewhere. See, for example, *Sämtliche Werke*, 5:397, 447, and passim.

with our sensuous nature: "Wouldn't the *imperative* form of the moral law already condemn and debase humanity itself and thus make the most sublime document of its greatness at the same time a testament to its frailty?" (5:467).[43] Schiller thus saw in the union of duty and inclination the possibility of demonstrating intellectual freedom without denying feeling, and when this occurred, it resulted in what Schiller had already identified in the *Kalliasbriefe* as moral beauty. In "Über Anmut und Würde," Schiller advanced even further and identified this coincidence as "the mark of perfected humanity and that which one understands by a *beautiful soul*. . . . It is in a beautiful soul, therefore, that sensuality and reason, duty and inclination, are harmonized, and grace is its expression in appearance" (5:468). With that one sentence, then, we have reached not only the culmination of Schiller's essay, but also in a sense that of the whole cultural development that allowed him—one could almost say impelled him—to write it.

We should pause here and reflect for a moment on the long path we have traveled to reach this station. Almost exactly one hundred years separate the publication of Schiller's treatise from the appearance of Locke's *Essay concerning Human Understanding*. Not the least of the developments seen by that intervening century of Enlightenment was the emergence of what we now generally take to be a distinctly modern consciousness. One vital part of that nascent modernity, and one dear to Schiller especially, was the insistence on personal autonomy unfettered by external forces, freedom in all of its gradations and forms. And the will to attain freedom from subservience to authority in all of its manifestations was not merely a political goal of the Enlightenment; it was reflected in its approach to virtually every human concern. But the task of liberating humanity from the tyrannies of the past seemed comparatively simple when weighed against the task of alleviating anxieties about the present. As oppressive, or merely paternalistic, as the Church may have been, it had at least managed to maintain a cohesive social order that was based on a clear and, largely for that reason, fairly effective ethical system. A major challenge to the transition from benighted subjugation toward Enlightened modernity had been to provide an alternative to that flawed but familiar order. The philosophers and writers we have been revisiting here had thus devoted an enormous amount of imaginative and narra-

---

43. Kant replied to this apparent criticism in a footnote to the second edition of his *Religion within the Limits of Reason Alone*, 19, and expressed his fundamental agreement with Schiller: "Now if one asks, What is the *aesthetic character*, the *temperament*, so to speak, *of virtue*, whether courageous and hence *joyous* or fear-ridden and dejected, an answer is hardly necessary. This latter slavish frame of mind can never occur without a hidden *hatred* of the law. And a heart which is happy in the *performance* of its duty (not merely complacent in the *recognition* thereof) is a mark of genuineness in the virtuous spirit. . . . This resolve, then, encouraged by good progress, must needs beget a joyous frame of mind, without which man is never certain of having really *attained a love* for the good, *i.e.*, of having incorporated it into his maxim." Schiller was elated at the response; see the letter to Körner from 18 May 1794, in *Briefe*, 3:438.

tive energy to fabricating a moral framework constructed entirely of the materials supplied by human nature itself. The idea of moral beauty, which contained an ethical code that was compelling not least of all because it entailed a cultivation of the self that paralleled artistic activity, seemed to answer most if not all of those urgent needs.

The beautiful soul, the seemingly real and irresistible embodiment of that highly abstract ideal, compliantly responded to this massive imaginative solicitation, and willingly bestowed its favors on anyone who devoutly desired them—and many did. The sexual language is appropriate here: from Plato's erotically vivid descriptions of the initiation into the realm of Ideas, through the equally explicit Pietistic fantasies of transforming the soul into the beautiful bride of Christ, to the unmaidenly experiences of Wieland's Danae and Rousseau's Julie—not to forget Humboldt's bizarre advocacy of prostitution as a means of attaining moral grace—the beautiful soul had always been the object of a particular, if conflicted, desire. Schiller, too, thought that "grace is found more in the *feminine* sex," and was thus "the expression of feminine virtue, which may often be lacking in the male" (5:469–70). (To a certain extent, of course, this conclusion was predetermined by the grammatical gender of the noun "soul," which in both German and French is feminine.) But with Schiller—although this generally holds true for the entire tradition as well—it became clearer than ever before that the beautiful soul was something like a narcissistic projection, and what he loved was in fact no more than an idealized image of himself, but one that he was committed to thinking possessed independent, objective reality.[44] Surprisingly few, among whom Kant of course stands as a singularly commanding presence, were able to see through the chimerical guise, and it seemed that most, like Schiller, were determined not to disturb the illusion: the more Schiller became entangled in logical contradictions in trying to prove the existence of moral beauty, the more ardently he clung to the apparition of the beautiful soul.

It is uncertain whether Schiller was aware, or if he even dimly felt, how weak his hold had become. But his conceptual grasp of the problem, as tenuous as it already was, betrayed further signs of slipping. For as Schiller then turned to the second half of the essay in which he treated the more

44. In the ninety-second "letter" of eighth collection of Herder's *Briefe zu Beförderung der Humanität,* which were published in 1796 and thus not too long after "Über Anmut und Würde" had appeared, Herder perceptively wrote on a closely related topic: "One could cite a series of examples from which it would clearly emerge how seldom we study the *ancients themselves* when we study antiquity, how even more seldom their *highest,* the 'kalon kagathon' of the Greek and Roman world, their rule of taste in the true, good, and beautiful. It is mostly the case that we look at them like Narcissus, thinking of what *we* have to say about *them,* and admire *our* figure in the liquid mirror of the old sacred source." See Johann Gottfried Herder, *Sämmtliche Werke,* ed. Bernhard Suphan (Berlin: Weidmann, 1877–1913), 18:80.

"masculine" concept of dignity (*Würde*), he appeared to undermine the position he had elaborately built up in the preceding part. "Just as grace is the expression of a beautiful soul," he wrote, "so too is *dignity* the expression of a sublime disposition" (5:470). In Schiller's view, as he just informed us, the beautiful soul *already* represented the condition of perfected morality, a state in which virtue had become so ingrained that goodness was realized with such effortless facility that it seemed to be a natural instinct, a state of being in which the claims of reason and sensuality were seamlessly fused. "But," Schiller admitted, "this beauty of character, the most mature fruit of humanity, is merely an idea, to which one strives to conform with continuous vigilance, but which, even with the greatest determination, one can never entirely achieve" (5:470). Schiller's reluctant concession that the beautiful soul, whose existence he had just spent so much effort trying to prove, was no more than an "idea," comes perilously close to negating his entire enterprise.

This impression is reinforced when he implies that it is not just difficult to achieve this state but practically impossible. For as Schiller saw it, whenever our physical nature was being solicited by some emotion or passion—whenever sensibility sought to press its own demands—it was inevitable that the equilibrium characterizing the beautiful soul will be upset, and quite possibly irretrievably lost. "Agreement with the law of reason is thus not possible under the assault of the affects except by contradicting the demands of nature" (5:474). Since it is depressingly obvious that moral choices in life must frequently be made in painful contradiction to our sensual wishes (the manifestation of which Schiller defined as "dignity"), it was not only the case that inner harmony thus defined was rare; it was strictly and absolutely incompatible with the exigencies of normal existence. Thus as Schiller himself also recognized, the two principles of grace and dignity were in complete opposition: "Since the ideal of perfect humanity demands not a conflict, but rather congruity between the moral and sensual, this ideal sits uneasily with dignity, which is an expression of that very conflict" (5:478). Despite this fundamental disparity between the two states of moral being, Schiller then wrote with breathtaking calm: "If grace and dignity—with the former supported by architectonic beauty, and the latter by strength—are *united* in the same person, then the expression of humanity is perfected, and the person stands there, vindicated in the realm of the mind, and acquitted in appearance" (5:481). With that statement, Schiller quite simply abdicated the domain governed by the laws of logic and rational argument and fled into a world of his own creation.[45]

45. See the argument in Hamburger, "Schillers Fragment 'Der Menschenfeind' und die Idee der Kalokagathie," 114–15. See as well Sharpe, *Friedrich Schiller*, 137, who, although largely uncritical of Schiller's thought, also admits: "If it is Schiller's purpose to replace the

It is important that we understand that Schiller's failure—as much as one hesitates to call such an articulate literary and cultural monument a "failure"—was not his alone, but rather the necessary result of his resolute adherence to an ideal that he himself saw was impossible to achieve. Schiller probably realized the insufficiency of his solution, although he responded to it with his customary aplomb and acted as if he had settled the question to his own satisfaction. His major philosophical work, for which "Über Anmut und Würde" acted as a sort of preparatory study, was the *Aesthetic Education of Humanity*, which although it does not contain the phrase "beautiful soul," does assume, as its title suggests, its reality.[46] The essay amounts to an attempt to move from the exclusive concentration on the "beautiful" individual to the level of the whole social sphere. Such a consideration of the social dimension of moral beauty had always been an essential element of the ideal, for morality can of course only make sense within the context of a larger civil order. So convinced was Schiller of the feasibility of his thesis that he envisioned beauty not simply as the guarantor of social tranquillity, but as the very agent that first enabled human beings to emerge from Hobbesian barbarism and coexist in relative peace. The terminology and impetus of the entire work were thus grounded in the ideology of moral beauty. Even the epigraph to the book—"Si c'est la raison, qui fait l'homme, c'est le sentiment, qui le conduit" [If it is reason that makes man, then it is sentiment that guides him]—was borrowed from Rousseau's *Julie*, further attesting to Schiller's desire to place his thought within a specific literary and ideational lineage.

At the end of the final letter of the *Aesthetic Education*, however, Schiller posed a rhetorical question that seemed to address as much his own doubts as those potentially raised by the reader. "But does such a State of Aesthetic Semblance really exist? And if so, where is it to be found? As a need, it exists in every finely attuned soul; as a realized fact, we are likely to find it, like the pure Church and the pure Republic, only in some few chosen circles, where conduct is governed, not by some soulless imitation of the manners and morals of others, but by the aesthetic nature we have made our own."[47]

---

polarity of the graceful and the dignified with complementarity, the absolute status of the 'schöne Seele' provides something of a logical problem."

46. The next and final mention of the phrase occurs in the famous essay "Über naive und sentimentalische Dichtung" (On naive and sentimental poetry), which Schiller began in conjunction with the *Aesthetic Education* but did not finish until the end of 1795. Yet Schiller did not appreciably advance the theoretical dimension of the discussion, and continued to compare the "sublime" character to the beautiful soul. But he did again resort to a concrete image by way of analogy to try to make his meaning clear: "In the beautiful soul . . . the ideal acts as nature, that is uniformly, and can thus show itself in a state of calm [*Ruhe*]. The deep ocean appears to be most sublime in its motion, the clear stream the most beautiful in its calm course." Schiller, *Sämtliche Werke*, 5:724.

47. Friedrich Schiller, *On the Aesthetic Education of Man in a Series of Letters*, ed. and trans. Elizabeth M. Wilkinson and L. A. Willoughby (Oxford: Oxford University Press, 1967), 219.

From the beginning it had been a feature of every effort to depict the actual realization of moral beauty that those few who were fortunate enough to participate in the project found themselves to be part of a very exclusive minority. In analogy to the institutions he named, Schiller imagined that beautiful souls would find themselves, if at all, in self-selected, intimate company. Perhaps he thought of the provincial court of Duke Carl August in Weimar as one such constellation, but Clarens could not have been very far from his mind as well. Although the diffident duke was no Monsieur de Wolmar, a more attentive reading of Rousseau's experimental community should have forewarned Schiller of the probable chances—not to speak of the desirability—of achieving what he had theoretically proposed. For as Clarens and even Schiller's own philosophical works had shown, moral beauty would always be constitutionally prevented from ever making an appearance by the very nature of its defining attributes.

Unswayed in the end by the doubts he had himself expressed, Schiller never completely abandoned the oasis described by the shimmering mirage of the beautiful soul. Yet for a concept that so intimately depended on the qualities of proportioned repose, classical balance, and undisturbed harmony for its meaning and coherence, the shrill dissonance that became increasingly impossible to ignore in Schiller's attempt to evoke the ideal inherently called that very concept into question with even greater insistence. Although many preferred simply to close their ears to these muffled but audible undertones, not everyone did. Two writers who faced up to the consequences of what they refused to disregard—Goethe and Hegel—possessed in almost every other way diametrically opposed sensibilities: one a poet very much bound to tangible reality, and the other a speculative philosopher *par excellence*. But by approaching the problem of the beautiful soul from these different directions, both Goethe and Hegel once again separated the elements of what Schiller—the philosopher-poet or poet-philosopher—had repeatedly tried to treat with such ambiguous results as one.

7

Goethe and Hegel:
The Sublation of the Beautiful Soul

Goodness, growing to a pleurisy,
Dies in his own too much.
                    —Shakespeare

After two decades of fairly desultory work, Goethe finally published his second novel, *Wilhelm Meisters Lehrjahre* (Wilhelm Meister's apprenticeship), in four volumes between 1795 and 1796. Abandoning the popular epistolary form that had brought him European fame with *Die Leiden des jungen Werther* twenty years before, Goethe chose this time to relate the adventures of his hero, the young Wilhelm Meister, in the third-person epic past, thus establishing a more comfortable distance between himself and his errant protagonist. But the sixth book of *Wilhelm Meister*, which is arguably the most famous—as well as the most enigmatic—of the novel, radically departs from this general scheme in both its form and its substance. It sharply interrupts the measured flow of the narrative devoted to the life and travels of the titular figure and introduces the autobiographical reflections of a character who otherwise plays no active role in the novel; indeed, the interpolated "manuscript" we read is said to have been written by someone who at that point in the tale, had already been dead for some time. Although few have questioned the artistic success of this vignette, its very existence has always troubled readers, many of whom have been alternately puzzled about the nature of the person it purports to reveal, its relevance to the whole, and even about Goethe's reasons for including it at all. As we will see, the "Bekenntnisse einer schönen Seele" (Confessions of a beautiful soul), as this section is called, does in fact occupy a rightful place in the novel, acting as a kind of contrapuntal accompaniment to its greater thematic development. More broadly, it can also be understood as performing an elaborate, melancholy coda to the complex of cultural motifs that obviously inspired its creation. Goethe's "Confessions of a Beautiful Soul," in other words, contains the most compelling portrait of the instantiation of perfected virtue that the eighteenth century produced; yet it was also destined to become the last legitimate descendant of that noble but barren lineage.

To those who are sensitive to the ironies of history it will seem somehow fitting that it was in the final years of the German Enlightenment—at the height of the "classical" period in Weimar—that the most fully realized incarnation of the beautiful soul appeared, only to turn out to have been the last viable representative of the genre. The paradoxes involved are palpable: precisely when German letters had finally regained a place of eminence that they had not enjoyed since the middle of the thirteenth century, the beautiful soul—which had been one of the chief forces fueling that very revival— had already begun to display unmistakable signs of morbidity. Characteristically, both Schiller and Goethe, the dioscuri of German classicism, took completely separate paths to the problem, but they ended up by confronting similar obstacles. Schiller, for whom the beautiful soul assumed, as we saw, an unprecedented and unparalleled importance, had approached the matter primarily in philosophical terms. But he soon encountered such serious difficulties in defining it that he found himself forced to avoid the phrase, and eventually, if only by implication, even the ideal itself. Goethe, on the other hand, possessed an almost congenital antipathy toward purely abstract thought (he only began to read Kant, for example, in 1789 and even then with conspicuous reluctance), and his own novelistic treatment of the beautiful soul, although in some ways no less ambiguous than Schiller's, is certainly more concrete. Yet in each case, although again for different but related reasons, the beautiful soul did not survive their authorial ministrations on its behalf. And only a few years after the turn of the century, it finally fell to Hegel to pronounce the formal eulogy.

This rather gloomy series of events was strangely prefigured, and perhaps even hastened, by the circumstances surrounding Goethe's first acquaintance with the beautiful soul, for he almost did not live long enough to tell his own version of the story. While the nineteen-year-old Goethe was pursuing his studies in Leipzig in 1768, the unexpected news of Winckelmann's sudden and gruesome death descended on him, as he later described it in his autobiography, "like a thunderbolt from a clear sky."[1] Almost as if in sympathetic reaction to the passing of the revered Philhellene—and, somewhat more prosaically, as a consequence of what seems to have been an

1. Johann Wolfgang von Goethe *From My Life: Poetry and Truth*, part 2, ed. Thomas P. Saine and Jeffrey L. Sammons, trans. Robert R. Heitner and Thomas P. Saine, in *Collected Works* (New York: Suhrkamp, 1987), 4:247. Henceforth cited in text and notes as "*Poetry and Truth*, part 2" by volume and page number from *Collected Works*. See the account of Goethe's university experiences, and more generally of this phase of his life, in the splendid new biography by Nicholas Boyle, *Goethe: The Poet and the Age* (Oxford: Oxford University Press, 1991), 1:62–71.

indifferent diet—Goethe's health also began to deteriorate shortly thereafter, and "one night I was awakened by a violent hemorrhage" (*Poetry and
Truth*, part 2, 4:248). Although the actual cause of his illness was then
unknown, it now appears certain that he was afflicted by a severe tubercular
condition, and for several days there were good grounds to fear for his life.
After just managing to survive this terrifying "gush of blood," as he remembered it, he returned to his native city of Frankfurt, where his family, especially his mother and sister, administered to his recuperation, which consumed most of the following year. Given this alarming development in his
physical constitution, Goethe understandably acquired a new interest in the
state of his soul. Confined to his bed, Goethe had the chance to subject both
his behavior and conscience to minute scrutiny and to think more generally
about the nature of contemporary religious and ethical thought. Reflecting
back on the time of his illness, he later wrote: "The Christian religion was
wavering between its own historical positivism and a pure deism which,
being based on ethical thought, was supposed to reestablish morality. Differences in character and ways of thinking were evident here in infinite gradations, but the underlying chief difference was over the question about how
much part reason, and how much part feelings, could and should play in
such convictions" (250). With that, Goethe had neatly circumscribed the
theoretical dilemma facing modern philosophers of ethics, to which the
conception of moral beauty had emerged as a viable solution. He had also
summarized the intellectual climate in which he had met his first beautiful
soul.

For it was while convalescing at home and weighing such ultimate matters
that Goethe came into close and regular contact with a noble relation of his
mother by the name of Susanna Katharina von Klettenberg. During the
years in which Goethe had been living and studying in Leipzig, his family
had begun to host Pietist conventicles at their house—Frankfurt had been,
after all, the birthplace of Spener's *collegia pietatis*—and Katharina von Klettenberg, who was a devout if not in every way typical Pietist, took frequent
part in these gatherings at the Goethe household to discuss the Bible and
other devotional literature.[2] In the course of his recovery, during which he
also participated in some of these meetings, Goethe clearly became very
fond of Katharina von Klettenberg, and she, in turn, became something of a
spiritual mentor to him, and until her death in 1774 Goethe often sought
out her company and solicited her advice even concerning his literary endeavors. In his autobiography, Goethe looked back over the tumultuous
early years of his life and recalled that from all of "these many distractions,
which usually gave rise to serious, and even religious meditations, I would

2. See the letter to Ernst Theodor Langer on 17 January 1769, in Johann Wolfgang von
Goethe, *Briefe*, ed. Karl Robert Mandelkow and Bodo Morawe (Hamburg: Christian Wegner,
1962–67), 1:83, in which Goethe described one such meeting at his house.

return again and again to my noble friend Miss von Klettenberg, whose presence would calm, at least for the moment, my impetuous, wide-ranging fancies and enthusiasms. After my sister, she was the one to whom I preferred giving an account of my projects" (*Poetry and Truth*, part 2, 4:464). It is obvious that this pious woman exerted a quiet but persistent influence over Goethe's imagination; indeed, as he later revealed, she was "the same person whose letters and conversations inspired the 'Confessions of a Beautiful Soul' that are to be found inserted in *Wilhelm Meister*" (253).

It probably can never be known how closely Goethe's literary monument to the friend of his youth corresponds to this actual historical figure.[3] Instead, we will examine the sixth book of *Wilhelm Meister* for its narrative value within the novel and for its relation to the tradition after which it is named. But it is not irrelevant to that immediate intention that the traumatic personal context in which Goethe came to know Miss Katharina von Klettenberg—one so strongly drawn by illness, confinement, and the possibility of death—indelibly colored his perception and later portrayal of the Beautiful Soul herself.

THE BILDUNGSROMAN TURNS AGAINST ITSELF

Although the sixth book of *Wilhelm Meister* may be its best-known individual section, the novel as a whole continues to be read as the most representative, and some might even say the only genuine, example of that supposedly quintessentially German literary genre, the bildungsroman. Wilhelm Dilthey—who, as we know, was not the first but the most influential person to use the word—elaborated his understanding of the concept in express reference to *Wilhelm Meister*. It thus seemed natural, in view of Dilthey's authority, that Goethe's work became the standard against which all potential contenders for the generic distinction subsequently came to be measured.[4] According to Dilthey, Goethe principally wanted to demonstrate in his novel the ideal of the purposeful shaping of an individual life, in which the native talents and resources of a person were allowed, but also subtly fostered by mentors or guides, to develop and finally to assume the form of a finished, mature personality. Dilthey's definition of *Bildung*, and

3. The degree to which Goethe might have altered the life story of Katharina von Klettenberg for his literary purposes has already been adequately explored by Robert Hering, *Wilhelm Meister und Faust und ihre Gestaltung im Zeichen der Gottesidee* (Frankfurt am Main: G. Schulte-Bulmke, 1952), 117–89.

4. Dilthey first used the term in his *Leben Schleiermachers*, which was published in 1870; see Wilhelm Dilthey, *Gesammelte Schriften* (Göttingen: Vandenhoeck & Ruprecht, 1970), 13.1. 299: "I would like to call those works 'Bildungsromane' which constitute the school of Wilhelm Meister (for Rousseau's related art form did not continue to have on effect on them). Goethe's work shows human development [*Ausbildung*] in various stages, figures, and periods of life."

his view of Goethe's novel generally, became canonical, and one of the primary preoccupations of criticism devoted to the book has been to show— or disprove—his contention that it embodied "the idea of a natural education in conformity with the inner development of the psyche."[5]

But the importance of *Bildung* itself went of course far beyond the relatively narrow sphere described by the concerns of literary criticism. Abstracted from the novel and applied as it was to an ever widening circle of activities and values, an expanded concept of *Bildung* became a kind of surrogate ideology for generations of German neohumanist scholars.[6] One of the consequences of this appropriation was that although the idea of *Bildung* is, or was, inherently teleological, for most of its nineteenth-century advocates it came to assume the status of a sovereign and independent good.[7] That is, *Bildung*, or the formation of one's innate abilities into a harmonious unity, the realization of one's character without regard to the purpose to which these talents would (or rather should) eventually be put— this concept of *Bildung* gradually came to be seen as an end in itself and as such stood as the central goal of humanist pedagogical theory and practice.[8] Indeed, promoting the achievement of *Bildung* in this particular sense became institutionalized in the nineteenth century as the proper, indeed only, role of the German university, which ensured the survival of this idea of *Bildung* until the present day. But it also guaranteed the almost unavoidable trivialization of *Bildung* into a merely mechanical means of self-definition.

The distillation of this concept into such a formalized procedure was bought, however, at great historical cost. For as a result of this same process of abstraction, the actual content of *Bildung*, the reason why it was undertaken in the first place, gradually receded before its purely functional importance. As opposed to the later neohumanistic emphasis on the primarily formal activity of personal refinement, eighteenth-century writers had always understood the aim of "inner development" to be specifically moral. Even Wilhelm von Humboldt—who as one of the organizing founders of the University of Berlin, is even more closely associated with the institutional

5. Wilhelm Dilthey, *Poetry and Experience*, in *Selected Works*, ed. Rudolf A. Makkreel and Frithjof Rodi (Princeton: Princeton University Press, 1985), 5:336.
6. E. L. Stahl's book *Die religiöse und die humanitätsphilosophische Bildungsidee und die Entstehung des deutschen Bildungsromans im 18. Jahrhundert* (Bern: Paul Haupt, 1934), is both a scholarly description and, in its uncritical orientation, a symptom of this development.
7. See, for example, the representative and influential comment by Hans-Georg Gadamer, *Truth and Method*, ed. Garrett Bareden and John Cumming (London: Sheed & Ward, 1975), 12: "Like nature, Bildung has no goals outside itself."
8. See the informative historical overview of the word in Rudolf Vierhaus's article "Bildung," in *Geschichtliche Grundbegriffe. Historisches Lexikon zur politisch-sozialen sprache in Deutschland*, ed. Otto Brunner, Werner Conze, and Reinhart Kosselleck (Stuttgart: Ernst Klett, 1972), 1:508–551. See also the critical study of this development by Günther Buck, *Rückwege aus der Entfremdung: Studien zur Entwicklung der deutschen humanistischen Bildungsphilosophie* (Munich: Wilhelm Fink, 1984).

notion of *Bildung* than is Goethe—did not conceive of it as something to be pursued for its own sake, but as having an eminently ethical source and object. In his early essay "Über Religion," for example, Humboldt had insisted that "the purpose of humanity lies in human beings themselves, in their inner moral cultivation [*moralische Bildung*]."[9] Using that very phrase, Goethe himself likewise emphasized more than once that "to work toward the development of one's moral cultivation is the simplest and most expedient task a person can undertake."[10] To be sure, some later commentators have recognized the importance of this neglected but necessary aspect of *Bildung*, and one critic has perceptively remarked that "to the condition of organic perfection naturally belongs the ethical stage of completion as well. 'Bildung' in the classical sense is thus simultaneously the embodiment of the true, the good, and the beautiful, it is humanity, kalokagathia."[11] Understood therefore in this, its "classical sense," the idea of moral beauty has always stood behind the conception of *Bildung* and the beautiful soul has always been its ultimate goal.

In every discussion of moral beauty we have considered, some sort of self-fashioning has been instrumental in the process of achieving a beautiful soul. Whether it was the convulsive, radical rebirth of the "new person" demanded by Pietist reformers, or the more genteel cultivation of personal manners advocated by Shaftesbury and his disciples, or even the venerable Platonic relationship between a wise preceptor and pliant pupil, inner beauty was thought to come about only as the result of the conscious and determined transformation of the soul it was intended to grace. But by emptying *Bildung* of its ethical significance and thus concentrating solely on what amounts to the predominantly *aesthetic* act of molding the materials of personality into a pleasant, concinnous design, the original impetus behind the desire for acquiring a beautiful soul could, at its worst, degenerate into the effete and sterile pursuit of solipsistic self-gratification. This vacuity is expressly stated, although with a clearly positive valuation, in one of the "classical" scholarly works devoted to the period, H. A. Korff's *Geist der Goethezeit*

9. Wilhelm von Humboldt, "Über Religion," in *Werke*, ed. Andreas Flitner und Klaus Giel (Darmstadt: Wissenschaftliche Buchgesellschaft, 1960–81), 1:32. Most Humboldt scholars gloss over this aspect of his thought and rarely mention ethics. See, for example, Paul R. Sweet, *Wilhelm von Humboldt: A Biography* (Columbus: Ohio State University Press, 1978–80), 1:51, who, in commenting on the word *Bildung*, writes that for "Humboldt it meant cultivating one's talents, molding one's self in terms of a cultural ideal." But Sweet is also rather vague about what this "cultural ideal" might have been for Humboldt.
10. See Johann Wolfgang von Goethe, *From My Life: Poetry and Truth*, part 4, *Campaign in France 1792, Siege of Mainz*, ed. Thomas P. Saine and Jeffrey L. Sammons, trans. Robert R. Heitner and Thomas P. Saine, in *Collected Works* (New York: Suhrkamp, 1987), 5:531.
11. Hans Heinrich Borcherdt, "Der deutsche Bildungsroman," in *Zur Geschichte des deutschen Bildungsromans*, ed. Rolf Selbmann (Darmstadt: Wissenschaftliche Buchgesellschaft, 1988), 186.

(The spirit of the age of Goethe). In a long section titled "The Idea of Beautiful Humanity" we find there a gloss devoted to *Wilhelm Meister* in which we read that "the idea of beauty as the final ideal of humanity is something so general, so purely formal, that in terms of its content it can be divided into countless particular forms and thus appears with each one of them in a new light."[12] Although this description is suffused with the reverential solemnity that used to typify similar studies of so-called German *Hochklassik*, the image it now evokes probably calls a more vacant figure to mind. For thus stripped of its moral stringency, transformed into "something so general, so purely formal," the beautiful soul rapidly runs the risk of becoming nothing more than a spiritual dandy.

Yet it is important to remember that even though this impoverishment of the beautiful soul is an obvious degradation of its original constitution, a similar emptiness had been at least latent in the conception from the very beginning. Deciding exactly what the moral benefits were of such evanescent beauty had, after all, persistently eluded even its most ardent and eloquent partisans. Goethe was certainly keenly aware of the numerous literary, religious, and philosophical attempts to justify or simply to define moral beauty in the century then coming to a close, and his own contribution to the already impressive accumulation of voices resonates with echoes from these earlier efforts. Yet Goethe's stance toward that complex constellation of ideas was not as uncomplicated or as uncritical as, for instance, Schiller's—not to mention the attitude struck by his later readers, who were for their part searching for edification and personal *Bildung* for themselves in his writings. There is reason, indeed, to believe that Goethe wrote his "Confessions of a Beautiful Soul" as a veiled cautionary tale about precisely that process of deluded diminishment performed in the name of inner expansion for which, paradoxically, his novel became famous.

Schiller himself, in fact, had notable difficulties in trying to pin down Goethe's position on the matter. It was not until Schiller had approached the senior poet with his celebrated "birthday letter" of 23 August 1794 that they began what became an intensive correspondence and eventually a highly productive artistic collaboration that continued until Schiller's death eleven years later. Coincidentally, in that very letter Schiller also asked Goethe whether he would be interested in publishing his unnamed "novel" in the journal (*Die Horen*) Schiller was then launching, and by December Goethe was sending him the revisions of *Wilhelm Meister*. Schiller, flattered and proud to be working so intimately with a man he admired, conveyed in his letters to Goethe nothing but suitably dutiful praise—until he received

12. H. A. Korff, *Geist der Goethezeit: Versuch einer ideellen Entwicklung der klassisch-romantischen Literaturgeschichte* (Leipzig: J. J. Weber, 1927–), 2:341.

the sixth book, and suddenly his enthusiasm seemed dampened. "In general," he diplomatically wrote in reference to this most recent installment, "the governing ideas of the whole are excellent, yet I am afraid a little too subtly drawn. I also can't guarantee that some readers won't think that the story has come to a standstill. It would perhaps not have been a bad idea to have condensed some things, shortened others a little, but to have expanded more on a few of the main ideas." As if hoping to encourage closer conformity with his own views by eliciting greater clarity of Goethe's opinion, Schiller also said (while being careful to use the less accusatory passive voice) that he felt "that too little has been said about the characteristic aspects of the Christian religion and of Christian enthusiasm; and the question of what this religion can be to a beautiful soul, or rather what a beautiful soul can make of it, has not been adequately indicated."[13] Besides referring to technical questions of compositional coherence, Schiller was clearly expressing his discomfort over the identification of the figure in the novel with his favorite symbol of moral perfection, and he may have even suspected Goethe of harboring a perspective antithetical to his own.[14] More than a year later, in fact, Schiller was still insisting—as much, one has the feeling, to restore his own peace of mind as to ensure the intelligibility of the novel—that Goethe provide a "somewhat clearer pronunciation of the main idea" (*Briefe*, 5:89).

Schiller's unease about the "main idea" of the "Confessions" has, as previously mentioned, been shared by many subsequent critics. Some, including the majority of Goethe's own contemporaries, regarded the autobiographical confessions that constitute it as an unclouded expression of eighteenth-century virtue, as a wholly transparent tribute to the "classical" ideal of noble and self-contained humanity.[15] More skeptical, and more modern, readers have detected instead a critically ironic and subtly provocative psychological analysis of Christian fanaticism and frustrated sexual desire.[16] Most recently,

13. Friedrich Schiller, *Briefe*, ed. Fritz Jonas (Stuttgart: Deutsche Verlags-Anstalt, 1892–96), 4:235. Henceforth cited parenthetically in the text as "*Briefe*" by volume and page number.
14. If Schiller did indeed sense this disagreement between them, then he was absolutely right. In an autobiographical sketch written after Schiller's death, Goethe described his initial disinclination toward Schiller at this time in their relationship and he specifically mentioned the essay "Über Anmut und Würde," which had appeared the year before and contained Schiller's most extensive treatment of the beautiful soul, as hardly being "a means of reconciling me [with Schiller]. . . . the enormous gulf separating our ways of thinking only gaped all the more decisively." See Goethe, "Glückliches Ereignis," in *Werke. Hamburger Ausgabe*, ed. Erich Trunz (Munich: C. H. Beck, 1981), 10:539–40.
15. See Daniel J. Farrelly, *Goethe and Inner Harmony: A Study of the "schöne Seele" in the Apprenticeship of Wilhelm Meister* (New York: Barnes & Noble, 1973); this positive evaluation is also endorsed by Martin Swales, *The German Bildungsroman from Wieland to Hesse* (Princeton: Princeton University Press, 1978), 57–58, who writes that "The Confessions of a Beautiful Soul" "catalogues a woman's growth to certainty of purpose and spiritual self-fulfillment."
16. Frederick J. Beharriell, "The Hidden Meaning of Goethe's 'Bekenntnisse einer schönen

and somewhat surprisingly, the character who is the Beautiful Soul of the title of Book 6 has become a protofeminist heroine, and her eventual contemplative withdrawal from society has been understood both as a rejection of the patriarchal order and as a positive alternative to Wilhelm's typically "masculine"—that is, active, linear, and obsessively goal-oriented—path toward *Bildung*.[17] Among those, finally, who try to link this sixth book with the overarching theme of the novel the claim is often made that the Beautiful Soul cultivates (or attempts to cultivate) the moral self by negating or denying certain aspects of her person. She thus misses the "true" essence of *Bildung*, which is supposed to consist in the harmonious development of *all* of one's mental and emotional faculties.[18] But moral beauty *did* give *Bildung* its true essence—or at least its eighteenth-century meaning—and Goethe must have had something else in mind than the representation of a false idol with some darkly parodic intent. Even though Schiller may not have dared, or even wanted, to express them so baldly, his apparent suspicions that Goethe did not share his unqualified endorsement of the beautiful soul thus appear to have been wholly justified, but to an extent that Schiller could never have afforded to acknowledge.

Turning now to the Beautiful Soul herself, we soon discover that the distinctive—and distinctively eighteenth-century—characteristic of her personality is the need for absolute self-determination, even at the expense of other social or individual requirements. Her first conscious experience occurs at the age of eight, when (and here, as so often in his work, Goethe established a primordial bond between his own past existence and his fictional creation) she "had a hemorrhage, and from that moment on I was feeling and memory."[19] Awakened to her inner life by a physical affliction,

Seele,'" in *Lebendige Form: Interpretationen zur deutschen Literatur, Festschrift für Heinrich E. K. Henel*, ed. Jeffrey L. Sammons and Ernst Schürer (Munich: Wilhelm Fink, 1970), 37–62.

17. See Marianne Hirsch, "Spiritual *Bildung*: The Beautiful Soul as Paradigm," in *The Voyage In: Fictions of Female Development*, ed. Elizabeth Abel, Marianne Hirsch, and Elizabeth Langland (Hanover: University Press of New England, 1983), esp. 26–33; Susanne Zantop, "Eignes Selbst und fremde Formen: Goethes 'Bekenntnisse einer schönen Seele,'" *Goethe Yearbook* 3 (1986): 73–92; Barbara Becker-Cantarino, "Die 'Bekenntnisse einer schönen Seele': Zur Ausgrenzung und Vereinnahmung des Weiblichen in der patriarchalen Utopie von *Wilhelm Meisters Lehrjahren*," in *Verantwortung und Utopie: Zur Literatur der Goethezeit*, ed. Wolfgang Wittkowski (Tübingen: Max Niemeyer, 1988), 70–90.

18. This is the argument made by Kurt May, "'Wilhelm Meisters Lehrjahre,' ein Bildungsroman?" *Deutsche Vierteljahrsschrift* 31 (1957): esp. 23–26. Although Michael Beddow, *The Fiction of Humanity: Studies in the Bildungsroman from Wieland to Thomas Mann* (Cambridge: Cambridge University Press, 1982), 148, generally disagrees with May, he also writes that "the life-history of the Schöne Seele" demonstrates an "incomplete development" and that her "somewhat isolated though highly refined spirituality is meant to appear a slightly less than perfect achievement."

19. Johann Wolfgang von Goethe, *Wilhelm Meister's Apprenticeship*, ed. and trans. Eric A. Blackall, in *Collected Works* (New York: Suhrkamp, 1989), 9:217. Henceforth cited parenthetically in the text as "*WMA*" by volume and page number from *Collected Works*.

she thus sets down the pattern of introspective concern and corporeal distrust that she would follow, with increasing intensity, forever thereafter. Born, like the woman after whom she was modeled, to a noble and wealthy family, she receives an unusually liberal education for a woman of her time and retains an inclination toward books and learning throughout the rest of her life. Being thus independent in both means and mind, she gradually comes to feel at liberty to consult and trust her own convictions about the matters that most directly affect her. Most dramatically, she breaks off two engagements to men who turned out to be less—or in some ways more— than she had originally imagined them to be and who cause her to feel that her own freedom would be imperiled by their attentions. "The thought of marriage," she laconically remarks, "inevitably has something frightening about it for a moderately discerning young girl" (*WMA*, 9:224). But it is in the realm of religious observance that the Beautiful Soul most decisively demonstrates the degree of her desire for absolute autonomy.

Again like Katharina von Klettenberg, the Beautiful Soul adheres to the spirit of Pietism even while—or rather, most particularly when—she has distanced herself from the constraints of its specific practices. As a young girl who possesses a vivid imagination, which her reading later gives additional substance and direction, she acquires a naive but fervid personal relationship to God, remarking that "I had moments when I intimately communed with the Invisible Being, and I can still remember some verses which I dictated to my mother at that time" (9:217). Although there are periods when she almost completely neglects her spiritual life, especially during the two tumultuous episodes involving her suitors, she still sustains her proclivity for what she calls "the Invisible." At the age of twenty-two, following the instinctive urgings of her nature, she comes to the conclusion that she has to renounce the immediate enjoyment afforded by the senses or face the possibility of forever forfeiting her eternal redemption. The sacrifice proves to be a relatively easy one for her to make, for she "knew from experiences which had come to me unsought, that there are higher emotions which guarantee us a pleasure not to be gained in idle entertainments, and that these higher pleasures provide a source of strength when misfortune overtakes us" (9:230). There is therefore a distinct progression in her development, and this focus on nonsensual edification is indicative of the direction that development takes. This course is made explicit when, a little later, her uncle manages to secure for her the position of canoness ("Stiftsdame"), which finally enables her to support herself. Thus liberated from all financial and social fetters, she is at last able to concentrate entirely on her inner being, and it is then that she submits herself "to the system of achieving conversion advocated by the pietist theologians at Halle" (9:236).

From Arndt to Spener and beyond, the *Bußkampf* had been the defining moment of Pietist existence, but August Hermann Francke, who had established his Pietist Foundation in Halle at the turn of the century, had been the first to contrive a codified "system" that could be easily learned and reproduced by neophytes who needed the reassuring assistance of such a spiritual template. As the Beautiful Soul describes it, the Halle method reflects the familiar, though now rigidified, process by which the "new person" is supposed to be reborn. "According to the stages of this system," she explains, "a change of heart must begin with a deep sense of alarm at one's sinfulness. In this state of extremity the heart must recognize the punishment one has deserved, and have a foretaste of hell which will sour the sweetness of sin. Then one should experience a noticeable assurance of grace, but this will not often come readily in the process but must be sought after" (9:236). For ten years she carefully arranges her life according to the rigid dictates of the formulaic rituals prescribed by the Halle school. But in true Pietist fashion (and in conformity with her own most pronounced character trait), she instinctively begins to resist these encroachments on her personal devotion and to enact a private revolt against these—ironically—orthodox strictures. Initially confining her skeptical opposition to silently entertaining opinions that differ from those of recognized theological authorities, she soon openly expresses her views and even rejects the advice of her friends, telling them that she needs to consult God alone with regard to her faith. "My decision to extricate myself in spiritual matters from the influence and advice of my friends resulted in acquiring the courage to pursue my own course in external relationships" (9:237). She had always been someone who preferred solitude to the company of others—she confesses that she is "often lonely in society, and complete isolation would have pleased [her] best" (9:227). But now she deepens the divide even further by delving more completely, and more exclusively, into her own conscience.

At this point in her tale the Beautiful Soul compares herself, not accidentally, to Wieland's Agathon, whom she sees as having been trained in a morally rigorous atmosphere in the sheltered isolation of Delphi, only to succumb to worldly temptations once he leaves that artificially regulated environment. "'You are not better than he,'" she persuades herself, and with that conclusion finally precipitates a genuine crisis of conscience that initiates her own, and not Francke's prefabricated, struggle for repentance. Until then, she says, "I had not experienced the reality of sinfulness in the least, but now the possibility of sin had become terrifyingly clear and conceivable to me" (9:238). Searching for some remedy for this discovery of a potential for evil, she asks herself: "How was this defect to be overcome? By virtuous actions? This I did not even contemplate, for during the past ten years my exercises of virtue had been far more than outward actions, and yet the horrors I now recognized had been deeply ingrained in my soul all the while" (9:239). She also consults various "treatises on morals," but finds them to be equally useless to her in her search for redemption. After fruitlessly seeking some external cure for her inner ills—real or imagined though they may have been—she finally finds solace from a source she has known all along, but which she had failed until then to embrace without reservation:

> How can I find the proper words to describe what I felt at that moment? A strong impulse lifted my soul to the cross on which Jesus died. I cannot call it other than an impulse, like that which carries one toward an absent friend, someone who loves dearly, making a connection that is more intense, more real than one would have imagined. My soul drew nigh to the incarnate, the crucified One, and at that moment I knew what Faith was. (9:240)

This mystical union with Christ is therefore the moment of her "rebirth," and it is while looking back over the divide between her "new" and former selves that she writes the "Confessions."

Goethe has thus given us a remarkably credible and detailed portrait, revealing a much more fully rendered personality than had ever previously been the case in either philosophical or fictional evocations of the beautiful soul. As the preceding account should have made clear, she is also presented with far too much sympathy and care to support the contention that Goethe merely wished to mock her behavior as nothing more than the compensatory conduct of a sexually repressed neurotic.[20] But it is also striking how little she seems to resemble the noble ideal that serves as her namesake. Oddly, this was a discrepancy noted by only a few contemporary readers. In a letter that Wilhelm von Humboldt wrote to Schiller on 4 December 1795, for example, he complained that she is "only very figuratively speaking a beautiful soul, and rather a petty, vain, and limited soul that has only a few larger aspects." Partly out of loyalty to Schiller, whom Humboldt adored, and partly because his own notions about moral beauty owed more to the Greek conception than to the Pietistic one, Humboldt could not subscribe to Goethe's rendition of the Beautiful Soul.[21] Trying to locate more precisely the source of his own dissatisfaction, Humboldt went on to suggest that to

20. Cf. Friedrich Strack, "Selbst-Erfahrung oder Selbst-Entsagung? Goethes Deutung und Kritik des Pietismus in 'Wilhelm Meisters Lehrjahre,'" in *Verlorene Klassik? Ein Symposium*, ed. Wolfgang Wittkowski (Tübingen: Max Niemeyer, 1986), 52–78; see also Michael Bell, "Narration as Action: Goethe's 'Bekenntnisse einer schönen Seele' and Angela Carter's *Nights at the Circus*," *German Life and Letters* 45 (1992): 22.
21. In view of this sympathetic affinity for the Greek conception, it is interesting that the great classical scholar Friedrich August Wolf once referred to Humboldt, who was himself an amateur philologist of no small distinction, as a "kalos kagathos." See Conrad Bursian, *Geschichte der classischen Philologie in Deutschland von den Anfängen bis zur Gegenwart* (Munich: R. Oldenbourg, 1883), 2:589.

have, as Goethe's figure does, "a completely isolated, eternally ill imagination, which is accompanied by coldness and a complete lack of true and
profound feeling; to have neither enough strength to feel enthusiasm in a
bold and great manner, nor enough ease and grace to produce beautiful
images: that is the most sterile thing one can imagine, and a character who
rests solely on such an imagination must necessarily be unpleasant and
dull."[22] Humboldt's censure is undoubtedly too strong and says more perhaps about his own predilections than about the character in question. But
he nevertheless put his finger on a crucial issue: namely, the marked paucity
of the "Beautiful Soul's" imagination (*Einbildung*), or more specifically her
inability to call forth a wealth of mental images (*Bilder*) to describe her inner
life. Although the linguistic link is not apparent in English, this poverty is
etymologically and conceptually related to the larger matter of *Bildung* itself.

Now a certain concept of *Bildung* obviously played an important role in
how the Pietist "rebirth" itself was conceived. In 1709, for instance, Gottfried Arnold published the *Wahre Abbildung des inwendigen Christentums* (True
depiction of inner Christianity), in which he stated that the soul had "to be
completely re-formed [*umgebildet*] and re-born." Arnold declared that we
must literally become inwardly "de-formed" (*entbildet*) in order to allow
Christ to enter our soul, which will then be formed (*gebildet*) in his likeness
(*Ebenbild*).[23] But Goethe's Beautiful Soul is never explicit about the actual
object or outcome of her own transformation; on the contrary, she appears
completely unable to give even an approximate notion of its nature. She
never refers to Christ as an "Ebenbild," much less does she render him in
the erotically saturated language used by many Pietists to describe their
spiritual experience. Instead, she typically, and here symptomatically, speaks
merely of an "Invisible Being." And at the significant juncture when she tries
to convey her state of mind when she experienced her conversion, she even
balks at the necessity of using figural language at all to represent emotional
phenomena: "Why must we always resort to images [*Bilder*] of external
conditions in order to speak of such innermost things?" (*WMA*, 9:239).

22. Cited in Goethe, *Werke*, 7:657–58.
23. Cited from Vierhaus, "Bildung," in *Geschichtliche Grundbegriffe*, 1:510. It is uncertain
whether Goethe knew this particular work by Arnold, but he certainly knew Arnold's most
famous book, the *Unparteyische Kirchen- und Ketzer-Historie* (Impartial history of heresy in the
Church) of 1699–1700, which he read and said "greatly influenced" him at the time of his
illness and first acquaintance with Katharina von Klettenberg. Goethe even noted that
Arnold's "sentiments were very much in agreement with mine"; see *Poetry and Truth*, part 2,
4:261. Interestingly, in 1794, while he was working on the revisions to *Wilhelm Meister*,
Goethe had this book sent to him in Weimar from his father's library in Frankfurt; see *Werke*,
9:759. For additional information on the relationship between the young Goethe and
Arnold, see Richard Brinkmann, "Goethes 'Werther' und Gottfried Arnolds 'Kirchen- und
Ketzerhistorie.' Zur Aporie des modernen Individualitätsbegriffs," in *Versuche zu Goethe:
Festschrift für Erich Heller, Zum 65. Geburtstag am 27.3.1976*, ed. Volker Dürr and Géza von
Molnar (Heidelberg: Lothar Stiehm, 1976), 167–89.

Finally, she capitulates before the ineffable and indicts language altogether, saying simply that "words fail us when we have such feelings. I could clearly distinguish what I felt from any fancies of the mind—there were no imaginings, no images [*Bilder*], and yet what I felt had the certainty of being attached to something definite" (9:240). A few lines later she similarly remarks that her "joy was beyond description."

This seemingly imageless inner condition of the Beautiful Soul need not have had a negative connotation. From the beginnings of Christianity, the demons of idolatry had restlessly pursued the pious conscience. And Protestantism as a whole had always had a different, and usually a much more critical, relationship to iconic representations of the Divine than had been the case in the Catholic Church. In the eighteenth-century religion of Greece, as well, it was not unusual to encounter the claim, as Winckelmann once reminded his readers, that "the Highest has, as Plato says, no image [*Bild*]."[24] But the absence of such "Bilder" in the Beautiful Soul is a symptom of a deficiency, not a sign of epiphanic plenitude, Platonic or otherwise. For she has no mental images because of her increasing isolation from their real source, namely, the external, physical world.[25] Even in basic epistemological terms (which Goethe, despite his wary avoidance of metaphysical speculation, also certainly knew), such a radical reduction of sensual stimuli inevitably creates a kind of cognitive imbalance, leaving the purely reflective faculties of thought bereft of the material they require to produce and process knowledge. This divorce from the physical sphere that ordinarily supplied the concrete ingredients of the imagination is further symbolized by the Beautiful Soul's troubled rapport with her own body. Once more emphasizing the difficulties of communication that this willful alienation from the senses produces, Goethe had her say that in "my many sleepless nights I had a feeling which I find hard to describe. It was as if my soul were thinking without the body; it looked on my body as a being foreign from itself, the way one views, say, a dress" (*WMA*, 9:252–53). She has become, as her name implies, a disembodied form, nothing more than a disconnected "soul," systematically drained of the vital "Bilder" that properly give density and consequence to *Bildung*. This disharmony, or disunion, between body and soul has arisen from an overemphasis on the inner realm and thus acts to disrupt the equilibrium between reason and nature, reflection and sensa-

24. Johann Joachim Winckelmann, *Geschichte der Kunst des Altertums* (Vienna: Phaidon, 1934; reprint, Darmstadt: Wissenschaftliche Buchgesellschaft, 1982), 222; Winckelmann did not indicate where "Plato says" this, but perhaps he was thinking of *The Statesman* 286a, in which Socrates remarks that "to the highest and most important class of existents there are no corresponding visible resemblances."
25. This connection is also made and developed by Stefan Fleischer, "'Bekenntnisse einer schönen Seele': Figural Representation in *Wilhelm Meisters Lehrjahre*," *Modern Language Notes* 83 (1968): 807–20.

tion, or duty and inclination that was necessary to the traditional conception of the beautiful soul. But—and this is decisive—the nature of this particular disjunction also makes it virtually impossible for her ever to escape the solipsistic prison she has thus created.

It is at this point in the narrative that Goethe performed one of the requisite rites in eighteenth-century treatments of the topos of moral beauty. He provided an emblematic, allegorical moment in which the novel comments on its own general significance. But instead of trying to make sense of the beautiful soul by closing the gap between figure and idea, which had always been the purpose of these moments, Goethe drove another wedge into that fissure by using the opportunity to subject the ideal to an explicit critique. In so doing, Goethe could in fact be considered as having merely made manifest a latent negativity that we have noticed before in these scenes of supposedly heightened meaning. Already an intrusive presence within *Wilhelm Meister* as a whole, the lone autobiographical voice of the Beautiful Soul is itself interrupted at this point by the insertion of words spoken by her Uncle. The scene in which their conversation takes place resonates with allegorical significance: the Uncle has arranged the marriage of the Beautiful Soul's sister and he holds the wedding ceremony at his manor. The house, we are told, seems "like a world of its own," and is alive with overt and subtle meaning. Even the Beautiful Soul displays uncharacteristic sensitivity to the eloquence of material things and remarks on entering the house that "the appearance of a well-formed person is as pleasant as the experience of a well-organized household that reveals the presence of an understanding and intelligent host. Just to come into a clean house is a pleasure in itself, even if it is otherwise lacking in taste and over-ornate, for it does show the presence of one aspect of a cultured [*gebildeter*] owner" (9:245). It is thus obvious that in the house, the adequate reflection of the person who has impressed his own mind onto its material form, someone of authority and station will impart some special wisdom. Accordingly, during the festivities, she and her Uncle engage in a discussion that quickly takes a reflective turn, and the Uncle reveals that he applies the same principles to the ordering of his life in general as he does to the arrangement of his living room. He sententiously tells his niece, while using the sorts of metaphors she is incapable of summoning herself:

> The greatest human achievement is no doubt to be able to determine circumstances as much as possible and to allow himself to be determined by them as little as possible. The whole world is spread out before us like a stone quarry before a master-builder, who deserves that name only if he can transform these raw natural materials into something corresponding to the image [*Urbild*] in his mind, with the utmost economy, purposefulness, and sure-

ness. Everything outside of us is just material, and I can well say the same about everything about us: but deep within us there lies the formative power that creates what ought to be, and will not allow us to rest until we have accomplished this in one way or another. You, my dear niece, have perhaps chosen the best part; you have striven to harmonize your moral being, your profoundly loving nature, within itself and with the Supreme Being, although we others are probably not to be criticized if we try to know the full extent of our sensual being and actively attempt to establish its unity. (9:246)

In his tactful yet pointed words the Uncle has outlined his (and, it is generally agreed, part of Goethe's own) vision of meaningful human activity in opposition to the progressively self-absorbed introspection exemplified by the Beautiful Soul. Instead of applying her energies to shaping or changing the world around her, he implies, she has instead privatively limited her activity to an ever more narrow and self-contained province of exquisite but sterile experience. In seeking to perfect her moral self she has neglected her physical person, and her Uncle suggests that in the end she may even compromise her precious virtue by being incapable of withstanding the ordinary sensual desires that are powerless over those who, unlike her, have had constant practice in warding off such carnal enticements. The Uncle explicitly mentions this potential threat in an openly critical comment. "One should not pursue moral cultivation [*Bildung*] in isolation and seclusion," he advises. "We are more likely to find that a person intent on moral culture will have every cause to cultivate his finer sensuality as well as his mind, so as not to run the risk of losing his foothold on those moral heights, slipping into the seductive allurements of uncontrolled fancy and debasing his nobler nature by indulging in idle frivolities, if not worse" (9:248).

But there is reason to believe that Goethe even meant to cast doubt on the kind of virtue that could be attained in this one-sided way. The Beautiful Soul's conversion came about as a result not of true sinfulness, for which she wanted to repent, but merely from an awareness of the mere possibility of sin, thus making her guilt purely imaginary. Her "sin" (which she came to realize, no less, through reading a novel, a fictional form infamous for its promotion of questionable morals) is entirely the product of fancy, which puts the reality of her virtue into justified doubt as well. For although much is made of her ostensible virtue, there is not a single instance throughout the entire "Confessions" in which the Beautiful Soul performs an act that could qualify as a "good" deed or that could even count as common kindness. On the contrary, because of her initially praiseworthy determination to preserve her absolute independence, which then came increasingly to nourish a consuming self-absorption, she has tended to bring unhappiness to others rather than the opposite. If as the Pietists believed, religion and hence morality were eminently practical affairs, then the Beautiful Soul, through her egoistic concern with her own inner life, has thus even failed to adhere to one of the basic articles of her chosen creed.

It is tempting to think that Goethe foresaw the creeping evisceration of the Enlightenment concept of *Bildung*. It is possible to imagine that he designed his portrait of the sickly Beautiful Soul as a warning not only to Wilhelm, who thus learns to avoid that particular path, but also to his future readers, who might otherwise have been inclined to abstract a "method" of self-fashioning from the novel instead of—to borrow her Uncle's image— mining the far richer, though far more sedimented, lodes of life itself. But Goethe may have had another quarry in sight as well. It is conceivable that he saw certain dangers within the very ideal of the beautiful soul itself. Perhaps, that is, Goethe discerned in the idea of moral beauty—then at the crest of its popularity—an inherent tendency toward the vacant aestheticization of the self that *Bildung* can produce when it is not grounded in genuinely ethical being, which is never selfishly sought as a means of private enjoyment, or even abstract satisfaction, but is always a matter of social or communal responsibility carried out in some sort of action. The "Confessions of a Beautiful Soul" would then have become something like an negative *Bildungsroman*, a cautionary morality tale that comments on, but also stands in pointed contrast to, the positive story of Wilhelm's own development. The achievement of moral beauty in the figure of a beautiful soul, which had occupied the center of European ethical consciousness for almost one hundred years as the very expression of consummate virtue, would have thus been reduced in Goethe's novel to a morally—and physically— consumptive condition.

Naturally this radical diminution of a cherished idol aroused Schiller's disapproval (tempered though it was by his deference to Goethe), and in a letter to Goethe he mildly protested that the Beautiful Soul did not deserve her title at all, suggesting instead her niece, Natalie, who will later marry Wilhelm, as a more suitable substitute. Schiller objected that he "wished that the canoness had not taken the predicate of a beautiful soul from her, for only Natalie is actually a purely aesthetic nature" (*Briefe*, 5:8). Relenting finally to Schiller's amicable but insistent prodding, Goethe responded a few days later with the peculiar formulation that "the predicate of 'beautiful soul' will be diverted [*abgeleitet*] to Natalie."[26] In the concluding pages of the novel Goethe fulfilled his promise to Schiller and allowed Natalie's brother, Lothario, to perform this "diversion" by saying:

> It is beyond belief what cultivated [*gebildeter*] people can achieve for themselves and others. . . . My sister Natalie is a living example of this. The ideal

26. Letter from 9 July 1796; cited in Goethe, *Werke*, 7:644.

of human activity which Nature has prescribed for her beautiful soul will always remain unattainable. She deserves this name more than many others —more even, if I may say so, than our noble aunt, who, when our good doctor assembled that manuscript, was the most beautiful personality we knew. But since then Natalie has developed, and everybody must rejoice at such a person." (*WMA*, 9:372).

But this description, and the rendering of Natalie generally, is so strangely noncommittal and even vaguely contradictory that it lacks any real conviction—a sense that the knowledge of how she only belatedly received her epithet merely enforces. Although several scholars have accepted Friedrich Schlegel's opinion that Natalie represented "the most beautiful form of the purest womanhood and goodness,"[27] others have remained less certain. Indeed, some have thought that she is so pallid and devoid of real vitality that she really amounts to an only slightly improved edition of her aunt (whom, incidentally, she is even said to resemble physically), but not a serious "salvation" of Schiller's ideal.[28]

Goethe's preferred notion of human fulfillment, his actual vision of substantial *Bildung*, was in fact much less lofty, but for that more vigorous, than the one entailed by the beautiful soul. In the Uncle's conversation with his pious niece, who strains after and necessarily fails to achieve the Absolute, he distributes some appropriately avuncular advice:

Man is born into a limited situation, he can comprehend aspirations that are simple, readily accessible and precise, and he accustoms himself to using means that are close at hand; but as soon as he branches out from his restricted sphere, he knows neither what he would like to do nor what he is obliged to do, and it is a matter of complete indifference whether he is confused by a multitude of objectives or disconcerted by their loftiness and importance. Either way he will be unhappy at having to strive after something that he cannot combine with ordinary regular activity. (*WMA*, 9:247)

The beautiful soul could not fit into such a program of more limited, but also more realistic, objectives. Goethe promoted an ethical ideal that saw to the pragmatic result, rather than the unknown and unknowable motive, of our actions. Diderot, someone whom Goethe greatly admired, once similarly wrote that "it is not the thoughts, it is the acts which distinguish the good

27. Friedrich Schlegel, *Prosaische Jugendschriften, 1794–1802*, ed. J. Minor (Vienna: Carl Konegen, 1906), 1:180.
28. See Hans Eichner, "Zur Deutung von 'Wilhelm Meisters Lehrjahren,'" *Jahrbuch des Freien Deutschen Hochstifts* (1966): 186–89. The similarity in appearance between Natalie and her aunt is mentioned at the beginning of chapter 3 of book 8, where Natalie and Wilhelm discuss the character of the Beautiful Soul.

man from the wicked one. The secret story of all souls is about the same."[29] Naturally, it is not the case that Goethe rejected *Bildung* itself. He forever affirmed it, but only when it was tempered by authentic moral energy outwardly directed, not when it was diluted by the enervating wish to acquire formal, which is to say a purely aesthetic, perfection of the self. This was a view that Hegel also came to endorse, but one that he addressed at a reach of generality that remained foreign to Goethe's desire for an ethics that was, as the Uncle had plainly put it, "simple, readily accessible and precise."

HEGEL'S *BILDUNG* AND THE BEAUTIFUL SOUL

What Goethe initiated on the novelistic level with his subtle derogation of the pretensions entertained by Natalie's ailing aunt, Hegel completed on the theoretical plane with the devastating description of the beautiful soul that he delivered toward the end of his *Phenomenology of Spirit.* Like the sixth book of Goethe's *Wilhelm Meister,* this section of Hegel's work has also attracted a fair amount of independent critical attention. But discussions devoted to Hegel's attitude toward the beautiful soul have frequently been marked by a disappointing indifference to the historical dimensions of the problem. Most accounts thus center on the internal significance of Hegel's argument alone, and those which venture into the murky waters of historical precedence go no further than Goethe himself or, at most, mention Schiller and other immediate contemporaries.[30] Yet it is impossible to measure the full weight of his achievement without realizing that just as Hegel both absorbed and transcended the Enlightenment at large, he seized upon the beautiful soul as the symbol of enlightened morality and, after acknowledging its necessary but contingent role, laid it to rest with the entire era that had conceived it.

As one might expect with a thinker of his stature and complexity, Hegel did not maintain a simple or even static relationship to the notion of the beautiful soul. Born in 1770 and raised, as were so many other leading

29. Denis Diderot, *Correspondance,* ed. G. Roth and Jean Varloot (Paris: Minuit, 1964), 11:149; cited in Carol Blum, *Rousseau and the Republic of Virtue: The Language of Politics in the French Revolution* (Ithaca: Cornell University Press, 1986), 58.

30. One of the best informed, and one of the briefest, treatments is by Jean Hyppolite, *Genesis and Structure of Hegel's Phenomenology of Spirit,* trans. Samuel Cherniak and John Heckman (Evanston: Northwestern University Press, 1974), 512–17. Almost everyone who discusses the *Phenomenology* comments at least cursorily on the passage concerning the beautiful soul. Typical of the focus I mentioned is the essay by Benjamin C. Sax, "Active Individuality and the Language of Confession: The Figure of the Beautiful Soul in the *Lehrjahre* and the *Phänomenologie*," *Journal of the History of Philosophy* 21 (1983): 437–66. The study by Karlheinz Well, *Die "schöne Seele" und ihre "sittliche Wirklichkeit": Überlegungen zum Verhältnis von Kunst und Staat bei Hegel* (Frankfurt am Main: Peter Lang, 1986), is less helpful than its title promises.

eighteenth-century German intellectuals, in the devoutly Pietistic state of Württemberg, Hegel imbibed as a youth that same heady mixture of religious enthusiasm and a passionate ardor for antiquity which we have so often witnessed before. After attending the prestigious Gymnasium Illustre in his home town of Stuttgart from 1777 to 1788, where he was introduced to the study of the classics and especially of Greece, Hegel studied theology for five years at the University of Tübingen, which then housed, as we know, some of the most influential and prominent Pietistic teachers of the day.[31] Between the poles of these two institutions, with each transmitting powerful though idiosyncratic versions of ancient and Christian culture, Hegel's mind gradually acquired its characteristic form. Indeed, one of his youthful efforts to combine their separate and complementary elements into a unified vision of the world offers a fairly primitive but illuminating instance of what also became his distinctive method of philosophizing. We see a precocious example of this synthesizing tendency in the title of one of his earliest extant essays, "Ueber die Religion der Griechen und Römer" (On the religion of the Greeks and Romans), which he wrote at the age of seventeen.[32] Even more clearly, in a speech that he later gave while serving as rector of the gymnasium in Nürnberg in 1809, but which was still representative of his previous opinions on the subject, he spoke of the benefits of studying Greek literature (which, predictably, he put "in the first place, and Roman in the second") in terms that demonstrate a remarkable fusion of sacred and profane concerns. Hegel explained that

> the perfection and glory of those masterpieces must be the spiritual bath, the secular baptism that first and indelibly attunes and tinctures the soul with respect to taste and knowledge. . . . While the first paradise was that of the human *nature*, this is the second, the higher paradise of the human *spirit*, the paradise where the human spirit emerges like a bride from her chamber, endowed with a more beautiful naturalness, with freedom, depth, and serenity. The first wild glory of its dawn in the East is restrained by the grandeur of form and tamed into beauty.[33]

31. The social and religious background to Hegel's thought has been best described by Laurence Dickey, *Hegel: Religion, Economics, and the Politics of Spirit, 1770–1807* (Cambridge: Cambridge University Press, 1987), esp. 1:33–137. Hegel's relationship to Pietism has recently been examined by Alan M. Olson, *Hegel and the Spirit: Philosophy as Pneumatology* (Princeton: Princeton University Press, 1992), 36–52. For a more focused discussion of Hegel's early education in Stuttgart and Tübingen, see H. S. Harris, *Hegel's Development: Toward the Sunlight, 1770–1801* (Oxford: Oxford University Press, 1972).

32. G.W.F. Hegel, "Ueber die Religion der Griechen und Römer," in *Frühe Schriften I*, vol. 1 of *Gesammelte Werke*, ed. Friedhelm Nicolin and Gisela Schüler (Hamburg: Felix Meiner, 1989), 42–45.

33. See G.W.F. Hegel, "On Classical Studies," in *Early Theological Writings*, trans. T. M. Knox, with intro. Richard Kroner (Chicago: University of Chicago Press, 1948), 324–25; transla-

Besides providing an example of Hegel's virtuosity in wielding vivid and memorable metaphors, the images elaborated in this passage enact precisely that union of contrasts which by then, two years after the *Phenomenology* had appeared, had already become the hallmark of his dialectic. The issue of the metaphorical convergence, as yet unnamed, that Hegel so skillfully evoked is undeniably present in the comparison of Hellas with a nuptial bride. It effortlessly joins the favorite Pietist means of imagining the soul's preparation to receive the Lord Christ with the no less common desire to envision Greece as the virgin soil in which the seeds of Western civilization were first planted, thus spawning European culture from an immaculately pure beginning. Behind, or rather at the intersection of, these potent images, standing like some ghostly apparition that is less fearsome than melancholy in its translucent beauty, is the figure we know so well. But as the middle term in Hegel's grand survey of the progress of Spirit, the beautiful soul had by this time already outlived its purpose, having been integrated in yet another, more comprehensive unity.

Hegel's strongly integrative habit of mind is apparent in his first approaches to the questions that had originally given rise to the discourse of moral beauty. Immediately after leaving the university, Hegel wrote, though never published, a series of essays that are now usually referred to as his *Early Theological Writings*, in which he grappled, among other things, with basic religious issues.[34] But it would be misleading to claim, as Laurence Dickey has done, that "Hegel's chief intellectual concern in the 1790s was not so much with philosophy as with theology."[35] One might more accurately state that Hegel was actually engaged in both at once, but with an even greater concern in view. As he expressed it in his 1795–96 essay *Die Positivität der christlichen Religion* (*The positivity of the Christian religion*), Hegel thought that "the aim and essence of all true religion, our religion included, is human

tion slightly modified. Knox's translation, *Early Theological Writings*, is henceforth cited as "Knox" by page number in text and notes. See also J. Glenn Gray, *Hegel and Greek Thought* (New York: Harper & Row, 1968).

34. As is well known, these essays were first edited and published by Dilthey's pupil and friend Herman Nohl in 1907 as the *Theologische Jugendschriften*, a title that Nohl himself had invented (although, in his defense, he was merely adopting terms Dilthey had used in his *Jugendgeschichte Hegels*). The designation of the essays as "theological" has become, however, the object of some controversy. Georg Lukács, *Der junge Hegel. Über die Beziehungen von Dialektik und Ökonomie* (Zurich: Europa, 1948), 45, rather implausibly but typically called the conception that there was "a youthful 'theological' period in Hegel's life a historical legend created by the reactionary apologists of imperialism." Lukács found a strange bedfellow in Walter Kaufmann, "The Young Hegel and Religion," in *From Shakespeare to Existentialism* (New York: Doubleday, 1960), 130, who flatly asserted that the essays are "antitheological." Charles Taylor, *Hegel* (Cambridge: Cambridge University Press, 1975), 55n, tries to steer a middle course. See also Dickey, *Hegel*, 150–57.

35. Dickey, *Hegel*, 6–7. Dickey also writes that "although Hegel is known primarily as a philosopher, he was basically a theologian *manqué*."

morality."[36] More emphatically still, in another fragment from approximately the same period, he wrote that "the highest purpose of humanity is morality" (*Werke*, 1:70). This was a belief, as we know, that had been consistently upheld by virtually every philosopher who had lived during the century in which Hegel was born. Always the dutiful son, he retained his faith in the central significance of ethical consciousness in human existence for the rest of his life as well.

Not only did Hegel share the Enlightenment's general conviction that morality was the most important problem confronting humanity, he also, and probably inevitably, addressed it from a perspective that bore the distinctive traces of his time. Although Hegel rarely mentioned Kant by name in these youthful writings, Kant's philosophy and especially his ethical thinking as he set it forth, in particular, in his *Religion within the Limits of Reason Alone* of 1793, formed the framework on which Hegel hung the armature of his own burgeoning philosophy. But in a fashion entirely typical of Hegel's thought more generally, he managed even here, in these earliest fragments, simultaneously to incorporate, criticize, and transcend the teachings of his mentors.

Following most eighteenth-century theologians, Hegel distinguished in these essays "natural" from "positive" (or revealed) religion, and he assigned to each a similarly conventional value. Calling the first "subjective," and the institutional variety "objective," Hegel felt that true religion—and thus true morality—originally sprang from the subjective realm of the heart, only to have been subsequently codified by the "objective" laws and regulations of the Church.[37] Clarifying and propagating these abstract laws, which as such appealed solely to the understanding, constituted the task of religious instruction and moral philosophy as they were understood during the Enlightenment. Kant's ethical philosophy, which Hegel saw as the modern culmination of this historical development, had thus demanded a rigid adherence to the moral law that reason prescribed to itself. "But," Hegel countered, "principles are never made practical through the understanding. . . . To be sure, Enlightenment of the understanding does make one smarter, but not better" (*Werke*, 1:21). To explain to a person in the most exact and rational terms why virtue was necessary for happiness will never cause that person, in the heat of some violent or nefarious passion, to adopt a more virtuous course. "Let us therefore not be alarmed if we find we have to believe that sensuality is the main element in all human actions and aspirations" (1:10).

36. G.W.F. Hegel, *Die Positivität der christlichen Religion*, in *Werke*, ed. Eva Moldenhauer and Karl Markus Michel (Frankfurt am Main: Suhrkamp, 1970), 1:105. See Hegel, *The Positivity of the Christian Religion*, in Knox, 68. Moldenhauer and Michel's edition of Hegel's *Werke* is henceforth cited as "*Werke*" by volume and page number in text and notes.
37. For a clear overview, see Raymond Keith Williamson, *Introduction to Hegel's Philosophy of Religion* (Albany: SUNY Press, 1984).

With that statement, in which the fundamental role of sensation in the motivation of moral behavior was not just recognized, but positively endorsed, Hegel seemed to have moved closer to Hume than to Kant, but in reality he had already left both behind.

Although the influence of the British moral philosophy on Hegel is hardly emphasized in the critical literature on his thought, it was stronger than most have apparently been willing to grant.[38] But given his insistence on the role of sensation in moral judgment, it should not surprise us to find Hegel claiming that "nature has sunk a germ of the finer sensations that stem from morality into every human being; she has placed in everyone a sense for the moral [*Sinn fürs Moralische*] for purposes other than mere sensuality. To prevent these beautiful germs from suffocating and to foster a true receptivity for moral ideas and sensations is the task of education, of *Bildung*" (*Werke*, 1:15–16). Elsewhere in these essays Hegel similarly spoke of the essential contribution of "moral feeling" and of "conscience" as "the inner sense for right and wrong" (1:18). And Hegel's knowledge, or at any rate his awareness, of the larger tradition that supplied the context for these concepts emerges from another early essay in which he praised those "men who developed the idea of morality purely from their own heart and saw therein, as if in a mirror, its beauty and became enchanted by it and whose souls were filled with respect for virtue and moral greatness—for example Spinoza, Shaftesbury, Rousseau, Kant" (1:74). For good reason, Hegel prided himself on his omnivorous reading habits, and these sketches read as if they were intended as synopses of the philosophical issues we have been pursuing in these pages. Hegel was thus not only acquainted with the various strains of thought that had contributed to the Enlightenment conception of moral beauty, he also formulated his own response to the moral dilemma it was designed to resolve by using the same conceptual resources as his predecessors.

But he did not come to the same conclusions. Kant had sought to eliminate all nonrational components from his explanation of the derivation of the moral law. Yet when Kant had tried to explain how it was that human beings were actually motivated to follow the dictates of practical reason, he betrayed the systematic consistency of his theory by appearing to resort to an enlistment of inducements drawn from just that sphere he had wanted to exclude. Hegel's solution to this dilemma was to attempt to overcome this strict dichotomy, and thus Kant's dilemma, by positing a mediating term that would combine both emotional elements and rational principles. To

38. Perhaps this is due to that general lack of interest in eighteenth-century moral philosophy as a whole which we have noted so often before. In the preface to his book *Hegel's Ethical Thought* (Cambridge: Cambridge University Press, 1990), xiii, Allen W. Wood flatly states that "Hegel's ethical theory has been neglected."

satisfy these requirements of abstract universality and subjective, immediate interest Hegel proposed the concept of "love." With more *élan* than originality, Hegel defined love as an inherently unifying force that could overcome the separation of body and mind and, more important, could even bridge the destructive chasm between individuals in society. Love is, of course, at once a profoundly Platonic and Christian notion, but Hegel used it for his own very specific philosophic purposes. Resisting Kant's rational dogmatism, Hegel remained convinced that the sensual, or "empirical," side of humanity had to be included in any viable moral program, and that love possessed the particular advantage of being structurally similar to Kant's universal law in that it is by definition nonegotistical. Love can only be realized, that is, by being given to someone else. But its main advantage is its ability to unify, or reconcile, the rational and emotional sides of human nature. "The fundamental principle of the empirical character is love, which has something analogous to reason insofar as love finds itself in other people, or, rather, by forgetting itself, love takes itself out of its own existence and, as it were, lives, feels, and acts in others—just as reason, as the principle of universally valid laws, recognizes itself in every rational creature as a fellow citizen of an intelligible world" (1:30). Although Hegel did not expressly say so at this point, and perhaps did not even realize it yet fully himself, his simple yet elegant suggestion of basing morality on love had thus just rendered the beautiful soul defunct.

But the concept of love did more than simply fulfill the demand for sensible motivation *and* intrasubjective universality that contemporary moral philosophy had created; it superseded that very frame of reference by making the rigid division between those two spheres blur and thus disappear. The idea of moral beauty, when it is understood properly, had represented the attempt to effect what amounted to no more than a reconciliation of sorts between the tug of inclination and the admonition of duty, with the hope that—in time—both would converge in practice. It was understood as the best and perhaps even the only real way of harnessing these two tendencies, which ordinarily conflicted more often than not. By striving to attain beauty of soul—that state of peaceful inner harmony in which the mind and the passions are meant to achieve a calm equilibrium, producing happiness in oneself and radiating benevolence toward others—one tried to achieve something like a spiritual armistice within oneself. But there was forever the danger that hostilities between the once-warring factions would break out again. Hegel's concept of love, besides inherently negating this threat, completely erased the boundary between, rather than simply held in check, the noumenal and physical halves of humanity.

More important still, however, and marking the greatest advance over the mainly inward focus of moral beauty, was the potential ability of love to overcome that even wider gulf dividing individuals within a larger transpersonal community. Demonstrating how beauty of soul could serve as the basis for social, and not simply subjective, harmony had always been one of the tougher tasks of its apologists. Usually the argument—or more frequently the assumption—was made that, if every person made the effort to become morally beautiful, then the effect on others would necessarily be that they would seek to reproduce the conditions within themselves that would create the pleasurable effect they had experienced while beholding such beauty in others. By dint of emulation, then, a society of beautiful souls would gradually, but inexorably, take shape, accompanied by the desired results of moral goodness in all. Yet as Shaftesbury had unabashedly acknowledged, and Rousseau and Schiller were both compelled to concede, such a society tended toward exclusivity, implicitly consigning those who lacked the means or the will to cultivate their souls in this way to baseness, servitude, and vice. Not only was there this built-in disposition toward the hierarchical formation of small coteries and cliques, the emphasis that the ideal of moral beauty placed on inward refinement made room for, and seemed even to encourage, an atomization of the self even within the breasts of the individual members of such select groups. The alienation that the Beautiful Soul in *Wilhelm Meister* suffers—from society at large, but also from her own physical existence—presents an extreme instance of the divisive consequences of this sort of self-indulgence. In Hegel's alternative conception, by contrast, love would bind all people from every class and station, thus obliterating even those poisonous barriers of prejudice and envy that helped to reinforce human misery and evil.

Although Hegel believed that the ancient Greeks had enjoyed something like this unconscious cultural homogeneity, a social unity that was composed of common and unquestioned beliefs, he clearly perceived its painful absence in modern society. If it were ever to be achieved again, he thought, it would have to be the result of careful moral instruction, of religious teaching; in short, it could take place only as the result of *Bildung*. The idea of *Bildung* in its eighteenth-century—that is to say its primarily *moral*—sense is crucial to Hegel's philosophy, and it occurs with particular frequency throughout these early writings. In view of Hegel's desire to transcend the psychic schism created by the Kantian insistence on a purely rational morality (ignoring for the moment whether Kant himself was able even theoretically to uphold this rigorous distinction), one could predict that Hegel also would have sought to exploit the full metaphorical range of the meaning of *Bildung*.[39] Hegel was not interested in ethical theories that dispensed gener-

39. The two most recent studies that have investigated the central position of *Bildung* in Hegel's thought are John H. Smith, *The Spirit and Its Letter: Traces of Rhetoric in Hegel's Philosophy of "Bildung"* (Ithaca: Cornell University Press, 1988); and although it concentrates largely on the *Phänomenologie*, Donald Phillip Verene, *Hegel's Recollection: A Study of Images in*

al maxims for regulating behavior and thus appealed solely to the intellectual ability to comprehend causes, effects, and other abstract relations. He favored instead an approach that presented strong sensuous images, or *Bilder*, to the imagination (*Einbildungskraft*) as well as one that produced proofs that satisfied reason; Hegel sought, that is, a means of addressing morality that engaged the sensuous and rational capacities at once.

It is here that Hegel's tendentious interpretation of Jesus comes into play. Although Hegel was occasionally quite critical of Jesus, he nevertheless appreciated Christ's historical, and even more his philosophical, significance. "Of very great practical importance," Hegel thus wrote, "is the history of Jesus, not merely his teachings, or those ascribed to him" (*Werke*, 1:81). To explain why it is his life, rather than his doctrines alone, that warrant our attention, Hegel began by citing Plato's dictum that "if virtue would visibly appear among people, all mortals would have to love it" (1:82). Comparing Jesus to that other great teacher of humanity, Socrates, Hegel wanted to show why the Greek philosopher had not become the founder of a popular religion, even though he had similarly devoted himself to the betterment of his fellow citizens. "What is lacking here," Hegel rhetorically asked of Socrates, "for a model [*Vorbild*] of virtue?" (1:82). Both Socrates and Jesus combined impeccable rectitude with sincere humility, both gave hope to the weak and dispossessed by exhorting the value of nonmaterial goods, and both believed in an afterlife. But Socrates detested physical nature, seeing it only as a source of impurity and temptation, and he relied essentially on the intellect alone as the seat of moral knowledge. Most of all, although he was an extraordinary man, he was in the end no more than that: a mortal human being. Jesus, however, represented an amalgam of the human and divine; he was a man and a god at once.

> And precisely the mixture, the addition of the Divine qualified the virtuous person Jesus to become an ideal of virtue—without the divinity of his person we would only have a human being, but here we have a superhuman ideal, which is still not foreign to the human soul, insofar as it has to think of itself as distanced from that ideal. In addition this ideal has the added advantage of not being a cold abstraction; its individualization, which we see speak and act, brings it even closer to our sensibility since it is already related to our mind. Here the faithful see, therefore, no longer a virtuous human being, but virtue itself. (1:83)

It is thus not so much the content of his teachings that was decisive—in another passage Hegel wrote that more or less the same expressions could be found in the works of Plato, Xenophon, and Rousseau (1:85)—rather,

the Phenomenology of Spirit (Albany: SUNY Press, 1985). See also the older work by Carl-Ludwig Furck, *Der Bildungsbegriff des jungen Hegel* (Weinheim: Julius Beltz, 1953).

what was crucial was the visible form and physical presence that Jesus alone gave to an otherwise intangible abstraction. He did not simply practice, he actually provided in his person a *Bild* of what he preached, thus literally offering a *Vorbild* for his followers to emulate, incarnating in an exemplary way both the essence and aim of *Bildung*. Or, as Hegel puts it a few pages later: "Belief in Christ is the belief in a personified ideal" (1:96). In Hegel's early "theological" essays the historical figure of Jesus therefore assumed the categorical position formerly occupied by the philosophical and literary figure of the beautiful soul.

It is difficult to determine whether Hegel deliberately or only intuitively effected this displacement, but the structural similarities between the two figures are striking. For what had the beautiful soul represented other than just such a personification of the ideal of moral beauty? The novels of Wieland and Rousseau had been attempts to dress a set of metaphysical notions in fictional garb with the intention of making those ideas accessible to a broader and more diverse audience; by thus painting, as it were, these concepts in poetic images they aimed to give them substance. This inherent tendency toward concretizing the ideal had reached its extravagant, even fanciful, apogee in Lavater's physiognomical theories, only then to undergo in Goethe's rendition a new intensification and metamorphosis. For Goethe's rendering gave the beautiful soul its most completely realized shape. But he had defined his "Beautiful Soul" by her endeavors to remove herself from precisely that sphere of sense, even in the guise of linguistic *Bilder*, which had been a prerequisite of her existence. In short, at the precise moment that the Beautiful Soul became most real, she desperately tried to rid herself of the very reality that had given her form.

It is this strange dissolution that seemed to result from the opposite desire to make the ideal more concrete that may have prompted Hegel to begin to examine the beautiful soul itself with a more critical eye. His fascination with how contrarieties seemed to veer into one another, despite one's best efforts to hold them apart, was one of the motivating interests behind *The Positivity of the Christian Religion*. In it Hegel mainly wanted to explore why Christianity, which he viewed as having been in his terms a "subjective" religion of morality at its inception, had gradually become ossified into an "objective" or "positive" religion that was no longer ruled by the heart, but by a bureaucratic and authoritarian Church apparatus. Hegel formulated the paradox this way:

How could we have expected a teacher like Jesus to afford any inducement to the creation of a positive religion, i.e., a religion which is grounded in authority and puts man's worth not at all, or at least not wholly, in morals? Jesus never spoke against the established religion itself, but only against the moral superstition that the demands of the moral law were satisfied by obser-

vance of the usages which that religion ordained. He urged not a virtue
grounded on authority (which is either meaningless or a direct contradiction
in terms), but a free virtue springing from man's own being. (Knox 71)

Here and in other passages such as these, Hegel is virtually indistinguishable
from the French *philosophes* he had surreptitiously but voraciously read in
school, and the most recent exciting innovation from France—the
Revolution—may have added a certain political pungency to his advocacy of
absolute freedom in matters of faith. His ideological hatred of the clergy,
and indeed of all organized religion, stemmed for the most part from his
recognition of how organized religion inhibited the development and independent exercise of moral judgment. By internalizing the rules governing
the regulation of conduct imposed by the Church and making one's actions
conform to that preestablished code, one forfeited, according to Hegel,
one's very humanity and practiced nothing but self-deception by willingly
submitting to indoctrination. One easily fell prey, Hegel wrote, to "the belief
that one has the prescribed feeling, that one's feeling corresponds with what
one finds described in the books, though a feeling thus artificially produced
could not possibly be equivalent to the true and natural feeling either in
force or value" (140). (In a revealing aside, Hegel made the acerbic remark
that it was exactly this sort of "system of rules and prescriptions for feelings
which is upheld and practiced by the Pietists more consistently than by
anyone else" [141–42].) The challenge, as he saw it, was to show how to
combine true individual, subjective freedom with binding obedience to the
abstract and generalized moral law. It was in the context of considering how
this fusion could be accomplished that Hegel explicitly discussed the beautiful soul for the first time.

During the final two years of the eighteenth century, Hegel composed
what became his last and greatest theological work, *Der Geist des Christentums*
(The spirit of Christianity). Although he was still largely preoccupied with
the problems of morality that had beset him throughout the early 1790s, he
now employed the tools of analysis he had acquired in those earlier essays
with greater precision and assurance. Returning to the themes he had elaborated in *The Positivity in the Christian Religion*, Hegel grappled again with the
difficulty of achieving the unification of individual, or "particular," inclination with "universal" duty so that neither would predominate over the other.
Anticipating the famous "master-slave dialectic" in the *Phenomenology*, Hegel
wrote here that Kant's solution had been inadequate on several accounts,
but mainly because "in the Kantian conception of virtue this opposition
remains, and the universal becomes the master and the particular the mas-
tered" (214). Even though the source of the moral law for Kant was not
located in the "positive" organization of the Church, but rather in the internal authority of autonomous reason, Hegel still detected here an insidious

subordination of subjective desire to objective imperatives. This situation created yet another enslavement, only this time one that takes place wholly within the breast of the individual. The deprivation of personal freedom in making moral choices in the Kantian system thus issued entirely, though paradoxically, from the subject itself. The subject necessarily—and for Hegel intolerably—became, so to speak, a slave to its own commands. The moral religion preached by Jesus, however, which had lent the spirit of Christianity its original power, conjoined these and other conflicting demands by resolving them, as Hegel wrote, into the various "modifications of love" (225). Love, Hegel's fundamental principal of unification, of reconciliation—in a word, of synthesis—thus returned in this essay as the harbinger of both cognitive and social harmony. One of most important among the liberal expressions of love was the act of "forgiveness," and Hegel demonstrated how this procedure worked in practice in his discussion of punishment and fate.

Although there are, naturally, many structural similarities between these two forms of forcing atonement for having transgressed against some law, fate has a greater effective compass than punishment since fate can visit pain and suffering on someone who is completely innocent of any crime.[40] Punishment is meted out by a specific human agent, but fate is diffuse to the point of being identical with life itself. There is the further peculiarity of fate that one can either bear it patiently and passively in silence or courageously attempt to defend oneself against unjust treatment. Hegel, forever in search of ways to reconcile antagonisms, saw an answer to this dilemma in moral beauty. "The truth of both opposites, courage and passivity, is so unified in beauty of soul that the life in the former remains though opposition falls away, while the loss of right in the latter remains, but the grief disappears. There thus arises a transcendence of right without suffering, a living free elevation above the loss of right and above struggle" (Knox, 235). If a situation arises in which someone or something tries to take away our possessions and we resist this attempt, we thereby automatically enter a relationship that defines *us*, rather than one that we actively determine, and depending on the outcome we will either cause or endure submission, a condition hateful to Hegel. By freely giving up whatever that external agent wishes to take away, however, or by forgiving the trespasses of others, the beautiful soul is able to preserve its autonomy intact. The blows of fate therefore strike a cheek that willingly offers itself, and by thus withdrawing from the scene of confrontation, by forgiving the aggressor, the integrity or unity of the self is preserved and protected. But Jesus, Hegel argued, took

40. See the discussion of this issue in Williamson, *Introduction to Hegel's Philosophy of Religion*, 53–55.

this maxim to its most radical conclusion: Jesus urged that if misfortune were to grow so great that it threatened the preservation of life itself, then this too—our very existence—must be gladly surrendered. As Hegel glossed this final sacrifice made in the name of absolute self-determination: "Beauty of soul has as its negative attribute the highest freedom, i.e., the potentiality of renouncing everything in order to maintain one's self" (236). To avoid being placed in another person's power, or in order to prevent any restriction of one's own liberty, it may be necessary to retreat so far that the only remaining option is to leave the life that is being impinged upon. Suicide, so it appears, or at least the willing relinquishment of one's own life, is the ultimate but consequential outcome of the beautiful soul's existence.[41]

Hegel's attitude toward this seemingly inexorable self-destruction is punctuated by a curious ambivalence, for it is clear that in theoretical terms the beautiful soul enabled at least a temporary reconciliation of the myriad contradictory requirements of virtue that he had identified in his moral philosophy. But the inner logic of moral beauty, as Hegel had described it, appeared to set a sequence of events into motion that, once started, could end only in the sort of radical dematerialization that we witnessed, for example, in the Beautiful Soul of *Wilhelm Meister's Apprenticeship*. Her desire for complete freedom and independence, even from the objects of sense, led to an inward withdrawal and a kind of self-cancellation that might very well be understood as a form of social suicide. (The parents of her niece, Natalie, perhaps reasonably concerned about the nature of the influence exerted on their children by the Beautiful Soul, eventually forbade them from visiting her, thus further increasing her isolation.) But in *The Spirit of Christianity*, Hegel had not yet completely rejected either the beautiful soul or the more general idea of the existence of moral beauty. And where he remained ambiguous with regard to his estimation of the final fate of Jesus, he showed no such hesitation about the only other "schöne Seele" to appear in the book. Indeed, the act carried out by this other person, Hegel asserted, was very much a "*kalon ergon*, a beautiful action—the only action in the history of the Jews that deserves the attribute *kalon*" (*Werke*, 1:311). This deed, which remained so singular, and so singularly meritorious, was performed, he wrote, by "the famous beautiful sinner, Mary Magdalene" (Knox, 245). Thus, according to Hegel, the only other person in the Bible in addition to Jesus who deserved the designation normally reserved for those who had risen to the highest level of human virtue was, in other words, a former prostitute.

This conclusion would be even more provocative than it already is had we

---

41. I thus disagree with the comment by Taylor, *Hegel*, 62, who claims that in "Hegel's portrait of Jesus' withdrawal is meant to be merely strategic, not ultimate."

not already seen several prostitutes appear in similar circumstances. It is improbable that Hegel was thinking of Agathon's hetaera, Danae, here, and in all likelihood he never knew of the essay containing Humboldt's scurrilous musings on the matter. He did not have to: Hegel had his own reasons for making this connection. That he did gives rise to the suspicion that the association between moral beauty and retailed love is more than coincidental. Given Hegel's theoretical commitment to overcoming oppositions, the very piquancy of this juxtaposition must have stimulated his interest. Even in formal terms, moreover, the biblical tale uncannily lent itself to his purposes. By borrowing his illustration from the Bible—the *Urtext* of Christian allegorical exegesis and the ethical breviary for European culture—Hegel conveniently found himself in the position of being able to follow the time-honored practice of relating, or in this case retelling, a story in order to present his readers with a beautiful soul.

When the guilt-ridden Mary Magdalene learns that Jesus is dining at the home of a prominent and respected Pharisee, she forces her way into the house and, on reaching Jesus, falls weeping to the ground and covers his feet with tears of remorse, which she then drys with her own hair. Scandalized by this intrusion, the host asks Jesus whether he knows what sort of woman he has allowed to approach him. In response, Jesus calmly says that although this woman had greatly sinned, she had also greeted him with more love than the host had shown to him. "Why do you trouble her?" Jesus asks in Hegel's rendition of the episode. "She has done unto me a *beautiful* deed" (Knox, 245). Showing how her past had been turned into a source of redemption, and drawing on his own philosophy of love, Hegel explained that "she is forgiven her many sins, Jesus says, for she has loved much" (244). The very enormity of her transgressions required an extraordinary act of contrition, an extreme effort of will—or as Jesus says, a pure instantiation of love. In other words, the same means by which Mary Magdelene sinned thus became the medium by which her sins were sublated.[42] Her "beautiful deed" is therefore the expression of this cancellation of contrarieties in her breast through all-embracing love. Already the preeminent expression of the fusion of sensuality and spirit, love here provided the theoretical cement to join the rent halves of humanity itself. So great is the redemptive power of this principle, Hegel implied, that it was able to bridge the gap between guilt and forgiveness, and could even overcome the ultimate division between life and death. Just as Jesus tells Mary Magdalene that she should "go in peace,

---

42. See Werner Hamacher, "*pleroma*—zu Genesis und Struktur einer dialektischen Hermeneutik bei Hegel," in G.W.F. Hegel, *"Der Geist des Christentums": Schriften 1796–1800, Mit bislang unveröffentlichten Texten,* ed. Werner Hamacher (Frankfurt am Main: Ullstein, 1976), 179–80. "Sublation" is the rather artificial word commonly used to render the untranslatable Hegelian term *Aufhebung*, which simultaneously means to lift up, cancel, and preserve.

your faith has saved you," so too he tells his disciples that with her tears "she has . . . anointed me for my burial in advance" (Knox, 245). Jesus, who would himself soon follow the logic of moral beauty to its suicidal end, thus allowed himself to be readied for his journey from earthly existence into the realm of pure spirituality by a person who was defined by her extensive involvement in pure carnality. Driving Hegel's argument to its finest and most scandalous point, one might say that Jesus was prepared for his impending physical death on the cross by a practiced executioner of *la petite mort.*

The dialectical bravura of the essay on the *Spirit of Christianity* is heightened by Hegel's exploitation of the iridescent instability of its denouement. In the end, one is left with the uncertain feeling that although Hegel seemed to admire the beautiful soul, he had also somehow transformed it here into an object of mild contempt. It was not, however, until the publication of his monumental philosophical *Bildungsroman,* the *Phenomenology of Spirit,* in 1807 that Hegel finally achieved his mature position regarding the beautiful soul.[43] The book is notoriously difficult, even impenetrable in parts, but it rewards the patient reader with, among many other things, an insight into Hegel's profound meditation on the problems of Enlightenment ethics. In end of the section devoted to his exposition of Spirit, Hegel once more confronted, without saying so directly, the inconsistencies that had plagued Kant's moral philosophy and which Kant had tried to escape by resorting to that equation of moral goodness with beauty which had been central to theoretical ethics since the beginning of the century. Hegel cast doubt on each of the terms that composed the Kantian system, first among them his conception of an absolutely purely rational concept of duty, devoid of any element of personal interest or subjective inclination, according to which all moral action was to be performed. Hegel argued that this very idea contained a debilitating contradiction, for in order to be absolutely pure, such a consciousness of duty *could not act,* because to act would be to sully oneself with reality, which is of course the antithesis of pure reason. But action is the very essence of morality; virtue only exists insofar as it is realized in concrete deeds and actions. Yet if one may disregard for the moment this external division, Hegel showed that it becomes clear that even in terms of its internal coherence, the theoretical goal of establishing inner purity or perfection is itself already an impossibility. Perfection by definition cannot be limited, it cannot be confined to only one aspect of our nature, but must encompass the entirety of experience and establish a true reconciliation of reason and sense. Inner perfection, by contrast, seeks by that adjectival qualification to establish just such a limitation and, moreover, it inexorably

---

43. Kaufmann, *Hegel,* 158, was the first to use this term in relation to the book, saying it "is the *Bildungsroman* of the *Weltgeist,* the story of its development and education."

tends in a direction that we have already repeatedly witnessed, namely toward dissolution. Thus, understood in this sense, Hegel wrote, "to advance in morality would really be to move towards its disappearance. That is to say, the goal would be the nothingness or the abolition . . . of morality and consciousness itself, but to approach ever nearer to nothingness means to diminish."[44] Not only was this sort of morality not perfect—for how could it be?—it was and had to remain decidedly imperfect, and "imperfect morality is therefore impure, or is immorality" (380).

Whereas Kant had been satisfied merely to discount the idea of perfection as being empty and thus useless in determining the ground of morality, Hegel took the further and wholly unprecedented step of declaring that the idea, and the desire to strive after it, was actually inherently immoral. Sounding as if he were preparing a summary of the numerous ethical treatises that we have traversed, Hegel declared that this immoral creature of virtue had a particular name and pattern of behavior:

> It lives in dread of besmirching the splendour of its inner being by action and an existence; and, in order to preserve the purity of its heart, it flees from contact with the actual world, and persists in its self-willed impotence to renounce its self which is reduced to the extreme of ultimate abstraction, and to give itself a substantial existence, or to transform its thought into being and put its trust in the absolute difference [between thought and feeling]. The hollow object which it has produced for itself now fills it, therefore, with a sense of emptiness. Its activity is a yearning which merely loses itself as consciousness becomes an object devoid of substance, and, rising above this loss, and falling back on itself, finds itself only as a lost soul. In this transparent purity of its moments, an unhappy, so-called "beautiful soul," its light dies away within it, and it vanishes like a shapeless vapour that dissolves into thin air. (400)

This description can have come only as a shock to those few contemporary readers who made it this far in the *Phenomenology*. The favorite model of eighteenth-century moral existence, the culminating moment of Enlightenment ethical exertion, had been found guilty of being covertly evil, and the punishment, which it perversely carried out itself, was a slow, but ineluctable, death. In fact, owing to the representative status of the beautiful soul, it must have seemed as if Hegel had meant to pass sentence on the whole age that had produced it. He certainly showed extreme severity in his judgment of how moral beauty tried to manifest itself. Hegel had ruled that the essence of the beautiful soul was to try to attain inner perfection by con-

---

44. G.W.F. Hegel, *The Phenomenology of Spirit*, trans. A. V. Miller (Oxford: Oxford University Press, 1977), 378.

forming to the pure conception of rational duty, but that this condition was necessarily upset when it became a matter of putting that conception into practice through action, namely, by performing a morally "good" deed. For at that instant the beautiful soul was forced to defile pure reason by contaminating it with antithetical subjectivity, or by engaging in the brute matter of reality. Yet as Hegel determined, "duty without deeds is utterly meaningless" (403). It was an impossible situation, and to pretend otherwise, Hegel warned, was no better than hypocritical.

Hegel abhorred hypocrisy in all of its forms and he insisted repeatedly that "hypocrisy must be unmasked" (401).[45] Although it may seem unfairly censorious to accuse all of the eighteenth-century advocates of the beautiful soul of having been nothing but hypocrites, it is nevertheless true that this ability to overlook certain discrepancies in one's own behavior or thought had characterized every previous attempt to give expression to the ideal. Rousseau's *Julie* remained the most extreme example of this peculiar form of clear-sighted blindness, but even Wieland remained sensitive yet vulnerable to the reproach of having tried to seem to be something other than what he was. With Lavater the issue had assumed a new, more disturbing dimension, for he had to work even harder to suppress the evidence that placed the thesis of moral beauty in doubt because he was the first to test it on real human beings and not just on fictional or philosophical fantasies. But it was Schiller who, owing to the greater acuity of his mind, coupled with his even more profound need to believe in the idea, had shown the strains of upholding it with unforgiving, though unintentional, clarity. At the end of his essay "Über Anmut und Würde," Schiller himself came to the realization that the beautiful soul could maintain its carefully calibrated equilibrium of reason and sensuality only when it remains in a state of calm passivity. As soon as it has to engage actively in the world around it—as soon as it attempts to become a viable moral force—it has to relinquish precisely those qualities which constitute its very character. "Agreement with the law of reason," Schiller also recognized, "is thus not possible under the assault of the affects except by contradicting the demands of nature."[46] The balance is disturbed, perfection marred, and beauty spoiled when the beautiful soul actually enters the world, which is neither harmonious, nor perfect, nor especially beautiful. Yet it is this very motion toward concretization that was essential to the beautiful soul as such. But Schiller would not—or could not—accept the consequences of his own conclusion. In desperation, he

---

45. See the perceptive comments by Judith N. Shklar, *Freedom and Independence: A Study of the Political Ideas of Hegel's Phenomenology of Mind* (Cambridge: Cambridge University Press, 1976), esp. 180–96.

46. Friedrich Schiller, "Über Anmut und Würde," in *Sämtliche Werke*, ed. Gerhard Fricke and Herbert G. Göpfert (Munich: Carl Hanser, 1958–59), 5:474.

tried to save the honor of the beautiful soul by marrying it to the concept of dignity, but it proved to be a logical *mésalliance*. As Natalie's Aunt well knew, the beautiful soul has to remain a maiden. But it was also precisely this self-imposed celibacy that condemned her and her lineage to extinction. Held motionless between incompatible alternatives, the beautiful soul had thus become ensnared in the irresolvable aporias that defined it; imprisoned by these inescapable antinomies, the beautiful soul gradually withered away. Hegel described the inexorable progression of this self-immolation this way:

> The "beautiful soul," lacking an *actual* existence, entangled in the contradiction between its pure self and the necessity of that self to externalize itself and change itself into an actual existence, and dwelling in the *immediacy* of this firmly held antithesis—an immediacy which alone is the middle term reconciling the antithesis, which has been intensified to its pure abstraction, and is pure being or empty nothingness—this "beautiful soul," then, being conscious of this contradiction in its unreconciled immediacy, is disordered to the point of madness, wastes itself in yearning and pines away in consumption.[47]

It is—or it should be—obvious that Hegel was not speaking of any particular instantiation of the ideal, nor was he referring to a specific historical personage.[48] He was, instead, addressing the dilemma of eighteenth-century moral philosophy as a whole, merely symbolized by its most representative invention.[49] Hegel had argued that because of the terms with which the beautiful soul, and indeed Enlightenment ethics at large, had been formulated—namely, that the conflicting spheres of reason and sense had to be brought into some semblance of harmony—because of this very demand, the idea could not in fact ever be realized. Yet this realization was essential to it as a moral principle: by definition it had to be practical, or realizable in concrete human action, and Hegel had been the first to see—or the first honest enough to say—that this "self-externalization" not only *did* not but also *never could* occur. The beautiful soul, the unstable sign of "empty nothingness," would quite simply dissolve on contact with life.

47. Hegel, *Phenomenology of Spirit*, 407.
48. It is reductive to imagine, as some commentators have done, that Hegel was merely making a historical reference to Novalis, who did in fact die of consumption. See Emanuel Hirsch, "Die Beisetzung der Romantiker in Hegels Phänomenologie. Ein Kommentar zu dem Abschnitte über die Moralität," *Deutsche Vierteljahrsschrift* 2 (1924): 520. This comparison also served as the basis for the article by J.-Y. Calvez, "L'age d'or. Essai sur le destin de la 'belle âme' chez Novalis et Hegel," *Études germanistiques* 9 (1954): 112–27.
49. Lewis P. Hinchman, *Hegel's Critique of the Enlightenment* (Gainesville: University Presses of Florida, 1984), 179–80, confuses the entire issue when he claims that the beautiful soul "stands for every attempt to recapture the lost wholeness of our lives by taking refuge in attitudes, forms, and customs that enlightenment had made impossible for us."

Hegel would not have been the thinker that he was, however, if he had merely left matters there. Immediately after performing last rites over the concept, he sought to console his readers with the promise that it had not died in vain. The very fact that it had passed away meant that a new, and previously unknown or unarticulated, possibility presented itself; the death of the beautiful soul opened a way to look at questions that went beyond the artificial boundaries separating the realms of subject and object, reason and sense, body and soul, and even good and evil. "The word of reconciliation is the *objectively* existent Spirit, which beholds the pure knowledge of itself *qua* absolutely self-contained and exclusive *individuality*—a reciprocal recognition which is *absolute* Spirit."[50] Although Hegel had therefore absorbed the figure into his larger conception of the absolute knowledge of the Spirit, and the beautiful soul had of course ceased to be what it was, Hegel could not pretend that it had never existed all. Thus although the beautiful soul did not survive, it did not entirely vanish either; it remained an important, though superseded, moment in Hegel's version of the development, or *Bildung*, of Spirit, which ultimately culminates in the self-awareness of God. "The 'beautiful soul' is its own knowledge of itself in its pure, transparent unity—the self-consciousness that knows this pure knowledge of *pure inwardness* as Spirit. It is not only the intuition of the Divine but the Divine's intuition of itself. Since this Notion holds itself firmly opposed to its realization, it is the one-sided shape which we saw vanish into thin air, but also positively externalize itself and move onward" (483).[51] The beautiful soul—which had provided to the Enlightenment imagination an absolute ideal of moral existence, one that no individual may completely achieve, but which no one should spare any effort to attain—no longer represented such a goal in Hegel's phenomenology, but at best a transitory stage.

During the decades that followed the publication of the *Phenomenology*, Hegel's thought continued to develop in new directions, even to the extent that he appeared to negate much of what he had set forth in that first great work. But he never changed his fundamental opinion about the beautiful soul itself. In his lectures on aesthetics, for example (which, although given in the mid-1820s, only began to be published four years after his death in 1831), Hegel again briefly mentioned the subject, but with no less disapproval than he had displayed almost two decades earlier:

There is an elevation and divinity of soul which in every way comes into a perverse relation with actuality, and the weakness which cannot endure and

50. Hegel, *Phenomenology of Spirit*, 408.
51. See the discussion of this transcendence, or sublation, of the beautiful soul in the article by Mitchell H. Miller, "The Attainment of the Absolute Standpoint in Hegel's *Phenomenology*," *Graduate Faculty Philosophy Journal* 7 (1978): esp. 202–6.

elaborate the genuine content of the existing world it conceals from itself by the superiority in which it spurns everything as unworthy of itself. After all, to the truly moral interests and sterling aims in life such a beautiful soul is not open; on the contrary, it spins its own web in itself and lives and weaves solely within the scope of its most subjective religious and moral hatchlings. . . . We cannot have any heart for this oddity of heart. For it is a property of a genuine character to have spirit and force to will and take hold of something actual.[52]

To take hold of something actual was just what the beautiful soul, or at least its patrons, had always tried but failed to do. By clearly stating what everyone else refused or was unable to mention, Hegel finally brought the one-hundred-year history of this magnificent, complex, but constitutionally flawed "oddity of heart" to a close.

52. G.W.F. Hegel, *Aesthetics. Lectures on Fine Art*, trans. T. M. Knox, (Oxford: Oxford University Press, 1975), 1:242. Interestingly, in his *Aesthetics* Hegel rejected in similar terms the allegorical mode in art, arguing there that "the first concern of allegory consists in personifying, and therefore conceiving as a *subject*, general abstract situations or qualities belonging to both the human and the natural world. . . . But this subjectivity in neither its content nor its external shape is truly in itself a subject or *individual*; on the contrary, it remains the abstraction of a universal idea which acquires only the empty *form* of subjectivity and is to be called a subject only, as it were, in a grammatical sense. An allegorical being, however much it may be given a human shape, does not attain the concrete individuality of a Greek god or of a saint or of some other actual person, because, in order that there may be congruity between subjectivity and the abstract meaning which it has, the allegorical being must make subjectivity so hollow that all specific individuality vanishes from it." Hegel, *Aesthetics*, 1:399.

Epilogue

D espite Hegel's notoriously self-assured estimate of his own place in the history of thought, the idea of the beautiful soul did not actually vanish from the European mind simply because he had so summarily dismissed it. Throughout the nineteenth century, it continued to play a substantial if often merely supporting role in many theoretical as well as popular accounts of the highest degree of perfection available to merely mortal beings. But there remained the decisive difference that despite these earnest efforts to keep it alive, the beautiful soul no longer represented a truly vital principle. As became increasing clear in the foregoing account, its internal possibilities had been fully probed and completely spent during the previous century. That it remained a part of ethical discourse for so long after it had ceased to promise a viable program says as much about the power of the original notion itself as it does about the intensity of the desire among those who adhered to it to persuade themselves of what they most wanted to believe. Although the beautiful soul thus retained a sizable following well into the industrial age, her new admirers—as opposed to her Enlightenment advocates—tended not to belong to the foremost ranks in the intellectual world. Like provincials who begin to adopt some fashion just as it has become passé in the capital, these later writers self-consciously adorned their thought with the mantle of moral beauty without realizing that to an informed and judicious observer, they had thereby made themselves more than a little ridiculous.[1]

---

1. Nietzsche, arguably the most important moral philosopher of the nineteenth century, completely rejected the beautiful soul, although he was certainly aware of its former status. In one of the sketches from the *Wille zur Macht*, Nietzsche derided the latter-day supporters of the beautiful soul: "They despised the body, they left it out of account; even more, they treated it like an enemy. They were insane enough to believe that one could carry around a

A single example of some of the potential consequences involved in this belated appropriation of the beautiful soul will suffice to illustrate how compromised that category had already become by the beginning of the nineteenth century. One of the most troubling, though as it turned out all too prophetic, instances of this post-Enlightenment enthusiasm for the ideal can be found in the fate of a once well-regarded and now virtually forgotten professor of philosophy by the name of Jakob Friedrich Fries. Born in 1773, Fries led a life that initially reads like that of many others we have encountered before: having received his earliest schooling at the rigidly Pietist institution in Niesky, Fries began studying law in Leipzig in 1795. He transferred two years later to Jena, where he took up philosophy under Fichte and thereby inaugurated his lifelong devotion to Kantian thought. After receiving his doctorate in 1801, Fries gave lectures in Jena alongside of, and apparently deliberately at the same time as, Hegel, who at that point enjoyed far fewer auditors than the highly popular Fries. When he become an *ordinarius* in 1805, Fries accepted an offer of a chair in philosophy at Heidelberg, where he stayed until 1816. During his tenure there he published an impressive number of works on a variety of philosophical subjects. And in 1813 he even tried his hand at writing fiction, which resulted in a book he conspicuously called *Julius und Evagoras; oder, Die Schönheit der Seele. Ein philosophischer Roman* (Julius and Evagoras; or, beauty of the soul. A philosophical novel).[2]

Given Fries's limitations as a thinker, it is unlikely that he was fully awake to the complexity of the tradition he was trying to keep alive. But by casting the beautiful soul in literary form Fries was, even if unconsciously, moving along a path that had been well marked out by his predecessors. He certainly carried his commitment to this ethical ideal into his more professional works as well. In his first major book on ethical philosophy, which appeared in 1818, he stated categorically (citing Schiller for support) that "we will discuss the doctrine of the value of a human life and of a human being's true purpose therein as a doctrine of the *beauty* and *sublimity of the soul,* according to the Greek conception of *kalokagathia.*"[3] In 1832, Fries pub-

---

'beautiful soul' in some cadaverous miscarriage. . . . And to make it comprehensible to others, they had to employ the concept 'beautiful soul' differently, to revalue its natural value, until finally a pale, sickly, idiotically enthusiastic creature was perceived as 'perfection,' as 'angelic,' as transfigured, as a higher form of human being." See Friedrich Nietzsche, "Aus dem Nachlaß der Achtziger Jahre," in *Werke,* ed. Karl Schlechta 3 (Munich: Carl Hanser, 1966), 3:769.

2. This is actually the title of the second edition, which appeared in 1822 and was almost a third longer than the first; see Jakob Friedrich Fries, *Julius und Evagoras; oder, Die Schönheit der Seele. Ein philosophischer Roman* (Heidelberg: Christian Friedrich Winter, 1822), especially the second and third "dialogues," "Die Schönheit der Seele," and "Sittliche Ausbildung des Geistes" (Moral education of the spirit), which were first added to this edition. Parts of the novel have been translated and published as Jakob Friedrich Fries, *Dialogues on Morality and Religion,* ed. and trans. D. Z. Phillips, David Walford, and Rush Rhees (Totowa, N.J.: Barnes & Noble, 1982).

3. Jakob Friedrich Fries, *Handbuch der praktischen Philosophie oder der philosophischen Zweck-*

lished the second part to his moral system, and there he still insisted that "virtue is beauty of the soul: perfection of the spirit and beauty of the spirit are one and the same." He went on to write that one could say that "ethics is the *aesthetics of the beauty of spirit.*"[4] Although Fries never ventured much further than issuing these sorts of very general claims, and although he never substantially amplified the theoretical dimensions of what had by then become a complex and differentiated debate, his views on morality nevertheless exerted a considerable influence on his many disciples, including one of the most important theologians of the early nineteenth century, Wilhelm Martin Leberecht de Wette.[5]

Still, it would be pointless to rehearse the specific details of Fries's notion of the "beauty of the soul." Reading like a brief compendium of eighteenth-century ideas about the subject, his comments amount to a derivative and uncritical review of familiar terrain. Strangely, however, it was this very superficiality that secured Fries his own, albeit ambivalent, measure of notoriety. For he might have disappeared from sight altogether had it not been for a particularly ill-tempered mention of his name in the preface of Hegel's *Grundlinien der Philosophie des Rechts* (Basic principles of the philosophy of right), which appeared in 1821. In drawing the lines demarcating his own thought from that of his contemporaries, which Hegel broadly characterized as having tried to dispense entirely with reason and to rely instead on the "heart, emotions, and enthusiasm," Hegel referred explicitly in a disparaging aside to one "Herr Fries." In particular, Hegel singled out Fries as the "ringleader of these hosts of superficiality" (*Heerführer dieser Seichtigkeit*), a man who so egregiously indulged in sophistic "pettifoggery" (*Rabulisterei*) in his discussions of moral and political questions that he had almost managed to make the name of philosophy itself disreputable.[6] Although Hegel did not mention the beautiful soul itself in his preface, Fries's enthusiastic and unreflective advocacy of the idea—an idea which Hegel had not so much destroyed as he had lain bare the inescapable internal contradictions that prevented its realization—must have only intensified Hegel's sense of the vacuousness of Fries's philosophy.

---

lehre. Erster Theil. Ethik, oder die Lehren der Lebensweisheit (Heidelberg: Mohr & Winter, 1818), § 19, 54.

4. Jakob Friedrich Fries, *Handbuch der praktischen Philosophie oder der philosophischen Zweck-lehre. Zweyter Theil. Die Religionsphilosophie oder die Weltzwecklehre. Handbuch der Religionsphiloso-phie und philosophischen Aesthetik* (Heidelberg: Christian Friedrich Winter, 1832), § 54, 194–95.

5. Although best known in his day for his commentary on and introduction to the New Testament, de Wette also published his lectures on ethics, which culminate in a paean to "intellectual beauty or beauty of the soul." See Wilhelm Martin Leberecht de Wette, *Vorlesungen über die Sittenlehre* (Berlin: G. Reimer, 1824), esp. 2.2: 342–401.

6. G.W.F. Hegel, *Grundlinien der Philosophie des Rechts oder Naturrecht und Staatswissenschaft im Grundrisse*, in *Werke*, ed. Eva Moldenhauer and Karl Markus Michel (Frankfurt am Main: Suhrkamp, 1970), 7:18–20.

But as much as we might tend to agree today with Hegel's accurate, if unusually harsh, description of Fries's thought, Hegel's own reputation came close to suffering irreparable damage as a result of his incautious outburst. The controversy that flared up around Hegel's criticism of Fries's emotionally based moral theory was less philosophical than political. Betraying here his deeper affinities to the Enlightenment, Hegel had insisted in the preface to his *Grundlinien der Philosophie des Rechts* that contrary to Fries's shallow ramblings about "feeling" as the basis of judgment, reality could be comprehended only by *rational* means, and that whatever could be understood rationally thus necessarily constituted reality for us. Hegel remained convinced, in other words, that—so goes the infamous phrase—"what is rational, is real; and what is real, is rational" (24). This statement was seen at once by Hegel's detractors as a brazen apology for the repressive government of the Prussian state, for which Hegel, whom it employed at the university in Berlin, now seemed to have evolved *de facto* into an ideological spokesman. More than thirty years later, the historian Rudolf Haym laid the most serious accusations at Hegel's feet when he described the entire preface to the *Philosophie des Rechts* as being "nothing other . . . than a scientifically formulated justification of the Carlsbad police system and the persecution of demagogues." Haym—a committed liberal writing in the aftermath of the unsuccessful 1848 revolution in Germany—thus interpreted Hegel's thought in a specifically political, if highly tendentious, fashion, and he condemned not just the preface alone but the entire work as containing "the classical statement of the spirit of Restoration, the absolute formulation of political conservatism, quietism, and optimism."[7] And because he appeared to share Haym's own progressive and democratic inclinations, Fries was thus made to emerge as the representative of the liberal opposition that Prussia, symbolized by Hegel, sought to repress by any means at hand.

Yet a closer look at the specific political forces—not to speak of the philosophical ones—that were operative at the time in which both Hegel and Fries were writing will reveal that the matter was not as simple as Haym had most persuasively portrayed it. Of Fries himself Haym had noticeably little to say, except for a sympathetic but otherwise unexplained comment that Hegel's attack deserved even more rebuke for having been unconscionably directed at a man who "was already outlawed by the police" (364). The reason Fries had been "outlawed" was that he had been one of the main speakers at the celebration at the Wartburg Fortress near Eisenach that had taken place on 18 October 1817. The *Wartburgfest* was ostensibly held to commemorate the three-hundredth anniversary of Martin Luther's defiant act of nailing his ninety-five theses to the door of the Schloßkirche in Witten-

---

7. Rudolf Haym, *Hegel und seine Zeit. Vorlesungen über Entstehung und Entwicklung, Wesen und Werth der Hegel'schen Philosophie* (Berlin: Rudolph Gaertner, 1857), 364–65.

berg; it actually served more immediate political ends. In the speech Fries gave at the event, he solemnly exhorted his students to take Luther as an example in their own struggle for "freedom of thought, equality of citizens!"[8] These were unmistakably revolutionary words, and his listeners not only understood, but also in some cases acted on, their political appeal. On 23 March 1819, an activist student by the name of Carl Ludwig Sand gained entrance under false pretences to the house of the dramatist August von Kotzebue, who was widely regarded as a governmental loyalist. Having forced his way to Kotzebue's study, Sand rushed up to the writer and, with an oath to the "Fatherland" on his lips, stabbed him to death.[9] It was a convenient pretext for the authorities to act against the student movement. In the aftermath of this sensational murder, students suspected of collaborating or even sympathizing with Sand were arrested. In the pocket of one such unfortunate young man was a letter from his teacher: F. J. Fries. As a result, and under direct instruction from the Prussian king Frederick William III, Fries was immediately suspended from his teaching duties at Jena and forced into early retirement.[10]

It was against this dramatic backdrop, then, that Hegel pronounced his severe criticism of Fries's philosophy, and from Haym's perspective, it must have seemed both unjust and reactionary indeed. But with even greater historical and emotional distance, Hegel's categorical rejection of Fries and his followers appears in a far different light. For in addition to freedom and equality, Fries also advocated an intensely nationalistic, or at least fervently patriotic, political orientation, and he repeatedly uttered phrases that in hindsight ring eerily familiar. In his address on the Wartburg, for instance, Fries said that "if the spirit of a people [*Volk*] were to achieve a true spirit of community, then there would prevail in this people justice, chastity, and self-sacrificing love of the Fatherland."[11] Even more fervently, Fries dedicated his *Ethik* of 1818 to the "Friends of the Wartburg" and in the preface he exclaimed with affected pathos:

> In this life, the majesty of the virtues of love of the Fatherland and of piousness have newly appeared to us Germans, and their meaning for the life of every individual has become clearer. The German *Volk* should be strengthened in the healthy spirit of the virtues of public life: this is our will and

8. Jakob Friedrich Fries, "Rede an die deutschen Burschen. Zum 18. October 1817," in *Das Wartburgfest am 18. Oktober 1817. Zeitgenössische Darstellungen, archivalische Akten und Urkunden*, ed. Hugo Kühn (Weimar: Alexander Duncker, 1913), 50.

9. See the account in Oscar Mandel, *August von Kotzebue. The Comedy, the Man* (University Park: Pennsylvania State University Press, 1990), 61–63.

10. Fries was allowed to return to the university in 1824, but he was not permitted to teach philosophy, and instead he gave lectures in physics and mathematics. In 1838 he was finally allowed to teach all subjects again. See the *Allgemeine Deutsche Biographie* (Leipzig: Duncker & Humblot, 1875–1912), 18:73–81.

11. Fries, "Rede an die deutschen Burschen," 54.

faith! . . . Thus it is your holy duty, You Germans, that you learn to believe
and trust in the spirit of the German *Volk!*[12]

We might initially be inclined to think that the expression of such *völkisch*
sentiments was typical enough for the time and not necessarily to be read
through the prism of their twentieth-century abuse. Yet other incidents
suggest that Fries used the word "German" in an ominously exclusionary,
and not simply benignly hortatory, sense. Among the assorted events that
took place at the *Wartburgfest,* following the formal procession to the fortress
and the official recitation of prepared speeches, there occurred an act that,
though meant apparently in jest, later assumed a deadly serious value. Some
of the students had brought along a large basket of books that "in their
opinion did not speak to the general mood of the German *Volk.*" Anticipating—or perhaps providing the model for—one of the darkest periods of
German history, the students consigned the offensive volumes to the flames
of a symbolic auto-da-fé.[13] It seems, in retrospect, not entirely accidental
that one of the incinerated books was by Kotzebue, who, as we know, fell
victim to the more literal-minded Sand less than two years later.

It is uncertain how Fries reacted to the book burning. But his general
attitude forces the assumption that he probably was not overly concerned
about its possible implications. On the contrary: a couple of years before the
Wartburgfest, in 1816, Fries had published a review essay that reinforces the
impression that he was more than open to such drastic measures and places
the preceding account into an even more insidious ideological context.
Titled *Über die Gefährdung des Wohlstandes und Charakters der Deutschen durch
die Juden* (On the endangerment of the well-being and character of the
Germans by the Jews), Fries's essay represents a relatively early and thus all
the more disturbing example of the virulent form of anti-Semitism in Germany that soon enough would not be confined to the destruction of books
alone. For here Fries made no secret of the objects of his antipathy: insisting
that Jews neither could nor should ever be assimilated into the German
state, he recommended that "the whole Jewish caste should be extirpated
root and branch" from German society because these "worthless . . . conniv-
ing second-hand peddlers" constituted "the gravest danger to the state."[14]

It would be difficult to decide which is the more painful to observe: the

12. Fries, *Ethik*, v–vi and xii.
13. See the account and the list of the burned books in the "Zugabe des Festes," in Kühn,
Das Wartburgfest, 85–88.
14. Jakob Friedrich Fries, *Über die Gefährdung des Wohlstandes und Charakters der Deutschen
durch die Juden* (Heidelberg: Mohr and Winter, 1816), 3 and 18; cited from Allen W. Wood,
Hegel's Ethical Thought (Cambridge: Cambridge University Press, 1990), 187. This work by
Fries originally appeared in the *Heidelbergische Jahrbücher der Litteratur* as a review of Friedrich
Christian Rühs's *Über die Ansprüche der Juden an das deutsche Bürgerrecht.*

sight of a person performing gestures—rhetorical and otherwise—that little more than one hundred years later, came to cause unprecedented and unspeakable suffering to those human beings whom he had just deemed to be utterly "worthless"; or, looking in the other direction on the temporal axis, the spectacle of a man who had written a novel on the "beauty of soul" here at least implicitly representing that ideal, which for more than a century had defined the quintessence of virtue, in the cause of its very opposite. In his prescient critique of the concept, Hegel himself had already foreseen the danger of this exemplar of moral goodness imperceptibly slipping into an immobile, passive state that in its effects (or rather in its lack thereof) could not be distinguished from moral baseness. In Hegel's view, Fries must have provided no more than concrete evidence of the fundamental correctness of what he had previously envisioned on a plane of great theoretical abstraction in his *Phenomenology*. Indeed, as Fries had demonstrated with brutal though unintentional clarity, the conceptual boundaries of the beautiful soul were so generously drawn, or so poorly defined, that evil itself could find room within its domain.

For us, too, who have attempted to assess the historical progression of the beautiful soul not only as a philosophical or literary ideal, but also as a broadly based social category during the Enlightenment, the Fries affair—as merely the most extreme example among many others—retrospectively casts a somber pall over that entire development. But perhaps for that very reason the beautiful soul can lend us a privileged means of access into the frequently invoked "dialectic" of that era and of its extension into our own. The Enlightenment, with its constitutive emphasis on the power of human reason to influence and change the world, has been forced to account for a great deal in this century that has been committed in its name. What is not often realized, however, is that by subjecting the Enlightenment to unrelenting scrutiny, its critics thereby ensure the continuation of its finest and most indispensible traits. The same might, in the end, turn out to be true of the idea of moral beauty as well: the only hope we may ever have of realizing the promise it held for establishing a binding private and public morality might be to examine critically the causes of its eventual—and probably inevitable—self-destruction and to bid the ideal a final and clear-eyed farewell. Only then may it eventually become possible to appreciate precisely what the eighteenth century has handed to us that we can take into the twenty-first.

Bibliography

Aarsleff, Hans. "The Berlin Academy under Frederick the Great." *History of the Human Sciences* 2 (1989): 193–206.

Addison, Joseph. *The Spectator.* Edited Donald F. Bond. 5 vols. Oxford: Oxford University Press, 1965.

Allgemeine Deutsche Biographie. 56 vols. Leipzig: Duncker & Humblot, 1875–1912.

Altmann, Alexander. *Moses Mendelssohn: A Biographical Study.* Philadelphia: Jewish Publication Society of America, 1973.

——. *Moses Mendelssohns Frühschriften zur Metaphysik.* Tübingen: J.C.B. Mohr, Paul Siebeck, 1969.

Aristotle. *The Athenian Constitution, The Eudemian Ethics, On Virtues and Vices.* Loeb Classical Library. 1935.

——. *Complete Works.* Edited by Jonathan Barnes. 2 vols. Princeton: Princeton University Press, 1984.

Arndt, Johann. *Vier Bücher vom Wahren Christenthum.* Magdeburg: C. L. Faber, 1727.

Astell, Ann W. *The Song of Songs in the Middle Ages.* Ithaca: Cornell University Press, 1990.

Babbitt, Irving. *Rousseau and Romanticism.* Boston: Houghton Mifflin, 1919.

Bachmann-Medick, Doris. *Die ästhetische Ordnung des Handelns: Moralphilosophie und Ästhetik in der Popularphilosophie des 18. Jahrhunderts.* Stuttgart: Metzler, 1989.

Bacon, Francis. *The Essayes or Counsels, Civill and Morall.* Edited by Michael Kiernan. Cambridge: Harvard University Press, 1985.

——. *Works.* Edited by James Spedding, Robert Leslie Ellis, and Douglas Denon Heath. 14 vols. 2d edition. London: Longmans, 1887–1901.

Baeumler, Alfred. *Das Irrationalitätsproblem in der Ästhetik und Logik des 18. Jahrhunderts bis zur Kritik der Urteilskraft.* Halle: Niemeyer, 1923.

Balguy, John. *A Collection of Tracts Moral and Theological.* London: J. Pemberton, 1734.

Bäppler, Klaus. *Der philosophische Wieland: Stufen und Prägungen seines Denkens.* Bern: Francke, 1974.

Barth, Karl. *Protestant Theology in the Nineteenth Century: Its Background and History.* Valley Forge: Judson Press, 1973.

Baruzi, Jean. *Leibniz: Avec de nombreux textes inédits.* Paris: Bloud, 1909.

Baumgarten, Alexander Gottlieb. *Theoretische Ästhetik: Die grundlegenden Abschnitte aus der "Aesthetica" (1750/58).* Translated and edited by Hans Rudolf Schweizer. Hamburg: Felix Meiner, 1983.

Beardsley, Monroe C. *Aesthetics from Classical Greece to the Present: A Short History.* New York: Macmillan, 1966. Reprint, Tuscaloosa: University of Alabama Press, 1975.

Beck, Lewis White. *A Commentary on Kant's Critique of Practical Reason.* Chicago: University of Chicago Press, 1960.

——. *Early German Philosophy: Kant and His Predecessors.* Cambridge: Harvard University Press, 1969.

——. *Kant's Latin Writings: Translations, Commentaries, and Notes.* In collaboration with Mary J. Gregor, Ralf Meerbote, and John A. Reuscher. New York: Peter Lang, 1986.

Becker, Carl L. *The Heavenly City of the Eighteenth-Century Philosophers.* New Haven: Yale University Press, 1932.

Becker-Cantarino, Barbara. "Die 'Bekenntnisse einer schönen Seele': Zur Ausgrenzung und Vereinnahmung des Weiblichen in der patriarchalen Utopie von *Wilhelm Meisters Lehrjahren.*" In *Verantwortung und Utopie: Zur Literatur der Goethezeit,* edited by Wolfgang Wittkowski. Tübingen: Max Niemeyer, 1988.

Beddow, Michael. *The Fiction of Humanity: Studies in the Bildungsroman from Wieland to Thomas Mann.* Cambridge: Cambridge University Press, 1982.

Beharriell, Frederick J. "The Hidden Meaning of Goethe's 'Bekenntnisse einer schönen Seele.'" In *Lebendige Form: Interpretationen zur deutschen Literatur, Festschrift für Heinrich E. K. Henel,* edited by Jeffrey L. Sammons and Ernst Schürer. Munich: Wilhelm Fink, 1970.

Bell, Michael. "Narration as Action: Goethe's 'Bekenntnisse einer schönen Seele' and Angela Carter's *Nights at the Circus.*" *German Life and Letters* 45 (1992): 16–32.

Berglar, Peter. *Wilhelm von Humboldt.* Hamburg: Rowohlt, 1970.

Berkeley, George. *Works.* Edited by A. A. Luce and T. E. Jessop. 9 vols. London: Thomas Nelson, 1948–57.

Bernard of Clairvaux. *On the Song of Songs.* Translated by Kilian Walsh and Irene Edmonds, with an introduction by M. Corneille Halflants et al. 4 vols. Spencer, Mass. and Kalamazoo, Mich.: Cistercian Publications, 1971–80.

Bernstein, John Andrew. *Shaftesbury, Rousseau, and Kant: An Introduction to the Conflict between Aesthetic and Moral Values in Modern Thought.* London: Associated University Presses, 1980.

Bianco, Bruno. "Freiheit gegen Fatalismus: Zu Joachim Langes Kritik an Wolff." In *Zentren der Aufklärung, vol. 1, Halle: Aufklärung und Pietismus,* edited by Norbert Hinske. Heidelberg: Lambert Schneider, 1989.

Blackall, Eric A. *The Emergence of German as a Literary Language, 1700–1775.* Cambridge: Cambridge University Press, 1959.

Blanc, André. "Le Jardin de Julie." *Dix-huitième Siècle* 14 (1982): 357–76.

Blasig, Uwe. *Die religiöse Entwicklung des frühen Christoph Martin Wieland.* Frankfurt am Main: Peter Lang, 1990.

Blum, Carol. *Rousseau and the Republic of Virtue: The Language of Politics in the French Revolution.* Ithaca: Cornell University Press, 1986.

Bode, Wilhelm. *Goethes Schweizer Reisen.* Leipzig: H. Haessel, 1922.

Bolingbroke, Henry St. John. *Works.* 8 vols. London, 1809.

Bowle, Jonathan. *Hobbes and His Critics: A Study in Seventeenth-Century Constitutionalism.* London: Jonathan Cape, 1951.

Boyle, Nicholas. *Goethe: The Poet and the Age.* Vol. 1. Oxford: Oxford University Press, 1991.

Brett, R. L. *The Third Earl of Shaftesbury: A Study in Eighteenth-Century Literary Theory.* London: Hutchinson, 1951.

Brinkmann, Richard. "Goethes 'Werther' und Gottfried Arnolds 'Kirchen- und Ketzerhistorie.' Zur Aporie des modernen Individualitätsbegriffs." In *Versuche zu Goethe: Festschrift für Erich Heller, Zum 65. Geburtstag am 27.3.1976,* edited by Volker Dürr and Géza von Molnar. Heidelberg: Lothar Stiehm, 1976.

Broome, J. H. *Rousseau: A Study of His Thought.* London: Edward Arnold, 1963.

Buck, Günther. *Rückwege aus der Entfremdung: Studien zur Entwicklung der deutschen humanistischen Bildungsphilosophie.* Munich: Wilhelm Fink, 1984.

Bühler, Karl. *Ausdruckstheorie: Das System an der Geschichte aufgezeigt.* With an introduction by Albert Wellek. 2d edition. Stuttgart: G. Fischer, 1968.

Burger, Heinz Otto, ed. *Begriffsbestimmung der Klassik und des Klassischen.* Darmstadt: Wissenschaftliche Buchgesellschaft, 1972.

Burke, Edmund. *A Philosophical Enquiry into the Origin of Our Ideas of the Sublime and Beatiful.* Edited by James T. Boulton. Notre Dame: University of Notre Dame Press, 1968.

Bursian, Conrad. *Geschichte der classischen Philologie in Deutschland von den Anfängen bis zur Gegenwart.* 2 vols. Munich: R. Oldenbourg, 1883.

Calvez, J.-Y. "L'age d'or: Essai sur le destin de la 'belle âme' chez Novalis et Hegel." *Études germanistiques* 9 (1954): 112–27.

Cassirer, Ernst. *Freiheit und Form: Studien zur deutschen Geistesgeschichte.* 1918. Reprint, Darmstadt: Wissenschaftliche Buchgesellschaft, 1975.

———. *The Philosophy of the Enlightenment.* Translated by Fritz C. A. Koelln and James P. Pettegrove. Princeton: Princeton University Press, 1951.

———. *The Platonic Renaissance in England.* Translated by James P. Pettegrove. New York: Gordian, 1970.

———. "Schiller and Shaftesbury." *Publications of the English Goethe Society* 11 (1935): 37–59.

Chytry, Josef. *The Aesthetic State: A Quest in Modern German Thought.* Berkeley and Los Angeles: University of California Press, 1989.

Clarke, G. W., ed. *Rediscovering Hellenism: The Hellenic Inheritance and the English Imagination.* Cambridge: Cambridge University Press, 1989.

Clarke, M. L. *Greek Studies in England, 1700–1830.* Cambridge: Cambridge University Press, 1945.

Colman, John. *John Locke's Moral Philosophy.* Edinburgh: Edinburgh University Press, 1983.

Cooper, John Gilbert. *The Life of Socrates.* 3d edition. London: Dodsley, 1750.

Courtine, Jean-Jacques and Claudine Haroche. *Histoire du visage: Exprimer et taire ses émotions XVIe–début XIX siècle.* Paris: Rivages, 1988.

Cowling, Mary. *The Artist as Anthropologist: The Representation of Type and Character in Victorian Art.* Cambridge: Cambridge University Press, 1989.

Cragg, Gerald R. *Reason and Authority in the Eighteenth Century.* Cambridge: Cambridge University Press, 1964.

Cranston, Maurice. *The Noble Savage: Jean-Jacques Rousseau, 1754–1762.* Chicago: University of Chicago Press, 1991.

Crawford, Donald W. *Kant's Aesthetic Theory*. Madison: University of Wisconsin Press, 1974.

Creery, Walter E., ed. *George Berkeley: Critical Assessments*. 3 vols. London: Routledge, 1991.

Crocker, Lester G. *Jean-Jacques Rousseau*. 2 vols. New York: Macmillan, 1968–73.

Cudworth, Ralph. *The True Intellectual System of the Universe: wherein all the Reason and Philosophy of Atheism is confuted, and its Impossibility demonstrated, with a Treatise concerning Eternal and Immutable Morality*. 3 vols. London: Thomas Tegg, 1845.

Darwin, Charles. *The Expression of the Emotions in Man and Animals*. Chicago: University of Chicago Press, 1965.

de Man, Paul. *Allegories of Reading: Figural Language in Rousseau, Nietzsche, Rilke, and Proust*. New Haven: Yale University Press, 1979.

———. *Blindness and Insight: Essays in the Rhetoric of Contemporary Criticism*. With an introduction by Wlad Godzich. 2d edition. Minneapolis: University of Minnesota Press, 1983.

de Wette, Wilhelm Martin Leberecht. *Vorlesungen über die Sittenlehre*. 4 vols. Berlin: G. Reimer, 1823–24.

Dickey, Laurence. *Hegel: Religion, Economics, and the Politics of Spirit, 1770–1807*. Cambridge: Cambridge University Press, 1987.

Diderot, Denis. *Oeuvres complètes*. Edited by Jules Assézat and Maurice Tourneux. 20 vols. Paris: Garnier Frères, 1875–77.

Dilthey, Wilhelm. *Gesammelte Schriften*. 18 vols. Stuttgart: B. G. Teubner; Göttingen: Vandenhoeck & Ruprecht, 1914–1977.

———. *Poetry and Experience*. In *Selected Works*, edited by Rudolf A. Makkreel and Frithjof Rodi. Vol. 5. Princeton: Princeton University Press, 1985.

Dockhorn, Klaus. *Macht und Wirkung der Rhetorik: Vier Aufsätze zur Ideengeschichte der Vormoderne*. Bad Homburg: Gehlen, 1968.

Dover, Kenneth James. *Greek Popular Morality in the Time of Plato and Aristotle*. Oxford: Basil Blackwell, 1974.

Duff, William. *An Essay on Original Genius and Its Various Modes of Exertion in Philosophy and the Fine Arts, Particularly in Poetry*. London, 1767. Reprint, edited by John L. Mahoney, Gainesville, Fla.: Scholars' Facsimiles & Reprints, 1964.

Eagleton, Terry. *The Ideology of the Aesthetic*. Oxford: Basil Blackwell, 1990.

Eckermann, Johann Peter. *Gespräche mit Goethe in den letzten Jahren seines Lebens*. Leipzig: Brockhaus, 1868.

Eichner, Hans. "Zur Deutung von 'Wilhelm Meisters Lehrjahren.'" *Jahrbuch des Freien Deutschen Hochstifts* (1966): 165–96.

Ellis, J. M. *Schiller's "Kalliasbriefe" and the Study of His Aesthetic Theory*. The Hague: Mouton, 1969.

Elson, Charles. *Wieland and Shaftesbury*. New York: Columbia University Press, 1913.

Encyclopédie, ou Dictionnaire raisonné des sciences, des arts et des métiers, par une société de gens de lettres. Edited by Denis Diderot and Jean Le Rond d'Alembert. 35 vols. Paris, 1751–67.

Engel, Johann Jakob. *Schriften*. 12 vols. Berlin: Mylius'sche Buchhandlung, 1844.

Engell, James. *The Creative Imagination: Enlightenment to Romanticism*. Cambridge: Harvard University Press, 1981.

Engfer, Hans-Jürgen. *Philosophie als Analysis: Studien zur Entwicklung philosophischer Analysiskonzeptionen unter dem Einfluß mathematischer Methodenmodelle im 17. und frühen 18. Jahrhundert.* Stuttgart: Friedrich Frommann Verlag; Bad Cennstatt: Günter Holzboog, 1982.

Farrelly, Daniel J. *Goethe and Inner Harmony: A Study of the "schöne Seele" in the Apprenticeship of Wilhelm Meister.* New York: Barnes & Noble, 1973.

Fleischer, Stefan. "'Bekenntnisse einer schönen Seele': Figural Representation in *Wilhelm Meisters Lehrjahre.*" *Modern Language Notes* 83 (1968): 807–20.

Fletcher, Angus. *Allegory: The Theory of a Symbolic Mode.* Ithaca: Cornell University Press, 1964.

Flew, R. Newton. *The Idea of Perfection in Christian Theology: An Historical Study of the Christian Ideal for the Present Life.* Oxford: Oxford University Press, 1934.

Foucault, Michel. "On the Genealogy of Ethics: An Overview of Work in Progress." In *The Foucault Reader,* edited by Paul Rabinow. New York: Random House, 1984.

Fowler, Thomas. *Shaftesbury and Hutcheson.* New York: G. P. Putnam's Sons, 1883.

Frankena, William. "Hutcheson's Moral Sense Theory." *Journal of the History of Ideas* 16 (1955): 356–75.

Fries, Jakob Friedrich. *Dialogues on Morality and Religion.* Edited and translated by D. Z. Phillips, David Walford, and Rush Rhees. Totowa, N.J.: Barnes & Noble, 1982.

———. *Handbuch der praktischen Philosophie oder der philosophischen Zwecklehre. Erster Theil. Ethik, oder die Lehren der Lebensweisheit.* Heidelberg: Mohr & Winter, 1818.

———. *Handbuch der praktischen Philosophie oder der philosophischen Zwecklehre. Zweyter Theil. Die Religionsphilosophie oder die Weltzwecklehre. Handbuch der Religionsphilosophie und philosophischen Aesthetik.* Heidelberg: Christian Friedrich Winter, 1832.

———. *Julius und Evagoras; oder, Die Schönheit der Seele. Ein philosophischer Roman.* Heidelberg: Christian Friedrich Winter, 1822.

Fuhrmann, Manfred. "Die *Querelle des Anciens et des Modernes,* der Nationalismus und die deutsche Klassik." In *Classical Influences on Western Thought, A.D. 1650–1870: Proceedings of an International Conference Held at King's College, Cambridge, March 1977,* edited by R. R. Bolgar. Cambridge: Cambridge University Press, 1979.

Fülleborn, Georg Gustav. *Beyträge zur Geschichte der Philosophie.* 5 vols. Züllichau and Freystadt: Friedrich Frommann Verlag, 1796–98.

Furck, Carl-Ludwig. *Der Bildungsbegriff des jungen Hegel.* Weinheim: Julius Beltz, 1953.

Gadamer, Hans-Georg. *Truth and Method.* Edited by Garrett Bareden and John Cumming. London: Sheed & Ward, 1975.

Gay, Peter. *The Enlightenment: An Interpretation.* 2 vols. New York: Alfred A. Knopf, 1966–69.

Gaycken, Hans-Jürgen. *Christoph Martin Wieland: Kritik seiner Werke in Aufklärung, Romantik und Moderne.* Frankfurt am Main: Peter Lang, 1982.

Gerhard, Melitta. *Der deutsche Entwicklungsroman bis zu Goethes "Wilhelm Meister."* Halle: Niemeyer, 1926.

Giamatti, A. Bartlett. *The Earthly Paradise and the Renaissance Epic.* Princeton: Princeton University Press, 1966.

Gibbon, Edward. *The History of the Decline and Fall of the Roman Empire.* Edited by J. B. Bury. 7 vols. London: Methuen, 1909–14. Reprint, New York: AMS Press, 1974.

Gibson, James. *Locke's Theory of Knowledge and Its Historical Relations.* Cambridge: Cambridge University Press, 1917.

Gleissner, Roman. *Die Entstehung der ästhetischen Humanitätsidee in Deutschland.* Stuttgart: J. B. Metzler, 1988.

Goethe, Johann, Wolfgang von. *Briefe.* Edited by Karl Robert Mandelkow and Bodo Morawe. 4 vols. Hamburg: Christian Wegner, 1962–67.

——. *From My Life: Poetry and Truth.* Parts 1 to 3. Edited by Thomas P. Saine and Jeffrey L. Sammons. Translated by Robert R. Heitner and Thomas P. Saine. Vol. 4 of the *Collected Works.* New York: Suhrkamp, 1987.

——. *From My Life: Poetry and Truth.* Part 4, *Campaign in France 1792, Siege of Mainz.* Edited by Thomas P. Saine and Jeffrey L. Sammons. Translated by Robert R. Heitner and Thomas P. Saine. Vol. 5 of the *Collected Works.* New York: Suhrkamp, 1987.

——. *Werke: Hamburger Ausgabe.* Edited by Erich Trunz. 12 vols. Munich: C. H. Beck, 1981.

——. *Wilhelm Meister's Apprenticeship.* Edited by and translated by Eric A. Blackall. Vol. 9 of the *Collected Works.* New York: Suhrkamp, 1989.

Graham, John. *Lavater's Essays on Physiognomy: A Study in the History of Ideas.* Frankfurt am Main: Peter Lang, 1979.

Gray, J. Glenn. *Hegel and Greek Thought.* New York: Harper & Row, 1968.

Grean, Stanley. *Shaftesbury's Philosophy of Religion and Ethics: A Study in Enthusiasm.* Athens: Ohio University Press, 1967.

Greschat, Martin, ed. *Zur neueren Pietismusforschung.* Darmstadt: Wissenschaftliche Buchgesellschaft, 1977.

Grudzinski, Herbert. *Shaftesburys Einfluss auf Chr. M. Wieland: Mit einer Einleitung über den Einfluss Shaftesburys auf die deutsche Literatur bis 1760.* Stuttgart: Metzler, 1913.

Günther, Hans R.G. "Psychologie des deutschen Pietismus." *Deutsche Vierteljahrsschrift* 4 (1926): 144–76.

Guthrie, W.K.C. *A History of Greek Philosophy.* 5 vols. Cambridge: Cambridge University Press, 1962–81.

Guyer, Paul. *Kant and the Claims of Taste.* Cambridge: Harvard University Press, 1979.

——. *Kant and the Experience of Freedom: Essays on Aesthetics and Morality.* Cambridge: Cambridge University Press, 1993.

Hall, H. Gaston. "The Concept of Virtue in *La Nouvelle Heloise.*" *Yale French Studies* 28 (1961–62): 20–33.

Hamann, Johann Georg. *Sämmtliche Werke.* Edited by Josef Nadler. 6 vols. Vienna: Herder, 1949–57.

Hamburger, Käte. *Philosophie der Dichter: Novalis, Schiller, Rilke.* Stuttgart: W. Kohlhammer, 1966.

Hampton, Jean. *Hobbes and the Social Contract Tradition.* Cambridge: Cambridge University Press, 1986.

Hankins, James. *Plato in the Italian Renaissance.* 2 vols. Leiden: E. J. Brill, 1990.

Harnack, Adolf. *Geschichte der königlich-preussischen Akademie der Wissenschaften zu Berlin.* 3 vols. Berlin: Reichsdruckerei, 1900.

Harris, H. S. *Hegel's Development: Toward the Sunlight, 1770–1801.* Oxford: Oxford University Press, 1972.

Harris, James. *Three Treatises, The First Concerning Art, The Second Concerning Music,*

Painting and Poetry, The Third Concerning Happiness. 4th edition. London: C. Nourse, 1783.

Hatfield, Henry. *Aesthetic Paganism in German Literature: From Winckelmann to the Death of Goethe.* Cambridge: Harvard University Press, 1964.

Havelock, Christine Mitchell. "Plato and Winckelmann: Ideological Bias in the History of Greek Art." *Source* 5 (1986): 1–6.

Haym, Rudolf. *Hegel und seine Zeit: Vorlesungen über Entstehung und Entwicklung, Wesen und Werth der Hegel'schen Philosophie.* Berlin: Rudolph Gaertner, 1857.

Hegel, Georg Wilhelm Friedrich. *Aesthetics: Lectures on Fine Art.* Translated by T. M. Knox. 2 vols. Oxford: Oxford University Press, 1975.

———. *Early Theological Writings.* Translated by T. M. Knox. Introduction by Richard Kroner. Chicago: University of Chicago Press, 1948.

———. *Frühe Schriften I.* Vol. 1 of *Gesammelte Werke.* Edited by Friedhelm Nicolin and Gisela Schüler. Hamburg: Felix Meiner, 1989.

———. *"Der Geist des Christentums": Schriften 1796–1800, Mit bislang unveröffentlichten Texten.* Edited by Werner Hamacher. Frankfurt am Main: Ullstein, 1976.

———. *The Phenomenology of Spirit.* Translated by A. V. Miller. Foreword by J. N. Findlay. Oxford: Oxford University Press, 1977.

———. *Theologische Jugendschriften.* Edited by Herman Nohl. Tübingen: J.C.B. Mohr, Paul Siebeck, 1907.

———. *Werke.* Edited by Eva Moldenhauer and Karl Markus Michel. 20 vols. Frankfurt am Main: Suhrkamp, 1970.

Hendel, Charles William. *Jean-Jacques Rousseau: Moralist.* 2 vols. Oxford: Oxford University Press, 1934.

Henrich, Dieter. "Hutcheson und Kant." *Kant-Studien* 49 (1957): 49–69.

———. "Über Kants früheste Ethik: Versuch einer Rekonstruktion." *Kant-Studien* 54 (1963): 404–31.

Herder, Johann Gottfried. *Sämmtliche Werke.* Edited by Bernhard Suphan. 33 vols. Berlin: Weidmann, 1877–1913.

———. *Werke.* Edited by Ulrich Gaier et al. 10 vols. Frankfurt am Main: Deutscher Klassiker Verlag, 1985

Hering, Robert. *Wilhelm Meister und Faust und ihre Gestaltung im Zeichen der Gottesidee.* Frankfurt am Main: G. Schulte-Bulmke, 1952.

Highet, Gilbert. *The Classical Tradition: Greek and Roman Influences on Western Literature.* Oxford: Oxford University Press, 1949.

Hinchman, Lewis P. *Hegel's Critique of the Enlightenment.* Gainesville: University Presses of Florida, 1984.

Hinderer, Walter. "Beiträge Wielands zu Schillers ästhetischer Erziehung." *Jahrbuch der deutschen Schillergesellschaft* 18 (1974): 348–87.

Hinrichs, Carl. *Preußentum und Pietismus: Der Pietismus in Brandenburg-Preußen als religiös-soziale Reformbewegung.* Göttingen: Vandenhoeck & Ruprecht, 1971.

Hirsch, Emanuel. "Die Beisetzung der Romantiker in Hegels Phänomenologie: Ein Kommentar zu dem Abschnitte über die Moralität." *Deutsche Vierteljahrsschrift* 2 (1924): 510–32.

Hirsch, Marianne. "Spiritual *Bildung*: The Beautiful Soul as Paradigm." In *The Voyage In: Fictions of Female Development,* edited by Elizabeth Abel, Marianne Hirsch, and Elizabeth Langland. Hanover: University Press of New England, 1983.

Hobbes, Thomas. *Leviathan, or the Matter, Forme and Power of a Commonwealth Ecclesiasticall and Civil.* Edited by Michael Oakeshott. Oxford: Basil Blackwell, 1946.

Holbach, Paul Henri Thiry, baron d'. *La morale universelle ou les devoirs de l'homme fondés sur sa nature.* 3 vols. Amsterdam, 1776. Reprint, Stuttgart: Friedrich Frommann Verlag; Bad Cannstatt: Günter Holzboog, 1970.

Hölderlin, Friedrich. *Sämtliche Werke.* Edited by Friedrich Beissner and Adolf Beck. 8 vols. Stuttgart: J. G. Cottasche Buchhandlung, 1946–85.

Home, Henry (Lord Kames). *Elements of Criticism.* 2 vols. New York: Campbell, 1823.

——. *Essays on the Principles of Morality and Natural Religion.* Edinburgh: R. Fleming, 1751.

Honig, Edwin. *Dark Conceit: The Making of Allegory.* Providence: Brown University Press, 1972.

Hostler, John. *Leibniz's Moral Philosophy.* London: Duckworth, 1975.

Humboldt, Wilhelm von. *Gesammelte Schriften.* Edited by Albert Leitzmann. 15 vols. Berlin: B. Behr, 1903–18.

——. *Werke.* Edited by Andreas Flitner and Klaus Giel. 5 vols. Darmstadt: Wissenschaftliche Buchgesellschaft, 1960–81.

Hume, David. *Enquiries concerning Human Understanding and concerning the Principles of Morals.* Edited by L. A. Selby-Bigge. 3d edition revised by P. H. Nidditch. Oxford: Oxford University Press, 1975.

——. *Essays and Treatises on Several Subjects.* 2 vols. London: J. Jones, 1822.

——. *Letters.* Edited by J.Y.T. Greig. 2 vols. Oxford: Oxford University Press, 1932.

——. *A Treatise of Human Nature.* Edited by L. A. Selby-Bigge. 2d edition edited by P. H. Nidditch. Oxford: Oxford University Press, 1978.

Hutcheson, Francis. *An Inquiry into the Original of Our Ideas of Beauty and Virtue.* 2d edition. London, 1726. Reprint, New York: Garland, 1971.

Hyppolite, Jean. *Genesis and Structure of Hegel's Phenomenology of Spirit.* Translated by Samuel Cherniak and John Heckman. Evanston: Northwestern University Press, 1974.

Isocrates. *Works.* Loeb Classical Library. 1945.

Jaeger, Werner. *Paideia: The Ideals of Greek Culture.* Translated by Gilbert Highet. 3 vols. New York: Oxford University Press, 1939–44.

Jauß, Hans Robert, ed. *Nachahmung und Illusion.* Munich: Eidos, 1964.

Jefferson, Thomas. *Writings.* Edited by Merrill D. Peterson. New York: Literary Classics of the United States, 1984.

Jones, James F. *La Nouvelle Héloïse: Rousseau and Utopia.* Geneva: Droz, 1978.

Justi, Carl. *Winckelmann und seine Zeitgenossen.* 3 vols. 2d revised edition. Leipzig: F.C.W. Vogel, 1898.

Jüthner, Julius. "Kalokagathia." In *Charisteria: Alois Rzach zum achtzigsten Geburtstag dargebracht.* Reichenberg: Gebrüder Stiepel, 1930.

Kaiser, Gerhard. *Pietismus und Patriotismus im literarischen Deutschland: Ein Beitrag zum Problem der Säkularisation.* Wiesbaden: Franz Steiner, 1961.

Kant, Immanuel. *Anthropology from a Pragmatic Point of View.* Translated by Mary J. Gregor. The Hague: Martinus Nijhoff, 1974.

——. *The Conflict of the Faculties. Der Streit der Fakultäten.* Translated by Mary J. Gregor. New York: Abaris Books, 1979.

——. *The Critique of Judgement.* Translated by James Creed Meredith. Oxford: Oxford University Press, 1952.

——. *Critique of Practical Reason and Other Writings in Moral Philosophy.* Translated and edited by Lewis White Beck. Chicago: University of Chicago Press, 1949.

——. *Critique of Pure Reason.* Translated by Norman Kemp Smith. New York: St. Martin's Press, 1965.

——. *Observations on the Feeling of the Beautiful and Sublime.* Translated by John T. Goldthwait. Berkeley and Los Angeles: University of California Press, 1965.

——. *Religion within the Limits of Reason Alone.* Translated by Theodore M. Greene and Hoyt H. Hudson. Chicago: Open Court, 1934.

——. *Werkausgabe.* Edited by Wilhelm Weischedel. 12 vols. Frankfurt am Main: Suhrkamp, 1968.

Kaufmann, Walter. *From Shakespeare to Existentialism.* New York: Doubleday, 1960.

——. *Hegel: Reinterpretation, Texts, and Commentary.* New York: Doubleday, 1965.

Käuser, Andreas. "Die Physiognomik des 18. Jahrhunderts als Ursprung der modernen Geisteswissenschaft." *Germanisch-Romanische Monatsschrift* Neue Folge 41 (1991): 129–44.

Kemal, Salim. *Kant and Fine Art: An Essay on Kant and the Philosophy of Fine Art.* Oxford: Oxford University Press, 1986.

Kenny, Anthony. *Aristotle on the Perfect Life.* Oxford: Oxford University Press, 1992.

Kerry, S. S. *Schiller's Writings on Aesthetics.* Manchester: Manchester University Press, 1961.

Kerslake, Lawrence. "Johann Georg Sulzer and the Supplement to the *Encyclopédie.*" *Studies on Voltaire and the Eighteenth Century* 148 (1976): 225–47.

King, Peter. *The Life of John Locke, with Extracts from His Correspondence, Journals, and Common-Place Books.* 2 vols. London: Henry Colburn & Richard Bentley, 1830.

Kleist, Ewald von. *Werke.* Edited by August Sauer. 3 vols. Berlin: Gustav Hempel, n.d.

Klettenberg, Susanna Katharina von. *Die schöne Seele: Bekenntnisse, Schriften, und Briefe.* Edited by Heinrich Funck. Leipzig: Insel, 1912.

Klopstock, Friedrich Gottlieb. *Ausgewählte Werke.* Munich: Carl Hanser, 1962.

Kontje, Todd Curtis. *Constructing Reality: A Rhetorical Analysis of Friedrich Schiller's Letters on the Aesthetic Education of Man.* New York: Peter Lang, 1987.

Korff, H. A. *Geist der Goethezeit: Versuch einer ideellen Entwicklung der klassisch-romantischen Literaturgeschichte.* 4 vols. Leipzig: J. J. Weber, 1927– .

Kristeller, Paul Oskar. *The Philosophy of Marsilio Ficino.* Translated by Virginia Conant. New York: Columbia University Press, 1943.

Kühn, Hugo, ed. *Das Wartburgfest am 18. Oktober 1817: Zeitgenössische Darstellungen, archivalische Akten und Urkunden.* Weimar: Alexander Duncker, 1913.

Kurth-Voigt, Lieselotte E. "Wielands 'Geschichte des Agathon': Zur journalistischen Rezeption des Romans." *Wieland-Studien* 1 (1991): 9–42.

Kuzniar, Alice A. "Signs of the Future: Reading (in) Lavater's *Aussichten.*" *Seminar* 22 (1986): 1–19.

Langen, August. *Der Wortschatz des deutschen Pietismus.* 2d edition. Tübingen: Niemeyer, 1968.

Lavater, Johann Caspar. *Ausgewählte Werke.* Edited by Ernst Staehelin. 4 vols. Zürich: Zwingli, 1943.

——. *Physiognomische Fragmente zur Beförderung der Menschenkenntnis und Menschenliebe.* 4 vols. Leipzig, 1775–78. Reprint, Zurich: Orell Füssli, 1968–69.

Lechler, Gotthard Victor. *Geschichte des englischen Deismus.* Stuttgart, 1842. Reprint, with an introduction by Günter Gawlick. Hildesheim: Georg Olms, 1965.

Leclerc, Ivor, ed. *The Philosophy of Leibniz and the Modern World.* Nashville: Vanderbilt University Press, 1973.

Leibniz, Gottfried Wilhlem. *Philosophical Essays*. Edited and translated by Roger Ariew and Daniel Garber. Indianapolis: Hackett, 1989.

——. *Philosophical Papers and Letters*. Translated and edited by Leroy E. Loemker. 2d edition. Dordrecht, Holland: D. Reidel, 1969.

——. "Trois dialogues mystiques inédits de Leibniz." Edited by Jean Baruzi. *Revue de Métaphysique et de Morale* 13 (1905): 1–38.

Lessing, Gotthold Ephraim. *Sämtliche Schriften*. Edited by Karl Lachmann and Franz Muncker. 23 vols. Stuttgart: G. J. Göschen; Berlin: Walter de Gruyter, 1886–1924.

Librett, Jeffrey Scott. "Rhapsodic Dispositions: Engenderments of the Ground in the Discourse of the 'Beautiful Soul' (Shaftesbury, Kant, Hegel, Heidegger)." Ph.D. diss., Cornell University, 1989.

Lichtenberg, Georg Christoph. *Aphorismen. Schriften. Briefe*. Edited by Wolfgang Promies and Barbara Promies. Munich: Hanser, 1974.

Livingston, Donald W., and King, James T., eds. *Hume: A Reevaluation*. New York: Fordham University Press, 1976.

Locke, John. *An Essay concerning Human Understanding*. Edited by Peter H. Nidditch. Oxford: Oxford University Press, 1975.

——. *Works*. 10 vols. London, 1823.

Lodge, R. C. *Plato's Theory of Ethics: The Moral Criterion and the Highest Good*. London: Routledge & Kegan Paul, 1928.

Lukács, Georg. *Der junge Hegel: Über die Beziehungen von Dialektik und Ökonomie*. Zurich: Europa, 1948.

Lütkemann, Joachim. *Der Vorschmack Göttlicher Güte Durch Gottes Gnade*. Edited by Philipp Julius Rehtmeyer. 2 vols. Braunschweig: Rudolph Schröder, 1720–25.

MacIntyre, Alasdair. *After Virtue: A Study in Moral Theory*. 2d edition. Notre Dame: University of Notre Dame Press, 1984.

Mackie, J. L. *Hume's Moral Theory*. London: Routledge & Kegan Paul, 1980.

Mandel, Oscar. *August von Kotzebue: The Comedy, the Man*. University Park: Pennsylvania State University Press, 1990.

Markley, Robert. "Style as Philosophical Structure: The Contexts of Shaftesbury's *Characteristics*." In *The Philosopher as Writer: The Eighteenth Century*, edited by Robert Ginsberg. Selinsgrove: Susquehanna University Press, 1987.

Marrou, H. I. *A History of Education in Antiquity*. Translated by George Lamb. New York: Sheed & Ward, 1956.

Martens, Wolfgang. *Die Botschaft der Tugend: Die Aufklärung im Spiegel der deutschen Moralischen Wochenschriften*. Stuttgart: J. B. Metzler, 1968.

Martini, Fritz. "Der Bildungsroman: Zur Geschichte des Wortes und der Theorie." *Deutsche Vierteljahrsschrift* 35 (1961): 44–63.

Mautner, Franz H. *Lichtenberg: Geschichte seines Geistes*. Berlin: Walter de Gruyter, 1968.

May, Kurt. "'Wilhelm Meisters Lehrjahre,' ein Bildungsroman?" *Deutsche Vierteljahrsschrift* 31 (1957): 1–37.

McCarthy, John A. *Christoph Martin Wieland*. Boston: Twayne, 1979.

——. *Fantasy and Reality: An Epistemological Approach to Wieland*. Frankfurt am Main: Peter Lang, 1974.

——. "Wieland as Essayist." *Lessing Yearbook* 8 (1976): 125–39.

McKeon, Michael. *The Origins of the English Novel: 1600–1740*. Baltimore: Johns Hopkins University Press, 1987.

McMahon, A. Philip. "Francis Bacon's Essay of *Beauty*." *PMLA* 60 (1945): 716–59.

McNeilly, F. S. *The Anatomy of Leviathan.* London: Macmillan, 1968.

Mendelssohn, Moses. *Gesammelte Schriften: Jubiläumsausgabe.* Edited by Fritz Bamberger et al. 19 vols. Stuttgart: Friedrich Frommann Verlag; Bad Cannstatt: Günter Holzboog, 1972–.

———. *Schriften zur Philosophie, Aesthetik, und Apologetik.* Edited by Moritz Brasch. 2 vols. Leipzig, 1880. Reprint, Hildesheim: Georg Olms, 1968.

Meyer, Herman. "Schillers philosophische Rhetorik." *Euphorion* 53 (1959): 313–50.

Miller, Mitchell H. "The Attainment of the Absolute Standpoint in Hegel's *Phenomenology.*" *Graduate Faculty Philosophy Journal* 7 (1978): 195–219.

Miller, R. D. *Schiller and the Ideal of Freedom: A Study of Schiller's Philosophical Works with Chapters on Kant.* Oxford: Oxford University Press, 1970.

Mintz, Samuel I. *The Hunting of Leviathan: Seventeenth-Century Reactions to the Materialism and Moral Philosophy of Thomas Hobbes.* Cambridge: Cambridge University Press, 1962.

Momigliano, Arnaldo. *Studies in Historiography.* New York: Harper & Row, 1966.

Montesquieu, Charles de Secondat, baron de. *Oeuvres complètes.* 2 vols. Paris: Hachette, 1862.

Müller, Walter. *Das Problem der Seelenschönheit im Mittelalter: Eine Begriffsgeschichtliche Untersuchung.* Bern: Paul Haupt, 1923.

Müller-Solger, Hermann. *Der Dichtertraum: Studien zur Entwicklung der dichterischen Phantasie im Werk Christoph Martin Wielands.* Göttingen: Vandenhoeck & Ruprecht, 1970.

Murphy, Roland E. *The Song of Songs: A Commentary on the Book of Canticles or The Song of Songs.* Edited by S. Dean McBride Jr. Minneapolis: Augsburg Fortress Press, 1990.

Nietzsche, Friedrich. *Werke.* Edited by Karl Schlechta. 3 vols. Munich: Carl Hanser, 1966.

Nivelle, Armand. *Kunst- und Dichtungstheorien zwischen Aufklärung und Klassik.* 2d expanded edition. Berlin: Walter de Gruyter, 1971.

Norton, David Fate. *David Hume: Common-Sense Moralist, Sceptical Metaphysician.* Princeton: Princeton University Press, 1982.

———. "Hutcheson on Perception and Moral Perception." *Archiv für Geschichte der Philosophie* 59 (1977): 181–97.

———. "Hutcheson's Moral Realism." *Journal of the History of Philosophy* 23 (1985): 397–418.

———. "Hutcheson's Moral Sense Theory Reconsidered." *Dialogue* 13 (1974): 3–23.

Norton, Robert E. *Herder's Aesthetics and the European Enlightenment.* Ithaca: Cornell University Press, 1991.

Olscamp, Paul J. *The Moral Philosophy of George Berkeley.* The Hague: Martinus Nijhoff, 1970.

Olson, Alan M. *Hegel and the Spirit: Philosophy as Pneumatology.* Princeton: Princeton University Press, 1992.

Parker, Harold T. *The Cult of Antiquity and the French Revolutionaries: A Study in the Development of the Revolutionary Spirit.* Chicago: University of Chicago Press, 1937.

Parker, Samuel. *A Free and Impartial Censure of the Platonick Philosophie, Being a Letter*

Written to his much Honoured Friend Mr. Nath. Bisbie. 2d edition. Oxford: Oxford University Press, 1667.

Passmore, John. *The Perfectibility of Man.* New York: Charles Scribner's Sons, 1970.

——. *Ralph Cudworth: An Interpretation.* Cambridge: Cambridge University Press, 1951.

Pattison, Mark. *Essays.* 2 vols. Oxford: Oxford University Press, 1889.

Paulsen, Wolfgang. *Christoph Martin Wieland: Der Mensch und sein Werk in Psychologischen Perspektiven.* Bern: Francke, 1975.

Peters, Richard. *Hobbes.* Harmondsworth, U.K.: Penguin, 1956.

Pfeiffer, Rudolf. *History of Classical Scholarship from 1300 to 1850.* Oxford: Oxford University Press, 1976.

Pfeiffer-Belli, Wolfgang. *Geschichte der deutschen Dichtung.* Freiburg: Herder, 1954.

Pinson, Koppel S. *Pietism as a Factor in the Rise of German Nationalism.* New York: Columbia University Press, 1934.

Plato. *The Collected Dialogues.* Edited by Edith Hamilton and Huntington Cairns. Princeton: Princeton University Press, 1963.

Plotinos. *Complete Works.* Edited by Kenneth Sylvan Guthrie. 4 vols. Alpine, N.J.: Platonist Press, 1919.

Pohlmeier, Heinrich. "Untersuchungen zum Begriff der schönen Seele im achtzehnten Jahrhundert und in der Goethezeit." Ph.D. diss., University of Münster, 1954.

Pope, Marvin H. *Song of Songs: A New Translation with Introduction and Commentary.* Garden City, N.Y.: Doubleday, 1977.

Poppe, Berhard. *Alexander Gottlieb Baumgarten: Seine Bedeutung und Stellung in der Leibniz-Wolffischen Philosophie und seine Beziehungen zu Kant.* Borna-Leipzig: Robert Noske, 1907.

Price, Richard. *A Review of the Principal Questions of Morals.* Edited by D. Daiches Raphael. Oxford: Oxford University Press, 1948.

Quilligan, Maureen. *The Language of Allegory: Defining the Genre.* Ithaca: Cornell University Press, 1979.

Ritschl, Albrecht. *Geschichte des Pietismus.* 3 vols. Bonn: Adolph Marcus, 1880–86.

Rogerson, Kenneth F. *Kant's Aesthetics: The Roles of Form and Expression.* Lanham, Md.: University Press of America, 1986.

Rohls, Jan. *Geschichte der Ethik.* Tübingen: J.C.B. Mohr, Paul Siebeck, 1991.

Rorty, Richard. "Freud and Moral Reflection." In *Pragmatism's Freud: The Moral Disposition of Psychoanalysis,* edited by Joseph H. Smith and William Kerrigan. Baltimore: Johns Hopkins University Press, 1986.

——. "Freud, Morality, and Hermeneutics." *New Literary History* 12 (1980): 177–85.

Rousseau, Jean-Jacques. *The Confessions.* Translated by J. M. Cohen. London: Penguin, 1953.

——. *Émile.* Translated by Barbara Foxley. London: J. M. Dent & Sons, 1938.

——. *La nouvelle Héloïse: Julie, or the New Eloise.* Translated and abridged by Judith H. McDowell. University Park: Pennsylvania State University Press, 1968.

——. *Oeuvres complètes.* Edited by Bernard Gagnebin and Marcel Raymond. 4 vols. Paris: Gallimard, Bibliothèque de la Pléiade, 1959–69.

Saine, Thomas P. *Von der Kopernikanischen bis zur Französischen Revolution: Die Auseinandersetzung der deutschen Frühaufklärung mit der neuen Zeit.* Berlin: Erich Schmidt, 1987.

Sax, Benjamin C. "Active Individuality and the Language of Confession: The Figure of the Beautiful Soul in the *Lehrjahre* and the *Phänomenologie.*" *Journal of the History of Philosophy* 21 (1983): 437–66.

Schaper, Eva. "Friedrich Schiller: Adventures of a Kantian." *British Journal of Aesthetics* 4 (1964): 348–62.

Schiller, Friedrich. *Briefe.* Edited by Fritz Jonas. 7 vols. Stuttgart: Deutsche Verlags-Anstalt, 1892–96.

——. *On the Aesthetic Education of Man in a Series of Letters.* Edited and translated by Elizabeth M. Wilkinson and L. A. Willoughby. Oxford: Oxford University Press, 1967.

——. *Sämtliche Werke.* Edited by Gerhard Fricke and Herbert G. Göpfert. 5 vols. Munich: Carl Hanser, 1958–59.

Schilpp, Paul Arthur. *Kant's Pre-Critical Ethics.* 2d edition. Evanston: Northwestern University Press, 1960.

Schlegel, Dorothy B. *Shaftesbury and the French Deists.* Chapel Hill: University of North Carolina Press, 1956.

Schlegel, Friedrich. *Prosaische Jugendschriften, 1794–1802.* Edited by J. Minor. 2 vols. Vienna: Carl Konegen, 1906.

Schmeer, Hans. *Der Begriff der "schönen Seele" besonders bei Wieland und in der deutschen Literatur des 18. Jahrhunderts.* Berlin: Emil Ebering, 1926.

Schmidt, Leopold. *Die Ethik der alten Griechen.* 2 vols. Berlin: Wilhelm Hertz, 1882.

Schmidt, Martin. *Pietismus.* 3d edition. Stuttgart: W. Kohlhammer, 1983.

Schmucker, Josef. *Die Ursprünge der Ethik Kants in seinen vorkritischen Schriften und Reflektionen.* Meisenheim am Glan: Anton Hain, 1961.

Schneewind, Jerome B., ed. *Moral Philosophy from Montaigne to Kant: An Anthology.* 2 vols. Cambridge: Cambridge University Press, 1990.

Schrader, Wolfgang H. *Ethik und Anthropologie in der englischen Aufklärung: Der Wandel der moral-sense-Theorie von Shaftesbury bis Hume.* Hamburg: Felix Meiner, 1984.

Scott, William Robert. *Francis Hutcheson: His Life, Teaching, and Position in the History of Philosophy.* Cambridge: Cambridge University Press, 1900.

Selbmann, Rolf, ed. *Zur Geschichte des deutschen Bildungsromans.* Darmstadt: Wissenschaftliche Buchgesellschaft, 1988.

Sengle, Friedrich. *Wieland.* Stuttgart: Metzler, 1949.

Seznec, Jean. *Essais sur Diderot et l'antinquité.* Oxford: Oxford University Press, 1957.

Shaftesbury, Anthony Ashley Cooper, third earl of. *Characteristicks of Men, Manners, Opinions, Times.* 2d edition. 3 vols. London, 1714.

——. *The Life, Unpublished Letters, and Philosophical Regimen of Anthony, Earl of Shaftesbury.* Edited by Benjamin Rand. London: Swan Sonnenschein, 1900.

Sharpe, Lesley. *Friedrich Schiller: Drama, Thought, and Politics.* Cambridge: Cambridge University Press, 1991.

Shelley, Percy Bysshe. *Complete Works.* Edited by Roger Ingpen and Walter E. Peck. 10 vols. New York: Charles Scribner's Sons, 1926–30.

Shklar, Judith N. *Freedom and Independence: A Study of the Political Ideas of Hegel's Phenomenology of Mind.* Cambridge: Cambridge University Press, 1976.

Shorey, Paul. *Platonism Ancient and Modern.* Berkeley and Los Angeles: University of California Press, 1938.

Shusterman, Richard. "'Ethics and Aesthetics Are One': Postmodernism's Ethics of Taste." In *After the Future: Postmodern Times and Places*, edited by Gary Shapiro. Albany: State University of New York Press, 1990.

Smith, Adam. *The Theory of Moral Sentiments*. 12th edition. 2 vols. Edinburgh, 1808.

Smith, John H. *The Spirit and Its Letter: Traces of Rhetoric in Hegel's Philosophy of "Bildung."* Ithaca: Cornell University Press, 1988.

Smith, Norman Kemp. *The Philosophy of David Hume: A Critical Study of Its Origins and Central Doctrines*. London: Macmillan, 1941.

Spence, Joseph. *Crito; or, A Dialogue on Beauty*. London, 1752. Reprint, New York: Garland, 1970.

Spener, Philip Jacob. *Pia Desideria*. Translated and edited by Theodore G. Tappert. Philadelphia: Fortress Press, 1964.

Spranger, Eduard. *Wilhelm von Humboldt und die Humanitätsidee*. Berlin: Reuther & Reichard, 1909.

Springorum, Friedrich. "Über das Sittliche in der Ästhetik Johann Georg Sulzers." *Archiv für die gesamte Psychologie* 72 (1929): 1–42.

Stafford, Barbara Maria. "Beauty of the Invisible: Winckelmann and the Aesthetics of Imperceptibility." *Zeitschrift für Kunstgeschichte* 43 (1980): 65–78.

———. *Body Criticism: Imaging the Unseen in Enlightenment Art and Medicine*. Cambridge: MIT Press, 1991.

Stahl, E. L. *Die religiöse und die humanitätsphilosophische Bildungsidee und die Entstehung des deutschen Bildungsromans im 18. Jahrhundert*. Bern: Paul Haupt, 1934.

Starobinski, Jean. *Jean-Jacques Rousseau: Transparency and Obstruction*. Translated by Arthur Goldhammer, with an introduction by Robert J. Morrissey. Chicago: University of Chicago Press, 1988.

Stephen, Leslie. *History of English Thought in the Eighteenth Century*. 3d edition. 2 vols. London: John Murray, 1902.

Stewart, Dugald. *Collected Works*. Edited by Sir William Hamilton. 11 vols. Edinburgh: Thomas Constable, 1854–60.

Stoeffler, F. Ernest. *German Pietism during the Eighteenth Century*. Studies in the History of Religions, vol. 24. Leiden: E. J. Brill, 1973.

———. *The Rise of Evangelical Pietism*. Studies in the History of Religions, vol. 9. Leiden: E. J. Brill, 1965.

Storz, Gerhard. "Schiller und die Antike." *Jahrbuch der deutschen Schillergesellschaft* 10 (1966): 189–204.

Stuckenberg, J.H.W. *The Life of Immanuel Kant*. London: Macmillan, 1882.

Sullivan, Roger J. *Immanuel Kant's Moral Theory*. Cambridge: Cambridge University Press, 1989.

Sulzer, Johann Georg. *Allgemeine Theorie der schönen Künste*. Edited by Christian Friedrich von Blankenburg et al., with an introduction by Giorgio Tonelli. 5 vols. 2d expanded edition. Leipzig, 1792. Reprint, Hildesheim: Georg Olms, 1967–70.

Summers, David. *The Judgment of Sense: Renaissance Naturalism and the Rise of Aesthetics*. Cambridge: Cambridge University Press, 1987.

Swales, Martin. *The German Bildungsroman from Wieland to Hesse*. Princeton: Princeton University Press, 1978.

Sweet, Paul R. *Wilhelm von Humboldt: A Biography*. 2 vols. Columbus: Ohio State University Press, 1978–80.

Taylor, Charles. *Hegel.* Cambridge: Cambridge University Press, 1975.

Taylor, Thomas. *Selected Writings.* Edited by Kathleen Raine and George Mills Harper. Princeton: Princeton University Press, 1969.

Thomé, Horst. "Menschliche Natur und Allegorie sozialer Verhältnisse: Zur politischen Funktion philosophischer Konzeptionen in Wielands 'Geschichte des Agathon.'" *Jahrbuch der deutschen Schillergesellschaft* 22 (1978): 205–34.

Torrey, Norman L. *Voltaire and the English Deists.* New Haven: Yale University Press, 1930.

Trevelyan, Humphrey. *Goethe and the Greeks.* Cambridge: Cambridge University Press, 1941.

Troeltsch, Ernst. *Aufsätze zur Geistesgeschichte und Religionssoziologie.* Vol. 4 of *Gesammelte Schriften.* Tübingen: J.C.B. Mohr, Paul Siebeck, 1925.

Turner, Frank M. *The Greek Heritage in Victorian Britain.* New Haven: Yale University Press, 1981.

Tuveson, Ernest Lee. *The Imagination as a Means of Grace: Locke and the Aesthetics of Romanticism.* Berkeley and Los Angeles: University of California Press, 1960.

Tytler, Graeme. *Physiognomy in the European Novel: Faces and Fortunes.* Princeton: Princeton University Press, 1982.

Unger, Rudolf. *Hamann und die Aufklärung: Studien zur Vorgeschichte des romantischen Geistes im 18. Jahrhundert.* 2 vols. Halle: Niemeyer, 1925.

Verene, Donald Phillip. *Hegel's Recollection: A Study of Images in the Phenomenology of Spirit.* Albany: State University of New York Press, 1985.

Vierhaus, Rudolf. "Bildung." In *Geschichtliche Grundbegriffe: Historisches Lexikon zur politisch-sozialen Sprache in Deutschland,* edited by Otto Brunner, Werner Conze, and Reinhart Koselleck. Vol. 1. Stuttgart: Ernst Klett, 1972.

Voltaire [François-Marie Arouet]. *Oeuvres complètes.* Edited by Louis Moland. 52 vols. Paris: Garnier Frères, 1877–85.

Vorländer, Karl. *Kant. Schiller. Goethe.* 2d expanded edition. Leipzig: Felix Meiner, 1923.

Waldberg, Max Freiherr von. *Studien und Quellen zur Geschichte des Romans.* Vol. 1, *Zur Entwicklungsgeschichte der "schönen Seele" bei den spanischen Mystikern.* Berlin: Emil Felber, 1910.

Walker, D. P. *The Ancient Theology: Studies in Christian Platonism from the Fifteenth to the Eighteenth Century.* Ithaca: Cornell University Press, 1972.

Wallmann, Johannes. *Philipp Jakob Spener und die Anfänge des Pietismus.* Beiträge zur historischen Theologie 42. Tübingen: J.C.B. Mohr, Paul Siebeck, 1970.

Walter, Julius. *Die Geschichte der Ästhetik im Altertum ihrer begrifflichen Entwicklung nach dargestellt.* Leipzig: O. R. Reisland, 1893.

Wankel, Hermann. "Kalos kai agathos." Ph.D. diss., University of Würzburg, 1961.

Ward, Keith. *The Development of Kant's View of Ethics.* New York: Humanities Press, 1972.

Watt, Ian. *The Rise of the Novel: Studies in Defoe, Richardson, and Fielding.* Berkeley and Los Angeles: University of California Press, 1959.

Webb, Timothy. *English Romantic Hellenism, 1700–1824.* Literature in Context. Manchester: Manchester University Press, 1982.

Weigelt, Horst. *Lavater und die Stillen im Lande: Distanz und Nähe. Die Beziehungen Lavaters zu Frömmigkeitsbewegungen im 18. Jahrhundert.* Göttingen: Vandenhoeck & Ruprecht, 1988.

Well, Karlheinz. *Die "schöne Seele" und ihre "sittliche Wirklichkeit": Überlegungen zum Verhältnis von Kunst und Staat bei Hegel.* Frankfurt am Main: Peter Lang, 1986.

Whichcote, Benjamin. *Works.* 4 vols. Aberdeen: J. Chalmers, 1751. Reprint, New York: Garland Publishing, 1977.

White, Stephen A. *Sovereign Virtue: Aristotle on the Relation Between Happiness and Prosperity.* Stanford: Stanford University Press, 1992.

Wieland, Christoph Martin. *Ausgewählte Briefe.* 4 vols. Zurich: Geßnersche Buchhandlung, 1815.

———. *Briefe.* Edited by Hans W. Seiffert. 10 vols. Berlin: Akademie, 1963–.

———. *Gesammelte Schriften.* Edited by the Deutsche Kommission der Königlich Preußischen Akademie der Wissenschaften. 3 Abteilungen. Berlin: Weidmann, 1909–.

———. *Sämmtliche Werke.* 39 vols. 6 supplementary vols. Leipzig: Göschen, 1794–1811.

———. *Werke.* Edited by Fritz Martini and Hans Werner Seiffert. 5 vols. Munich: Carl Hanser, 1964–68.

Wiese, Benno von. *Friedrich Schiller.* Stuttgart: J. B. Metzler, 1959.

Wild, John. *George Berkeley: A Study of His Life and Philosophy.* New York: Russell & Russell, 1962.

Williamson, Raymond Keith. *Introduction to Hegel's Philosophy of Religion.* Albany: State University of New York Press, 1984.

Wilson, Arthur M. *Diderot.* New York: Oxford University Press, 1972.

Winckelmann, Johann Joachim. *Geschichte der Kunst des Altertums.* Vienna: Phaidon, 1934. Reprint, Darmstadt: Wissenschaftliche Buchgesellschaft, 1982.

———. *Kleine Schriften. Vorreden. Entwürfe.* Edited by Walther Rehm. Berlin: Walter de Gruyter, 1968.

———. *Versuch einer Allegorie besonders für die Kunst.* Dresden: Walther, 1766.

Winkler, Kenneth P. "Hutcheson's Alleged Realism." *Journal of the History of Philosophy* 23 (1985): 179–94.

Wittgenstein, Ludwig. *Tractatus Logico-Philosophicus.* London: Routledge & Kegan Paul, 1963.

Wittkowski, Wolfgang, ed. *Verantwortung und Utopie: Zur Literatur der Goethezeit.* Tübingen: Max Niemeyer, 1988

———, ed. *Verlorene Klassik? Ein Symposium.* Tübingen: Max Niemeyer, 1986.

Wolff, Christian. *Vernünfftige Gedancken von der Menschen Thun und Lassen, zu Beförderung ihrer Glückseeligkeit.* 4th edition. Frankfurt and Leipzig, 1733. Reprint, edited by Hans Werner Arndt, Hildesheim: Georg Olms, 1976.

Wolff, Robert Paul. *The Autonomy of Reason: A Commentary on Kant's "Groundwork of the Metaphysic of Morals."* New York: Harper & Row, 1973.

Wood, Allen W. *Hegel's Ethical Thought.* Cambridge: Cambridge University Press, 1990.

Wundt, Max. *Die deutsche Schulphilosophie im Zeitalter der Aufklärung.* Tübingen: J.C.B. Mohr, Paul Siebeck, 1945.

———. *Geschichte der griechischen Ethik.* 2 vols. Leipzig, 1908–11. Reprint, Aalen: Scientia, 1985.

———. "Die Wiederentdeckung Platons im 18. Jahrhundert." *Blätter für deutsche Philosophie* 15 (1941): 149–58.

Wundt, Wilhelm. *Völkerpsychologie: Eine Untersuchung der Entwicklungsgesetze von Sprache, Mythos und Sitte.* 10 vols. Leipzig: Engelmann, 1900–1928.

Xenophon. *Memorabilia and Oeconomicus.* Loeb Classical Library. 1923.

Yolton, John E., ed. *John Locke: Problems and Perspectives, A Collection of New Essays.* Cambridge: Cambridge University Press, 1969.

———. *Locke and the Compass of Human Understanding: A Selective Commentary on the "Essay."* Cambridge: Cambridge University Press, 1970.

Zantop, Susanne. "Eignes Selbst und fremde Formen: Goethes 'Bekenntnisse einer schönen Seele.'" *Goethe Yearbook* 3 (1986): 73–92.

Zelle, Carsten. "Physiognomie des Schreckens im achtzehnten Jahrhundert: Zu Johann Caspar Lavater und Charles Lebrun." *Lessing Yearbook* 21 (1989): 89–102.

Ziolkowski, Theodore. "Language and Mimetic Action in Lessing's *Miss Sara Sampson.*" *Germanic Review* 40 (1965): 261–76.

Index

Abbt, Thomas, 89
Addison, Joseph, 20n, 34, 178n
aesthetics, 6, 27, 39, 72, 81, 84–87, 137,
    180, 192–94, 219–24, 289
  and ethics as one, 4, 28, 39
  of existence, 2–3, 8
Alembert, Jean Le Rond d', 10, 21n, 87,
    104, 192
allegory, 65, 149–50, 190
  Agathon as, 154–60, 164
  Goethe and, 260
  Hegel on, 282n
  Julie and, 173–74
  Schiller and, 231, 234–36
analysis, 11, 12, 110, 179
Ancients *vs.* Moderns, 10, 48, 105
antiquity. *See* Greece
anti-Semitism, 196–97, 288–89
Aristotle, 49, 135, 150, 160, 177–78,
    199n
  Eudemian Ethics, 132
  Magna Moralia, 132
  Metaphysics, 133
  Physiognomonica, 178
Arndt, Johann, 60–64, 66–70, 79, 226,
    255
  *Postilla; Oder, Auslegung der Sonntages und
    aller Festen Evangelien*, 60
  Vier Bücher vom Wahren Christenthum,
    60–64
Arnold, Gottfried, 258
art, and didacticism, 4, 148–54, 193
atheism, 15, 56

Bach, Johann Sebastian, 56
Bacon, Francis, 15, 102, 199n
  The Essayes or Counsels, Civill and Morall,
    183
  Novum Organum, 11

Balguy, John, 44
Baumgarten, Alexander Gottlieb, 81, 83–
    87, 90, 139, 180–81, 192–93, 203,
    214, 228
  Aesthetica, 84–87, 196
  Ethica, 84
  Metaphysica, 84
Baumgarten, Siegmund Jakob, 84
beautiful soul
  as category, 69, 86
  collapse, 8, 142, 209
  death of, 278–82
  as epitome of human existence, 6, 210,
    281
  Hegel on, 266, 272, 278–82
  Jesus takes place of, 272
  Lavater on, 181–82, 189–91
  literary work as, 164
  as problem, 211
  prostitute as, 161–63, 275–77
  reality of, 6, 7, 138–39, 142, 175, 181,
    272
  Rousseau on, 168–75
  Schiller on, 229, 241–45
  Wieland on, 154–64
beauty, definition of
  Baumgarten on, 86
  Berkeley on, 47–48
  and Church, 65–66
  Greeks and, 121–22
  Hutcheson on, 42
  Leibniz on, 77
  Mendelssohn on, 203–5
  Plato on, 127–31
  Plotinos on, 133–36
  Schiller on, 229–31
  Shaftesbury on, 34–38
  as symbol of morality, 223–24
  Xenophon on, 124

beauty of soul, 36–37, 66–70, 84, 89, 96–
    97, 134–35, 151, 190, 213
  Hegel on, 275–76
  Plato on, 127–31
beauty of virtue, 26, 39, 42, 44–46, 48–50,
    52, 95–97, 115, 146–48, 284
  Burke disputes, 96
Becker, Carl, 56
Bell, Sir Charles, 207
Bengel, Johann Albrecht, 226
Berkeley, George, 116, 210
  Alciphron, or, the Minute Philosopher, 44–
    50
Berlin Academy. *See* Royal Academy of Sci-
    ence and Letters in Berlin
Beulwitz, Caroline von, 228
Bildung, 63, 116–18, 149–50, 152–53, 161,
    171, 188, 213, 239, 249–51, 258, 261–
    62, 281
  beautiful soul as goal of, 251
  Goethe on, 263
  Hegel on, 268, 270–72
  moral beauty as essence of, 254
  as neohumanist ideology, 250
Bildungsroman, 152–53, 155, 168, 249–50
Blackwell, Thomas, 49n
Blake, William, 107
Bodmer, Johann Jakob, 144–45, 149n
Bolingbroke, Henry St. John, 102–3
Bonnet, Charles, 207
  La Palingénésie philosophique, 201
Breitinger, Johann Jakob, 149n
British moral philosophy, influence of, 55,
    69, 75, 82, 87, 89, 93–94, 96, 115,
    144, 268
Buffon, Georges-Louis Leclerc de, 185
Burke, Edmund, 228
  *Philosophical Enquiry into the Origin of
    Our Ideas of the Sublime and Beautiful*,
    95–96
Burnet, Thomas, 32n
Butler, Bishop Joseph, 27

Caesar, Julius, 101
Cambridge Platonists, 15–17, 28–29, 32,
    39
Cassirer, Ernst, 5, 27n
Catt, Henri de, 179n
Christianity, 13–14, 17, 26, 43, 56–74,
    104, 106, 119, 140, 144, 166, 180,
    200–201, 202n, 211, 253
  Goethe on, 248
  Hegel on, 265–67, 273–75
  idolatry and, 259
  and love, 269
  and Plotinos, 135
Chytry, Josef, 4n, 7–8
Cicero, 10, 45n, 101, 104, 150, 163

clergy, suspicion of, 14
  Hegel and, 273
Coleridge, Samuel Taylor, 107
collegia pietatis, 60, 66, 145, 226, 248
Condillac, Étienne Bonnot de, 159
conscience, 92
Cooper, John Gilbert, 184–85
Crawford, Charles, 103
Crébillon (Prosper Jolyot), 165
Cudworth, Ralph, 21, 31, 39
  *Treatise concerning Eternal and Immutable
    Morality*, 15–17
Cuyret, Adrien, seigneur de Margency,
    175

Darwin, Charles, 207
death, 127–28, 249
  of Winckelmann, 247
deconstruction, 2
Deism, 25, 44, 55, 140, 211
de Man, Paul, 173
Descartes, René, 81, 83, 213
  Discourse on Method, 11
de Wette, Wilhelm Martin Leberecht, 285
Diderot, Denis, 21n, 27, 43, 104, 110,
    139–40, 192, 207, 263
Dilthey, Wilhelm, 152, 249–50
Duff, William, 106–7

Eckermann, Johann Peter, 114, 142
education, 24, 34, 36, 38, 123, 136, 152,
    213
  Plato on, 126–31
  Rousseau and, 140
  Wieland on, 116–18, 140
  See also Bildung
egotism in morals, 12–14, 30n, 42
Ekhof, Hans Conrad Dietrich, 206–7n
elitism in morals, 25, 37, 44, 47, 78
Elizabeth I, queen of England, 178
Ellis, J. M., 232
empiricism, 19, 23, 92, 98
Encyclopédie, 21n, 43, 137–38, 185, 192
Engel, Johann Jakob, 208, 238
  Ideen zu einer Mimik, 206–7
Enlightenment, character of, 5–9, 45, 54,
    56–57, 98, 100, 102, 137–38, 142,
    224, 228, 247, 264, 267, 277, 280, 289
epistemology, 1, 6, 17, 19, 22, 88
evil, 22, 172, 199, 289
  attraction of, 37
  beautiful soul as, 278
  Hobbes and, 13
  as result of bad taste, 35

Ferguson, Adam, 106
Fichte, Johann Gottlieb, 284
Ficino, Marsilio, 103

Fielding, Henry, 154–55
Fleury, Cardinal, 55
Foucault, Michel, 3, 5
Francke, August Hermann, 59, 71–72, 84, 143, 148n, 256
freedom, 56, 77
    of will, 82, 91–92, 217, 230
French influence on Germany, 10, 87
Freud, Sigmund, 2, 3, 92
Friedländer, David, 197
Friedrich II, king of Prussia, 10, 87–88
Friedrich Wilhelm I, king of Prussia, 72
Friedrich Wilhelm III, king of Prussia, 287
Fries, Jakob Friedrich, 284–89
    Julius und Evagoras; oder, Die Schönheit der Seele. Ein philosophischer Roman, 284
    Über die Gefährdung des Wohlstandes und Charakters der Deutschen durch die Juden, 288

Galen, 178
Garrick, David, 207n
Gay, Peter, 106
Gibbon, Edward, 17
Gleim, Ludwig, 145
Goethe, Johann Wolfgang von, 27, 112, 114–15, 142, 176, 180, 186n, 189, 192n, 202n, 228, 245–54, 257–64
    illness of, 247–48
    Die Leiden des jungen Werther, 246
    Wilhelm Meister's Apprenticeship, 246, 249, 252–64, 270
good, definition of, 13–14, 16, 18, 22, 24, 30, 32, 41, 94
Gottsched, Johann Christoph, 108
Greece, ancient, 3, 7, 49, 78, 99–136, 144, 154, 181, 227
    Hegel and, 265, 270
    importance for Germans, 108–21
    opposed to Rome, 100–102
    See also kalokagathia
Gujer, Jakob, 189–91, 231

Halle, 59, 79, 84, 255–56
Hamann, Johann Georg, 62, 184
    Aesthetica in nuce, 187
    Sokratische Denkwürdigkeiten, 184n
happiness, connected with virtue, 12, 19, 20–21, 33, 37, 75–78, 81, 137, 147, 210, 267
    Kant on, 215
    Plato on, 126
harmony, 34, 41, 43, 76–78, 185, 212, 241, 243, 245, 261, 279–80
Harris, James, 50
Haym, Rudolf, 286–87

Hegel, Georg Wilhelm Friedrich, 206, 226, 245
    on Fries, 285
    on Kant, 267–68, 273, 277–78, 283–87, 289
    Aesthetics. Lectures on Fine Art, 281–82
    Der Geist des Christenthums, 273–75
    Grundlinien zur Philosophie des Rechts, 285–86
    "On Classical Studies," 265
    Die Phänomenologie des Geistes, 206, 264, 266, 273, 277–81, 289
    Die Positivität der christlichen Religion, 266–67, 272–73
    Theologische Jugendschriften, 266
    "Ueber die Religion der Griechen und Römer," 265
Herder, Johann Gottfried, 27, 65n, 85, 86n, 106, 115, 121, 122, 126
    Briefe zu Beförderung der Humanität, 120n, 242n
    Über den Ursprung der Sprache, 120
    Ueber die neuere deutsche Literatur. Fragmente, 114, 119–20, 177
Hermes, Johann Timotheus, 162n
Herodotus, 101, 109
Hirzel, Hans Kaspar, 190–91
    Die Wirthschaft eines philosophischen Bauers, 189
Hobbes, Thomas, 5n, 16–18, 22, 29, 30n, 53–54, 56, 70, 77, 81, 88, 158, 165–66, 189, 244
    Leviathan, 11–15, 21, 94
Holbach, Baron Paul Henri Dietrich d', 104–5
Hölderlin, Friedrich, 113, 226
    "Griechenland," 112
Home, Henry (Lord Kames), 228
    Elements of Criticism, 236n
    Essays on the Principles of Morality and Natural Religion, 50
Homer, 100–101, 108–9, 118
Horace, 100–101, 150, 153n, 160
Humboldt, Wilhelm von, 169, 179n, 236n, 250–51, 257–58, 276
    "Geschichte des Verfalls und Unterganges der griechischen Freistaaten," 114
    "Über Religion," 161–62
Hume, David, 5n, 6, 15, 27, 43, 57, 88, 93, 109, 144, 151n, 213, 220, 268
    Enquiry concerning the Principles of Morals, 51–53, 212
    Treatise of Human Nature, 51, 53–54
Hutcheson, Francis, 27, 32, 46n, 51, 77, 89–90, 94, 106, 117, 144, 185
    An Inquiry into the Original of Our Ideas of Beauty and Virtue, 38–43, 183–84
    System of Moral Philosophy, 43
hypocrisy, 68, 70, 170, 172, 279

innate knowledge, 16, 17–18, 21, 29, 30, 122
interest, 26, 42, 220–22
irrationalism, 16, 58
Isocrates, 123

Jaeger, Werner, 121
Jaucourt, chevalier de, 185
Jefferson, Thomas, 125
Jesus Christ, 26, 61, 64, 66–69, 71, 187,
    242, 257, 266
  Hegel on, 271–72, 274–75
  as model, 258
Judaism, 200–201
justice, 13, 16, 30, 67, 69, 171

kalokagathia, 7, 49, 116–19, 144, 153, 157,
    227, 284
  aristocratic origins of, 122
  Aristotle on, 132–33
  and education, 149
  as highest good, 121–23
  history of, 122
  place in Greek society, 121–23
  Plato on, 126–31
  Plotinos on, 135
  Xenophon on, 123–26
Kant, Immanuel, 5n, 27, 43, 62, 83, 87,
    91–92, 192, 205–6, 211, 228, 230,
    240, 241n, 247, 268–70, 277–78, 284
  on beautiful soul, 215, 221–25
  on moral beauty, 218, 221–24
  on moral law, 215–16
  Anthropologie in pragmatischer Hinsicht,
    206
  Beobachtungen über das Gefühl des Schönen
    und Erhabenen, 95
  Critique of Judgement, 99, 219–24, 233
  Critique of Pure Reason, 98, 214, 224
  Grundlegung zur Metaphysik der Sitten, 95,
    97, 215–19, 234
  Religion within the Limits of Reason Alone,
    98, 241n, 267
  "Untersuchung über die Deutlichkeit
    der Grundsätze der natürlichen
    Theologie und moral," 93–95
Kempis, Thomas à, 64
Kleinjogg. See Gujer, Jakob
Kleist, Ewald von, 145
Klettenberg, Susanna Katharina von, 248–
    49, 255, 258n
Klopstock, Friedrich Gottlieb, 144, 151
Korff, H. A., 251–52
Körner, Christian Gottfried, 228–31, 233,
    235, 241n
Kotzebue, August von, 287–88

Lambert, Johann Heinrich, 89, 196
language, theory of, 186–87, 189

Lavater, Johann Caspar, 238, 272, 279
  Aussichten in die Ewigkeit, 181, 186–87
  Physiognomische Fragmente, 176–81, 185–
    90, 197, 205, 208–9
law, moral, 12, 22–24, 26, 30, 97, 147,
    215–17, 267
Leibniz, Gottfried Wilhelm, 56, 72, 81,
    83–84, 87, 89, 119, 181, 192, 196
  character of thought, 73
  Discourse on Metaphysics, 74
  "Discours sur les beaux sentiments,"
    78–79
  neglect of his ethics, 74
  "On Happiness/On Wisdom," 75–78
  Principles of Nature and Grace, Based on
    Reason, 74
  Principles of Philosophy, or, the Monadology,
    74
  Théodicée, 73
Lessing, Gotthold Ephraim, 27, 43, 119–
    20, 143n, 201
  Briefe, die neueste Literatur betreffend, 12
  Hamburgische Dramaturgie, 207n
  Laokoon, 118, 149n
  Nathan der Weise, 202
Lichtenberg, Georg Christoph, 196, 200,
    202, 205, 238
  "Über Physiognomik," 197–99
Locke, John, 9, 16, 29, 30, 37, 38, 41, 55,
    74, 88–89, 98, 102–3, 158–59, 210, 214
  Essay concerning Human Understanding,
    18–25, 103, 241
  The Reasonableness of Christianity, 25–26,
    211
Louis XIV, king of France, 122n
love, 13, 35, 64, 77–78, 95, 162, 197, 209
  as eros, 129–31
  Hegel on, 269–70, 274, 276
Lucretius, 101
Luther, Martin, 58, 62–63, 226, 286
Lütkemann, Joachim, 66–69, 70

MacIntyre, Alasdair, 1, 2, 5
Magdalene, Maria, 275–77
Malebranche, Nicolas de, 105n
Mandeville, Bernard de, 39, 45
Mann, Thomas, 125
Marx, Karl, 165
mathematics, 11–12, 17, 22, 40, 76, 79,
    87–88, 93
Maupertuis, Pierre-Louis Moreau de, 87
McKeon, Michael, 138
Meier, Georg Friedrich, 139
Mendelssohn, Moses, 27, 43, 94, 184,
    196–97, 200–201, 205–6, 214, 218–
    19, 228, 240
  "Die Idealschönheit in den schönen
    Wissenschaften," 89

Mendelssohn, Moses (*cont.*)
  "Die Verwandschaft des Guten und
    Schönen," 90
  "Rhapsodie oder Zusätze zu den
    Briefen über die Empfindungen,"
    90n, 219
  "Ueber die Evidenz in metaphysischen
    Wissenschaften," 89–93
  "Ueber einige Einwürfe gegen die Phys-
    iognomik, und vorzüglich gegen die
    von Herrn Lavater behauptete Har-
    monie zwischen Schönheit und
    Tugend," 202–4
  "Zufällige Gedanken über die Har-
    monie der inneren und äußeren
    Schönheit," 202
method, 11–12, 15, 18, 22, 25, 28, 40, 53–
    54, 75, 87–89, 93, 110, 178–79
Meusel, Johann Georg, 166
Molyneux, William, 24
Montaigne, Michel Eyquem de, 105n
Montesquieu, Charles de Secondat, baron
    de, 27, 105, 109
moral beauty, 26, 37, 41, 46–48, 55–56,
    69, 80–81, 87, 89, 92, 96–98, 182,
    210, 257
  Balguy on, 44
  Berkeley on, 45
  from literature to reality, 182
  from philosophy to literature, 138–
    39
  gives essence to *Bildung*, 254
  Hegel on, 268–70, 275, 278
  Home on, 50
  Hume on, 53
  Hutcheson on, 39
  Kant on, 218, 221–24
  origin of, 211–12
  reevaluation of, 138
  Schiller on, 228–29, 232–33, 242
  Shaftesbury on, 36
  Sulzer on, 192–94
  Wieland on, 146–51, 162–63
moral feeling, 94, 95, 96, 157, 193
  Hegel on, 268
  Kant on, 215
moral sense
  Berkeley on, 48
  Hegel on, 268
  Home on, 50
  Hutcheson on, 40–42
  Kant on, 94
  Mendelssohn on, 90
  Shaftesbury on, 32–33, 213
More, Henry, 15, 178n
Morgenstern, Karl, 152–54, 168
mysticism, 58, 70, 102

natural state of humanity
  Christian conception of, 14, 166
  Hobbes on, 13, 18, 166
  Pietism and, 61
  Rousseau on, 167
Neoplatonism, 33, 108, 133, 229
Newton, Isaac, 18, 55–56, 87, 93–94, 102–
    3, 216–17, 222
Nicolai, Philipp, 63
Nietzsche, Friedrich, 283n
Norton, Kurt, 27
Novalis, 280n
novels and morals, 2, 6, 138–40

Origen, 64
Ovid, 101

paedaeia, 126, 130n
Parker, Samuel, 106
  *A Free and Impartial Censure of the Pla-
    tonick Philosophie*, 102–3
pathognomy, 199–200, 207
Pattison, Mark, 17, 57
pedantry, 20, 31, 147
perfection in morality, 1, 26, 31, 34,
    68, 77, 81–82, 85, 91–92, 95, 147,
    193
  in Christianity, 71
  Hegel on, 277, 279
  Kant rejects, 96, 215
  Leibniz on, 74–75
  Mendelssohn on, 203
  Schiller on, 229–30
  Wieland on, 144
Pernety, Antoine Joseph, 179n
physiognomy, 7, 176, 238–39
  appeal of, 177, 179
  Bacon on, 183
  disreputability of, 178
  Hegel on, 206
  history of, 177–78
  Humboldt on, 208
  Hutcheson on, 183–84
  Kant on, 205–6
  Lichtenberg on, 197–200
  Mendelssohn on, 202–6
  St. Bernard on, 183
  Schiller on, 205, 238
  as science, 178–79, 188–89
Pietism, 56–72, 83–84, 108, 116, 251,
    256–57
  character of, 58, 69, 71, 256
  ethics of, 58–59, 61–62
  and Goethe, 248
  and Hegel, 264–65, 273
  and Kant, 62, 96, 98
  pragmatism of, 148, 261–62

Pietism (*cont.*)
  and Schiller, 226–27
  and Wieland, 143–44
Plato, 16, 35, 48, 51n, 71, 75, 76n, 101,
    112, 117–18, 123–34, 140, 144, 146,
    158–60, 182, 213, 242, 251, 259, 269,
    271
  concern with beauty, 127
  importance in Germany, 108–9
  response to, 102–9, 125–26
  style of, 102–3, 105–6, 126
  theory of Forms, 128–29, 155, 182, 242
  Definitions, 126n
  Gorgias, 126
  Phaedo, 127–28
  Phaedrus, 128–29
  Philebus, 127
  Republic, 182
  Statesman, 259n
  Symposium, 129–31
  Timaeus, 104
Platonism, 15, 35, 40, 65, 104, 145, 216,
    229
pleasure in morals, 33–34, 37–38, 40–42,
    75, 77–78, 80–83, 91, 127, 212, 233
Plotinos, 16, 48
  Enneads, 133–36
Pope, Alexander, 101, 115
Porphyry, 133
postmodern condition, 3
poststructuralism, 2
Price, Richard, 50
prostitution, 161–62, 169, 242, 275–77

Quintilian, 150

Ramberg, Johann Heinrich, 233
reason, moral contribution of, 14–18, 22–
    23, 25–26, 28, 31–33, 36, 40, 42, 47,
    52–53, 81–82, 90, 94, 97, 147, 157,
    217
rebirth (*Wiedergeburt*), 61–63, 67, 70, 109,
    144, 226, 251, 258. *See also* Pietism
reformation, 58, 61
Reid, Thomas, 106
Reiske, Johann Jakob, 108
relativism in morals, 21, 22, 24, 40
religion and morals, 3, 4, 7, 11, 12–15,
    18–19, 23, 26, 30–31, 37, 55–79, 97–
    98. *See also* Hegel; Kant; Leibniz;
    Locke; Pietism
repentence (*Bußkampf*), 61–62, 255–56
Richardson, Samuel, 56, 154, 165, 182
romanticism, 4, 34
Rome, 100–101, 133
Rorty, Richard, 2, 3, 5

Rousseau, Jean-Jacques, 1, 10, 27, 100,
    105–6, 138, 142, 159, 181–82, 245,
    270–72
  reactions to, 165–66
  First *Discours*, 141
  Second *Discours*, 167
  Émile, 140, 159
  Julie: ou, la Nouvelle Héloïse, 141, 165–75,
    190–91, 235, 244, 279
Royal Academy of Science and Letters in
    Berlin, 10, 87–89, 93, 115, 179, 191,
    203, 214
Rudolf August, duke of Brunswick, 74

St. Augustine, 65, 67
St. Bernard of Clairvaux, 64–66, 183
St. John of the Cross, 64
St. Petersburg, 10
St. Teresa of Avila, 64, 70
Sand, Carl Ludwig, 287–88
Schelling, Friedrich Wilhelm Joseph, 226
Schiller, Friedrich, 27, 111–12, 142, 195,
    205, 211, 216n, 252–54, 257, 264,
    270, 279, 284
  and Goethe, 247, 262
  Greece and, 227–28, 233–36
  importance of beautiful soul for, 225,
    262
  influence of Pietism on, 225, 262
  and Kant, 225–26, 232
  philosophy and, 228–29
  style of, 233, 235–37
  The Aesthetic Education of Man, 244
  "Brief eines reisenden Dänen (Der An-
    tikensaal zu Mannheim)," 227–28
  "Die Götter Griechenlands," 111–12,
    227
  Die Horen, 252
  Kalliasbriefe, 229–33, 235
  "Die Künstler," 234
  "Über Anmut und Würde," 216n, 233–
    43, 253n, 279
  "Über naive und sentimentalische
    Dichtung," 244n
  "Versuch über den Zusammenhang der
    tierischen Natur des Menschen mit
    seiner geistigen," 205
Schlegel, Friedrich, 263
Scholten, Johann Andreas von, 196
Scottish philosophy, 15, 106–7
self-interest in morals. *See* egotism
sensation in morals, 18, 32–33, 52, 80, 83,
    85, 90, 92, 94, 158–59
sexuality, 64–65, 159, 161–62, 165, 169,
    171–72, 174n, 253
Shaftesbury, Anthony Ashley Cooper, earl
    of, 43–50, 52–53, 77–80, 89–90, 97n,

Shaftesbury, Anthony Ashley Cooper
(*cont.*)
    105n, 106, 116–20, 144, 146, 148,
    163, 212–13, 229, 237n, 251, 270
    Characteristicks of Men, Manners, Opin-
    ions, Times, 26–39
Shelley, Percy Bysshe, 102, 107
Smith, Adam, 106, 213–14
Smith, John, 15
Socrates, 10, 47, 104–5, 124–31, 146, 182,
    184, 190, 271
Song of Songs, 64–66
Sophocles, 109
Spence, Joseph (Sir Harry Beaumont),
    50
Spener, Philipp Jakob, 59, 63, 66, 68, 73,
    79–80, 82, 145, 148, 226, 248, 255
    Pia desideria, 60, 69–71
Springorum, Friedrich, 194
Starobinski, Jean, 170, 172
Stephen, Sir Leslie, 45
Stewart, Dugald, 15
Stoics, 52, 78
Sulzer, Johann Georg, 214, 228, 235n
    Allgemeine Theorie der schönen Künste,
    192–95
Sydenham, Floyer, 107

taste, 31, 34–36, 38, 47, 90, 92, 96, 111,
    204, 213
Tauler, Johann, 63
Taylor, Thomas, 107, 109
Trembley, Abraham, 207
Tyrrell, James, 19

ugliness, as moral baseness, 67, 134, 186,
    198–99, 209
unconscious, 2, 92
unio mystica, 64, 257

Virgil, 101, 111
virtue, definition of, 13, 30–32, 37–38, 41,
    69, 83, 95
Voltaire (François-Marie Arouet), 18, 27,
    55, 82, 84, 87, 102–4, 109

Wartburgfest, 286–88
Weigel, Valentin, 63
Weimar, 140, 245, 247
Whichcote, Benjamin, 15, 29
Wieland, Christoph Martin, 27, 101, 116–
    20, 181, 228, 235, 242, 256, 272
    character of, 142–43, 145
    Der goldene Spiegel, 140
    Geschichte des Agathon, 141, 150–69. See
        also allegory
    "Plan einer Akademie zu Bildung des
        Verstandes und des Herzens junger
        Leute," 116–18, 149
    "Platonische Betrachtungen über den
        Menschen," 147–48
    "Timoklea. Ein Gespräch über schein-
        bare und wahre Schönheit," 146
    "Theages, oder Unterredungen von
        Schönheit und Liebe," 148–49, 155,
        160
Winckelmann, Johann Joachim, 27, 109,
    114–15, 125, 181, 227
    "Gedancken über die Nachahmung der
        Griechischen Wercke in der Mahlerey
        und Bildhauer-Kunst," 111
    Geschichte der Kunst des Altertums, 259
    Versuch einer Allegorie, 155
Wittgenstein, Ludwig, 4
Wolf, Friedrich August, 257n
Wolff, Christian, 72, 79, 87, 88–89, 91, 98,
    119, 158, 181, 185, 188, 192, 193,
    203, 210, 211
    *Vernünfftige Gedancken von der Menschen
    Thun und Lassen*, 80–81, 83, 185
Wordsworth, William, 107

Xenophon, 101, 105, 117, 123, 190, 271
    Memorabilia, 124–25
    Oeconomicus, 124–25

Young, Arthur, 190

Zimmermann, Johann Georg, 145
Zinzendorf, Count Nicholas Ludwig von,
    59, 67n